LEST WE *forget*

Daily Devotionals

Other books by George R. Knight include:

LEST WE *forget*

Daily Devotionals

George R. Knight

REVIEW AND HERALD®
PUBLISHING ASSOCIATION
Since 1861 | www.reviewandherald.com

Copyright © 2008 by Review and Herald® Publishing Association

Published by Review and Herald® Publishing Association, Hagerstown, MD 21741-1119

Review and Herald® titles may be purchased in bulk for educational, business, fund-raising, or sales promotional use. For information, e-mail SpecialMarkets@reviewandherald.com

The Review and Herald® Publishing Association publishes biblically based materials for spiritual, physical, and mental growth and Christian discipleship.

The author assumes full responsibility for the accuracy of all facts and quotations as cited in this book.

This book was
Edited by Gerald Wheeler
Cover photo illustration and design by Trent Truman
Interior designed by Tina Ivany
Cover photos/Review and Herald® Library
Typeset: 11.5/13 Bembo

PRINTED IN U.S.A.
12 11 10 09 08   5 4 3 2 1

Library of Congress Cataloging-in-Publication Data
Knight, George R.
  Lest we forget / George R. Knight.
      p. cm.
  1. Devotional calendars--Seventh-Day Adventists. I. Title.
  BV4811.K58 2008
  286.7'32--dc22
                                        2008031873

ISBN 978-0-8280-2337-5

Abbreviations for E. G. White References

CM	*Colporteur Ministry*
COL	*Christ's Object Lessons*
CT	*Counsels to Parents, Teachers, and Students*
DA	*The Desire of Ages*
Ed	*Education*
Ev	*Evangelism*
EW	*Early Writings*
FE	*Fundamentals of Christian Education*
GC	*The Great Controversy*
LS	*Life Sketches of Ellen G. White* (1915 edition)
1888 LS	*Life Sketches of James and Ellen White* (1888 edition)
Lt	letter
MH	*The Ministry of Healing*
MM	*Medical Ministry*
MS	manuscript
PP	*Patriarchs and Prophets*
PT	*Present Truth*
RH	*Review and Herald*
SG 1-4	*Spiritual Gifts*, volumes 1-4
SM 1-3	*Selected Messages*, books 1-3
SW	*Southern Work*
T 1-9	*Testimonies for the Church*, volumes 1-9
TM	*Testimonies to Ministers and Gospel Workers*
WLF	*A Word to the "Little Flock"*

A WORD TO MY FELLOW TRAVELERS

Welcome to the journey as we spend 365 days walking through the formative years of Adventist history.

I have written this devotional from the firm convictions (1) that God has guided the Seventh-day Adventist Church in the past and continues to do so in the present, (2) that Adventism is a movement of prophecy rather than merely another denomination, and (3) that the greatest danger that it faces in the twenty-first century is that it will forget its identity and thus lose its purpose and reason for being. Thus the title—*Lest We Forget*.

Unlike the general run of devotionals that focus on uplifting and inspiring thoughts related to some portion of scripture, *Lest We Forget* takes a historical approach that seeks both to enlighten its readers on the development of Adventism and to inspire at the same time. That marriage of purposes has not always been an easy one to carry out in one-page segments, but I have tried in spite of the difficulties, ever operating under the firm conviction that most church members understand little of Adventism's history. Thus I must admit that my conscious purpose in preparing this book has been instructional as well as devotional. In the long run the two realms aren't really separate. After all, all true devotion must be rooted in fact rather than fiction. A chronological list of the year's readings has been included at the back of the volume as a handy reference of the topics covered.

I trust that his year's readings will bring each reader closer both to the church and to its Lord. Beyond that, it is my prayer that an understanding of how God has led His people in the past will provide insight and courage as we move into the future toward the goal of the Second Advent.

The preparation of this volume would have been impossible without the skilled help of my wife and my editors at the Review and Herald Publishing Association—Gerald Wheeler and Jeannette Johnson.

George R. Knight
Rogue River, Oregon

"We have nothing to fear for the future, except as we shall forget the way the Lord has led us, and His teaching in our past history."

—Ellen G. White

STONES OF REMEMBRANCE

And those twelve stones, which they took out of the Jordan, Joshua set up in Gilgal. And he said to the people of Israel, "When your children ask their fathers in time to come, 'What do these stones mean?' then you shall let your children know, 'Israel passed over this Jordan on dry ground.'" Joshua 4:20-22, RSV.

Those weren't just any old rocks! Each had special meaning. They were stones of remembrance, stones of history.

The rocks themselves were common enough, resembling millions of others on the hills of Palestine. But these 12 pointed to something. They looked back to God's leading in Israel's experience.

The Bible is a historical book based upon a series of events beginning with Creation and the entrance of sin and flowing through God's covenant with Abraham, the Exodus, Israel's captivity and restoration, the incarnation and virgin birth of Jesus, His sinless life and death on the cross, the resurrection, and the Second Advent.

Thus the Bible is a book of remembrance of God's miraculous leading of His people.

When churches lose the significance of those remembrances they are in trouble. Adrift from their mooring, they have lost their way. In the Judeo-Christian realm losing the way begins with forgetting the past—more specifically, forgetting God's leading in the past.

When that happens Christians lose their sense of identity. And with a lack of identity comes a vanishing mission and purpose. After all, if you don't know who you are in relation to God's plan, what do you have to tell the world?

Christian history is littered with religious bodies who have forgotten where they have come from, and, as a result, have no direction for the future. And that forgetting is a very real temptation for Adventism.

It was no accident that an aging Ellen White alerted her readers to the topic. "In reviewing our past history," she penned, "having traveled over every step of advance to our present standing, I can say, Praise God! As I see what the Lord has wrought, I am filled with astonishment, and with confidence in Christ as leader. We have nothing to fear for the future, except as we shall forget the way the Lord has led us, and His teaching in our past history" (LS 196).

As we shall see in our journey through Adventism's history this year, our church has its own stones of remembrance.

We neglect them at our peril.

THE TIMES WERE EXCITING—1

But thou, O Daniel, shut up the words, and seal the book, even to the time of the end: many shall run to and fro, and knowledge shall be increased. Dan. 12:4.

Amerca in the early nineteenth century," claims historian Ernest Sandeen, "was drunk on the millennium." Christians of all stripes believed they were on the very edge of God's kingdom.

The frightfully destructive Lisbon earthquake of 1755 had directed the minds of many to the topic of the end of the world, but the most important stimulus had its roots in the events of the French Revolution of the 1790s. The social, political, and religious upheavals taking place reminded people of biblical descriptions of the end of the world. The violence and magnitude of the French catastrophe turned the eyes of scholars on both sides of the Atlantic to the biblical prophecies of Daniel and the Revelation.

In particular, many Bible students soon developed an interest in the time prophecies and the year 1798. In February of that year Napoleon's general Berthier had marched into Rome and dethroned Pope Pius VI. Thus 1798, for many biblical scholars, became the anchor point for correlating secular history with biblical prophecy. Using the principle that in prophecy a day equals a year, they saw the capture of the pope as the "deadly wound" of Revelation 13:3 and the fulfillment of the 1260 year/day prophecy of Daniel 7:25 and Revelation 12:6, 14, and 13:5.

Bible scholars, writes Sandeen, believed they now had a "fixed point in the prophetic chronology of Revelation and Daniel. Some of them felt certain that they could now mark their own location in the unfolding prophetic chronology."

At last, many suggested, the prophecy of Daniel 12:4 was coming to fruition. Six hundred years before the birth of Christ, the prophet had written: "But thou, O Daniel, shut up the words, and seal the book, even to the time of the end: many shall run to and fro, and knowledge shall be increased." Because of such world events, many now came under conviction that they had arrived at the "time of the end." As never before, the eyes of Bible students literally ran "to and fro" over Daniel's prophecies as they sought to get a clearer understanding of end-time events. The late eighteenth and early nineteenth centuries witnessed an unprecedented number of books published on Bible prophecy.

Bible prophecy was being fulfilled. Not only were people examining the writings of Daniel as never before, but knowledge of those prophecies was rapidly increasing. It was a time of prophetic excitement.

THE TIMES WERE EXCITING—2

And this gospel of the kingdom shall be preached in all the world for a witness unto all nations; and then shall the end come. Matt. 24:14.

The study of Bible prophecy wasn't the only religious reaction to the French Revolution. A second was the greatest religious revival to ever shake America.

Beginning in the 1790s and running up into the 1840s the Second Great Awakening did more than anything else in the history of the young country to transform the United States into a Christian nation.

Accompanying the religious revival was a wave of social and personal reform. Many had come to believe that the political and technological breakthroughs of the late eighteenth and early nineteenth centuries had begun to provide the machinery for the creation of heaven on earth. Hundreds of reform movements arose for the betterment of human society.

Reform societies arose in the early nineteenth century in almost every conceivable area of human interest. It was in those decades that campaigns for the abolition of slavery, war, and the use of alcohol became major factors in American culture. In addition, societies emerged to promote public education; better treatment of the deaf, blind, mentally incapacitated, and prisoners; the equality of the sexes and races; and so on. Beyond the social realm, one finds organizations sponsoring personal betterment in such areas as moral reform and health—including the American Vegetarian Society.

Both religionists and secularists pooled their energies and resources in the hope of perfecting society through reform. But religionists went beyond their contemporaries through the establishment of Bible societies, home and foreign mission societies, Sunday school unions, and associations for the promotion of Sunday sacredness. For the first time Protestant Christians felt the need to preach the gospel to all the world.

Because of the reforms and mission outreach enthusiasm, millennial expectations were omnipresent in the 1830s. Charles Finney, the greatest American evangelist of the day, set forth the prevailing opinion of the churches when he penned in 1835 that "if the church will do her duty" in reform, "the millennium may come in this country in three years."

The idea was that the reforms and other aspects of the Awakening would prepare the world for the beginning of the millennium of Revelation 20, during which the earth would continue to improve until Christ returned at the end of the 1,000 years.

It was into a world of millennial excitement that William Miller came preaching his Advent message. As a result, churches everywhere welcomed him with open arms.

God had prepared the way. He always does. It is our job to follow His leading.

AN UNLIKELY CANDIDATE FOR MINISTRY

I tell you the truth, no one can see the kingdom of God unless he is born again.
John 3:3, NIV.

It was in the hopeful and expectant exuberance of the Second Great Awakening that we discover what appeared to be a rather hopeless candidate for ministry.

In fact, in his 20s William Miller (born in 1782) was more interested in making fun of preachers than in emulating them. In particular, he found the ones in his own family to be especially good targets for that brand of fun. Those "favored" by such activity included his grandfather Phelps (a Baptist minister) and his uncle Elihu Miller, of the Low Hampton Baptist Church.

Miller's mimicking of his grandfather's and uncle's devotional peculiarities afforded great entertainment for his skeptical associates. He imitated, with "ludicrous gravity," his relatives' "words, tones of voice, gestures, fervency, and even the grief they might manifest for such as himself."

Beyond entertainment for his friends, such exhibitions functioned as a statement of who young Miller was. Like other young people in times of rapid cultural transition, Miller had gone through his own identity crisis. Part of his rebellion against his family had undoubtedly been an aspect of the perennial struggle of adolescents to discern who they are in contradistinction to their parents.

That struggle, unfortunately, is equally hard on both parents and adolescents. Such was the case of William's deeply religious mother, who knew of his antics but found them anything but funny. To her, the actions of her eldest son were "the bitterness of death."

William, however, hadn't always been a religious rebel. In his earliest years he had been intensely and even painfully devout. The first page of his diary (which he began to keep in his teens) contains the statement: "I was early taught to pray the Lord." Being the only descriptive statement about himself in the diary's introduction, it must have seemed important to him as a distinguishing characteristic.

But it was not to last. In early adulthood Miller left Christianity and became an aggressive and skeptical deist, who would lampoon not only his grandfather but Christianity itself.

But old Grandpa Phelps never gave up on him. "Don't afflict yourself too deeply about William," he consoled his mother. "There is something for him to do yet in the cause of God."

And so there was. But, unfortunately for her, it would take time for that prophecy to reach fulfillment.

Phelps never stopped praying for his children and grandchildren. Here is something important for those of us who live in the twenty-first century.

HOPELESSNESS POINTS TO HOPE

"When I realized that my fate's the same as the fool's, I had to ask myself, 'So why bother being nice?' It's all smoke, nothing but smoke. The smart and the stupid both disappear out of sight. In a day or two they're both forgotten." "Humans die. . . . We all end up as dust." Eccl. 2:14-16; 3:19, 20, Message

Miller's service as a captain in the second war against Britain (1812-1814) provided a turning point in his life. Even before the conflict he had begun to harbor doubts about the adequacy of his deistic belief. Part of the problem was that deism promised an afterlife, but in actual fact Miller had concluded that it logically led to nothingness after death.

About the same time, Miller began to contemplate his own mortality and its meaning. On October 28, 1814, he wrote to his wife concerning a deceased army friend: "But a short time, and, like Spencer, I shall be no more. It is a solemn thought."

The hard facts of life were pushing Captain Miller toward the faith he had once so vigorously rejected.

But he still had one hope. If only he could find true patriotism in the ranks of the army he would be able to conclude that his faith in deism was not in error. "But," he penned, "two years in the service was enough to convince me that I was in an error on this thing also." The negative biblical picture of human nature appeared to be more accurate than the deistic perspective, which taught that human nature was basically good and upright. But Miller could not find that verified in history. "The more I read," he wrote, "the more dreadfully corrupt did the character of man appear. I could discern no bright spot in the history of the past. Those conquerors of the world, and heroes of history, were apparently but demons in human form. . . . I began to feel very distrustful of all men."

Miller's final belief crisis in deism had to do with what appeared to be an act of God in history at the Battle of Plattsburg in September 1814. In that battle an American "apology of an army" defeated a superior force of crack British regulars, some recently having been victorious over Napoleon.

America had been all but certain to lose. "So surprising a result against such odds," Miller concluded, "did seem to me like the work of a mightier power than man."

Like the author of Ecclesiastes, Miller was being forced by the hard facts of life to take another look at God. The good news is that the hard facts of life are still in our day performing the same function.

GOD WORKS IN STRANGE WAYS

So faith comes from hearing, and hearing through the word of Christ. Rom. 10:17, ESV.

Miller's turning away from the inadequacies of deism didn't mean that he was all that excited to become a Christian.

But he did begin to attend church. At least when he felt like it.

The next turning point in Miller's life came in May 1816 when he discovered himself "in the act of taking the name of God in vain." He had acquired the practice in the army but had come under conviction that it was wrong.

That action might seem insignificant to most people, but the topic of religion had agitated Miller's mind for some time. As a result, the event precipitated a crisis in his life. "In the month of May 1816," he later wrote, "I was brought under conviction; and O, what horror filled my soul! I forgot to eat. The heavens appeared like brass, and the earth like iron. Thus I continued till October, when God opened my eyes."

Two things happened in September 1816 that prepared Miller for his October crisis. The first was the celebration of the Battle of Plattsburg. While preparing for a time of "high glee," the veterans attended a sermon the evening before the big party. They returned in deep thought. Prayer and praise had replaced mirth and thoughts of the dance as they recalled the circumstances of the bitter battle and their "surprising" victory.

The second event took place the following Sunday. Miller's mother had discovered that he absented himself from church whenever the pastor was out of town. On such occasions one of the deacons would read poorly a sermon.

Miller made the mistake of intimating that if he could do the reading he would always be present. Thus the still deistic Miller regularly received invitations to present the sermons that the deacons selected. It was on September 15, 1816, that he read a sermon that so choked him up that he was forced to sit down in the midst of the message. He had reached a spiritual crisis.

A few weeks later, as he put it, "God opened my eyes; and O, my soul, what a Savior I discovered Jesus to be!" That discovery propelled the young convert into regular Bible study. Before long he noted that the Bible "became my delight, and in Jesus I found a friend."

God is a Diety of miracles. That He could take a skeptic such as Miller and lead him to conversion through his own public reading of a sermon is a wonder. We serve a God who utilizes a multitude of means to accomplish His will.

A MAN OF THE WORD

Thy word is a lamp unto my feet, and a light unto my path. Ps. 119:105.

Although well-read as a deist intellectual, upon his conversion to Christianity in 1816 Miller became a man of essentially one book—the Bible. Some years later he wrote to a young minister friend that "you must preach *Bible,* you must prove all things by *Bible,* you must talk *Bible,* you must exhort *Bible,* you must pray *Bible,* and love *Bible,* and do all in your power to make others love *Bible* too."

On another occasion he stated that the Bible is "a treasure which the world cannot purchase." It not only brings peace and "a firm hope in the future" but it "sustains the mind" and "gives us a powerful weapon to break down infidelity." Beyond that, "it tells us of future events, and shows the preparation necessary to meet them." He wanted young ministers to study the Bible intensively rather than having them indoctrinated in "some sectarian creed. . . . I would make them study the Bible for themselves. . . . But if they had no mind, I would stamp them with another's mind, write bigot on their forehead, and send them out as *slaves!*"

Miller not only pointed others to the Bible, but he practiced what he preached. It was his own extensive Bible study that brought him to his rather startling conclusions. His approach was thorough and methodical. Regarding his early study of the Bible, he commented that he began with Genesis and read each verse, "proceeding no faster than the meaning of the several passages should be so unfolded, as to leave me free from embarrassment respecting any mysticism or contradictions." "Whenever I found any thing obscure," he explained, "my practice was to compare it with all collateral passages; and by the help of *Cruden,* I examined all the texts of Scripture in which were found any of the prominent words contained in any obscure portion. Then by letting every word have its proper bearing on the subject of the text, if my view of it harmonized with every collateral passage in the Bible, it ceased to be a difficulty."

Miller's study of the Bible was not only intensive but also extensive. His first time through it took about two years of what appears to have been full-time study. At that point he "was fully satisfied that [the Bible] is its own interpreter," that "the Bible is a system of revealed truths, so clearly and simply given, that the 'wayfaring man, though a fool, need not err therein.'"

We can thank God that He still guides us through His word.

MILLER'S STARTLING DISCOVERY

And he said unto me, Unto two thousand and three hundred days; then shall the sanctuary be cleansed. Dan. 8:14.

Miller didn't avoid what some consider the more fruitless aspects of Scripture, such as chronology. "As I was fully convinced that 'all Scripture given by inspiration of God is profitable,' that it came not at any time by the will of man, but was written as holy men were moved by the Holy Ghost, and was written for our learning, that we through patience and comfort of the Scriptures might have hope, I could but regard the chronological portion of the Bible as being as much a portion of the word of God, and as much entitled to our serious consideration, as any other portion of the Scriptures.

"I therefore felt, that in endeavoring to comprehend what God had in his mercy seen fit to reveal to us, I had no right to pass over the prophetic periods. I saw that as the events predicted to be fulfilled in prophetic days had been extended over about as many literal years; as God in Numbers 14:34, and Ezekiel 4:4-6, had appointed each day for a year; . . . I could only regard the time as symbolical, and as standing each day for a year, in accordance with the opinions of all the standard Protestant commentaries. If, then, we could obtain any clue to the time of their commencement, I conceived we should be guided to the probable time of their termination; and as God would not bestow upon us an useless revelation, I regarded them as conducting us to the time when we might confidently look for the coming" of Christ.

Building upon Daniel 8:14, Miller interpreted the cleansing of the sanctuary as the purifying of the earth by fire at the Second Advent. Since biblical scholars generally agreed that the beginning date for the 2300 days was 457 B.C., he concluded, in harmony with scores of writers on the prophecies, that Daniel's prophecy would be fulfilled about the year 1843.

The difference of opinion on Daniel 8:14 was not the timing, but the nature of the event itself. By 1818 Miller had come to the startling conclusion that "in about twenty-five years . . . all the affairs of our present state would be wound up; that all its pride and power, pomp and vanity, wickedness and oppression would come to an end; and that in place of the kingdoms of this world, the peaceful and long desired kingdom of the Messiah would be established."

Jesus' coming is still the hope of all hopes, the event that will usher in ultimate joy.

THE JOY OF DISCOVERY

And I went unto the angel, and said unto him, Give me the little book. And he said unto me, Take it, and eat it up; and . . . it shall be in thy mouth sweet as honey. Rev. 10:9.

Revelation 10 is a fascinating interlude in the flow of the seven trumpets. From an examination of Revelation 9:13 and 11:15-18 it is clear that Revelation 10 takes place between the sixth and seventh trumpets. It is also obvious that the sounding of the seventh trumpet has to do with events at the Second Advent, when "the kingdoms of this world are become the kingdoms of our Lord, and of his Christ" and then "he shall reign for ever and ever" (Rev. 11:15).

The focal point of chapter 10 is "a little book" (verses 2, 8-10) that the verb tense (verse 2) indicates will be unsealed or opened up (in the context of the chapter) at the end of time. Now, the Old Testament tells us of only one book that will be sealed until the end of time: "But thou, O Daniel, shut up the words, and seal the book, even to the time of the end: many shall run to and fro, and knowledge [of the book of Daniel] shall be increased."

Interestingly enough, the book of Daniel has only two parts that it explicitly states would remain sealed until the time of the end. One has to do with the 1260-year time prophecy of chapter 12 (see verses 7-9). The other is Daniel 8:26, in which we read: "The vision of the evenings and mornings that has been given you is true, but seal up the vision, for it concerns the distant future" (NIV). Joyce Baldwin in her commentary on Daniel 12:4 perceptively notes that "the reason why Daniel was to keep his last two visions sealed was that they were not yet relevant (8:26; 12:9), at least not in all their detail." As Leon Wood points out in his commentary on Daniel, "since the only mention" in chapter 8 "of an evening and morning is in verse 14, it must be that reference [in verse 26] is to the 2,300 evening-mornings."

It is also of interest that Gabriel explicitly tells Daniel twice that his vision of Daniel 8 would extend to the "time of the end" (verses 17, 19). In the angel's explanation three of the four symbols of Daniel 8 have their completion in history (verses 20-25), with only one (the 2300 days) being left for fulfillment at the end of time (verse 26).

Miller perceived these things. Thus he could indicate in a time chart in the *Signs of the Times* of May 1841 that Revelation 10 had been fulfilled and the little book had been opened. And sweet indeed was the opening. "I need not speak of the joy that filled my heart in view of the delightful prospect" of the soon coming of Jesus.

The message of the sealed little book had been sweet indeed. But Miller, like most of us, cherished those parts of prophecy that he thought he understood and skipped over the rest. As a result, he somehow missed the conclusion that the opening of the prophecies of the little book would in the end bring bitterness and disappointment (Rev. 10:8-10).

Lord, help us to learn to read with both eyes open.

MILLER'S UNDERSTANDING OF PROPHECY

No prophecy of scripture is a matter of one's own interpretation, because no prophecy ever came by the impulse of man, but men moved by the Holy Spirit spoke from God. 2 Peter 1:20, 21, RSV.

Miller was in good company in his interpretation of prophecy. Prophetic understanding divides into three major schools. Preterists view prophetic fulfillment as having taken place by the time or at the time of the writing of a prophetic book. Thus, for example, the book of Revelation is speaking primarily about events at the end of the first century of the Christian Era.

Futurism, a second school of prophetic interpretation, holds that the bulk of apocalyptic prophecy will come to pass in a short space of time just before the Second Advent. The immensely popular *Left Behind* series of our day is grounded in futurism.

The third view, historicism, regards the fulfillment of prophecy as beginning in the time of the prophet, continuing across the spectrum of history, and climaxing at the Second Coming.

The historicist understanding of prophecy is best illustrated by Daniel 2, whose fulfillment commences during the lifetime of Nebuchadnezzar and Daniel, extends through the next three kingdoms that dominate the Mediterranean world, runs up through the divisions of Rome, and reaches its fulfillment at the end of time with the arrival of the kingdom of God. The visions of Daniel 7, 8-9, and 10-12 replicate the historicist model, as does Revelation 12, which traces world history from the time of the Christ child up to the end of time in verse 17, thus setting the stage for the end-time events that unfold in chapters 13-22.

Miller was an historicist, as was the early church and nearly all Protestant interpreters up through the middle of the nineteenth century. Futurism and Preterism, while capturing important aspects of Bible prophecy, didn't have much of a presence in Apocalyptic study until the Reformation of Martin Luther, when certain expositors of the dominant church sought to escape what they considered to be problematic historicist interpretations of such topics as the great red dragon and the whore of Babylon. The late nineteenth and twentieth centuries witnessed a surge of futurism and preterism, partly in response to the perceived failures of Millerism.

But the failures of Millerite Adventism haven't changed the obviously historicist perspective of Daniel 2 or even the year-for-a-day principle, which is so built into Daniel 9 that the Revised Standard Version translators rendered verse 24 as "seventy weeks or years" in spite of the fact that the Hebrew has only "seventy weeks." The addition was necessary even to individuals who didn't believe in predictive prophecy if they were to make sense of a prophecy claiming to extend from the time of the restoration of Jerusalem to the Messiah.

THE SIN OF BIBLE STUDY

Son of Man, I have made you a watchman for the house of Israel; whenever you hear a word from my mouth, you shall give them warning from me. If I say to the wicked, "You shall surely die," and you give him no warning, nor speak to warn the wicked from his wicked way, in order to save his life, that wicked man shall die in his iniquity; but his blood I will require at your hand. Eze. 3:17, 18, RSV.

William Miller's 1818 discovery that Jesus would return to earth in "about twenty-five years filled him with joy." That was good.

But, he noted, "the conviction came home to me with mighty power regarding my duty to the world in view of the evidence that had affected my own mind." If the end was near, it was important that the world should know it.

He supposed that his conclusions about the Advent might find opposition among the "ungodly," but he had no doubt that Christians everywhere would gladly accept them as soon as they had a chance to hear about them. But he feared to present his findings, "lest by some possibility I should be in error, and be the means of misleading any." As a result, he spent another five years (1818-1823) in continued study of the Bible. As he eliminated one objection to his view of the Advent another would come to his mind, such as "of that day and hour knoweth no man." During that five-year period, Miller noted in 1845, "more objections arose in my mind, than have been advanced by my opponents since; and I know of no objection that has been since advanced, which did not occur to me." But after continued study he believed that he could answer all of them from the Bible. Thus after seven years of study Miller had fully convinced himself that Christ would return "about the year 1843."

At that point Miller reports that "the duty of presenting the evidence of the nearness of the advent to others—which I had managed to evade while I could find the shadow of an objection remaining against its truth—again came home to me with great force."

As a result, he began to speak more openly of his views in private conversations with his neighbors and minister. But to his astonishment, "very few . . . listened with any interest."

Miller continued to study the Bible. But the more he did, the more convicted he was that he had a duty to tell others. "Go and tell the world of their danger" was the message that assailed him day and night.

But that was the last thing he wanted to do. You see, like many of us, Miller loved studying the Bible, but he lacked ambition to do anything. Such is the sin of Bible study. We are all tempted to make it an end in itself rather than a means of motivation to action.

BE CAREFUL WHAT YOU PROMISE GOD!

Eli perceived that the Lord was calling the boy. Therefore Eli said to Samuel, "Go, lie down; and if he calls you, you shall say, 'Speak, Lord, for thy servant hears.'" 1 Sam. 3:8, 9, RSV.

But sometimes we don't want to hear. Such was the case of William Miller. Even though the ears of his conscience rang with the command to warn the world of danger to come, he had no desire to do so.

"I did all I could to avoid the conviction that anything was required of me; and I thought that by freely speaking of it to all, I should perform my duty, and that God would raise up the necessary instrumentality for the accomplishment of the work. I prayed that some minister might see the truth, and devote himself to its promulgation."

Now, there's a handy solution. Get some minister to do our work. I have come to the conclusion that if the church relies on the ministers to "finish the work" it will take a little longer than eternity. The bad news about the good news is that God calls each of us to do our part.

But that is just what the very human William Miller didn't want to do. Hoping to witness by proxy, he eventually arrived at the Moses excuse. "I told the Lord that I was not used to public speaking, that I had not the necessary qualifications to gain the attention of an audience," and so on. But he could get no relief. For nine more years Miller struggled with the conviction that he had a task to do for God. Then one Saturday about the year 1832 he sat down at his desk to examine a detail of Bible teaching. Suddenly he felt overwhelmed with the belief that he needed to become active for the Lord.

In agony he cried out that he couldn't go.

"Why not?" came the reply.

And then he recited all of his threadbare excuses.

Finally his distress became so great that he promised God that he would perform his duty if he got an invitation to speak publicly on the topic of the Lord's coming. With that he experienced a sigh of relief. After all, he was 50 years old, and no one had ever asked him to present the topic before. He felt free at last. But within a half hour he received just such an invitation. And with it came a flash of anger that he had ever promised God anything. Without answering he stormed out of the house. After struggling with God and himself for about an hour, he finally agreed to preach the next day. That sermon was the beginning of one of the most fruitful ministries of the mid-nineteenth century.

The moral: Be careful what you promise God. He may have more in mind for your life than you have ever dreamed of.

POWERFUL MESSAGE/ORDINARY PACKAGE

And he said, Go forth, and stand upon the mount before the Lord. And, behold, the Lord passed by, and a great and strong wind rent the mountains, and broke in pieces he rocks before the Lord; but the Lord was not in the wind: and after the wind an earthquake; but the Lord was not in the earthquake: and after the earthquake a fire; but the Lord was not in the fire: and after the fire a still small voice.
1 Kings 19:11, 12.

O ften God uses the ordinary things of life. And that's good, because most of us are ordinary. So was William Miller.

The experience of Timothy Cole, pastor of the Christian Connexion congregation in Lowell, Massachusetts, illustrates that fact. Having heard in the late 1830s of Miller's outstanding success as a revivalist, Cole invited him to hold a series of meetings in his church. He went to greet the successful evangelist at the train depot, expecting a fashionably dressed gentleman whose demeanor matched his reputation. Cole watched closely as the passengers debarked the train, but saw no one who corresponded with his mental image. Eventually an unimpressive old man, shaking with palsy, alighted from the passenger coach. To Cole's dismay, the "old man" turned out to be Miller. At that point he quickly repented of inviting him. Someone of Miller's appearance, he concluded, couldn't know much about the Bible.

More than a little embarrassed, Cole led Miller through the back door of his church and, after showing him the pulpit, took a seat among the congregation. Miller felt a bit ill-used, but proceeded with the service. But if Cole was unimpressed with Miller's appearance, the opposite held true for Cole's reaction to his preaching. After listening for 15 minutes, he arose from the congregation and went up and sat behind William on the platform. Miller lectured daily for a week and returned the next month for a second series. The revival was a success, with even Cole being converted to Miller's views.

The plain fact is that God can do extraordinary things with ordinary people. The *Maine Wesleyan Journal* characterized Miller as a "plain farmer," but reported that he "succeeds in chaining the attention of his auditory for an hour and a half to two hours." It wasn't the man but his message. William's message was sincere, logical, and biblical. And he also had a bit of spunky humor. On one occasion, when under criticism for his beliefs, he told his audience, "They have reported that I was insane, and been in a mad-house seven years; if they had said a mad world for fifty-seven years, I must plead guilty to the charge."

An ordinary person with a powerful message. God used him. He can use you also if you let Him.

THE MIDNIGHT CRY

And at midnight there was a cry made, Behold, the bridegroom cometh;
go ye out to meet him. Matt. 25:6.

It was quite natural for Miller and his followers to find themselves attracted to Jesus' great sermon on the Advent found in Matthew 24 and 25. But the parable of the 10 virgins found in Matthew 25:1-13 especially caught their attention. They saw their own movement and message in the passage. In the process they historicized the details of the parable.

Thus they saw the 10 virgins as humanity in general in its probationary state. The five wise virgins were believers in God, while the foolish ones represented unbelievers.

The lamps were the word of God, and the oil represented faith.

The marriage for them was the focal point of the parable. That was the time when Christ the bridegroom would appear in the clouds of heaven. The marriage was the great event toward which all history moved. The coming of the bridegroom was the hope that motivated them to sacrifice their means to support the preaching of their message.

The sleeping condition of the virgins for the Millerites indicated the apathy and ignorance of both Christians and unbelievers in the nearness and timing of the Advent.

The "'midnight cry,'" Miller wrote, "is the watchman, or some of them, who by the word of God discover the time as revealed, and immediately give the warning voice, 'Behold, the bridegroom cometh; go ye out to meet him.'" In other words, the midnight cry was the final wake-up call to get people ready for the arrival of the divine Bridegroom.

But not all would respond. Thus, as Miller saw it, the reaction to the proclamation of the midnight cry would produce a division between the wise and the foolish, between those who accepted the message and got ready for the approaching Bridegroom and those who kept on sleeping.

At the Second Advent itself the wise would enter into the kingdom with the Bridegroom. But for the rest "the door was shut." Miller saw the shutting of the door as the close of human probation.

Thus the urgency of his message. People needed to be warned so that they could get ready for the event of the ages.

That message is still of importance in our day. Miller may have been in error regarding the timing of the Advent, but the Second Advent itself is still the hope of the ages. And the function of God's people continues to be to wake up sleeping sinners to the ultimate reality that our world will not last forever.

THE NAPOLEON OF THE PRESS

And I saw another angel . . . saying with a loud voice, Fear God, and give glory to him; for the hour of his judgment is come. Rev. 14:6, 7.

The man who put Millerite Adventism on the map was not Miller but Joshua V. Himes, a young Christian Connexion minister who had learned the skills of a publicist by working with William Lloyd Garrison, the inflammatory sparkplug in the movement to free the slaves.

Himes on first meeting Miller in November 1839 was convicted by his message but wondered how come it wasn't better known.

"Do you *really* believe this message?" Himes asked the older preacher.

"Certainly I do, or I would not preach it."

But "what are you doing to spread or diffuse it through all the world?"

"All I can," Miller replied.

"Well, the whole thing is kept in a corner yet. There is but little knowledge on the subject, after all you have done. If Christ is to come in a few years, as you believe, no time should be lost in giving the church and world warning, in thunder-tones, to arouse them to prepare."

"I know it, I know it, Bro. Himes, but what can an old farmer do? . . . I have been looking for help—I want help."

It was at that point, Himes recalled, "that I laid myself, family, society, reputation, all upon the altar of God, to help him, to the extent of my power, to the end."

With the entrance of Himes, Millerism took on a dynamic that it never possessed before. A dynamo of energy and ingenuity, between 1840 and 1844 Joshua put the movement into high gear and made Millerism a word that everyone recognized.

Nathan Hatch, a leading historian of American religion, has described Himes' publishing efforts as "an unprecedented media blitz" and "an unprecedented communications avalanche." One of Himes' detractors styled him as the "Napoleon of the press."

Within a short space of time the constantly active Himes had begun *The Midnight Cry* and *The Signs of the Times,* periodicals that would take the Advent message to the ends of the earth, and sent forth a never-ending stream of books and tracts. Within a few years he had, with rather primitive technology, distributed millions of pieces of printed matter. Himes may have been a publicist and Miller an idea man, but it took both of them, and a whole lot of other less-visible people, to make a dynamic movement. The good news is that God needs all of us. Each of us has some talent that we can use for His glory. In fact, this very day God is calling on you to rededicate your life and your skills to Him and His work on earth.

An Urgent Message

Go ye therefore into the highways, and as many as ye shall find, bid to the marriage. Matt. 22:9.

Millerite believers felt a sense of urgency to warn the world to prepare for the coming of Christ. One of the major instruments they utilized would be the camp meeting, a form of religious gathering employed by the Methodists and others since about 1800.

The initiative for the first Millerite camp meeting took place at the Boston general conference in May 1842. By that date the year 1843 loomed perilously close, with most of the world yet to be warned.

L. C. Collins expressed the faith of many when he wrote: "My faith is *strong* in the coming of Christ in '43. I make no calculations for any thing beyond, but glory. . . . But with so short a time to awake the slumbering virgins, and save souls, we must *work; work* night and day. God has thrust us out in haste, to give the *last* invitation, and we must labor in earnest, and *compel* them to come in, so that his house may be filled. . . . Strong men in Israel are rallying to our help. The midnight cry must yet be made to ring, and ring through every valley and over every hilltop and plain. An awful trembling must yet seize upon sinners in Zion. A crisis *must come,* before the door of mercy is everlastingly shut against them. They must be made to feel that it is *now or never."*

A sense of urgency and responsibility rested heavily upon the Millerites by mid-1842. The day after Collins penned his letter, the momentous Boston general conference opened, with Joseph Bates, at the helm. That conference not only voted to hold camp meetings—it also appointed a committee to superintend them. The principal object of the meetings was "to awake sinners and purify Christians by giving the Midnight Cry."

Some Millerites felt that the very attempt to hold such meetings was a bit presumptive. After all, a camp meeting was a great undertaking. "What," declared some, "a little handful of Adventists hold a camp meeting! Why, they are hardly able to hold a house meeting." But the key word was that they would "TRY" in spite of appearances.

And God rewarded their faith. Josiah Litch estimates that 500-600 were converted to God during the first two Adventist camp meetings. There is a lesson here. It is not outward appearances that count, but God's blessings. And He is still willing to bless those who step out in faith and "TRY."

THE ZEALOUS CHARLES FITCH

The zeal of thine house hath eaten me up. Ps. 69:9.

In 1838 a copy of Miller's published lectures on the Second Advent fell into the hands of Charles Fitch, a Presbyterian minister and abolitionist of some prominence.

"I have *studied* it," he penned to Miller on March 5, "with an overwhelming interest, such as I never felt in any other book except the Bible. I have compared it with scripture and history and I find nothing on which to rest a single doubt respecting the correctness of your views."

Fitch, true to his zealous and sincere character, wasn't satisfied with merely one reading. Before long he had read Miller's book *six times,* noting that his "mind was greatly overwhelmed with the subject."

Impelled by Miller's message, he immediately "wrote and preached to the people of Boston" about his newfound faith. Preaching his first two sermons on Miller's views on March 4, he exuberantly wrote to William the next day, noting that he desired to be "a watchman on the walls," and wanted "to *give the trumpet a certain sound."*

As a major step in faithfully acting the part, Fitch announced to Miller that the very next day, March 6, he was scheduled to read a paper on the Advent doctrine before the Boston ministerial association. But sometimes zeal outruns knowledge and wisdom. And so it was for Charles Fitch on March 6, 1838. The zealous preacher, who had barely had time to examine the doctrine himself, was both intimidated and shocked by the response he received. To his ministerial colleagues it was "moonshine." "There was much laughter over the subject," Fitch recalled, "and I could not help feeling that I was regarded as a simpleton." After that he gave up preaching the Advent near. As he later saw it, "the fear of man brought me into a snare."

But not for long. In 1841 he restudied the Bible on the topic. He subsequently became one of the most prominent advocates of the movement. He would be the only one of Millerism's leading preachers not to go through the October 1844 disappointment. While in Buffalo, New York, during late September he baptized a group of believers in frigid Lake Erie on a cold, windy day. After starting for his lodging in wet clothes, he twice turned back to baptize more candidates. The extended exposure led to illness and death on October 14. But even his approaching death did not dampen the zeal of the 39-year-old believer. He knew that "he would only have to take a short sleep, before he should be waked in the resurrection morn."

THE NOISE OF ANGELS

And there followed another angel, saying, Babylon is fallen, is fallen, that great city, because she made all nations drink of the wine of the wrath of her fornication. Rev. 14:8.

The Millerites believed that they were preaching the first angel's message of Revelation 14:6, 7: "And I saw another angel fly in the midst of heaven, having the everlasting gospel to preach unto them that dwell on the earth, and to every nation, and kindred, and tongue, and people, saying with a loud voice, Fear God, and give glory to him; for the hour of his judgment is come: and worship him that made heaven, and earth, and the sea, and the fountains of waters."

For them the "hour of his judgment" was the Second Advent. Thus it was equivalent to the cleansing of the sanctuary of Daniel 8 and the coming of the bridegroom of Matthew 25. All three passages, they believed, pointed to the return of Jesus.

The preaching of that message seemed harmless enough at first. But the nearer the expected date came, the more friction arose between the Advent believers and others in their churches. We need to remember that the Millerites before 1843 did not have separate congregations. To the contrary, they worshipped with the non-Adventist members of their local church. But they couldn't just be quiet as the expected time of the Advent neared. It was the hope closest to their hearts. The Second Coming was all they could talk about.

That was good in itself. However, many of their fellow church members had heard too much on the topic, setting the stage for conflict as the Millerites entered what they believed would be their last year on earth. Many congregations eventually concluded that they had heard more than enough from the Adventists. The only solution seemed to be to disfellowship them and expel Adventist ministers from their pulpits.

The Adventists reacted with Charles Fitch's preaching of the second angel's message: "Babylon is fallen" (Rev. 14:8), "come out of her, my people" (Rev. 18:4). To Fitch and his fellow believers, any church member who wasn't looking forward to the soon appearing of Jesus was truly confused (i.e., Babylon).

The second angel's message provided a theological justification for Adventists to separate from their congregations and form their own. More important, it gave them the independence needed to continue to study their Bibles as God led them from the message of the second angel to that of the third in the months following the October 1844 disappointment. The progressive path of truth isn't always smooth, but God is leading even when we can't see through the noise and smoke of earthly confusion.

JOSEPH BATES INVADES THE SOUTH

My God sent his angel and shut the lions' mouths, and they have not hurt me. Dan. 6:22, RSV.

Millerism, given the fact that most of its leaders were abolitionists, wasn't welcome in the South. Yet requests for preachers kept coming. The May 1843 Millerite general conference, however, decided not to send lecturers into the slave states because of the danger and difficulty.

But in early 1844 Joseph Bates came under conviction that God had called him to minister to both the slaves and their owners. The intrepid missionary, after experiencing some modest success in Maryland, found himself challenged and denounced by a Methodist lay leader who attacked the "doctrine of the Advent in a violent manner." In the midst of his attack the man "began to talk about *riding us [out of town] on a rail."*

"We are ready for that, sir," Bates shot back. "If you will put a saddle on it, we would rather ride than walk."

"You must not think," he continued, "that we have come six hundred miles through the ice and snow, at our own expense, to give you the Midnight Cry, without first sitting down and counting the cost. And now, if the Lord has no more for us to do, we had [gladly] lie at the bottom of the Chesapeake Bay as anywhere else until the Lord comes. But if he has any more work for us to do, you can't touch us!"

The *Newark Daily Advertiser* reported the incident, noting that "the wreck of matter and the crush of worlds is but a small consideration to one who can take things so coolly."

On another occasion during that same tour a Southern judge accosted Bates, saying that he understood that he was an abolitionist who had come "to get away our slaves."

"Yes judge," Bates replied, "I am an abolitionist, and have come to get your slaves, and *you too!"*

Bates and his companion were especially gratified in being able to give their message to slaves. At times they even chose to walk from one appointment to another so that they would be able to talk to the slaves they met outside of the hearing of other Whites. "The poor slaves," he reported "feasted upon" the Advent message, "especially when they learned that the Jubilee was so near at hand. They seemed to drink it down as the ox drinks water, and from what I have since heard, I believe that many of them will be ready when Jesus comes."

God never ever said our path through life would be easy. But He has promised that if we are faithful to Him, He will bless us and be with us.

As Christians we can praise God for all His blessings every day.

THE AFRICAN-AMERICAN FACE OF MILLERISM

The Spirit of the Lord is upon me, because he has anointed me to preach good news to the poor . . . , to proclaim release to the captives . . . , [and] to set at liberty those who are oppressed. Luke 4:18, RSV.

Millerism was largely a movement among Northern Whites at a time when most Blacks still lived in the South. Yet we find consistent evidence that African-Americans attended Advent services and camp meetings. By mid-1843 the responsibility to work aggressively among the Black population was becoming more obvious to the Millerite leaders. As a result, Charles Fitch made a successful motion at a major meeting in May "to take up a collection for a laborer to go among our colored brethren." The next day the attendees collected funds to enable John W. Lewis, "a highly esteemed colored preacher," to work full-time "among that much neglected class of our brethren, with whom he is most closely connected."

By February 1844 Himes could report that "many of the colored people have received the doctrine" in Philadelphia. "One of their most efficient ministers has embraced the doctrine in full, and will devote himself wholly to the proclamation of it."

Another Black lecturer who preached the Advent message was William E. Foy, who had several visions beginning on January 18, 1842. Those visions led him to a belief in the soon coming of Jesus, even though, as he put it, "I was opposed to the doctrine of Jesus' near approach" until receiving the visions. Beyond a belief on the soon return of Jesus, Foy wrote that "the duty to declare the things which had thus been shown me, to my fellow creatures, and warn them to flee from the wrath to come, rested with great weight upon my mind."

Foy resisted his convictions for some time, partly because the Advent message was "so different" from what people expected and partly because of "prejudice among the people against [those] of my color." But in the midst of a prayer of deep distress, he received a definite impression that God would be with him if he shared the message. As a result, he began preaching his new faith.

The message of Advent hope has always found receptive hearts among the oppressed of the world, no matter what their race or culture. It is those who have been building their kingdom on this earth who are hardened to the message. What we need to remember is that all of earth's inhabitants are under the slavery of sin and need to be liberated by the One who came to set the captives free. The Advent hope is the dream of freedom for every person eternally.

ADVENT WOMEN ON THE MOVE

And Miriam sang to them: "Sing to the Lord, for he has triumphed gloriously; the horse and his rider he has thrown into the sea." Ex. 15:21, RSV.

Women have always had a part in God's work. And so it was in Millerite Adventism.

Lucy Maria Hersey, for example, had been converted at the age of 18 and felt the Lord had called her to preach the gospel.

In 1842 she accepted Miller's doctrine. Soon after she accompanied her father on a trip to Schenectady, New York, where a believer asked her father to address a non-Adventist group on the evidences of his faith. The people were "so opposed to *female speaking*" that the host thought it best if the father made the presentation. But miracle of miracles, Hersey found himself speechless.

After a long silence, the host introduced Lucy as one able to talk on the topic. And talk she did, finding a response so great that they soon had to shift to a larger auditorium to hold the crowds. That was the beginning of a fruitful ministry that resulted in the conversion of several men who became Advent preachers.

Even more successful was Olive Maria Rice. Converted to Millerism in 1842, she was "convinced that the Lord had something more for me to do than to assist in prayer meetings." By March 1843 God had blessed her ministry with hundreds of conversions. She wrote to Himes that "there are constantly four or five places calling for my labors at the same time."

Rice recognized that many opposed her work because she was a female, but she declared that she "dare not stop for the only reason that I am a sister. Though men may censure and condemn, I feel justified before God, and expect with joy to render my account for thus warning my fellow beings."

Elvira Fassett had to overcome the opposition of her husband. She had been taught that a woman should not speak in public. But being pressed by others, she finally gave in, only to find that the Lord blessed her labors. One of her most important converts was her husband, who had witnessed the impact of her preaching and had come to realize the importance of the prophecy of Joel 2 that in the last days God would pour out His Spirit on young women. Subsequently the Fassetts preached the Advent message as a ministerial team.

The good news is that God summons all of us to proclaim His message. And He will bless us as we yield to His will.

THE YEAR OF THE END OF THE WORLD

Behold, he is coming with the clouds, and every eye will see him. Rev. 1:7, RSV.

This year . . . is the last year that Satan will reign in our earth. Jesus Christ will come. . . . The kingdoms of the earth will be dashed to pieces. . . . The shout of victory will be heard in heaven. . . . Time shall be no more." Thus wrote William Miller in his "New Year's Address to Second Advent Believers" on January 1, 1843. At long last the year of the end of the world had arrived.

And, as we might expect, the excitement was high. But they weren't quite sure as to when in the year they should be looking. Miller himself, knowing that Christ had said that no person knew the day or the hour, had been quite cautious on the topic. "About the year 1843" was about as precise as he wanted to be.

But by December 1842 his disciples were pushing him to be more specific. After all, the very next month would begin 1843. Miller concluded that he could indeed be more specific. Basing his calculations on the Jewish feast of Passover, he wrote that he believed that Jesus would appear in the clouds of heaven sometime between March 21, 1843, and March 21, 1844.

Those who thought that they had discovered some formula for pinpointing the exact day set many specific dates between the two points. Miller himself held for a late-in-the-year fulfillment, since he thought their faith would be tried.

And tried it was. The Second Advent did not occur on March 21, 1844. The hopeful decided that they had miscalculated the date for Passover. Perhaps it was April 21. But that date also passed. And thus the Millerite groups went through their first or spring disappointment.

The movement avoided disintegration at that time because they had not put too much hope in a specific date. On the other hand, they did feel downhearted. They continued to study their Bibles to discern where they were in prophetic time. Then in early summer they discovered Habakkuk 2:3, "For the vision is yet for an appointed time, but at the end it shall speak, and not lie: though it tarry, wait for it; because it will surely come, it will not tarry." They concluded that they were in the "tarrying time." After all, didn't Matthew 25:5 plainly teach that the "bridegroom tarried"?

Their faith had a resilience that we must admire. Yes, they were disappointed. But rather than give up, they turned to their Bibles to discover their whereabouts in prophetic history. That is not what they wanted to be doing, but it is the only option for those of us who continue to cry out "how long, O Lord" (Rev. 6:10).

THE SEVENTH MONTH MOVEMENT

On exactly the tenth day of this seventh month is the day of atonement.
Lev. 23:27, NASB.

Hope found rebirth in the ranks of the somewhat-listless Millerite Adventists in August 1844 when a Methodist minister by the name of Samuel S. Snow demonstrated from the Bible that they had been looking at the wrong dates for the fulfillment of the 2300-day prophecy of Daniel 8:14.

Miller himself had put forth the logic of the new understanding in a *Signs of the Times* article on May 17, 1843. At that time he argued that the first advent of Christ had fulfilled the spring feasts of the ceremonial year set forth in Leviticus 23, but that the autumn or seventh-month feasts needed to be connected with the Second Advent.

That logic is sound enough. After all, the offering of the first-fruits, Christ's death as the Passover lamb, and the Pentecostal outpouring had all taken place according to the New Testament. But none of the seventh-month feasts tied to harvesttime had met any fulfillment during the New Testament period.

Those facts led Miller to suggest that his followers should look to the seventh month of the Jewish religious year for the fulfillment of the prophecy they had identified with the Second Advent.

Miller may have developed the seventh-month argument in May 1843, but he let the matter drop and reverted back to a first-month or Passover dating. Snow, however, followed William's logic to its natural conclusion. Looking for Christ's return at the end of the 2300 days, he predicted that Jesus would come on October 22, 1844, the seventh month of the Jewish year, the Day of Atonement.

Snow had first published his findings in *The Midnight Cry* of February 22, 1844, but no one was ready to listen. By August, though, they were all ears.

The seventh-month movement took Millerism by storm. In the October 3 issue of *The Midnight Cry* George Storrs wrote that "I take up my pen with feelings such as I never before experienced. *Beyond a doubt,* in my mind, the *tenth day* of the *seventh month* will witness the revelation of our Lord Jesus Christ in the clouds of heaven. We are then within a *few days* of that event. . . . Now comes the TRUE *Midnight Cry.* The previous was but the alarm. NOW THE REAL ONE IS SOUNDING: and oh, how solemn the hour."

Now, here's true excitement. How would you live if you believed you could calculate mathematically that Jesus would appear in less than three weeks? That is precisely how we need to live every day.

SWEET IN THE MOUTH/BITTER IN THE BELLY

*And I took the little book out of the angel's hand, and ate it up; and it was
in my mouth sweet as honey: and as soon as I had eaten it, my belly was bitter.
Rev. 10:10.*

And how sweet it was!

Writing on October 6, the day he finally accepted the October 22 date, Miller exclaimed in the headline article of *The Midnight Cry* of October 12, "I see a glory in the seventh month which I never saw before. Although the Lord had shown me the typical bearing of the seventh month, one year and a half ago [the May 1843 article], yet I did not realize the force of the types. . . . Thank the Lord, O my soul. Let Brother Snow, Brother Storrs, and others be blessed for their instrumentality in opening my eyes. I am almost home, Glory! Glory!! Glory!!! I see that the time is correct. . . .

"My soul is so full I cannot write. . . . I see that we are yet right. God's word is true; and my soul is full of joy; my heart is full of gratitude to God. Oh, how I wish I could shout. But I will shout when the 'King of kings comes.' Methinks I hear you say, 'Brother Miller is now a fanatic! Very well, call me what you please; I care not; Christ will come in the seventh month, and will bless us all. Oh! glorious hope. Then I shall see him, and be like him, and be with him forever. Yes, forever and ever."

Nothing was sweeter than the hope of the soon-coming Christ!

Yet He did not come! And bitter was the disappointment.

On October 24 Millerite leader Josiah Litch wrote to Miller and Himes from Philadelphia that "it is a dark day here—the sheep are scattered—and the Lord has not come yet."

Hiram Edson reported that "our fondest hopes and expectations were blasted, and such a spirit of weeping came over us as I never experienced before. It seemed that the loss of all earthly friends could have been no comparison. We wept, and wept, till the day dawn."

A young Millerite preacher by the name of James White penned that "the disappointment at the passing of the time was a bitter one. True believers had given up all for Christ, and had shared his presence as never before. . . . The love of Jesus filled every soul, . . . and with inexpressible desire they prayed, 'Come, Lord Jesus, and come quickly.' But he did not come. And now to turn again to the cares and perplexities of life, in full view of the jeers and revilings of unbelievers who now scoffed as never before, was a terrible trial of faith and patience."

The opening of the little book of Daniel had truly been sweet in the mouth but bitter in the belly.

RETROSPECT: ERROR AND GOD'S LEADING

We had hoped that he was the one to redeem Israel. Luke 24:21, RSV.

William Miller and his fellow believers had obviously been wrong in certain aspects of their Bible interpretation and understandings. After all, Jesus did not return to earth on October 22, 1844, or anywhere near the 1840s.

The question that begs asking is "Could God have been leading such a movement?"

We find the best answer in the New Testament. There we see the disciples repeatedly misinterpreting Christ's words regarding His future crucifixion and the nature of His kingdom. Not until after His resurrection did they even begin to understand what Jesus had so intently sought to teach them. But because they did not have ears to hear, they had to go through a shattering disappointment that shook the very foundations of their belief in God's leading. It would take further study and a growth in understanding before they could comprehend what had happened to them.

The problem is that God has chosen to work through human agents in the plan of salvation. Thus even those earthly situations in which God is leading have both divine and human elements. And everything touching humanity is tainted with fallibility. Such is the long history of God's seeking to work in and through human beings down through history.

More specifically to Millerism, one can only wonder, since Miller believed that the opening of the prophecies of the little book of Daniel reflected upon in Revelation 10 had seen their fulfillment in his day, why he didn't read the rest of the chapter. That is, if he believed that the book had been opened and its message was sweet in the mouth, why didn't he notice that it would be bitter in the belly (verse 10) and that another movement would arise out of the ashes of bitterness, one with a worldwide message for "many peoples, and nations, and tongues, and kings" (verse 11). Miller's own logic would have led him to see that God had foreseen the bitter disappointment, just as Jesus had predicted that of His disciples.

Again, if Miller could hold that he was preaching the first angel's message (Rev. 14:6, 7), and many of his followers believed they were sounding the second (verse 8), why is it that they failed to give due emphasis to the third (verses 9-12)? All three progressively lead to the Second Advent pictured in verses 14-20.

The sad fact is that God has chosen to use fallible humans in His mission on earth. The good news is that He continues to work with us in spite of our weaknesses. For that we can praise Him.

THE SCATTERING TIME–1

The hour is coming, indeed it has come, when you will be scattered. John 16:32, RSV.

Josiah Litch used words full of biblical meaning when he wrote two days after the October disappointment that "it is a dark day here—the sheep are scattered—and the Lord has not come yet." Profound spiritual disappointments have always tended toward disillusionment and the scattering of believers.

So it was with the Millerite Adventists in late 1844 and early 1845. To put it mildly, they were disoriented and confused as they sought to find meaning in their recent experience. The height of their hope had led to the depth of their despair.

It is impossible to get a completely accurate picture of the disappointed Millerites, but it is probable that the majority abandoned their Advent faith and either went back to their previous churches or drifted into secular unbelief.

We can view those who maintained their hope in the soon return of Christ as belonging to one of three general groups. The big question that faced all of them was What, if anything, had happened on October 22 at the close of the 2300 days of Daniel 8:14?

The first identifiable group to arise in the wake of the Disappointment was the spiritualizers. This sector of Adventism claimed that the movement had been correct on both the date and the event. That is, Christ had come on October 22. But it had been a spiritual entrance into their hearts rather than a visual return in the clouds of heaven.

With that interpretation they took a major step away from Miller's understanding of the Bible. They began to spiritualize its meaning, even in places where it was obviously speaking of literal events. And with that, they opened themselves to all sorts of deception.

Fanaticism easily arose among the spiritualizers. Some claimed that since they were in the kingdom they were of necessity sinless and beyond sin. Among that group some took "spiritual" husbands and wives, with some very unspiritual results. Others held that since they were in the seventh millennium it was wrong to work. And still others, following the biblical injunction that members of the kingdom would be as little children, discarded forks and knives, ate with their hands, and crawled around on their hands and knees. Needless to say, outbreaks of charismatic enthusiasm swept through their ranks.

There is an important lesson for us here. We need to be careful and intelligent in our reading of God's Word. To spiritualize away the plain meaning of Scripture is to open ourselves to spiritual disaster.

THE SCATTERING TIME—2

Then Jesus said to them, . . . "I will strike the shepherd, and the sheep of the flock will be scattered." Matt. 26:31, RSV.

If William Miller dreaded one thing above others, it was fanaticism. His movement had been fairly free from it up until October 1844. But by spring 1845 fanaticism and charismatic excesses were running wild among certain segments of the spiritualizers.

By April 1845 Miller was beside himself with the developing fanaticism. That month he wrote to Himes that "this is a peculiar time. The greatest variety of fanciful interpretations of Scripture are now being prescribed by new luminaries, reflecting their rays of light and heat in every direction. Some of these are wandering stars, and some emit only twilight. I am sick of this everlasting changing; but, my dear brother, we must learn to have patience. If Christ comes this spring, we shall not need it long; and if he comes not, we shall need much more. I am prepared for the worst, and hope for the best."

Unfortunately for Miller, time continued to last, and he and his followers witnessed something less than the hoped-for "best." Eighteen months later an ailing Miller penned: "I have not done with pain. I have been troubled with head-ache, teeth-ache, bones-ache, and heart-ache, since you left; but much more of the last ache, when I think of so many of my once dearly beloved brethren, who have since our disappointment gone into fanaticism of every kind, and left the first principles of the glorious appearing of the great God and our Saviour, Jesus Christ."

He wasn't the only one confused and perturbed by the welter of disorientation among the spiritualizers in early 1845. Himes noted in May that "the seventh month movement [had] produced mesmerism seven feet deep."

The problem of all Millerites in early 1845 was the question of identity. Different sectors of the movement produced different answers to it, but they were all dealing with the same issues.

To put it bluntly, it is hard to keep straight in times of great trouble. It always has been and it always will be. Our daily prayer must be that God will help us keep both feet on the ground and our mind at its clear-thinking best, especially in troublous times.

And like Miller, we must enter such times of trial hoping for the best, but prepared for the worst.

Help us this day, our Father, to have both a balanced attitude and a prayer in our heart.

THE SCATTERING TIME—3

Let all things be done decently and in order. 1 Cor. 14:40.

To bring order out of confusion. That was what Adventists needed in the spring of 1845. At least that's what Joshua V. Himes thought. He could plainly see that the fanatical spiritualizers would drive the movement into ruin.

But their fanaticism wasn't the only point on which Himes differed from the spiritualizers. He also disagreed as to whether prophecy had been fulfilled in October 1844. As we saw earlier, the spiritualizers said it had been—that Jesus had come into their hearts on October 22, 1844, that the 2300-day prophecy had met its completion, and that they had been correct on both the timing and the event.

Himes would eventually decide that Millerism had been wrong on the time but correct on what should have taken place at the end of the 2300 days. To put it another way, no prophecy had been fulfilled on October 22, but they should continue to expect the return of Jesus in the clouds of heaven in the next few years of "disputed time." In the process of arriving at that conclusion, Himes as early as November 1844 had begun to give up Miller's understanding of prophecy. Eventually he would lead those in his segment of the movement away from the prophetic understanding that had given force and point to Millerite evangelism.

But that end wasn't clear to anyone during the spring of 1845. All Himes knew was that they had to escape from the false teachings of the fanatics. It was that same fear that drove the ever-ailing and ever-weakening Miller into Himes' camp by late April 1845. Himes had persuaded William to join him at a conference slated to open on April 29 at Albany, New York. There the majority group of Adventists organized into a quasi-denomination with a doctrinal base and a rudimentary organizational approach along the lines of congregationalism.

The Albany event was a good thing in the sense that it sought to bring order out of chaos. It was unhelpful, however, when it divorced its segment of Millerism from an understanding of the prophecies that had given it birth and meaning. The underlying problem was that their major motivation was to define their movement in terms of what they were against. They had fallen into the pit of doing theology primarily against their neighbor. And with that comes a failure of balance.

Help us, Lord, to keep our eyes on Your Word rather than on the problems of our neighbors as we seek to navigate through the day.

THE SCATTERING TIME—4

Through faith we understand. Heb. 11:3.

Understanding doesn't come easily. Especially when we need it most, when our confusion shakes the very foundation of our life.

It is almost impossible for those of us who live more than 160 years after the event to comprehend the depth of confusion and chaos in Millerite ranks in the wake of the October disappointment.

The answers to what had happened in October 1844, as we have noted the past three days, were several. The spiritualizer segment, holding that they had been right on the time and the event, claimed that Christ had indeed come on October 22. The Albany Adventists, on the other hand, said that they had been wrong on the time but right on the event to take place at the end of the 2300 days. That is, no prophecy had been fulfilled in October, but the cleansing of the sanctuary was indeed the Second Advent, an event yet to occur.

Both groups had given up something essential. For the spiritualizers it was a literal understanding of the Bible, while for the Albany group it was Miller's grasp of prophecy.

But there was a third possible position regarding a fulfillment of the prophecy of the 2300 days in October 1844. That is, that Millerites had been correct on the time but wrong on the event. In other words, the 2300-day prophecy had been fulfilled, but the cleansing of the sanctuary was obviously not the Second Advent.

The interesting thing about that third perspective is that, unlike the other two answers as to what had happened, this one had no visible adherents. Whereas thousands in mid-1845 identified themselves with the ideas, leaders, and periodicals of the spiritualizers and the Albany Adventists, the orientation that held that something had happened on October 22 but that the cleansing of the sanctuary was not the Second Advent had no visible presence.

Yet it is out of the third position that the largest of the Adventist groups, the Seventh-day Adventists, would eventually emerge. But that development awaited three things: (1) the rise of leaders, (2) the evolution of doctrines that explained the Millerite experience and clarified wrong notions, and (3) the development of periodicals and organizational strategies that could spread those teachings. The rest of this year's journey will follow this third group.

Meanwhile, we can be thankful for God's patience—that He waits for us, even in our day, as we seek to iron out life's difficulties.

MEET JOSEPH BATES

I am with you and will watch over you wherever you go. Gen. 28:15, NIV.

Joseph Bates is the core individual during the earliest period of Seventh-day Adventism. He not only stands at the center of the development of the movement's doctrinal position, but he will eventually introduce Seventh-day Adventism's other two founders to the Sabbath. Bates, as we will see, was not only the key founder of Adventism, but he would be its most zealous missionary. It is safe to say that there would be no Seventh-day Adventism as we know it without his pioneering leadership.

But Bates hadn't always been a Christian. Born in Massachusetts on July 8, 1792, he gave up the faith of his father early in life. His hometown was becoming the whaling capital of the United States, and he dreamed day and night of an adventurous life at sea.

His father, who had larger plans for the boy, finally gave his permission in the hopes that a voyage would "cure" him. But it had the opposite effect.

In June 1807, just before his fifteenth birthday, Joseph sailed as a cabin boy on a voyage to Europe. His early seagoing experiences might have led a more timid person to give up his dreams and return home. For example, on the return voyage from England the young seaman managed to fall off of one of the mast-heads into the ocean near a large shark that some of his mates had been baiting. If the creature hadn't shifted its position at that precise moment, Bates would have had a very short career at sea.

In the spring of 1809 Bates had another near-fatal experience when his ship struck an iceberg off Newfoundland. Trapped in the ship's hold, he and another sailor held each other in the dark and prepared to die as they heard from time to time "the screams and cries of some of our wretched companions, on the deck above us, begging God for mercy."

Years later Bates wrote of his spiritual stirrings at the time: "Oh, the dreadful thought! Here to yield up my account and . . . sink with the wrecked ship to the bottom of the ocean, so far from home and friends, without the least . . . hope of heaven."

The rugged young man had had a wake-up call, but he wasn't ready to offer his life to God yet.

We can be thankful that God didn't give up. And the blessed truth is that He is still working, even for our very own loved ones.

PRISONER BATES

Sufficient unto the day is the evil thereof. Matt. 6:34.

It took me quite a bit of living before I finally understood that verse. The New International Version puts it more plainly: "Each day has enough trouble of its own."

Young Bates certainly would have agreed with that. His adventures between 1807 and 1809 were but a small foretaste of the difficulties he would yet face.

A major turning point in his life took place on April 27, 1810. That evening a press-gang consisting of an officer and 12 men entered his boarding house in Liverpool, England, and seized him and several other Americans and dragged them at sword point as "recruits" for the British navy in spite of their documents declaring that they were United States citizens.

To us such treatment may reside at the edges of our imagination. But those were different times. Britain was in the midst of a death struggle with Napoleon, and its navy needed men. Because of low pay, filthy living condition, poor rations, and customary floggings, it was almost impossible to gain enough recruits. By the beginning of America's war with Britain in 1812 the British navy contained approximately 6,000 Americans.

Seventeen-year-old Bates would spend the next five years (1810-1815) as a "guest" of the British government, serving about half of his time as a sailor in the Royal Navy and the other half as a prisoner of war. His experiences indicate the tough stuff the young man was made of. At the outbreak of the War of 1812 the British urged the 200 Americans in Bates' squadron to fight for them against the French. Only six, including Bates, declined. His principle-based refusal cost him dearly.

On one occasion, in a conflict with the French fleet, all of the Americans except him, Bates reported, assisted the British. For his intransigence a British officer knocked Bates to the floor and ordered him put in leg irons. Bates responded that he was free to do so, but that he would not work because he was a prisoner of war. At that point the officer notified Bates that when the action began he would have him "lashed up on the main rigging for a target for the Frenchmen."

That spirit of independence and determination would characterize Joseph Bates for the rest of his life. And it is that principle-based and courageous approach to life that made him the forceful sort of person who would put his energies into building a movement on the ruins of Millerism.

May his tribe increase. God needs Joseph Bateses in every congregation.

BATES GETS RELIGION

I sought the Lord, and he heard me. Ps. 34:4.

Bates' father had been a religious man and attempted without much luck to raise his son to be spiritual. In 1807, however, one of the revivalistic waves of the Second Great Awakening deeply stirred young Joseph. But the interest was short-lived after a career at sea diverted his life.

But the sea has a way of turning a sailor's eyes to God, especially when they rode in small wooden ships. As Bates later put it, there was nothing in the stormy seas but "the thickness of a plank separating us from Eternity." It was in the face of losing such a plank that Bates dates his earliest religious stirrings. In the midst of a furious four-day hurricane that sent waves as high as the mast heads the young captain in desperation did two things—threw 40 tons of iron into the sea and took the unprecedented step of asking his cook to pray.

The cook wasn't the only one praying. So was Bates' wife, Prudy. Beyond that, believing that her husband packed too many novels and romances for his trips, Prudy stowed a New Testament and other Christian publications in his luggage. Through them the Holy Spirit did its proper work. Soon Bates had lost interest in reading just for entertainment and began devouring such books as Philip Doddridge's *Rise and Progress of Religion in the Soul*. The 32-year-old captain was getting religious, but feared that his officers and men might discover it and make fun.

The turning point came at the death of a sailor by the name of Christopher. As captain, it was Bates' duty to oversee the burial. Yet he felt so unworthy.

Having done his best, four days after the burial he gave his life to God and "promised the Lord that I would serve him the remainder of my life."

The meaning of Christopher's burial not only affected Bates—he used the event to stir up his crew, the next Sunday preaching a sermon on everlasting life.

Bates looked back on his conversion as finding "the Pearl of great price which was worth more riches than my vessel could contain." His only wish, he noted, "is that I could teach [others] the way of life and salvation."

And teach he would. That mission dominated the rest of his life.

We serve a powerful God, who can change the lives of our sons and daughters, and us also.

REFORMER ON THE LOOSE

Let us search and try our ways, and turn again to the Lord. Lam. 3:40.

B ates on his last voyage (the one after he was converted) believed his duty was not only to convert his crew to Christianity, but to make sure they behaved like Christians, even before they actually became such.

Thus at sunset on August 9, 1827 (the day they departed port), he assembled his crew and stated the rules and regulations that would govern the voyage. It must have been a shock to the rough seafaring men who stood before him. Not only were they to give up swearing, but they were to show respect for one another by using their proper names rather than nicknames. Much more radical was the rule that they would have no shore leave on Sunday while in port. Rather, proclaimed the captain, "we shall observe the Sabbath" on board ship.

The crew mostly sat in stunned silence to the proclamations. Some voiced contrary opinions, but what were they to do? After all, they were already out to sea on a journey that would probably take some 18 months.

But the real bomb hadn't yet dropped. *The Empress,* Bates announced, would be a temperance ship. There would be no liquor or intoxicating drinks on board, and if he could he would persuade them never to drink at all, even when on shore.

At that point Bates knelt and dedicated himself and his crew to God.

Such was the atmosphere of what must have been a strange voyage for the crew. We don't know all their feelings, but one of the crew exclaimed that they were off to "a very good beginning." And at least one held that it was a very bad beginning.

On that voyage Bates began to get a better understanding of the Sabbath. The voyage witnessed his reading at least twice Seth Williston's *Five Discourses on the Sabbath.* On the first reading Bates declared that he did not know that the Bible had so much to say about the topic. Of course, he noted, "it was altered to the first day of the week" as a remembrance that on that day "our Saviour arose triumphant from the grave." A few weeks later he wrote that "the more I read and reflect on this holy day [Sunday] the more I am convinced of the necessity of keeping it entirely holy."

Christianity made a difference in Bates' life. It changed every part of it. And so it must if we have found Christ as both Savior and Lord. To follow in His steps is to lead a life radically different from that of the world around us.

BATES DISCOVERS THE ULTIMATE REFORM

But according to his promise we wait for new heavens and a new earth in which righteousness dwells. 2 Peter 3:13, RSV.

B ates first encountered the teaching of Christ's soon return through a local minister. But the idea didn't make much progress in his mind until 1839. In the fall of that year he heard about William Miller's preaching that Christ would come about 1843.

When Bates objected to the idea, someone told him that Miller used a great deal of Scripture to prove his point. Soon Bates attended an Adventist series of meetings and was "very much surprised to learn that any one could show anything about the *time* of the Saviour's second coming." On the way home from the first lecture he declared, "That is the truth," to his wife.

His next step was to read Miller's *Evidence From Scripture and History of the Second Coming of Christ, About the Year 1843.* Bates wholeheartedly accepted Miller's teaching, thus becoming the first of those who would later become Seventh-day Adventists to embrace and participate in the Millerite Advent movement.

Millerism soon dominated Bates' life, eventually usurping the time that he had previously devoted to social reform. At that point some of his friends asked him why he no longer attended the meetings of the temperance and abolitionist societies. "My reply was," he told them, "that in embracing the doctrine of the second coming of the Saviour, I found enough to engage my whole time in getting ready for such an event, and aiding others to do the same, and that all who embraced this doctrine would and must necessarily be advocates of temperance and the abolition of slavery."

Bates went on to tell his friends that "much more could be accomplished in working at the fountainhead" of the problem. After all, the vices that the various reform societies sought to eradicate were the product of sinful existence. But Christ's return would result in a "sudden and total obliteration of all evil." Thus Millerism became for Bates "the ultimate reform." He had concluded that "corrupt humanity could not reform corruption." The advent of Christ would be the only real and permanent solution.

From the beginning Bates became a significant leader in Millerism, being one of 16 people who called the first General Conference session in 1840 and chairing the one in May 1842.

Those responsibilities placed him in a position from which he could eventually engineer the rise of Sabbatarian Adventism in the late 1840s.

God directed Bates' life step by step. And He does the same for you and me. Our job is not to run ahead but to follow His leading day by day.

MEET JAMES WHITE

Now the word of the Lord came to Jonah . . . saying, "Arise, go to Nineveh, that great city, and cry against it; for their wickedness has come up before me." But Jonah rose to flee to Tarshish from the presence of the Lord. Jonah 1:1-3, RSV.

Some of us hear the call of the Lord to preach the Word, but aren't all that eager to do so. So it was with James White, the second person instrumental in the founding of Seventh-day Adventism.

James was born in Palmyra, Maine, on August 4, 1821. "At the age of fifteen," he reports, "I was baptized, and united with the Christian [Connexion] church. But at the age of twenty I had buried myself in the spirit of study and school teaching and had lain down the cross. I had never descended to the common sin of profanity, and had not used tobacco, tea and coffee, nor had I raised a glass of spirituous liquor to my lips. Yet I loved this world more than I loved Christ and the next, and was worshiping education instead of the God of heaven."

Young James had heard about Millerism, but regarded it "as wild fanaticism." In that state of mind he was shocked to hear his mother, whom he trusted, speak favorably of the Advent doctrine. He was unprepared for its impact upon him, partly because he had already made plans for his life. But conviction as to its truth he could not avoid.

"As I returned to the Lord," he reports, "it was with strong conviction that I should renounce my worldly plans and give myself to the work of warning people to prepare for the day of God. I had loved books generally, but, in my backslidden state, had neither the time nor taste for the study of the sacred Scriptures, hence was ignorant of the prophecies."

More specifically, James White felt impressed to visit the students he had been instructing in a local public school. "I prayed to be excused from that task," he wrote, "but no relief came." In that state of mind he went to work in his father's fields, "hoping I could work off the feelings under which I suffered."

But he couldn't. James then prayed for relief, but none came. Finally "my spirit rose in rebellion against God, and I recklessly said, I will not go." With a stomp of his foot he put an end to the matter and set out to do his own thing.

The experience of James White is not altogether unlike that of some of the rest of us. We hear the call of God to do this or that and we stomp our feet and resist.

But God doesn't give up. He has a plan for each of us. What is His plan for you today? And, more important, how will you relate to His will?

A Preacher in Spite of Himself

I charge thee therefore before God, and the Lord Jesus Christ. . . . Preach the word; be instant in season, out of season; reprove, rebuke, exhort with all longsuffering and doctrine. 2 Tim. 4:1, 2.

We left James White yesterday still rebelling against the call of God. "Finally," he reports, "I resolved that I would do my duty." Soon afterward a "sweet peace from God flowed into my mind, and Heaven seemed to shine around me. I raised by hands and praised God with the voice of triumph." His struggles with his earthly ambitions did not end, but at least he was moving in the right direction.

James' witnessing made an impact from the very beginning. At one place a woman called together about 25 of her neighbors, none of whom professed to be Christians. He gave his witness, then bowed to pray. I "was astonished," he wrote, "to find that these twenty-five sinners all bowed with me. I could but weep. They all wept with me."

He was having success, but felt constantly torn between his earthly ambitions and God's call to preach the Advent near. "The struggle," he penned, "was a severe one." After one occasion in which he "felt embarrassed" because his preaching was so impoverished because of a lack of biblical knowledge, he was shocked to hear some of his hearers address him as "Elder White." "The word Elder," he recalled, "cut me to the heart. I was confused and about paralyzed."

Things went along fairly well until he attempted to speak in the presence of two preachers who had not accepted the Advent doctrine. After 20 minutes he became "confused and embarrassed, and sat down." At that point he notes, "I finally gave up all for Christ and his gospel, and found peace and freedom."

Beyond surrender, James saw that if he was to be a successful preacher he needed to prepare himself for the task. As a result he tells us, I purchased "Advent publications, read them closely, studied my Bible," and spoke publicly as God opened the way.

We can find a lesson in James White's experience for all of us. Of course, we are not all called to become ministers, but God summons each of us to use the talents that He has given us. Some of us have an ongoing struggle in responding. The good news is that God does not lose patience with us. Just as He did with James, He will continue to work *with* us so that He can work *through* us. Our daily prayer must be that God will not only show us His will but that we will accept His will for our lives.

NO ONE SAID IT WOULD BE EASY

Keep your head in all situations, endure hardship, do the work of an evangelist, discharge all the duties of your ministry. 2 Tim. 4:5, NIV.

No one said that doing God's will would be easy. At least it wasn't for the newly committed preacher James White. For one thing he was poor. As he set out for "the great harvest-field," he recalled, "I had neither horse, saddle, bridle, nor money, yet felt I must go. I had used my last winter's earnings in necessary clothing, in attending Second-Advent meetings, and in the purchase of books and the [prophetic] chart. But my father offered me the use of a horse for the winter, and Elder Polley gave me a saddle with both pads torn off, and several pieces of an old bridal."

Poor he was, but go he did. But not everyone was happy with his arrival. At one place he reports a snowball barely missing his head while he was praying. Then came a deluge of them along with the noise of a mob that he had to shout to overcome. "My clothing and also my Bible," he recalled, "were wet from the melted fragments of a hundred snowballs."

What to do became the challenge. "That was no time for logic," he concluded, "so I closed my Bible and entered into a description of the terrors of the day of God. . . . Repent and be converted" was his appeal. At the end of the meeting nearly 100 arose for prayer.

God never said it would be easy. But just because the going is hard does not mean that God's blessing is not with us. James White as a young preacher learned to grow in spite of difficulties. And in the process he developed innovative approaches that spoke to the hearts and minds of people.

In one noisy place where he had a difficult time even making it to the pulpit, the first words they heard from his lips were a song loud and clear:

"You will see your Lord a coming,
You will see your Lord a coming,
You will see your Lord a coming,
In a few more days,
While a band of music,
While a band of music,
While a band of music,
Shall be chanting through the air."

His song not only stilled the crowd, but it expressed the hope of the soon approaching Advent to which he had given his life. God never told us that it would be easy to follow Jesus. But He did promise blessings unlimited when we do.

MEET ELLEN WHITE

Remember now thy Creator in the days of thy youth. Eccl. 12:1.

While I was praying at the family altar, the Holy Ghost fell upon me, and I seemed to be rising higher and higher, far above the dark world. I turned to look for the Advent people in the world, but could not find them, when a voice said to me, 'Look again, and look a little higher.' At this I raised my eyes, and saw a straight and narrow path, cast up high above the world. On this path the Advent people were traveling to the city, which was at the farther end of the path" (EW 14). Those words record part of 17-year-old Ellen G. Harmon's first heavenly vision in December 1844.

Ellen and her twin sister were born the youngest of a family of eight children in Gorham, Maine, on November 26, 1827. Her father, a maker and seller of hats, eventually moved the family to Portland, Maine.

It was in Portland that 9-year-old Ellen experienced an accident that deeply affected her. Hit in the face by a rock thrown by a classmate, she hovered near death for several weeks. Eventually she recovered, but the experience left her in such poor health that she was unable to continue her formal schooling, even though she tried with all her heart. Poor health would continue to plague her for much of her life.

Her inability to attend school, however, did not stop her informal education. Her autobiographical sketches reflect a young woman with both a probing mind and a sensitive nature. And the size of her personal library at the time of her death indicates that she was well-read in a variety of subjects.

Her sensitively appears not only in her relationship to other people, but also toward God. In fact, even a casual reading of her autobiography leads to the conclusion that she was desperately in earnest about religion from her earliest recollections.

The thought that Jesus might return in a matter of years especially traumatized young Ellen. She first came across that teaching at age 8 when on the way to school she picked up a scrap of paper indicating that Jesus could arrive in a few years. "I was seized with terror," she wrote. "Such a deep impression was made upon my mind . . . that I could scarcely sleep for several nights, and prayed continually to be ready when Jesus came" (LS 20, 21).

Her early experience helps us to see the truth that some things that we fear can eventually become the hope of our lives, especially as we come to understand God's character better.

STRUGGLING WITH GOD

"I believe; help my unbelief!" Mark 9:24, RSV.

The religious journey isn't equally pleasant for everyone. That is especially true of those with a sensitive nature. And young Ellen was one of those sensitive ones.

Yesterday we found her "seized with terror" when as a child she first read about the nearness of the Advent. Her fear of the Second Coming stemmed from several sources. One was a deep sense of unworthiness. "There was in my heart," she penned, "a feeling that I could never become worthy to be called a child of God. . . . It seemed to me that I was not good enough to enter heaven" (LS 21).

For years Ellen struggled with her fears. Two false beliefs compounded her problem. The first was that she had to be good—or even perfect—before God could accept her. The second was that if she was truly saved she would have a feeling of spiritual ecstasy.

Her emotional darkness began to dissipate during the summer of 1841 when she attended a Methodist camp meeting at Buxton, Maine. There she heard in a sermon that all self-sufficiency and effort were worthless in gaining favor with God. She realized that "it is only by connecting with Jesus through faith that the sinner becomes a hopeful, believing child of God" (*ibid.*, 23).

From that point forward she earnestly sought pardon for her sins and strove to give herself entirely to the Lord. "All the language of my heart was," she later penned, "'Help, Jesus; save me, or I perish!'" "Suddenly," she tells us, "my burden left me, and my heart was light" (*ibid.*).

But, she thought, this is too good to be true. As a result, she tried to reassume the load of distress and guilt that had been her constant companion. As she put it: "It seemed to me that I had no right to feel joyous and happy" (*ibid.*). Only gradually did she understand the wonder of the fullness of God's redeeming grace.

But in spite of her new understanding she continued to struggle with doubts because she did not always have the ecstatic feelings that she believed she had to have if she were truly saved. As a result, she continued to fear that she was not perfect enough to meet her Savior at His advent.

Does Ellen's reaction seem familiar? Many of us find it hard to believe that the gospel is really as good as God claims it is. In the end the solution is not feelings but reading God's promises for what they really say.

Help us, Lord, today in our unbelief.

A YOUNG MILLERITE—1

In My Father's house are many mansions; if it were not so, I would have told you. I go to prepare a place for you. And if I go and prepare a place for you, I will come again and receive you to Myself; that where I am, there you may be also. John 14:2, 3, NKJV.

Ellen Harmon had first heard William Miller in a series in Portland, Maine, during March 1840. When he returned for a second set of meetings in June 1842 she gladly attended.

She had accepted Miller's message but still could not escape the nagging fear that she wasn't "good enough." Beyond that, the thought of God torturing people in a never-ending hell troubled her.

While Ellen was in that mental state, her mother suggested that she counsel with Levi Stockman, a Methodist minister who had accepted Millerism. Stockman relieved Ellen's mind by telling her "of the love of God for His erring children, that instead of rejoicing in their destruction, He longed to draw them to Himself in simple faith and trust. He dwelt upon the great love of Christ and the plan of redemption."

"Go free," he told her, "return to your home trusting in Jesus, for He will not withhold His love from any true seeker" (1T 30). That interview was one of the major turning points in Ellen Harmon's life. From then forward she looked upon God "as a kind and tender parent, rather than a stern tyrant compelling men to blind obedience." Her heart "went out toward Him in a deep and fervent love. Obedience to His will [now] seemed a joy; it was a pleasure to be in His service" (LS 39).

Her new understanding of God as a tender parent aided young Ellen in several ways. Not the least of which was the nature of hell, a topic that we will examine in a future reading.

The kindly parent view of God also helped her look forward to the Second Advent with joyful enthusiasm. She saw that she had nothing to fear from such a Being, but everything to hope.

And what a blessed hope it is! All too often we in the twenty-first century get caught up with our daily lives to such an extent that we fail to realize the magnitude of the promises of the Second Coming.

Whatever good things our "tender parent" has given us on this earth, we know from the Bible that what is yet to come will be infinitely better.

We can be thankful for our "tender parent."

A YOUNG MILLERITE—2

For the Lord himself will descend from heaven with a cry of command, with the archangel's call, and with the sound of the trumpet of God. And the dead in Christ will rise first; then we who are alive, who are left, shall be caught up together with them in the clouds to meet the Lord in the air; and so we shall always be with the Lord. Therefore comfort one another with these words. 1 Thess. 4:16-18, RSV.

Αnd comforting words they are! They had become especially so to young Ellen Harmon. Her discovery of God as a "tender parent" energized her to sound the news of the Second Coming so that others could prepare for the joyous event.

Thus, contrary to her naturally shy nature, she began to pray in public, to share with others in the Methodist class meetings her belief in Jesus' saving power and His soon return, and to earn money to buy printed material to spread the Advent doctrine.

The last activity particularly taxed her. Because of her poor health she had to sit propped up in bed to knit stockings at 25 cents a day to do her part. Intensely sincere, her conviction showed up in every aspect of her life. It led many of her young friends to faith in Jesus.

Not only was Ellen zealous for the Advent truth preached by Miller, but so were her parents and siblings. But their local Methodist congregation, which taught that Christ would not come until after the 1,000 millennial years of peace and plenty, did not appreciate the constant agitation of the teaching on the soon return of Christ. As a result, in September 1843 it expelled the Harmon family from its membership.

Their experience reflected that of many others as Millerite Adventists everywhere refused to remain quiet on the topic of the return of Jesus in the near future.

But Ellen and most other Millerites were not overly concerned with their expulsion from the various denominations. After all, Jesus would appear in a few short months, and then all their troubles would be over. With that hope in mind, the Millerite believers continued to meet together for encouragement as the predicted time approached.

Joy filled their hearts. As Ellen would later put it, the period extending from 1843 into 1844 "was the happiest year of my life" (LS 59). Looking back, we realize that those believers were in error on the time of the Advent, but they were not wrong about the hope itself. The blessed hope of the Advent of Jesus is still a joy that fills our hearts with anticipation.

A PEOPLE OF THE BOOK—1

All scripture is given by inspiration of God, and is profitable for doctrine, for reproof, for correction, for instruction in righteousness. 2 Tim. 3:16.

The most basic issue for any religious group is authority. Those who initiated the Seventh-day Adventist movement were clear on the topic. As James White put it in early 1847, *"the Bible* is a perfect and complete revelation. It *is our only rule of faith and practice"* (italics supplied).

The Sabbatarians, as we shall see in the days to come, developed their distinctive doctrinal beliefs on the basis of Bible study. That fact was not always obvious to their detractors. Miles Grant, for example, argued in 1874 in the *World's Crisis* (a leading first-day Adventist periodical) that "it is claimed by the Seventh-day Adventists that the sanctuary to be cleansed at the end of the 1300 [2300] days mentioned in Dan. 8:13, 14, is in heaven, and that the cleansing began in the autumn of A.D. 1844. If any one should ask why they thus believe, the answer would be, the information came through one of Mrs. E. G. White's visions."

Uriah Smith, editor of the Seventh-day Adventist *Review and Herald,* vigorously responded to that accusation. "Hundreds of articles have been written upon the subject [of the sanctuary]. But in no one of these are the visions once referred to as any authority on this subject, or the source from whence any view we hold has been derived. Nor does any preacher ever refer to them on this question. The appeal is invariably to the Bible, where there is abundant evidence for the views we hold on this subject."

Smith, we should point out, made a statement that any person willing to go back into early Seventh-day Adventist literature can verify or disprove. Paul Gordon has done that on the subject of the sanctuary in *The Sanctuary, 1844, and the Pioneers* (1983). His findings support Smith's claims.

The facts of the case are that whereas many later Adventists have tended to lean on Ellen White's authority or that of Adventist tradition, the early Adventists were a people of the "Book." Current Seventh-day Adventists of all persuasions need to note that fact as they seek to discover the genuine Adventism of history. The good news is that God has given in His Book the words of life. We can rejoice today with the psalmist, who declared, "Thy word have I hid in mine heart, that I might not sin against thee" (Ps. 119:11).

A PEOPLE OF THE BOOK–2

They received the word with all eagerness, examining the Scriptures daily to see if these things were so. Acts 17:11, ESV.

Ellen White was in full harmony with Bates and her husband on the centrality of the Bible. In her first book (1851) she wrote: "I recommend to you, dear reader, the Word of God as the rule of your faith and practice" (EW 78). And 58 years later she stood before the 1909 General Conference session with a Bible in her hands, saying, "Brethren and sisters, I commend unto you this Book." Her last spoken words to a General Conference session of the church, they reflected the sentiment of her ministry across its more than six decades.

James White in 1847 touched on the unique role of the Bible in Adventist doctrinal formation, claiming that Scripture is "our only rule of faith and practice." In the context of his wife's prophetic ministry he wrote that "true visions are given to lead us to God, and his written word; but those that are given for a new rule of faith and practice, separate from the Bible, cannot be from God, and should be rejected."

Four years later he again made that point explicit. "Every Christian," he wrote, "is therefore duty bound to take the Bible as a perfect rule of faith and duty. He should pray fervently to be aided by the Holy Spirit in searching the Scriptures for the whole truth, and for his whole duty. He is not at liberty to turn from them to learn his duty through any of the gifts. We say that the very moment he does, he places the gifts in a wrong place, and takes an extremely dangerous position. The Word should be in front, and the eye of the church should be placed upon it, as the rule to walk by, and the foundation of wisdom, from which to learn duty in 'all good works.'"

In short, early Seventh-day Adventists rejected tradition, church authority, and even the gifts of the Spirit in their doctrinal formation.

With that in mind, it is important to ask where we are as Adventists (both individually and collectively) today on the topic of authority. In all too many cases, it appears, we are weak on the Bible.

Today is the best day possible to reverse that problem. Right now as you pray I want you to recommit yourself to serious Bible study on a daily basis. Why not begin with the Gospels, the letters of Paul, or the Psalms.

The important thing, however, is not where you start your study, but that in the spirit of the Adventist pioneers you commit yourself to at least one-half hour of Bible study every day. I know this will interfere with your TV time. But that is good.

THE CENTRALITY OF THE SHUT DOOR

*And while [the foolish virgins] went to buy, the bridegroom came; and they that were
ready went in with him to the marriage: and the door was shut. Afterward came also
the other virgins, saying, Lord, Lord, open to us. But he answered and said, Verily
I say unto you, I know you not. Matt. 25:10-12.*

Some biblical symbols pick up more than one meaning across time. Thus it
was with that of the shut door in post-Millerite Adventism during the late
1840s.

Earlier we saw that Miller as early as 1836 had viewed the shut door of
Matthew 25:10 as the close of human probation. That is, before Christ comes
every human being will have made a decision for or against Him.

Since Miller had tied the Second Advent to the October 1844 date, he held
that probation would cease by that time. He continued to hold that view after the
October disappointment. On November 18, 1844, for example, he wrote that
"we have [finished] our work in warning sinners. . . . God, in his providence has
shut the door; we can only stir up one another to be *patient.*"

But that wasn't the only viewpoint on the confusing happenings of the autumn of 1844. J. V. Himes, for example, as early as November 5 had concluded
that no prophecy had been fulfilled in October 1844. And if that were the case,
the door of probation had not shut. Therefore God's people still needed to give
the message of salvation.

As strange as it may seem to us today, it was differing understandings of the
shut door that separated the various strands of Adventism in 1845 and beyond. In
order to grasp the issues it is important to realize that by early 1845 the phrase "the
shut door" had picked up two meanings:

(1) the close of probation

(2) that prophecy had been fulfilled in October 1844

With that recognition in mind, we can think of the Albany Adventists who
followed Himes as "open-door Adventists" and the fanatical spiritualizers and the
developing Sabbatarians as "shut-door Adventists."

James White was so intent on the fact that prophecy had been fulfilled at the
end of the 2300-day prophecy that he came to characterize the Sabbatarians as
"the seventh day shut door people." (We can be thankful that the name didn't
stick.)

Meanwhile, the theological task of the Sabbatarians during the late 1840s was to
separate themselves from their fanatical cousins in the shut door sector of Adventism.
That could only happen through further Bible study and God's leading.

NEW LIGHT ON THE SANCTUARY—1

And he said to him and to me, For two thousand and three hundred evenings and mornings; then the sanctuary shall be cleansed and restored. Dan. 8:14, Amplified Bible.

We must never forget that those who would become Sabbatarian Adventists were of the shut-door persuasion. That is, they believed that the prophecy of Daniel 8:14 had met its completion in October 1844. They had no doubts about the dating of the prophecy. The historicist interpreters of Daniel had always widely agreed that the 2300-day prophecy would be fulfilled between 1843 and 1847. The controversy hadn't been about the date but about what would happen at the close of the prophetic time period. In other words, there had been a general consensus about the interpretation of the symbolic figure related to the date, but widespread disagreement over the interpretation of the other two prophetic symbols of Daniel 8:14.

The theological task that Adventists needed to accomplish in the wake of the October disappointment was to unlock the meaning of the sanctuary and the cleansing.

Miller, we noted earlier, had interpreted the sanctuary to be the earth and the cleansing to be its purifying by fire at the Second Advent. His viewpoint had obviously failed. We should recognize that some had expressed doubts as to Miller's interpretation before the October disappointment. Josiah Litch, for example, wrote in April 1844 that "it has not been proved that the cleansing of the sanctuary, which was to take place at the end of the 2300 days, was the coming of Christ or the purification of the earth." Again he noted, as he wrestled with the meaning of the text, that they were most likely to be "in error relative to the event which marked its close."

That line of thought rose again soon after the October disappointment. Thus Joseph Marsh could acknowledge in early November: "We cheerfully admit we have been mistaken in the *nature* of the event we expected would occur . . . ; but we cannot yet admit that our great High Priest did not *on that day* accomplish *all* that the type would justify us to expect."

We can glean a lesson here. At times we are more certain of a particular interpretation of Scripture than we have a right to be. We need to be humble and do our homework as we study God's word.

Help us, Father, to keep our minds open to Your progressive leading as we study Your Word.

NEW LIGHT ON THE SANCTUARY—2

We have such a high priest, who has taken His seat at the right hand of the throne of the Majesty in the heavens, a minister in the sanctuary and in the true tabernacle, which the Lord pitched, not man. Heb. 8:1, 2, NASB.

Years after the event, Hiram Edson wrote about an experience he claimed he had on October 23, 1844, the day after the disappointment. "I began," he penned, "to feel there might be light and help for us in our present distress. I said to some of my brethren, let us go to the barn. We entered the granary, shut the doors about us and bowed before the Lord.

"We prayed earnestly; for we felt our necessity. We continued in earnest prayer until the witness of the Spirit was given that our prayer was accepted, and that light should be given, our disappointment be explained, and made clear and satisfactory. After breakfast I said to one of my brethren [probably O.R.L. Crosier], 'Let us go and see, and encourage some of our brethren.'

"We started, and while passing through a large field I was stopped about midway of the field. Heaven seemed opened to my view, and I saw distinctly, and clearly, that instead of our High Priest coming out of the Most Holy of the heavenly sanctuary to come to the earth on the tenth day of the seventh month, at the end of the 2300 days, that he for the first time entered on that day the second apartment of that sanctuary; and that he had a work to perform in the Most Holy before coming to this earth."

Edson's recollections are generally well known among Seventh-day Adventists. And some seem to think that it was through his "vision" that the church got its sanctuary doctrine.

But, we need to ask, are his visions or insights (or anyone else's) the proper grounding for a doctrine? Again, what if Adventism never had a report of Edson's experience? Would it make a difference? Not at all!

Hiram goes on to state that Crosier (who was living with him part of the time) and Dr. F. B. Hahn studied the topic of the sanctuary with him from the Bible. Crosier did an in-depth study, which Edson and Hahn agreed to finance for publication.

Here is the important point. At most, Edson's experience pointed out one possible interpretation of the meaning of the sanctuary. But Bible study and Bible study only could provide a solid foundation.

We must build all our teachings on solid Bible study. *ALWAYS!*

NEW LIGHT ON THE SANCTUARY—3

[The earthly sanctuary services serve as] a copy and shadow of the heavenly sanctuary; for when Moses was about to erect the tent, he was instructed by God, saying, "See that you make everything according to the pattern which was shown you on the mountain." Heb. 8:5, RSV.

Yesterday we met O.R.L. Crosier, the friend of Hiram Edson who devoted his time to intensive and extensive biblical study on the meaning of the sanctuary and the cleansing that would take place at the end of the 2300 days of Daniel 8:14. Writing in the *Day Dawn,* published by Edson and F. B. Hahn, Crosier very systematically set forth his findings. One of his first conclusions is that Miller's interpretation was wrong since "the word Sanctuary cannot be applied to the earth upon any principle whatever." Crosier obviously has his concordance at hand when he notes that "the word Sanctuary occurs 104 times in the Bible—100 in the Old Testament, . . . and 4 times in the New Testament, all in the Epistle to the Hebrews."

Later in his article Crosier concludes that the sanctuary of Daniel 8:14 could not possibly be the Jewish sanctuary, because it had been "irrecoverably destroyed." "Yet, though the Jewish Sanctuary ceased to be *the* Sanctuary 1800 years ago, something else existed to the end of the 2300 days which was called *the Sanctuary,* and was at the end of that period, to undergo a change which is expressed by the word 'cleansed,' 'justified,' 'vindicated,' or 'declared just.'"

One thing is clear from the book of Hebrews, Crosier pointed out: "That Christ at his ascension entered the place of which the Jewish Sanctuary was a figure, pattern or type, and that is the place of his ministry during the Gospel dispensation." The book of Hebrews unquestionably indicates that "'we have such an High Priest, *who is set on the right hand of the throne of the Majesty* IN THE HEAVENS: A MINISTER OF THE SANCTUARY . . . .' This is the only text in the New Testament in which the word Sanctuary is found, except the three that speak of the Jewish Sanctuary. And now we feel safe in stating, that there is no Scripture authority for calling anything else the Sanctuary under the Gospel dispensation, but the place of Christ's ministry in the heavens, from the time of his ascension to the Father till his second coming."

Today we can thank God that we have Jesus as our high priest in the heavenly sanctuary. "Consequently he is able for all time to save those who draw near to God through him, since he always lives to make intercession for us" (Heb. 7:25, RSV). Amen!

NEW LIGHT ON THE SANCTUARY—4

He is able to save to the uttermost those who draw near to God through him, since he always lives to make intercession for them. Heb. 7:25, ESV.

Crosier had begun to write about the heavenly sanctuary as early as March 1845. But it was on February 7, 1846, that he presented his fullest understanding of the topic in an article entitled "The Law of Moses."

We can summarize the most important conclusions of "The Law of Moses" as follows: 1. A literal sanctuary exists in heaven. 2. The Hebrew sanctuary was a complete visual representation of the plan of salvation *patterned* after the heavenly sanctuary. 3. Just as the earthly priests had a two-phase ministry in the wilderness sanctuary, so Christ has a two-phase ministry in the heavenly. The first phase began in the holy place at His ascension, the second on October 22, 1844, when Christ moved from the first apartment of the heavenly sanctuary to the second. Thus the antitypical or heavenly day of atonement started on that date. 4. The first phase of Christ's ministry dealt with forgiveness, while the second involves the blotting out of sins and the cleansing of both the sanctuary and individual believers. 5. The cleansing of Daniel 8:14 was a purification from sin and was therefore accomplished by blood rather than fire. 6. A period of time would take place between the beginning of Christ's second apartment ministry and the Second Advent.

The results of Crosier's Bible study had answered the questions on the identity of the sanctuary and the nature of the cleansing. In addition, they indicated what had occurred at the conclusion of the 2300 day prophecy of Daniel 8:14.

Crosier's article did not go unnoticed by those who would become the leaders of the Sabbatarian Adventists. As early as May 1846 Joseph Bates recommended Crosier's treatment of the sanctuary as being "superior to any thing of this kind extant."

The next year Ellen White penned that "the Lord shew me in vision, more than one year ago, that Brother Crosier had the true light, on the cleansing of the Sanctuary, etc.; and that it was his will that Brother C. should write out the view which he gave us in the *Day-Star, Extra,* February 7, 1846" (WLF 12).

We can be thankful that God not only has a plan for saving His people from their sins, but that it is moving toward its completion as Christ ministers on our behalf in heaven.

NEW LIGHT ON THE SANCTUARY—5

Thus it was necessary for the copies of the heavenly things to be purified with these rites, but the heavenly things themselves with better sacrifices than these. For Christ has entered, not into a sanctuary made with hands, a copy of the true one, but into heaven itself, now to appear in the presence of God on our behalf. Heb. 9:23, 24, RSV.

Given the importance of Daniel 8:14's teaching about the cleansing of the sanctuary at the end of the 2300 days to shut-door Adventism, it isn't surprising that we find more than just Hiram Edson, O.R.L. Crosier, and F. B. Hahn concerned with the identity of the sanctuary and the cleansing and with what happened at the completion of the 2300-day prophecy.

Other published students of the topic include Emily C. Clemons, who edited a periodical in mid-1845 graphically entitled *Hope Within the Veil,* and G. W. Peavey, who was teaching in April 1845 that Christ had "closed the work typified by the daily ministrations previous to the 10th day of the 7th month, and on that day went into the holiest of all."

Peavey also saw an interrelationship between Daniel 8:14, Hebrews 9:23-24, and Leviticus 16, and concluded that the Most Holy Place of the heavenly sanctuary needed purification by Christ's blood in the antitypical day of atonement. He believed, however, that the cleansing of the heavenly sanctuary had taken place on October 22, 1844, whereas Crosier and his friends regarded the atonement as an unfinished process that had begun on that date. It was Crosier's understanding that would eventually find its way into Sabbatarian Adventism.

Ellen Harmon's early visions also touched upon the topic of the sanctuary. In early 1845 she reported a vision during which she "saw the Father rise from the throne, and in a flaming chariot go into the holy of holies within the veil, and sit down," at the beginning of the second phase of Christ's heavenly ministry (EW 55).

While her vision harmonized with the Bible-based conclusions of Crosier and others, we must remember that she had no prominence or authority in Adventism at that time. She was basically unknown to the major players in the developing sanctuary theology. To them she was merely a 17-year-old girl claiming to have visions amidst the conflicting voices of a shut-door Adventism literally overrun by a multitude of individuals claiming charismatic gifts.

Thank You, Father, that You are willing to guide our minds as we seek knowledge of Your great plan of redemption.

ELLEN WHITE'S FIRST VISION—1

And it shall come to pass afterward, that I will pour out my spirit upon all flesh; and your sons and your daughters shall prophesy. Joel 2:28.

In December 1844 Ellen Harmon was praying with four other women in the house of a Mrs. Haines of Portland, Maine. "While we were praying," Ellen notes, "the power of God came upon me as I had never felt it before" (LS 64).

During the experience, she wrote, "I seemed to be rising higher and higher, far above the dark world. I turned to look for the Advent people . . . , but could not find them, when a voice said to me, 'Look again, and look a little higher.' At this I raised my eyes, and saw a straight and narrow path, cast up high above the world. On this path the Advent people were traveling to the city, which was at the father end of the path. They had a bright light set up behind them at the beginning of the path, which an angel told me was the midnight cry [the preaching of the October 22 date as the fulfillment of Daniel 8:14].

"This light shone all along the path and gave light for their feet so that they might not stumble. If they kept their eyes fixed on Jesus, who was just before them, leading them to the city, they were safe.

"But soon some grew weary, and said the city was a great way off, and they expected to have entered it before. Then Jesus would encourage them. . . .

"Others rashly denied the light behind them and said that it was not God that had led them out so far. The light behind them went out, leaving their feet in perfect darkness, and they stumbled and lost sight of the mark and of Jesus, and fell off the path down into the dark and wicked world below. . . .

"Soon our eyes were drawn to the east, for a small black cloud had appeared, about half as large as a man's hand, which we all knew was the sign of the Son of man. We all in solemn silence gazed on the cloud as it drew nearer and became lighter, glorious, and still more glorious, till it was a great white cloud. . . .

"Then Jesus' silver trumpet sounded, as He descended on the cloud. . . . He gazed on the graves of the sleeping saints, then raised His eyes and hands to heaven, and cried, 'Awake! awake! awake! ye that sleep in the dust, and arise'" (EW 14-16).

ELLEN WHITE'S FIRST VISION—2

And in the last days it shall be, God declares, that I will pour out my Spirit upon all flesh, and your sons and your daughters shall prophesy. Acts 2:17, RSV.

Surprisingly, Ellen White's first vision did not deal with the sanctuary or its cleansing. Rather, its intent was to encourage the disappointed Millerite Adventists by offering them assurance and comfort. More specifically, it provided instruction along several lines.

First, it indicated that the October 22 movement had not been a mistake. To the contrary, October 22 had witnessed a fulfillment of prophecy. As such, it was a *"bright light"* behind them to help the disappointed Adventists get their bearings and guide them in the future. It is of interest that Ellen Harmon had given up her belief in the October message during the month before her first vision. Thus the vision reversed her own thinking.

Second, the vision indicated that Jesus would continue to lead them, but they needed to keep their eyes fixed on Him. Thus Adventism had two foci for its guidance—the October event in its past history and Jesus' continuing direction in the future.

Third, the vision seemed to imply that it would be longer than expected before Jesus would come again.

Fourth, that it was a serious mistake to give up their past experience in the 1844 movement and claim that it had not been from God. Those who made that conclusion would drift into spiritual darkness and lose their way.

Ellen White's first vision provided a number of positive lessons. But please note one thing: It did not indicate *what* had happened on October 22, 1844. That knowledge would become clear through Bible study. Rather than providing specific explanations, Ellen's first vision merely highlighted the fact that God was indeed still leading a people in spite of their disappointment and confusion. It was the first sign of His prophetic care and guidance through Ellen Harmon.

The theme of God's directing His people through the perils and pitfalls of history would become the central theme of her ministry. It would come to its maturity in the five important volumes tracing the history of God's leading from the entrance of sin in *Patriarchs and Prophets* up through the completion of God's plan in *The Great Controversy*.

Thank God today for His continuing guidance.

THE CALL TO WITNESS

Do not be afraid, but speak and do not be silent. Acts 18:9, RSV.

About a week after her first vision Ellen experienced a second one, telling her to relate to other Adventists what God had revealed to her. It also instructed her that she would meet great opposition.

She balked at her duty. After all, she reasoned, she had poor health, was only 17 years of age, and was naturally timid. "For several days," she explained later, "I prayed that this burden might be removed from me, and laid upon someone more capable of bearing it. But the light of duty did not change, and the words of the angel sounded continually in my ears, 'Make known to others what I have revealed to you'" (LS 69). She went on to note that she preferred death to the task ahead of her. Having lost the sweet peace that had come with her conversion, she once again found herself in despair.

It is little wonder that Ellen Harmon felt dismayed at having to go public. After all, the population at large openly scorned Millerites, and serious doctrinal error and a wide variety of fanaticism plagued post-disappointment Millerism's own ranks.

More specifically, the prophetic gift had become especially suspect in 1844 by both the larger culture and the Millerite Adventists. The summer of 1844 had seen Joseph Smith, the Mormon "prophet," lose his life to a mob in Illinois, while late 1844 and early 1845 saw the rise of a large number of Adventist "prophets" of questionable character, a fair number of them operating in Maine. And in the spring of 1845 the Albany Adventists would vote that they had "no confidence in any new messages, visions, dreams, tongues, miracles, extraordinary gifts, revelations," and so on.

In that climate it is not surprising that young Ellen Harmon sought to avoid her call to prophetic office. But in spite of her personal fears, she ventured forth and began to present God's comforting counsel to the confused Adventists.

Even a cursory glance at her several early autobiographical statements indicates that she encountered a great deal of both fanaticism and personal opposition. Some of her early visions dealt with fanaticism and opposition by giving counsel and rebuke that was often quite personal in nature.

Today, O Lord, help us to be faithful in the place where You have put us to sound the message that You have given us.

RELATIONSHIP OF SPIRITUAL GIFTS TO THE BIBLE—1

And he gave some as apostles, and some as prophets, and some as evangelists, and some as pastors and teachers, for the equipping of the saints for the work of service, to the building up of the body of Christ; until we all attain to the unity of the faith, and of the knowledge of the Son of God. Eph. 4:11-13, NASB.

E arly Sabbatarian Adventists held that the Bible taught that spiritual gifts, including the prophetic one, would exist in the church until the Second Advent.

Uriah Smith provided them with an illustration that makes the point nicely. "Suppose," he wrote, "we are about to start upon a voyage. The owner of the vessel gives us a book of directions, telling us that it contains instructions sufficient for our whole journey, and that if we will heed them, we shall reach in safety our port of destination.

"Setting sail, we open our book to learn its contents. We find that its author lays down general principles to govern us in our voyage, and instruct us as far as practicable, touching the various contingencies that may arise, till the end; but he also tells us that the latter part of our journey will be especially perilous; that the features of the coast are ever changing by reason of quicksands and tempests; 'but for this part of the journey,' says he, 'I have provided you a pilot, who will meet you, and give you such directions as the surrounding circumstances and danger may require; and to him you must give heed.'

"With these directions we reach the perilous time specified, and the pilot, according to promise, appears. But some of the crew, as he offers his services, rise up against him. 'We have the original book of directions,' they say, 'and that is enough for us. We stand upon that, and that alone; we want nothing of you.'

"Who now heeds that original book of directions? Those who reject the pilot, or those who receive him, as that book instructs them? Judge ye.

"But some . . . may meet us at this point like this: 'Then you would take Sister White as our pilot, would you?' It is to forestall any efforts in this direction, that this sentence is penned. We say no such thing. What we do say is distinctly this: that the gifts of the Spirit are given for our pilot through these perilous times, and whenever or in whomever we find genuine manifestations of these, we are bound to respect them, nor can we do otherwise without in so far rejecting the Word of God, which directs us to receive them."

A SIDE LESSON ON RESTORATIONISM

Those from among you shall build the old waste places; You shall raise up the foundations of many generations; And you shall be called the Repairer of the Breach, the Restorer of Streets to Dwell In. Isa. 58:12, NKJV.

Arising independently in several sections of the United States around 1800, restorationism aimed at reforming the churches by recovering all of the New Testament's teachings. The restorationists rejected the view that the Reformation was something that happened only in the sixteenth century. Rather, the Reformation began then but would continue until the last vestiges of tradition were gone and the teachings of the Bible were firmly in place in the church. The task of the restorationist movement was to complete the unfinished reformation.

The restorationists espoused a radical view of *sola scriptura*. They wanted Bible evidence for every position they set forth. Scripture was to be their only foundation for faith and practice. The movement was also anti-creedal. A popular statement among its adherents was that "we have no creed but the Bible itself."

The spirit of the restorationist movement set the stage for a great deal of the theological agenda for the majority of American Protestants during the early nineteenth century. It fostered the attitude of getting back to the Bible that permeated the American Protestant mentality of the times.

One branch of the restorationist movement had special importance to Seventh-day Adventists: the Christian Connexion. James White and Joseph Bates (two of Adventism's three founders) were members of it.

Those two men brought with them into Adventism both the Bible-oriented philosophy of the Christian Connexion and its drive to return to the church *all* the lost teachings of the Bible. They were convinced that such a restoration must take place before the Second Advent.

A restorationist view of history continues to influence Adventism today. Take, for example, the opening words of the denomination's Statement of Fundamental Beliefs: "Seventh-day Adventists accept the Bible as their only creed." Beyond that, Ellen White's *The Great Controversy* is built upon a restorationist pattern, tracing the recovery of those Bible teachings lost in the early centuries of Christianity, beginning with the Reformation and extending to the eschaton.

As Seventh-day Adventists we can be thankful that we belong to a movement that is strong on Scripture.

RELATIONSHIP OF SPIRITUAL GIFTS
TO THE BIBLE—2

God has appointed in the church first apostles, second prophets, third teachers, then workers of miracles, then healers, helpers, administrators, speakers in various kinds of tongues. 1 Cor. 12:28, RSV.

The Christian Connexion made a large impact upon early Sabbatarian Adventism, including its view of spiritual gifts.

We learn of the connexionist view on the topic through the writings of William Kinkade (b. 1783), one of the movement's foremost theologians. Kinkade wrote in 1829 that he had in his early years refused to call himself by "any name but that of *Christian*" and that he would take no book for his "standard but the *Bible.*"

He was certainly clear on the supreme authority of the Bible in religious matters. However, in his extended discussion of the "restoration of the ancient order of things" he claimed that he could not settle for "one inch short" of the New Testament order.

And at the center of New Testament order, he argued, were spiritual gifts, including, he wrote, "the gift of prophecy, set forth in such places as 1 Corinthians 12:8-31 and Ephesians 4:11-16. The presence of spiritual gifts in the church, *is the ancient order of things;* everyone opposed to this, is opposed to primitive Christianity. To say that God caused these gifts to cease, is the same as to say, God has abolished the order of the New Testament church. . . . These gifts constitute the ancient order of things."

Kinkade argued that they were not temporary gifts that ended with the apostolic age. Rather, "these gifts, as they are laid down in the scripture, compose the gospel ministry" as set forth in the New Testament.

William Kinkade's New Testament theology of the perpetuity of spiritual gifts in the context of the Bible as the only source of authority is important for understanding early Seventh-day Adventism since two of the denomination's three founders had been active in the Christian Connexion. James White and Joseph Bates entered Sabbatarian Adventism from a movement that held to both the Bible as the only determiner of faith and practice and the continuation of spiritual gifts.

The delicate balance between the two is reflected in the writings of James White, which set the tone for the proper function of spiritual gifts in the church.

God our Father, we thank You that You have cared enough for Your church to pour out the gifts of the Spirit. Help us to be wise in our use of Your gifts.

RELATIONSHIP OF SPIRITUAL GIFTS TO THE BIBLE—3

Quench not the Spirit. Despise not prophesyings. Prove all things; hold fast that which is good. 1 Thess. 5:19-21.

How easy it is to despise anyone who claims to have the gift of prophecy. After all, we have the Bible. Then again, a lot of crazy and questionable people have made such claims down through history. In the light of such facts it is only natural to doubt if not to despise.

But then there's the Bible's own counsel on the topic: "Do not quench the Spirit. Do not despise prophecies, but test everything; hold fast what is good" (1 Thess. 5:19-21, ESV).

Despising outright those who claim the gift of prophecy is not an option for New Testament Christians. To the contrary, Scripture requires them to "test" such claimants.

The Bible, fortunately, not only tells us to evaluate them, it also suggests some ways of how to do it. One appears in the Sermon on the Mount, in which Jesus commands us to "beware of false prophets, who come to you in sheep's clothing but inwardly are ravenous wolves. You will know them by their fruits. . . . Every sound tree bears good fruit, but the bad tree bears evil fruit" (Matt. 7:15-17, RSV).

Applied to a prophetic claimant, one needs to evaluate the results of the principles they advocate and whether their own lives reflect New Testament Christianity.

Another test occurs in 1 John 4. It tells us to "test the spirits to see whether they are of God; for many false prophets have gone out into the world. By this you know the Spirit of God: every spirit which confesses that Jesus Christ has come in the flesh is of God, and every spirit which does not confess Jesus is not of God" (verses 1-3, RSV).

We must ask ourselves, What's a prophetic claimant's witness to Jesus?

Isaiah 8:20 presents a third test: Do such a person's teachings agree with the Bible?

Those are all important criteria, but even more important is whether their teachings point to themselves and their own word or to Jesus and the Bible.

Those early Adventists found themselves forced to their Bibles as they sought to evaluate the claims of young Ellen Harmon/White and others in the late 1840s. And it wasn't always easy to make their decisions.

It still isn't easy. But that is not the point. We have a command.

Help us today, Father, to become zealous students of Your Word, so that we might be better evaluators of all things spiritual.

TESTING THE PROPHET—1

Beware of false prophets, who come to you in sheep's clothing. . . . You will know them by their fruits. Matt. 7:15, 16, RSV.

Yesterday we noted the Bible command to test those who claim the prophetic gift. The early Sabbatarian Adventists did just that.

Take Joseph Bates, for example. After witnessing Ellen White in vision several times, he declared himself to be a "doubting Thomas." "I do not believe in [her] visions," he said. "But if I could believe that the testimony the sister has related tonight was indeed the voice of God to us, I should be the happiest man alive."

He claimed that her message deeply moved him, believed that she was sincere, and was somewhat mystified as to her experience. "Although I could see nothing in [the visions] that militated against the word," he later wrote, "yet I felt alarmed and tried exceedingly, and for a long time [was] unwilling to believe that it was anything more than what was produced by a protracted debilitated state of her body."

But even though he had his doubts, he did not just tune her out. Coming out of the Christian Connexion, he was at least open to the idea that the New Testament gifts of the Holy Spirit (including that of prophecy) would remain active in the church until the return of Christ.

As a result, Bates decided to investigate what Ellen believed to be a divine gift of prophecy. "I therefore," he penned, "sought opportunities in presence of others, when her mind seemed freed from excitement (out of meeting), to question, and cross question her and her friends which accompanied her, especially her elder sister, to get if possible at the truth. When she was in vision, Bates added, "I listened to every word, and watched every move to detect deception or mesmeric influences."

With Bates we find a case study of a person struggling between the natural proclivity to reject an individual's claim to the prophetic gift and the Bible command to test and accept that which is good (1 Thess. 5:19-21).

We will return to Bates' struggle on the topic. But we need to be honest with our own selves. How is it with me? Are my mind and heart really open? Or am I so full of prejudice against (or for) such a gift that I am blind to evidence? May God grant each of us clear vision and open hearts on the topic.

TESTING THE PROPHET—2

Beloved, do not believe every spirit, but test the spirits to see whether they are from God, because many false prophets have gone out into the world. 1 John 4:1, NASB.

The turning point in Bates' evaluation of Ellen White's gift came during November 1846 in Topsham, Maine, when she had a vision that included astronomical data. As an ex-seaman Bates was well acquainted with the topic.

He later told J. N. Loughborough of his experience in Topsham. "One evening, in the presence of Bro. Bates, who as yet was an unbeliever in the visions," Loughborough reports, "Sr. White had a vision, in which she soon began to talk about the stars. She gave a glowing description of the rosy-tinted belts which she saw across the surface of some planet, and then added, 'I see four moons.' 'Oh,' said Bro. Bates, 'she is viewing Jupiter.'" She went on to describe several other astronomical phenomena.

After Ellen White came out of vision, Bates asked her if she had ever studied astronomy. "I told him," she recalled, that "I had no recollection of ever looking into an astronomy" (2SG 83).

James White was of the same opinion regarding her total lack of knowledge on the topic. "It is well known," he wrote in describing the Topsham vision in early 1847, "that she knew nothing of astronomy, and could not answer one question in relation to the planets, before she had this vision."

The evidence had been enough for the skeptical Bates. From that point on he firmly believed that she had a divine gift. He had concluded by April 1847 that God had given her gift "to comfort and strengthen his 'scattered,' 'torn,' and 'peeled people,'" since their disappointment in 1844.

And in January 1848 Bates urged his readers not to reject Ellen White's work "because of her childhood and diseased bodily infirmities, and lack of worldly knowledge." After all, he pointed out, "God's manner has ever been to use the weak things of this world to confound the learned and mighty." The Lord was, according to Bates, employing her to "encourage the little flock" at the very time many of the previous leaders were deserting it.

"I was once slow," he noted, "to believe that this sister's visions were of God. I did not oppose them," however, "for the word of the Lord is positively clear that spiritual visions will be given to his people in the last days."

And so they will. Our task is not to despise but to test. May God help us with that assignment.

BATES GETS THE SABBATH—1

Remember the Sabbath day, to keep it holy. Six days shalt thou labour, and do all thy work: but the seventh day is the sabbath of the Lord thy God. Ex. 20:8-10.

Seventh-day Adventists regard Joseph Bates as the apostle of the Sabbath. But, we need to ask, how did he come across the topic?

The answer to that question has more than one branch. For one thing, ever since he had become a Christian he had kept Sunday as the Sabbath, even going so far as to enforce his position on his crew when he captained a ship.

A second avenue undoubtedly involved his study of prophecy. After all, a student of the book of Revelation has no difficulty in seeing that the commandments of God would be kept at the end of time (see Rev. 12:17; 14:12).

But how did Bates become sensitized to the fact that the Sabbath of the New Testament is Saturday rather than Sunday?

That's where the Seventh Day Baptists come in. That group has never been an aggressive evangelistic people. The United States had only 6,000 of them in 1840. And by the year 2000 their numbers had shrunk to 4,800—a 20 percent loss in membership in 160 years. To put it bluntly, evangelism has never been their strong suit.

But during at least one time in their history they did become aggressive. Their 1841 General Conference session concluded that God "required" evangelism on the topic of the Sabbath. Then in 1842, Merlin Burt reports, the denomination's publication society "began publishing a series of tracts with the objective of 'introducing the Sabbath' to the 'Christian public.'" Again, at their 1843 General Conference session they once more resolved that it was their "solemn duty" to enlighten their fellow citizens on the topic of the seventh-day Sabbath.

Their efforts had some positive results. At their 1844 meeting the Seventh Day Baptists thanked God that "a deeper and wider-spread interest upon the subject has sprung up than has ever before been known in our country."

The story of these Baptists tells us that truth is a good thing. But it also indicates that even truth can do no good if people merely sit on it.

It wasn't until they made a conscious decision to let their light shine on the topic that things began to happen. We still need those kinds of light-shining decisions today.

BATES GETS THE SABBATH—2

So God blessed the seventh day and hallowed it, because on it God rested from all his work which he had done in creation. Gen. 2:3, RSV.

Yesterday we noted that the Seventh Day Baptists had had some results in their effort in the early 1840s to stimulate attention among other Christians regarding the biblical Sabbath.

Interestingly, a significant part of that interest had developed among the Millerite Adventists. As a result, the *Sabbath Recorder* reported in June 1844 "that considerable numbers of those who are looking for the speedy appearance of Christ, have embraced the seventh day, and commenced observing it as the Sabbath." The *Recorder* went on to suggest that obedience to the Sabbath was part of "the best preparation" for the Advent.

We do not know exactly what the *Recorder* meant by saying that "considerable numbers" of Millerites had begun to keep the Sabbath by the summer of 1844, but we do know that the issue of the seventh-day Sabbath had become problematic enough by September for the Millerite *Midnight Cry* to publish two lengthy articles on the topic.

"Many persons," we read, "have had their minds deeply exercised respecting a supposed obligation to observe the seventh day." The editors decided that "there is no particular portion of time which Christians are required by law to set apart as holy time." But if such a conclusion was incorrect, "then we think the seventh day is the only day for the observance of which there is any law."

The final article concluded with the thought that the "seventh-day brethren and sisters . . . are trying to mend the old broken Jewish yoke, and put it on their necks." The article also suggested that Christians should not call Sunday the Sabbath.

The Seventh Day Baptists responded to the *Midnight Cry* articles by noting that "the new discovery of the Second Advent believers, which makes it morally certain to them that Christ will come on the tenth day of the seventh month, has probably unfitted their minds in a great measure for the consideration of the claims of the Sabbath upon their attention."

And so it had. But biblical truth is persistent. And for that we can be thankful. God leads His people as a whole and each of us as individuals step by step in the pathway of His Word.

BATES GETS THE SABBATH—3

For truly, I say to you, until heaven and earth pass away, not an iota, not a dot, will pass from the Law until all is accomplished. Matt. 5:18, ESV.

A mong those Seven Day Baptists who interacted with the Millerites, one of the more significant is Rachel Oakes. By early 1844 she had not only accepted the Advent message, but had shared her Sabbath perspective with the Adventist congregation in Washington, New Hampshire, where her daughter (Mrs. Cyrus Farnsworth) was a member.

Her first convert, apparently, was William Farnsworth, who had earlier convinced her on the Millerite teachings.

Another person she brought to the Sabbath was Frederick Wheeler, who, while preaching in the Washington church, remarked that all persons confessing communion with Christ should "be ready to follow Him, and obey and keep God's commandments in all things."

Later Rachel Oakes reminded Wheeler of his remarks. "I came near getting up in the meeting at that point," she told him, "and saying something."

"What was it you had in mind to say?" Wheeler asked.

"I wanted to tell you that you would better set that communion table back and put the cloth over it, until you begin to keep the commandments of God."

Wheeler was somewhat in shock from her frontal assault. He later told a friend that Mrs. Oakes' "words cut him deeper than anything that he had ever had spoken to him." But he thought them over, studied the Bible on the topic, and soon began to observe the seventh-day Sabbath.

That was apparently in March 1844. Subsequently, several members of the Washington congregation joined Wheeler and William Farnsworth in honoring the biblical Sabbath.

When I get to the kingdom, one person I want to look up is Rachel Oakes. She must have been a real character. The least we can say about her is that she certainly wasn't bashful about sharing her beliefs. God had given her a voice, and she used it in spreading His Sabbath truth. I don't know if her approach was Christ-centered or somewhat offensive, but I trust that it was the former since Wheeler, a Methodist minister, did not turn away from her in disgust.

One of the lessons of Rachel Oakes is that we never know the widespread influence we have on other people. And that goes for all of us. Even you!

BATES GETS THE SABBATH—4

If you love me, obey my commandments. John 14:15, NLT.

The Adventist experience with the Sabbath in Washington, New Hampshire, during the spring of 1844 was significant. But of even more impact was the conversion of Thomas M. Preble to the biblical Sabbath. Preble, the pastor of the Free Will Baptist congregation in nearby Nashua, had been a Millerite since 1841. It appears that he got the Sabbath from Frederick Wheeler, whose Washington congregation was about 35 miles from his home. Preble tells us he began to observe the Sabbath in the summer of 1844.

We have no record of any publications from Preble on the Sabbath issue before the October disappointment, although it is probable that he was part of the agitation that resulted in the several responses published in the *Midnight Cry* in September to put a damper on the discussion of the seventh day.

But in early 1845 Preble came out strong on the topic, publishing an article on the Sabbath in the *Hope of Israel* on February 28. He concluded his study by noting that "all who keep the first day for 'the Sabbath,' are [the] *Pope's Sunday-keepers!!* and GOD'S SABBATH-BREAKERS!!!"

"If I had but one day on this earth to spend," Preble declared, "I would give up error for truth, as soon as I could see it. May the Lord give us wisdom, and help us keep all 'his commandments that we may have right to the tree of life.' Rev. 22:14."

A 12-page pamphlet entitled *A Tract, Showing That the Seventh Day Should Be Observed as the Sabbath, Instead of the First Day; "According to the Commandment"* soon followed the article.

By April 1845 Bates had discovered Preble's article on the Sabbath in the *Hope of Israel.* He tells us that he "read and compared" Preble's evidence with the Bible and became convinced "that there never had been any change" of the Sabbath to the first day of the week.

"THIS IS TRUTH!" he declared to himself. And "in a few days," he reports, "my mind was made up to begin to keep the fourth commandment."

One of the impressive things about Bates is that he was willing to change firm opinions when faced with proper biblical evidence. God desires each of us to have teachable hearts and minds as He leads us in the path of life.

BATES SPREADS THE SABBATH—1

And I heard the voice of the Lord saying, "Whom shall I send, and who will go for us?" Then I said, "Here am I! Send me." Isa. 6:8, RSV.

Soon after accepting the Sabbath, Bates traveled to Washington, New Hampshire, to meet with Wheeler, the Farnsworth brothers, and other Adventists who observed it. Wheeler's son George reports that Bates arrived about 10:00 in the evening, "after the family were all in bed." George heard his father let someone in. And during the night he woke from time to time to hear their voices. They talked all night long, and then continued on until noon. At that point Bates headed for home.

Back in Massachusetts Bates met James Madison Monroe Hall on the bridge that linked the towns of Fairhaven and New Bedford.

It was at that encounter that Hall blurted out the fateful question that probably diverted his activities for the rest of the day and certainly changed his life forever. "What's the news, Captain Bates?"

"The news," he replied, is that "the seventh day is the Sabbath, and we ought to keep it."

I don't know how long they spent on that bridge, but given Bates' usual style, it could have been all day. What we do know is that Hall went home, studied his Bible on the topic, and observed the next Sabbath. His wife followed him a week later. Hall was Bates' first convert to an understanding that would shape both men's lives from that day onward.

For his part, Hall thereafter held Bates in such high regard that he named his only son Joseph Bates Hall.

Ever afterward Joseph Bates was a man with a mission. And he would not slack in that endeavor until he was on his deathbed. Nothing could stop him.

In the early 1850s, for example, Bates reports a five-week missionary tour in Canada during which for more than 20 days he struggled with heavy snow and extreme cold, on one occasion "wading through deep snow for 40 miles" to take his message to an interested family.

Another time he cut through three feet of ice so that he could find enough water to baptize seven people in -30° F weather.

And we thought we were zealous! Look again.

God help me this day to take Your message more seriously. Help me to move beyond my comfort zone.

71

BATES SPREADS THE SABBATH—2

Be ready always to give an answer to every man that asketh you a reason of the hope that is in you. 1 Peter 3:15.

To put it mildly, Joseph Bates was an enthusiastic witness for his new-found understanding of the seventh-day Sabbath. In 1854, for example, young Stephen N. Haskell (a first-day Adventist preacher) met that whirlwind of energy, conviction, and enthusiasm. The 21-year-old Haskell had been introduced to the seventh-day Sabbath, but was not totally convicted on the topic.

Then someone directed Bates to Haskell's house. Haskell reports that Joseph spent 10 days with them, preaching every night as well as on Sabbath and Sunday. But beyond that the irrepressible Bates held a Bible study for Haskell and a few others "from morning until noon, and from noon until night, and then in the evening until the time we went to bed."

"He did that for ten successive days," Haskell later reported, "and I have been a Seventh-day Adventist ever since." He never once doubted the importance of the Sabbath thereafter. Bates had done it again.

But he wasn't always successful in his witness. One of his greatest failures took place in August 1846, the month he first met a young Christian Connexion preacher and his girlfriend—James White and Ellen Harmon. Bates, of course, let loose with one of his extensive Bible studies on what had become his favorite topic. The result? Failure! Total failure!

Both rejected his teaching on the seventh-day Sabbath. Ellen recalled that "Elder Bates was keeping the Sabbath, and urged its importance. I did not feel its importance, and thought that Elder B. erred in dwelling upon the fourth commandment more than upon the other nine" (1888 LS 236, 237).

His meeting of James White and his future wife weren't the only important events to take place in August 1846. That month saw the marriage of James and Ellen and it also witnessed the publication of Bates' first little book on the Sabbath, entitled *The Seventh-day Sabbath, a Perpetual Sign.*

But before turning to those events we need to look a bit longer at Bates. We can learn at least three lessons from him. First, that it is easy to become one-sided and unbalanced in our presentation of the biblical message. Second, that even the most zealous fail from time to time. Third, that failure is not an excuse to stop trying.

JAMES WHITE CHANGES HIS MIND ABOUT MARRIAGE

Have you not read that he who made them from the beginning made them male and female, and said, "For this reason a man shall leave his father and mother and be joined to his wife, and the two shall become one flesh." Matt. 19:4, 5, RSV.

It will undoubtedly come as a shock for most sheltered Seventh-day Adventists to discover that James White did not believe in marriage.

Yes, you heard me right. James opposed marriage in 1845. Thus he could publish in the *Day-Star* that an Adventist couple in announcing their marriage had "denied their faith." Marriage, White held, was "a wile of the Devil. The firm brethren in Maine who are waiting for Christ to come have no fellowship with such a move." And why, you may be asking, did he take such a position? The answer appears in his next sentence: "We are looking for redemption in the Morning Watch."

The facts of the case are that he expected Jesus to return in October 1845. Beyond that, the early Adventists believed that time was extremely short. And from that perspective, getting married and setting up a home appeared to be a denial of the faith in the *soon* coming of Jesus. After all, if Jesus came when they expected, there would be no need for earthly homes and marriages.

Thus James later reported that "most of our brethren who believed with us that the second advent movement was the work of God, were opposed to marriage because they believed that time was very short, and they considered that it was a denial of our faith to get married, as such a step seemed to contemplate years of life in this world."

But time continued on. And with that came reevaluation.

As a result, James and Ellen were married in August 1846. The reason: "God had a work for both of us to do, and he saw that we could greatly assist each other in that work." After all, young Ellen needed a "legal protector" if she was to travel the country bearing her "important . . . message to the world."

The lesson: Sometimes we are wrong. And when we are, the only sensible thing to do is admit it and make a course correction.

But for some of us that is not easy.

Help me, Lord, to see Your leading in spite of my errors. Help me to be humble enough to adjust when I am wrong.

BATES SPREADS THE SABBATH—3

And he shall speak great words against the most High, . . . and think to change times and laws. Dan. 7:25.

Augustus 1846 saw the publication of Bates' first little book on the Sabbath—*The Seventh-day Sabbath, a Perpetual Sign, From the Beginning to the Entering Into the Gates of the Holy City, According to the Commandment.*

That's quite a title! But it indicates his firm belief in the importance of the Sabbath at the end of time.

The 1846 edition of that little book (it was only 48 pages) presented a largely Seventh Day Baptist concept of the Sabbath. Thus Bates set forth the ideas that the seventh-day Sabbath was the correct day of worship and that the Papacy had attempted to change God's law (Dan. 7:25).

But two points of special interest in the 1846 edition of that book indicate that Bates was beginning to interpret the Sabbath in the light of an Adventist theological framework.

The first is the thought in the preface that "the *seventh* day" is "to be restored before the second advent of Jesus Christ." That idea derived from the restorationist platform that Bates brought with him from the Christian Connexion. Thus the Reformation was not complete and would not be until all the great Bible truths neglected or perverted down through history found their rightful place in God's church.

The second very Adventist tilt in the 1846 edition is Bates' interpretation of the Sabbath within the context of the book of Revelation. He tied the Sabbath to Revelation 14:12: "Here is the patience of the saints: here are they that keep the *commandments* of God, and the faith of Jesus." He also pointed out in alluding to verse 7, with its command to "worship him that made heaven and earth, and the sea, and the fountains of waters," that "the seventh-day Sabbath is more clearly included in these commandments" than the other nine.

It is that very emphasis that had turned off Ellen Harmon. But Bates didn't back off just because he ran into criticism and rejection.

Help us, Lord, to keep our eyes open to the implications of Your word. And give us strength when we discover important truths.

AND WHAT HAPPENED TO
T. M. PREBLE AND RACHEL OAKES?

Choose you this day whom ye will serve. Joshua 24:15.

Today we need to ask about the fate of T. M. Preble and Rachel Oakes, two of those instrumental in the chain of events that led Joseph Bates to the Sabbath.

Preble, unfortunately, gave up the seventh-day Sabbath. "After conscientiously observing the seventh day for the Sabbath, for about three years," he wrote in 1849, "I have satisfactory reasons for giving it up, and now keep the first day as heretofore." In 1867 he published *The First-day Sabbath: Clearly Proved by Showing That the Old Covenant, or Ten Commandments, Have Been Changed, or Made Complete, in the Christian Dispensation.*

Commenting on that book from a Seventh-day Adventist perspective, Uriah Smith suggested in no uncertain terms that Preble's volume on the seventh-day Sabbath had been the better of the two.

And Preble's brother-in-law doubted his sincerity in the change back to Sunday. According to him, Preble had become the administrator of a large estate, and when the Sabbath interfered with his business, he gave it up. "The no law theory was his after excuse in the matter."

But even though Preble rejected the Sabbath in his personal experience, he made an impact on the heart and mind of Joseph Bates that nothing could reverse.

And Bates wouldn't be the only major leader of Sabbatarian Adventism influenced by Preble's 1845 tract. In the spring of that year it fell into the hands of 15-year-old John Nevins Andrews and converted him on the topic of the seventh day. Andrews would later become Adventism's major scholar on the Sabbath, publishing the first edition of his important *History of the Sabbath and First Day of the Week* in 1873.

What about Rachel Oakes, the person indirectly responsible for bringing the Sabbath to Preble? She observed the Sabbath for the rest of her life, but did not join the Seventh-day Adventist Church because of certain rumors she had heard about James and Ellen White. When those rumors were cleared up in the late 1860s, she was baptized a short time before her death.

"She sleeps," S. N. Haskell wrote in her obituary, "but the result of her introducing the Sabbath among Adventists lives."

Praise God for the mysterious ways He leads His children!

BATES SPREADS THE SABBATH—4

Do not be afraid, but go on speaking and do not be silent. Acts 18:9, ESV.

B ates, as we have noted, didn't have a bashful bone in his body when it came to telling others about the Sabbath. But one of his most conspicuous failures on the topic was his own wife. Even though he wrote book after book on the topic and must have badgered her constantly, she must have been as stubborn as he was. As a result, "he kept the Holy Sabbath alone."

Fairhaven tradition has it that "Captain Bates used to take his wife in their carriage to the Christian church on Sunday, but he himself would not enter to worship 'on the pope's Sabbath'; he would return for her after church." The good news is that Prudence Bates accepted the seventh day in 1850. His prayers, example, and impatient patience had finally paid off. Like many of our friends and family, she was apparently listening when she appeared not to be doing so.

More good news for Bates came with the conversion of James and Ellen White to the seventh day, probably in November 1846. James later reported that "by reading" Bates' *Seventh-day Sabbath, a Perpetual Sign,* "I was established upon the Sabbath, and began to teach it."

That acceptance set the stage for the formation of Seventh-day Adventism. From that point on Bates and the Whites began to work together.

Events were finally beginning to move. By December 1846 Bates' *Seventh-day Sabbath* had apparently reached western New York. Late in the year Bates and James had hoped to meet with Hiram Edson, O.R.L. Crosier, and F. B. Hahn (the developers of the heavenly sanctuary understanding) at Edson's Port Gibson, New York, home, but circumstances detained White in the east.

One item on the agenda was the seventh-day Sabbath, which Edson claims he had been favorable toward for some months, but without any definite conviction.

But after Bates' presentation, during which Edson "could scarcely keep his seat," "Edson was on his feet and said, 'Brother Bates, that is light and truth. The seventh day is the Sabbath, and I am with you to keep it.'"

Thus by late 1846 we find a group of believers uniting on three key doctrines—the Second Advent, the Sabbath, and the heavenly sanctuary. The stage was set for the rise of Seventh-day Adventism.

God may, from our perspective, lead slowly, but He leads certainly.

Help us, Lord, to be patient with Your direction.

THE TEMPTATION TO LEGALISM

No human being will be justified in his sight by works of the law, since through the law comes knowledge of sin. Rom. 3:20, RSV.

Not everything Bates taught was pure gold. While no one can have the slightest doubt about his devotion to the seventh-day Sabbath from 1846 to the end of his life, his understanding of the Sabbath in relation to the plan of salvation is much less clear.

At times the good captain comes across as extremely legalistic:
- "Doing these commandments saves the soul."
- "The keeping of GOD'S SABBATH HOLY SANCTIFIES AND SAVES THE SOUL! But the keeping of one, or all the other nine without it will not."
- "We must keep the whole [law] if we would be saved."
- "God's children are to be saved, if at all, by doing or keeping the commandments."

While Bates could make gospel-sounding statements, there is no doubt that he was entangled in a legalism that ran through the course of his life.

One of his favorite texts to support his legalistic approach to the Sabbath is the account of the rich young ruler in Matthew 19. Repeatedly Bates goes back to that story to make his point. "The young man came and said to him, 'Good Master, what good thing shall I do that I may have eternal life?' Jesus answered, 'If thou wilt enter into life, keep the commandments.'" Bates interpreted that teaching to mean that "the only way, to enter life, was to keep the commandments." Furthermore, he added, if Jesus did not mean what he said, "then he deceived the lawyer."

Twenty years after expressing those thoughts Bates was still on the same track with the rich young ruler, concluding that "if you really desire to have eternal life when Jesus comes, be sure, oh! Be sure, that you keep all the ten commandments of God."

Sadly enough, in the 1888 era Uriah Smith and G. I. Butler were still employing Matthew 19 in the same manner. In fact, I recall published Bible studies still using that text as a proof for commandment keeping during the 1960s. For some, commandment keeping was still the route to life eternal.

That is exactly the point that Paul was attacking in today's text (Rom. 3:20). It is unfortunate that sincere believers can use good Bible texts in bad ways.

Help us, O Lord, as we grapple with the true meaning of Scripture.

GLIMPSES OF THE GOSPEL

By grace you have been saved through faith; and this is not your own doing, it is the gift of God—not because of works, lest any man should boast. Eph. 2:8, 9, RSV.

Bates may have been able to convince the other two founders of Seventh-day Adventism regarding the Sabbath, but they didn't buy into his legalism.

James White, for example, was explicitly clear when he wrote: "Let it be distinctly understood that there is no salvation in the law, that is, there is no redeeming quality in the law."

For White it was all-important to have "living active faith in Jesus." Speaking of the Millerite message in 1850, he declared that it "led us to the feet of Jesus, to seek forgiveness of all our sins, and a free and full salvation through the blood of Christ."

While James appealed to people to "obey and honor [God] by keeping his commandments," he also wrote that "we must seek a full and free pardon of all our transgressions and errors, through the atonement of Jesus Christ, now while he pleads his blood before the Father."

Ellen was of the same mind as her husband. Especially enlightening is her use of the rich young ruler of Matthew 19 throughout her long ministry. It varied greatly from that of Bates, Smith, and Butler. Never did she quote Jesus in that context as saying that the way to gain heaven was to keep the commandments.

Rather, invariably she pointed beyond what she called the "external and superficial" understanding of the young ruler (and Bates) to the deeper need of a total transformation that could come only through a personal relationship with Christ.

To her the lesson of Matthew 19:16, 17 was not that one could gain salvation by the law, but that the rich young ruler had totally failed. While it was true, she pointed out, that he obeyed the external aspects of the Ten Commandments, he did not see that the law was rooted in the love of God. For her the rich young ruler had not been saved by keeping the commandments, but was totally lost (see, e.g., 2SG 239-243; DA 518-523; COL 390-392).

Dear friend, one of the most important understandings we need for daily living is the relationship of the law to the saving gospel. We will review the gospel message extensively later this year. But we need to begin our journey on the topic today.

THE SABBATH AND THE APOCALYPTIC VISION—1

And the temple of God was opened in heaven, and there was seen in his temple the ark of his testament. Rev. 11:19.

A few days ago we examined the little book that Joseph Bates published on the Sabbath in August 1846. We noted that the first edition of *The Seventh-day Sabbath, a Perpetual Sign* set forth largely a Seventh Day Baptist understanding of the Sabbath. That is, that the seventh day is the correct one and that the church had changed it in the medieval period.

We also saw how that book converted the Whites and Hiram Edson and other students of the heavenly sanctuary to the Sabbath. Discussions between Bates and those individuals led him to a fuller understanding of the implications of the seventh-day Sabbath in the period immediately prior to the Second Advent. Bates set forth his enriched understanding in January 1847 in a second edition of *The Seventh-day Sabbath*. While it had only an additional 14 pages, they presented the interpretive framework within which all future Sabbatarian theological thinking would take place.

One major insight was his emphasis on Revelation 11:19: "And the temple of God was opened in heaven, and there was seen in his temple the ark of his testament." Joseph had grasped a fact that harmonized with his new second apartment understanding of the heavenly sanctuary related to Daniel 8:14. Whereas every vision in Revelation begins with a sanctuary scene, in the first half of the book they take place in the holy place. But from Revelation 11:19 on the focus shifts to the Most Holy. In other words, Bates saw that the book of Revelation itself ties the opening of the Most Holy place of the heavenly sanctuary to end-time events.

But even more important to him was the contents of the ark. As he put it, "this Temple has been opened for some purpose." That purpose, as he saw it, was to highlight the Ten Commandments, the most important item in the ark of the covenant (Deut. 10:5).

Bates had begun to understand that the very core of the book of Revelation ties together the Second Advent, the opening of the Most Holy Place of the heavenly temple at the end of time, and the importance of the Ten Commandments right before Christ's coming. That understanding would become even more evident to him in Revelation 12-14.

Help us to see, Lord, what You are trying to teach us in that important end-time passage.

THE SABBATH AND THE APOCALYPTIC VISION—2

The dragon was wroth with the woman, and went to make war with the remnant of her seed, which keep the commandments of God, and have the testimony of Jesus Christ. Rev. 12:17.

Bates' discovery of the sanctuary teaching of Revelation 11:19 naturally led him to Revelation 12. That chapter is a historical portrayal of the Christian church from Christ's birth up to the end of time, during which the dragon (identified as "the Devil and Satan" in verse 9) becomes angry with the woman (the church) and goes off "to make war on the rest of her offspring" who "keep the commandments of God." (Rev. 12:17, RSV).

At that point Joseph found the link between Revelation 11:19 and 12:17. Not only would the second apartment of the heavenly sanctuary be opened at the end of time, revealing the ark containing the Ten Commandments, but those very commandments were featured at the end-time climactic point of chapter 12.

In his study Bates concluded that not only would the Ten Commandments be restored at the end of time, but that conflict would arise over them. As he viewed it, the conflict would mainly involve one commandment—the Sabbath, the one that had been changed by the church (see Dan. 7:25). He would read on to see that commandment pinpointed in Revelation 14:7.

As Bates put it, "that there will yet be a mighty struggle about the restoring and keeping of the seventh day Sabbath, that will test every living soul that enters the gates of the city, cannot be disputed. It is evident the Devil is making war on all such. See Rev. 12:17. 'Remember the Sabbath day and keep it holy.' Amen." With those words he closed the 1847 edition of his *Seventh-day Sabbath*.

His discoveries in the book of Revelation overwhelmed Bates. Not only would God have a "remnant" who would keep the Sabbath at the end of time, but there would be discord over that commandment. That conclusion would become even firmer as he studied Revelation 13 and 14.

It is impossible to know how clearly Bates saw it, but Revelation 12:17 is the key text of the rest of Revelation. Most immediately, chapter 13 expands on the dragon power of 12:17 and chapter 14 the last-day woman. Both chapters reflect conflict over the allegiance of God's people in the last days. Beyond that, Revelation 15-19 builds upon chapters 13 and 14, as they flesh out end-time prophetic events.

Help us, Lord, to study these momentous passages with more care.

THE SABBATH AND THE APOCALYPTIC VISION—3

Here is the patience of the saints: here are they that keep the commandments of God, and the faith of Jesus. Rev. 14:12.

In our last reading we saw that by January 1847 Joseph Bates had concluded from Revelation 12:17 that God would not only have a people at the end of time who would honor the Ten Commandments contained in the ark of the covenant (Rev. 11:19), but that the dragon would make war with those commandment keepers. It didn't take too much more study to see that end-time conflict reflected in such passages as Revelation 13:7, 8, which describes those who "worship" the beast as making "war" with those who follow the Lamb.

From chapter 13 he went to Revelation 14, which describes the end-time worshippers of the Lamb as following "the Lamb wherever he goes" (verse 4, RSV).

At that juncture, Revelation 14 became the focal point of Bates' study in the second edition of *The Seventh-day Sabbath, a Perpetual Sign.* Before looking at his conclusions, we should note the outline of chapter 14 itself.

1. Verses 1-5 introduce the end-time 144,000, who follow the Lamb in all of His teachings and have "his Father's name written on their foreheads" (verse 1, RSV).
2. Verses 6 and 7 present the first angel's message.
3. Verse 8 reflects on the second angel's message.
4. Verses 9-12 set forth the message of the third angel.
5. Verse 13 highlights the fate of those followers of the Lamb caught in the end-time persecution of Revelation 13.
6. And chapter 14 climaxes with the coming of Christ in the clouds of heaven to reap the harvest of the earth (verses 14-20).

That progression did not escape Bates as he struggled to understand where God's people were in the flow of end-time events. Interestingly enough, certain Millerites had emphasized the first and second angels' messages. Miller himself had believed that the judgment hour message of the first angel was being preached in his day. To Miller the judgment of verse 7 was the Second Advent.

Charles Fitch began to proclaim the second angel's message on the fall of Babylon in 1843 when the denominations began to persecute the Second Advent believers. But it would be the content of the third angel's message that would capture Bates' attention.

Before you pray this morning, it would be a good idea to read Revelation 14.

THE SABBATH AND THE APOCALYPTIC VISION—4

Fear God, and give Him glory, because the hour of His judgment has come; worship Him who made the heaven and the earth and sea and springs of waters. Rev. 14:7, NASB.

We have been studying the past few days Bates' growing understanding of Revelation 12-14. He was particularly fascinated with the three angels' messages of chapter 14, pictured as the last ones that God would give to the world before the Second Advent.

He found verse 12 especially pertinent. It once again (see Rev. 12:17) highlights the fact that just before the end of time God will have a commandment-keeping people. Of course, he did not miss the implications of verse 7, which indicates what commandment would be at issue in the end-time struggle. He correctly recognized the fact that the words "worship him that made heaven, and earth, and the sea, and the fountains of waters" allude to the Sabbath commandment of Exodus 20:8-11 (cf. Gen. 2:1-3). He also plainly saw from Revelation 14:7, 9 that worship would be the central issue at the end of the world's history. According to Revelation 14, people before the Second Advent would either be worshipping the beast of Revelation 13 (see Rev. 14:9) or the Creator of heaven and earth (verse 7). That latter group, of course, would obey *all* of God's commandments as they patiently waited (verse 12) for Jesus to come in the clouds of heaven (verses 14-20).

Bates' reading of Revelation 12:17-14:20 led him to several conclusions. First, that since 1845 God had been raising up a people who would honor all His commandments, including the Sabbath. "Now," he penned in 1847, "that such a people can be found on the earth as described in the 12 v. and have been uniting in companies for the last two years, on the commandments of God and faith or testimony of Jesus, is indisputable and clear."

Second, "John further shows that this is a remnant (which of course means the last end) made war with (his meaning is clear,) for 'keeping the commandments of God . . .' (12:17)."

And third, Bates noted that Revelation portrays only two groups at the end of time. "One is keeping the commandments and faith of Jesus. The other has the mark of the beast."

His insights set the stage for the development of Seventh-day Adventist theology. He had in essence developed by 1847 what has become known in Adventist circles as great controversy theology.

Father, once again give us clear minds as we meditate upon Your last message to a sinful world.

THE SABBATH AND THE APOCALYPTIC VISION—5

And I looked, and behold a white cloud, and upon the cloud one sat like unto the Son of man, having on his head a golden crown, and in his hand a sharp sickle. Rev. 14:14.

The past few days we have been meditating upon Joseph Bates' development of great controversy theology. By early 1847 he had come to the conclusion that what was becoming the Sabbatarian Adventist movement was not just another drive toward denominationalism but a movement of prophecy.

Another thing that we need to note is that the great controversy theme is firmly rooted in Scripture. Too many believe that it has its genesis in the writings of Ellen White. As early as April 7, 1847, she also would highlight that teaching. But her report of her vision on the topic would be one of confirmation of Bates' Bible study rather than one of origination. Let's take a look at her earliest great controversy vision.

"Dear Brother Bates," she wrote on April 7, 1847, "Last Sabbath we met with the dear brethren and sisters here. . . . Soon I was lost to earthly things, and was wrapped up in a vision of God's glory. . . . After viewing the glory of the Holy, Jesus raised the second veil, and I passed into the Holy of Holies.

"In the Holiest I saw the ark . . . . In the ark, was . . . the tables of stone. . . . Jesus opened them, and I saw the ten commandments written on them with the finger of God. . . . On one table was four, and on the other six. The four on the first table shone brighter than the other six. But the fourth (the Sabbath commandment) shone above them all; for the Sabbath was set apart to be kept in honor of God's name. . . . I saw that God had not changed the Sabbath, for He never changes. . . .

"I saw that the holy Sabbath is, and will be, the separating wall between the true Israel of God and unbelievers; and that the Sabbath is the great question, to unite the hearts of God's dear waiting saints" (WLF 18, 19).

She went on to note that the faithful preaching of the Sabbath and the keeping of it would become a powerful message, but that "at the commencement of the time of trouble" it would bring about persecution, even to the point at which all who "would not receive the mark of the Beast, and of his image, . . . could not buy or sell." The vision ends in persecution and deliverance at the Second Advent by Jesus coming on a "great white cloud," (*ibid.*, 19, 20).

Father, we look forward to that cloud with all of its meaning and blessing. Amen.

THE KEYNOTE OF SABBATARIAN ADVENTIST SELF-UNDERSTANDING

Set thee up waymarks, make thee high heaps: set thine heart toward the highway. Jer. 31:21.

Joseph Bates never separated history and theology. Rather, in his mind they were two aspects of the same topic. That unity shows up in the titles of most of his books, including his two editions of *The Seventh-day Sabbath, a Perpetual Sign* (1846, 1847), which carry the subtitle of *From the Beginning to the Entering Into the Gates of the Holy City, According to the Commandment.* That same historical bent appears most explicitly in his 1847 *Second Advent Way Marks and High Heaps: Or a Connected View, of the Fulfilment of Prophecy, by God's Peculiar People, From the Year 1840 to 1847.*

For Bates Sabbatarian Adventism was a movement and a message anchored in prophetic history. The "waymarks and high heaps" is an obvious takeoff of Jeremiah 31:21, which speaks of them as guides for God's people on their homeward journey. Back on January 1 we saw in our first reading (Joshua 4:20-22) how God used a pile of stones of remembrance to help His people not to forget how He had guided them in the past. Bates employed the same metaphor to indicate that God is still leading His people.

James White was excited about Bates' *Second Advent Way Marks and High Heaps.* He praised it to a friend a month after its publication, noting that "Brother Bates is out with a book on our past experience." Three months later James wrote that Bates' "works on the Lord's Sabbath and our past experience are very precious to us in this time of trial." He went on to "thank God for qualifying our Brother Bates so that he has so clearly harmonized our past experience with the Bible, and also so clearly defended the Sabbath question."

In White's mind Bates' central contribution was what James would later describe as the "chain of events" perspective of how God was leading his people as portrayed in Revelation 14. That sequence of events understanding began with William Miller's preaching of the good news of the Second Advent (Rev. 14:6, 7), continued on with Charles Fitch's sounding of the message that Babylon had fallen (verse 8), and was climaxing in the preaching of Revelation 14:12, with its message on end-time commandment keeping. Bates and now the Whites saw that that chain leads to the Second Advent.

Thank You, Lord, that You have given prophetic guideposts. Help us to discern their relevance.

STEPPING OUT IN FAITH

And she said, "As the Lord your God lives, I have nothing baked, only a handful of meal in a jar, and a little oil in a cruse; and now, I am gathering a couple of sticks, that I may go in and prepare it for myself and my son, that we may eat it, and die." And Elijah said to her, "Fear not; go and do as you have said; but first make me a little cake of it and bring it to me, and afterward make for yourself and your son." 1 Kings 17:12, 13, RSV.

And she did! But neither her meal nor her oil ran out until the famine ended. The Widow of Zarephath had stepped out in faith, and God had rewarded her.

Joseph Bates had several similar experiences. By the age of 36 he had accumulated enough money to retire. But by the end of 1844 he had given nearly all of it to further the Millerite message. His generosity positioned him where he also would have to step out by faith.

That thought brings us back to his little books. He found that it was easier to write them than to pay to get them published. Thus it was in the fall of 1847 that he sat down to write a book of more than 100 pages with only 12½ cents in his possession.

Just before he went to the printer his wife asked him to buy some flour. But having only 12½ cents, he could buy only four pounds. She, not knowing his circumstances, asked how it was that a man who had sailed ships around the world had come home with only a little flour.

At that point he told her two things. First, that he had used all his savings. And, second, that he was writing another book on the Sabbath.

The news really frustrated her. After all, she hadn't even accepted the Sabbath. As Bates put it, "she does not comprehend my duty." As usual, he told Prudy that God would take care of them.

And He did!

Soon after that, he felt impressed to go to the post office, where he found $10 in the mail. With it he was able to buy sufficient groceries and at least think about producing the book.

But even then he arrived at the printer without enough money, only to discover that someone else had already covered the publishing expenses.

Faith or foolishness?

That remains a crucial question in our day. God continues to bless those who step out in faith. And He still at times uses others as His agents in "paying the bill."

THE GATHERING TIME—1

"Go therefore to the thoroughfares, and invite to the marriage feast as many as you find." And those servants went into the streets and gathered all whom they found. Matt. 22:9, 10, RSV.

We saw back in January that the Great Disappointment of October 1844 had shattered Millerism. The once powerful movement had split into several factions, and many had given up Adventism altogether. The scattering time had begun in late 1844.

But all was not lost. Three and one half years of zealous Bible study had enabled Joseph Bates and the Whites to arrive at some powerful conclusions regarding the cause of the Disappointment and the shape of prophetic history according to the book of Revelation.

By early 1848 they had a message based on the heart of the Apocalypse of John that tied together the Second Advent, the opening of the second apartment of the heavenly sanctuary, and the end-time importance of the Sabbath into a unified theology. To Bates and the Whites those were not three distinct doctrines or "fundamental beliefs" but a unified last-day message. They saw its evangelistic delivery package in terms of the three angels of Revelation 14.

Let's eavesdrop on James in his letter to a Brother Bowles on November 8, 1849: "By the proclamation of the Sabbath truth in connection with the Advent movement," White wrote, "God is making known those that are His. The scattering time we have had; it is in the past, and now the time for the saints to be gathered into the unity of the faith, and be sealed by one holy, uniting truth has come. Yes, Brother, it has come. It is true that the work moves slowly, but it moves sure, and it gathers strength at every step. New ones are entering the fields . . . and are proclaiming the sealing, separating message . . . of the 3rd angel of Rev. 14. . . . O my soul, what a message.

"Our past Advent experience, and present position and future work is marked out in Rev. 14 . . . as plain as the prophetic pencil could write it. Thank God that we see it. . . . I believe that the Sabbath truth is yet to ring through the land, as the Advent never has. Let us all keep awake and be ready at any time to work for God. . . . Our home, our resting place, our Heaven, is yonder, just yonder. . . . Jesus is coming to gather the poor outcasts home."

It's hard not to catch his excitement. I'm still excited as I read God's promises and His prophecies. Our home is not here, but just "yonder."

THE GATHERING TIME–2

And the master said to the servant, "Go out to the highways and hedges, and compel people to come in, that my house may be filled." Luke 14:23, RSV.

By mid-1847 the leaders of what was becoming Sabbatarian Adventism had generally come to accept a core of beliefs. The next step would be to share them with others. Their primary tactic was to organize a series of conferences whose purpose, according to James White, was the "uniting [of] the brethren on the great truths connected with the message of the third angel."

By 1848 many Adventists in New England and western New York had become convinced of the truth of one or more of the Sabbatarian doctrines, but they lacked a consensus.

The series of conferences beginning in 1848 would spread the Sabbatarian message evangelistically. Given the fact that the Sabbatarians were shut door Adventists who believed that probation had closed for all but those who had accepted Miller's message, the invitees to the conferences were limited to those Adventists who had accepted the first angel's message and hopefully the second. The task of the evangelists was to present the third angel's message as part of the answer to what took place at the end of the 2300 days, thus revealing where they stood in prophetic history.

James White, reporting on the first conference in April 1848, noted that about 50 people attended, "They were not all fully in the truth. . . . Bro. Bates presented the commandments in a clear light, and their importance was urged home by powerful testimonies. The word had effect to establish those already in the truth, and to awaken those who were not fully decided."

The goals of the conferences emerged even more clearly in Ellen White's report of the one held in "Bro. Arnold's barn" in August 1848. Noting that there were about 35 present, she reported that "there were hardly two agreed. . . . All were anxious for an opportunity to . . . preach to us." But "they were told that we had not come so great a distance to hear them, but had come to teach them the truth." She also gladly observed that after a strenuous meeting the participants eventually united "upon the third angel's message" (2SG 97-99).

God still uses men and women who grasp His Word to guide others into biblical understanding. He may even desire to use you in that endeavor this very day.

THE GATHERING TIME—3

*How beautiful upon the mountains are the feet of him that bringeth good tidings,
that publisheth peace; that bringeth good tidings of good, that publisheth salvation.
Isa. 52:7.*

The initial phase of what White termed the gathering time lasted from 1848 through 1850. The Sabbatarian conferences of those years were the avenue that Bates and the Whites utilized to form a core of believers on the platform of the three angels' messages of Revelation 14. But conferences weren't the only means that God would use.

At the one held in Dorchester, Massachusetts, in November 1848 Ellen White had a vision that would forever change the shape of Adventism.

After coming out of vision, she said to her husband, "I have a message for you. You must begin to print a little paper and send it out to the people. Let it be small at first; but as the people read, they will send you means with which to print, and it will be a success from the first. From this small beginning *it was shown to me to be like streams of light that went clear round the world*" (LS 125; italics supplied).

Now 160 years later that statement may not seem all that impressive. After all, in the early twenty-first century Adventist publications do circle the earth, pumped out by the millions each year in hundreds of languages from scores of publishing houses.

But that is the fulfillment, not the prophecy.

What must have the early believers thought of such a vision? After all, in November 1848 there were probably less than 100 Sabbatarian Adventists, and most of those were poor.

Beyond that, they all believed in the shut door concept, including Ellen White herself. As she later put it, "With my brethren and sisters, after the time passed in forty-four I did believe no more sinners would be converted. But I never had a vision that no more sinners would be converted" (1SM 74).

The publishing vision, in fact, contradicted her personal belief and that of her fellow Sabbatarians. Here was an open door vision in the midst of a shut door people.

Yet, in spite of their beliefs, Adventist publications, including the "little paper," have gone like streams of light "round the world."

Thank You, God, that Your sight is better than ours. Help me today to see with Your eyes rather than mine.

PUBLISHING THE MESSAGE—1

You will receive power when the Holy Spirit comes upon you; and you will bear witness for me in Jerusalem, and throughout all Judea and Samaria, and even in the farthest corners of the earth. Acts 1:8, REB.

Small beginnings were the way of the early Christian church. So would they be for Sabbatarian Adventism. One can hardly imagine a more humble start for what would become a worldwide publishing endeavor.

In response to his wife's publishing vision, the financially prostrate and homeless James White stepped out in faith to write and print the "little paper." Looking back at the experience, he later wrote: "We sat down to prepare the matter for that little sheet, and wrote every word of it, our entire library comprising a three-shilling pocket Bible, *Cruden's Condensed Concordance,* and Walker's old dictionary, minus one of its covers. Destitute of means, our hope of success was in God."

Not having much choice, White sought out a non-Adventist printer who produced the eight-page pamphlet for a total stranger and was willing to wait for his pay until contributions filtered back from the hoped-for readers. James White found such a printer in Charles Pelton of Middletown, Connecticut.

The first 1,000 copies of the *Present Truth* came off the press in July 1849. "When he brought the first number from the printing office," Ellen White recalled, "we all bowed around it, asking the Lord, with humble hearts and many tears, to let his blessing rest upon the feeble efforts of his servant. He [James] then directed the paper to all he thought would read it, and carried it to the post office [eight miles distant] in a carpetbag. . . . Very soon letters came bringing means to publish the paper, and the good news of many souls embracing the truth" (1888 LS 260).

The content of the *Present Truth* was what the Sabbatarians saw as God's special message for their time—the Sabbath, the three angels' messages, and related topics. The "little paper" played an important part in the gathering time of the late 1840s.

God, from a human perspective, often works in strange ways. We are impressed with bigness and power in any endeavor. But the Lord values humility and dedication. Stepping out in humble faith isn't just something for James White. He can use you and me also if we will give Him the little that we have in humble dedication.

THE NATURE OF PRESENT TRUTH—1

Wherefore I will not be negligent to put you always in remembrance of these things, though ye know them, and be established in the present truth. 2 Peter 1:12.

Each of the founders of Sabbatarian Adventism had a dynamic understanding of what they called "present truth." Of course, the use of the term wasn't unique to them. The Millerites earlier had employed the term to refer to the imminent return of Jesus. And later they applied it to the seventh-month movement (i.e., the proclamation that Jesus would arrive in October 1844). Thus even in the Millerite use of *"present truth"* we find a progressive dynamic in understanding.

It was no accident that James White chose the title *Present Truth* for the first Sabbatarian Adventist periodical. Bates had used it as early as January 1847 to refer to the Sabbath and related truths.

James White in the first edition of his little publication in July 1849, after quoting 2 Peter 1:12, which speaks of being "established in the PRESENT TRUTH," wrote that "in Peter's time there was present truth, or truth applicable to that present time. The church [has] ever had a present truth. The present truth now, is that which shows present duty, and the right position for us who are about to witness the time of trouble." He agreed with Bates on the content of present truth. The first two angels of Revelation 14 had sounded—now it was time for the third.

The early Sabbatarians definitely believed they had something the world needed to hear, but they realized that God still had more to reveal to them. That is, they saw truth as dynamic and progressive. As a result, Ellen White could write in relation to the theological issues related to the 1888 General Conference session that "that which God gives His servants to speak today would not perhaps have been present truth twenty years ago, but it is God's message for this time" (MS 8a, 1888).

The Whites and Bates were open to further development of truth. And younger leaders evidenced the openness of the founders. Thus Uriah Smith, for example, wrote in 1857 that the Sabbatarians had discovered increasing truth since 1844. "We have," he noted, "been enabled to rejoice in truths far in advance of what we then perceived. But we do not imagine that we yet have it all. . . . We trust to progress still, our way growing continually brighter and brighter."

How is it with me today? Is my mind still open for God's leading as He reveals truth in His Word?

THE NATURE OF PRESENT TRUTH—2

And another angel, a third, followed them, saying with a loud voice . . .
Rev. 14:9, RSV.

One way to grasp the founders of Sabbatarian Adventism's understanding of present truth is to examine one of James White's evangelistic sermons. As we glimpse its powerful flow we need to remember that he was preaching to and writing to ex-Millerites—men and women who had already accepted the first and perhaps the second angels' messages of Revelation 14.

"Then," James declares, "the sixth verse of the fourteenth chapter introduces the second advent message, and commences another *chain of events* related to the successive messages which were to be proclaimed to the people of God" before the Second Advent.

"All advent believers agree that the first angel's message" was fulfilled in the proclamation of Christ's second advent in the 1840s. "With what solemnity, zeal and holy confidence the servants of the Lord proclaimed the time. And O, how their words fell upon the people, melting the hardest sinner's heart."

The second angel *"followed* after the first delivered the burden of his message." He "called us out from the . . . churches where we are now free to think, and act for ourselves in the fear of God. It is an exceedingly interesting fact, that the Sabbath question began to be agitated among second advent believers immediately after they were called out of the churches by the second angel's message. God's work moves in order. The Sabbath truth came up in just the right time to fulfill prophecy. Amen."

"He called us from the bondage of the churches in 1844, and there humbled us, and has been proving us, and has been developing the hearts of his people, and seeing whether they would keep his commandments. . . .

"Many stopped at the first angel's message, and others at the second, and many will refuse the third; but a few will 'follow the Lamb withersoever he goeth,' and go up and possess the land."

Present truth for the founders of Sabbatarian Adventism had to do with the flow of prophetic history. God was summoning a people. Step by step He was revealing His truth to them. Never did they view themselves as merely another denomination. To the contrary, they consistently saw their movement as one of prophecy. They had a special message to give before Jesus would come—a message spelled out in Revelation 14:6-12 and forming the core of God's end-time proclamation.

PUBLISHING THE MESSAGE—2

Thou shalt go before the face of the Lord to prepare his ways. Luke 1:76.

Something about an exciting message makes people want to share it with others. That is especially true if the message is one of hope from God.

By 1849 the Sabbatarian Adventists, though few in number, were more than eager to spread their message through the printed page. James White had not only initiated the *Present Truth* to present the new understandings about the Sabbath and the third angel, but in the summer of 1850 he began publishing the *Advent Review,* a periodical that sought to impress the scattered Millerites with the forcefulness and truthfulness of the arguments undergirding the 1844 movement.

White's approach had a plan behind it. If the *Advent Review* was to awake the disappointed Millerites to the truthfulness of the first and second angels' messages, the *Present Truth* urged them to accept the third. He combined the two periodicals into one in November 1950 and called it the *Second Advent Review and Sabbath Herald* (today known as the *Adventist Review*).

The Sabbatarians were convicted that they had God's last day message. We find their enthusiasm for their message and their willingness to sacrifice to publish reflected in the first general Adventist census in 1860. Taken by D. T. Taylor of the Advent Christian movement, the census found 54,000 Adventists of various types, of which about 3,000 were Sabbatarians. The remarkable thing about Taylor's numbers was the relative interest in publications by the different Adventist groups. The larger bodies with nearly 20 times the membership of the Sabbatarians had a circulation list of only 5,000, whereas the smaller body had one of 4,300. Taylor went out of his way to point out that the Sabbatarians, "though a decided minority, are very devoted, zealous, and active in the promulgation of their peculiar views of Sunday and Sabbath."

And they were. They had a message for God's people at the end of time, and they knew it.

Their aggressiveness paid off. Membership growth among the Sabbatarians during the gathering time zoomed from about 100 at the end of 1848 to about 2,500 four years later. Others also, thanks to their publication ministry, began to see the logic of their message.

God still uses Adventist publications to spread His message. In this each of us can have a part through both our means and our prayers.

EVEN GOOD FRIENDS GET INTO BIG ARGUMENTS

And there arose a sharp contention, so that they [Paul and Barnabas] separated from each other. Acts 15:39, RSV.

They looked like the perfect evangelistic team. But problems can arise even between good Christian friends. So it was when Paul and Barnabas clashed over Mark's fitness for ministry. As a result, both went their own way in what appears to have been a huff. But God blessed in spite of the problem. He now had two evangelistic teams instead of one.

The record of that high-powered disagreement reminds me of one that threatened to tear apart the two Sabbatarian leaders in 1850. The issue was the "little paper" of the Dorchester vision. While it is true that after the vision Ellen White told her husband—perhaps personally—that he was to publish a periodical that would eventually be "like streams of light that went clear round the world," Bates had his own view of the topic.

The older man was quite certain that White's periodical was drawing off money that should go to evangelism. White, on the other hand, thought money was being squandered in other areas that could and should have been used to support the paper.

James penned that "Brother Bates wrote me a letter that threw me down as low as I ever was." "I [had] already been in a hot furnace for some time on account of the burden I felt for the little paper." But Bates' letter made it even worse—"the burden grew heavier and heavier on me" and "I gave it up forever." "I think" the paper "will die. . . . I think I shall hang all up for the present."

The battle rumbled on for the better part of 1850 and threatened to destroy Sabbatarian Adventism. The devil never sleeps, my friends. After years of struggle and sacrifice, Bates and James White finally had a message to preach and had finally arrived at the gathering time, only to have the movement founder on the stubborn personalities of its two leaders. Ellen White in her role as mediator between the two men feared that they would destroy what they loved. The good news is that God helped them face themselves and work through their differences.

Things haven't changed all that much. The church in the twenty-first century is still full of opinionated, strong personalities.

And the devil is still trying to separate.

And God is still trying to heal.

And we still need to be open to the softening impact of His Spirit.

HYMNS FOR GOD'S PECULIAR PEOPLE

They sing the song of Moses the servant of God, and the song of the Lamb.
Rev. 15:3.

When a Christian movement begins to take a definite shape it usually develops its own hymnal. James White undertook that task for Sabbatarian Adventism, publishing *Hymns, for God's Peculiar People, That Keep the Commandments of God, and the Faith of Jesus* in 1849.

Hymns and hymn books, of course, are never neutral. They reflect the message that is of utmost importance to those who write the songs and compile the hymnals. And just as many people in the days of the Roman Empire sung their way into orthodox Christian doctrine, so it was that many in the nineteenth century sung their way into the Adventist message.

James White knew the power of song. He also knew its doctrinal function. With that in mind, it is not surprising to find that the first hymn in James' collection is titled "Holy Sabbath." Its message speaks for itself.

"1. The Pure, unfailing word of God—
   Fountain ever sure—
   Its statutes, precepts, and its laws,
   Are written for the pure.

"2. In paradise where man was led,
   The word will safely guide;
   And if he should this law evade,
   His steps would surely slide.

"3. The Holy Sabbath here was made,
   Which God did sanctify;
   And if we would our God obey,
   We must with this comply.

"4. In after times, when Moses liv'd,
   This law was ratified:
   And all who kept this holy word,
   May know they're sanctified.

"5. Still farther down the streams of time,
   We hear the prophet say—
   Hearken, fear not reproach nor shame,
   Who keep the seventh day.

"6. For thus the Mighty God hath said
   To those who truly rest,
   Thou shalt on the high places ride,
   And feed among the blest.

"7. Here too are they who patient are,
   And keep commandments pure,
   They'll in the Holy city share,
   If to the end endure.

"8. Then let us still pursue this road,
   Till we fair Canaan gain,
   Then we shall walk the street of gold,
   And in that rest remain."

Since James' book only had words and no tunes, you will have to figure out how to sing it. But even if the tune is missing, the poem leaves no doubt about the message.

MORE ADVENT SINGING

The ransomed of the Lord shall return, and come to Zion with songs and everlasting joy upon their heads. Isa. 35:10.

As we might guess, James White's *Hymns, for God's Peculiar People* had a large number of songs about the Second Advent and heaven. But since most people had been Christian before they had become Sabbatarians, he apparently did not feel the need to supply many hymns on grace and worshipping the majesty of God. Those were well known. James apparently made his selections to fill a doctrinal gap. Some were quite specific, such as one simply titled "Washing Feet."

While "Washing Feet" didn't make it into the current *Seventh-day Adventist Hymnal,* some of James' selections did. My favorite is "I'm a Pilgrim." While that song was number 666 in the 1941 hymnal, I'm glad to say that it now sports the more sanctified enumeration of 444. Why not sing it with me this morning?

"1. I'm a pilgrim, and I'm a stranger;
  I can tarry, I can tarry but a night;
 Do not detain me, for I am going
   To where the fountains are ever flowing.
"2. There the glory is ever shining!
   O, my longing heart, my longing heart is there:
 Here in this country so dark and dreary,
   I long have wandered forlorn and weary.
"3. There's the city to which I journey;
   My Redeemer, my Redeemer is its light!
 There is no sorrow, nor any sighing,
   Nor any tears there, or any dying."

The refrain is a message in itself:

"I'm a pilgrim, and I'm a stranger;
  I can tarry, I can tarry but a night."

Really? Is it true that we modern Adventists see ourselves as pilgrims and strangers on this earth who can tarry but a night? For all too many of us this earth has become our home. We are comfortable here. And we like it. After all, we think to ourselves, "I am rich, and increased with goods, and have need of nothing" (Rev. 3:17).

And then comes that policeman's knock on the door to tell us about our daughter; the physician's report that says we have an advanced stage of cancer; the spouse who out of the blue demands a divorce. Suddenly we are back to reality. This earth is *not* our home.

Help me today, Father, to reevaluate my priorities and my daily life.

PROVIDENTIAL DREAMS

Behold, the dwelling place of God is with man. He will dwell with them,
and they will be his people, and God himself will be with them as their God.
Rev. 21:3, ESV.

While we are thinking about early Advent hymns we need to take a look at the short but productive life of Annie Smith, who has three hymns in the *Seventh-day Adventist Hymnal*—"How Far From Home?" "I Saw One Weary," and "Long Upon the Mountains."

Annie's mother had been a Millerite and by 1851 had become a Sabbatarian Adventist and had met Joseph Bates. The two of them agreed to pray for her children, who had no interest in Adventism. Shortly afterward, Bates scheduled himself to hold meetings near Annie's residence. Her mother urged her to attend, but the daughter wasn't much interested. Perhaps to please her mother, though, she agreed to go.

The night before the meeting Bates dreamed of it. All seats were filled except one by the door. He dreamed that he changed his subject from the one he had planned to the topic of the sanctuary. They sang the first hymn, prayed, and sang a second hymn. And just as he was opening his Bible and was reading "Unto two thousand and three hundred days; then shall the sanctuary be cleansed" and pointing to the drawing of the sanctuary on his large prophetic chart, the door opened and a young woman entered and took her seat in the vacant chair. Bates also dreamed that the person was Annie Smith, for whom he and her mother had been praying. That same evening Annie had essentially the same dream. In hers she also saw herself arriving late just as the preacher began reading from Daniel 8:14.

The next evening, Annie started out in plenty of time, but lost her way, and so failed to arrive until the second hymn. She quickly took the seat by the door just as the preacher began reading the text that she had dreamed of.

Bates had not thought about his dream until she entered the room. As he closed the meeting, he went to Annie, addressing her as Mrs. Smith's daughter whom he had dreamed about the night before. Annie Smith's life would never be the same. That night she accepted the Sabbatarian Adventist message.

God works in wondrous ways. And He still does so in our day. All of us have loved ones who need to realize God's love and care more fully. The God who cares for us also cares for our loved ones. Let us never cease praying for them.

MORE ON ANNIE SMITH

He will wipe away every tear from their eyes, and death shall be no more, neither shall there be mourning nor crying nor pain anymore, for the former things have passed away. Rev. 21:4, ESV.

Yesterday we met Annie Smith at the time of her conversion. Soon afterward, she wrote for the *Review and Herald* on November 21, 1851, that "I trust that I have forsaken all to follow the Lamb withersoever he leads the way. Earth has lost its attractions. My hopes, joys, affections, are now all centered in things above and divine.

"I want no other place than to sit at the feet of Jesus, and learn of him—no other occupation, than to be in the service of my heavenly Father—no other delight, than the peace of God, which passeth all understanding.

"O praise his name for what he has done for me, I feel a sweet foretaste of the glories of that better world—an earnest of that inheritance—and I am determined by his grace to overcome every obstacle, endure the cross, despising the shame, so that an entrance may be administered into the everlasting kingdom of our Lord and Saviour Jesus Christ."

Up to that point in her life her hopes and ambitions had been on a teaching career in a first-class secondary school. In fact, not long before her conversion she had received an offer of a prestigious position at an excellent salary. In short, by 1851 she had everything she had ever hoped for on this earth.

But after accepting the Advent message through Joseph Bates, all her ambitions changed. Hearing that James White needed help in editing the *Review*, she volunteered to assist him at no salary but room and board. She was excited to be in the Lord's work so that she could enable others to learn of the coming kingdom.

For three years she worked with James White, but pulmonary tuberculosis cut short her life in 1855 in her twenty-seventh year.

The day before her death she wrote the preface to her poem "Home Here and Home in Heaven," thanking God for the work He had given her here below, but turning her eyes to heaven as her years "ceased to flow."

Annie's life may have been a short one, but her influence lived on, especially in her hymns and in her brother Uriah, who her experience had helped bring to the Lord in late 1852.

Lord, as I consider Annie Smith, help me to get my values and priorities straight. This day I give myself to Your service. Thank You for life.

AND WHAT ABOUT DEATH?—1

But I would not have you to be ignorant, brethren, concerning them which are asleep. 1 Thess. 4:13.

Some time ago we learned how the early Sabbatarians discovered the Bible truths about the seventh-day Sabbath and the two-phase ministry of Christ in the heavenly sanctuary, teachings that they integrated with their understanding of the Second Advent as found in Revelation 11:19-14:20. Those three "pillar truths" stood at the very center of Sabbatarian Adventism.

But observant readers may have noticed a fourth Adventist pillar missing from our discussion—what Adventist have traditionally called "the state of the dead." We need to take a look at how those early Sabbatarians developed their understandings on hell and what happens to individuals when they die.

Such issues deeply trouble many people. Take young Ellen Harmon, for example. "In my mind," she wrote, "the justice of God eclipsed His mercy and love. The mental anguish I passed through at this time was very great. I had been taught to believe in an eternally burning hell. . . . The horrifying thought was ever before me, that my sins were too great to be forgiven, and that I should be forever lost. The frightful descriptions that I had heard of souls in perdition sank deep into my mind. Ministers in the pulpit drew vivid pictures of the condition of the lost. . . . The tortures of thousands upon thousands of years," during which "the fiery billows would roll to the surface the writhing victims, who would shriek, 'How long, O Lord, how long?' Then the answer would thunder down the abyss, 'Through all eternity!' . . .

"Our heavenly Father was presented before my mind as a tyrant, who delighted in the agonies of the condemned; not as the tender, pitying Friend of sinners, who loves His creatures with a love past all understanding, and desires them to be saved in His kingdom. When the thought took possession of my mind that God delighted in the torture of His creatures, who were formed in His image, a wall of darkness seemed to separate me from Him" (LS 29-31).

Needless to say, young Ellen could not harmonize the traditional teaching of hell with the loving Jesus. Yet that thought itself made things worse, since now she feared that she was rejecting God's Word and thereby deserved hell even more than before.

Help us, Lord, as our finite minds grapple with the difficult teachings of Scripture.

AND WHAT ABOUT DEATH?—2

For the wages of sin is death; but the gift of God is eternal life through Jesus Christ our Lord. Rom. 6:23.

Given the struggles that young Ellen had with the traditional teachings on hell, it is no wonder that in her mature years she would write that "it is beyond the power of the human mind to estimate the evil which has been wrought by the heresy of eternal torment. The religion of the Bible, full of love and goodness, and abounding in compassion, is darkened by superstition and clothed with terror. . . . The appalling views of God which have spread over the world from the teachings of the pulpit have made thousands, yes, millions, of skeptics and infidels." She went on to indicate that the traditional teaching was a part of the Babylonish or confused teachings of the church that mingled human theory with the truth of God (GC 536).

I have to admit that the same issues have troubled me. So much so that in 1997 I wrote an article for the *Signs of the Times* entitled "The Infinite Hitler." The basic idea was that if the traditional teaching of the church was true it would make Hitler and Stalin look like pretty nice guys. After all, their victims eventually died, whereas God could roast His in conscious agony throughout the ceaseless ages of eternity. Others must have seen the logic of the article, since it received the Award of Merit from the Associated Church Press in June 1998.

Of course, I knew that many others were in agreement, since I had cited such evangelical leaders as John R. W. Stott and Clark Pinnock and others as having rejected the traditional view for the biblical.

But what is the biblical view? And how did the Adventists arrive at it? We will begin to examine those questions tomorrow. But first it is important to recognize that the basic issue involves whether humans are born with immortality. Greek philosophy says yes, but the Bible, while admitting that God has it (1 Tim. 6:16), declares that the only humans who will receive it are those who believe in Jesus, and that they will not get it until the second advent of Jesus (1 Cor. 15:51-55).

Now, immortality means not subject to death. Thus if the wicked have it, they by definition will live in some form throughout eternity. But if they don't have it, they must, as Romans 6:23 says so plainly, die. No other options exist.

Lord, we are thankful that You make the gift of immortality available to those who believe in Jesus. And we are equally thankful that sin and sinners are not immortal.

AND WHAT ABOUT DEATH?—3

And the serpent said unto the woman, ye shall not surely die. Gen. 3:4.

Two streams brought the biblical truth of death and hell into Sabbatarian Adventism. George Storrs, whom we met earlier as a leading proponent of the seventh-month movement, stimulated one. Back in 1837 Storrs had come across a book by Henry Grew that dealt with the final destiny of the wicked. Grew argued for the "entire extinction of being and not endless preservation in sin and suffering."

Up to that time Storrs had never doubted that people possessed immortal souls. But Grew's work drove him to a thorough study of the Bible on the topic. As a result, Storrs "became settled that man has no immortality by his creation, or birth; and that 'all the wicked will God destroy'—*utterly exterminate.*" He had come to believe in what theologians refer to as conditionalism (i.e., people receive immortality only through the condition of faith in Christ) and annihilationism (the final eternal destruction of the wicked rather than their preservation alive in the fires of hell throughout ceaseless ages).

The teaching of those doctrines brought Storrs into conflict with the Methodist establishment and contributed to his resignation as a minister in 1840. Storrs set forth his views in such books as *An Inquiry: Are the Souls of the Wicked Immortal? In Six Sermons* (1842). He argued that the devil's proclamation to Eve in the Garden of Eden, "Ye shall not surely die," was the biggest lie ever.

By 1842 Storrs had become a Millerite through the ministry of Charles Fitch. Unfortunately, all the Millerite leaders except Fitch vigorously reacted to Storrs' views. On January 25, 1844, Fitch wrote him of his convictions: "As you have long been fighting the Lord's battles alone, on the subject of the state of the dead, and of the final doom of the wicked, I write this to say that I am at last, after much thought and prayer, and a full conviction of duty to God, prepared to take my stand by your side. I am thoroughly converted to the Bible truth, that 'the dead know not anything.'"

Not wanting to hide his "light under a bushel," Fitch soon preached two sermons on the topic to his congregation in late January. "They have produced a great uproar," he penned to Storrs. "Many thought I had a devil before, but now they feel sure of it. But I have no more right my Brother, to be ashamed of God's truth on this subject than on any other."

Fitch, as we noted earlier, was a man willing to stand by his convictions once he was certain of the Bible's teaching. May we emulate his spirit.

AND WHAT ABOUT DEATH?—4

Can we know what this new doctrine is that you are teaching? Some of the things you say seemed startling to us and we would like to find out what they mean. Acts 17:19, 20, New Jerusalem.

If Paul's respondent at Athens had a desire to learn more about the new doctrine the apostle taught, the same certainly can not be said about the Millerite leaders in relationship to Storrs' understanding on the state of the dead.

On May 7, 1844, Miller published a letter in which he disclaimed "any connection, fellowship, or sympathy with Br. Storrs' views on the intermediate state, and end of the wicked." In April Josiah Litch went so far as to begin publishing a periodical entitled *The Anti Annihilationist*. The general Millerite approach was to steer clear of the topic. Jesus would come in a few weeks, and then we would all know the truth of the matter.

Such pronouncements, of course, did not do much to silence Storrs and his colleagues.

And their agitation bore fruit. In subsequent years the two largest denominations to come out of Millerism—the Advent Christians and the Seventh-day Adventists—would both adopt conditionalism and annihilationism.

If Storrs' teaching was one avenue through which conditionalism entered Adventism, the Christian Connexion was another. Elias Smith, one of the Connexion's founders, had accepted the teaching early in the century. And many Connexionists, with their desire to restore all the lost Bible teachings, emphasized both conditionalism and annihilationism. That influenced both James White and Joseph Bates, who had both been members of the Connexion.

The Connexion position on the topic would also sway young Ellen Harmon after her mother accepted it at the Casco Street Christian (Connexion) Church in Portland, Maine. After hearing her mother discuss it with a friend, she investigated it in the Bible and accepted it. Those insights brought her great relief of both mind and heart. Not only did they dissipate her doubts about God's love and justice, but they helped her see the reason for the resurrection. After all, as she put it, "if at death the soul entered upon eternal happiness or misery, where was the need of a resurrection of the poor moldering body?" (LS 49, 50).

Thus all three of Sabbatarian Adventism's founders were conditionalists from the very founding of the movement.

Thank You, Lord, for both Your great promises and for beliefs that make consistant and vital sense.

THE PILLAR DOCTRINES

Preach the word; be instant in season, out of season; reprove, rebuke, exhort with all longsuffering and doctrine. For the time will come when they will not endure sound doctrine. 2 Tim. 4:2, 3.

By early 1848 the Sabbatarian Adventist leaders, through extensive and intensive Bible study, had come to basic agreement on at least four points of doctrine:

1. The personal, visible, premillennial return of Jesus.
2. The cleansing of the heavenly sanctuary, with Christ's ministry in the second apartment having begun in October 1844—the beginning of the antitypical day of atonement.
3. The obligation to observe the seventh-day Sabbath and its role in the great end-time conflict prophesied in Revelation 12-14.
4. That immortality is not an inherent human quality but something people receive only through faith in Christ.

Sabbatarian Adventists, and later Seventh-day Adventists, came to see those teachings as "landmarks" or "pillar" doctrines. Together they set this branch of Adventism off from not only other Millerites, but from Christians in general. Those four distinctives stood at the heart of developing Sabbatarian Adventism and defined them as a distinctive people. The so-called landmark doctrines formed the nonnegotiable core of the movement's theology.

The careful reader may wonder how come I did not include the doctrine of spiritual gifts as it relates to Ellen White in the above list. While that is a unique Adventist perspective, it didn't really, as we shall see, receive attempts at doctrinal formation until the 1850s and 1860s. Beyond that, Ellen White herself did not see that teaching as one of the pillars.

The Sabbatarians, of course, shared many beliefs with other Christians, such as salvation by grace through faith in Jesus' sacrifice and the efficacy of prayer. But their teaching in the early years, like their hymnal, focused on where they differed from other Christians rather than on where they were like them.

That neglect would eventually bring about theological problems that they would have to deal with in the 1880s. But more on that topic later.

For now we can be thankful for the clarity with which the founders of Seventh-day Adventism did their theological homework. The good news is that their belief system makes sense.

LIVING ON THE FINANCIAL EDGE

I appeal to you therefore, brethren, by the mercies of God, to present your bodies as a living sacrifice, holy and acceptable to God, which is your spiritual worship. Rom. 12:1, RSV.

I t's easier to be a dead sacrifice than a living one. At least in death the sacrifice is over, but in life it goes on and on. So it was for the founders of Adventism.

Bates, as we noted earlier, had had a fair portion of wealth. But having given everything to Millerism except his home, he spent the rest of his life on the thin edge of financial reality.

But he wasn't the only one. In April 1848 James White was able to write of himself and Ellen that "all we have including clothes, bedding, and household furniture we have with us in a three-foot trunk, and that is but half full. We have nothing else to do but to serve God and go where God opens the way for us."

But travel wasn't always easy in those days, especially if a person was broke. Bates for example, felt deeply impressed in early 1849 that it was his duty to preach the message in Vermont. Having no money, he decided to walk from southern Massachusetts.

However, he wasn't the only one under conviction regarding that missionary tour. Ellen White's sister Sarah, impressed that she should help him, requested advance pay from her employer and worked for $1.25 per week as a hired girl to pay his way.

But the trip was fruitful. James White wrote that Bates "had a hard time, but God was with him and much good was done. He found or left quite a number on the Sabbath."

For those of us living in more prosperous times, it is difficult to grasp the privations that the early Adventists underwent in accomplishing their mission. James White later commented that "the few that taught the truth traveled on foot, in second-class cars, or on steamboat decks, for want of means." Such travel, his wife noted, exposed them to "the smoke of tobacco, besides the swearing and vulgar conversation of the ship hands and the baser portion of the traveling public" (1T 77). At night they often slept on the floor, cargo boxes, or grain sacks with their suitcase for a pillow and overcoat for a covering. In winter they walked the deck to keep warm.

And we imagine that we have it hard, that we have lived a sacrificial life. Think again. Most of us haven't got the foggiest idea of the sacrifices it took to establish our church.

WHAT ABOUT DATE SETTING?—1

But of that day and hour no one knows, not even the angels of heaven, nor the Son, but the Father only. Matt. 24:36, RSV.

I n spite of Jesus' clear words on the topic, and in spite of the Millerite crisis in trying to set the date for the Second Advent, it has proved to be a constant temptation for Adventists to either set a date or to come as close as possible to one. And we must admit that it is an exciting possibility. But the inevitable failure has a deadening affect on the church and its members.

After the failure of the prediction that Christ would return in October 1844, it seemed only natural for the disappointed Adventists to continue to establish dates for that event on the basis of the various prophecies. Thus William Miller and Josiah Litch came to expect that Jesus would appear before the end of the Jewish year 1844 (that is, by the spring of 1845). H. H. Gross, Joseph Marsh, and others projected dates in 1846, and when that year passed Gross discovered reasons to look for Christ in 1847,

The early Sabbatarian Adventists were not immune from date setting. In September 1845 James White firmly believed that Jesus would arrive on the tenth day of the seventh Jewish month in October of that year. That is the reason that he argued publicly that an Adventist couple who had announced their marriage had fallen for a "wile of the Devil," and had "denied their faith" in the Second Advent, since "such a step seemed to contemplate years of life in this world."

Yet "a few days before the time passed," James recalled, "I was at Fairhaven and Dartmouth, Mass., with a message on this point of time. At this time Ellen was with the band at Carver, Mass., where she saw in vision, that we should be disappointed, and that the saints must pass through the 'time of Jacob's trouble,' which was future. Her view of Jacob's trouble was entirely new to us, as well as herself."

That experience apparently cured James White of speculating on the date of the Second Advent. But, as we will see tomorrow, it certainly didn't halt Joseph Bates.

Date setting for the Second Advent!

It certainly seems natural to most of us. That is what the disciples wanted Jesus to do in Matthew 24. But He refused. And He still refuses. There is an important lesson here that we need to learn.

WHAT ABOUT DATE SETTING?—2

Watch therefore, for you do not know on what day your Lord is coming.
Matt. 24:42, RSV.

I s Jesus really sure about that? Surely there must be some way to determine the time, at least by us faithful Adventists.

At least Joseph Bates thought that in 1850. The passage of time must have been getting him down. After all, it had been six long years since the Millerite disappointment. He could certainly discover the date if he worked at it hard enough. And by 1850 Bates was quite sure that he had.

In that year he wrote that "the seven spots of blood on the Golden Altar before the Mercy Seat, I fully believe represents the duration of the judicial proceedings on the living saints in the Most Holy."

Most of us have heard about the quite valid year-for-a-day principle of prophetic interpretation. But Bates had a new one: the spot-of-blood-for-a-year principle. Using his "new light," Bates had concluded that the pre-Advent judgment would last seven years and would conclude in October 1851, at which time Christ would come.

Given his stature in Sabbatarian circles, Bates soon gathered a following for his new scheme. But both of the Whites would vigorously resist him.

In November 1850 Ellen publicly claimed that "the Lord showed me that TIME had not been a test since 1844, and that time will never again be a test" (PT, Nov. 1850).

Then on July 21, 1851, as excitement on the topic mounted, she wrote in the *Review and Herald* that "the Lord has shown me that the message of the third angel must go, and be proclaimed to the scattered children of the Lord, and that it should not be hung on time; for time never will be a test again. I saw that some were getting a false excitement arising from preaching time; that the third angel's message was stronger than time can be. I saw that this message can stand on its own foundation, and that it needs not time to strengthen it, and that it will go in mighty power, and do its work."

The church today needs to listen to these insights. As I look at Adventism, I see it as a people who have forgotten the power of their message. I still remember how the forcefulness of the flow of Revelation itself struck me when I first grasped it nearly 50 years ago. The years have not diminished that power. One of the great needs of Adventism today is to recover its message.

WHAT ABOUT DATE SETTING?—3

Now after a long time the master of those servants came and settled accounts with them. Matt. 25:19, RSV.

Yesterday we found Joseph Bates struggling mightily with the "long time" aspect of Jesus' sermon in Matthew 24 and 25. On the basis of the one spot of blood for a year principle he had determined that Jesus would return in October 1851. We also saw Ellen White challenging Bates. But she isn't finished with him. Let's listen in a bit more.

"I saw," she wrote in the *Review* of July 21, 1851, "that some were making everything bend to the time of this next fall—that is, making their calculations in reference to that time. I saw that this was wrong, for this reason: Instead of going to God daily to know their PRESENT duty, they look ahead, and make their calculations as though they knew the work would end this fall, without inquiring their duty of God daily."

The next month James cut loose on Bates, claiming that he had been against his time teaching from its inception a year earlier. Referring specifically to Joseph's theory, White wrote that "some who have thus taught we esteem very highly, and love 'fervently' as brethren, and we feel that it becomes us to be slow to say anything to hurt their feelings; yet we cannot refrain from giving some reasons why we do not receive the *time*." He then launched into six reasons that he believed Bates was wrong.

The combined confrontation by the Whites apparently convinced Bates (who believed Ellen to be a prophet) that he had been wrong on the time issue. Soon he and most of those who had followed him dropped the emphasis. As a result, James could report in early September that the "seven years time" was a nonissue in his recent tour among the churches. But some, Ellen noted in November, had held on to the time expectation and were very "low and dark," confused, and distracted (Lt 8, 1851).

The "seven spots" crisis cured Bates of time setting. After that, although he would see the end as near, he never set a date for the Second Advent.

It's too bad that some of his spiritual followers haven't gotten the point. The time-setting temptation, with its resulting excitement and eventual letdown, is still with us. It is unfortunate that all too many Adventists are still more interested in Second Advent excitement than in "PRESENT duty." We cannot expect God's blessing until we get our priorities reversed.

Lord, help us to focus today on "present duty."

WHAT ABOUT DATE SETTING?—4

As the bridegroom was delayed, they all slumbered and slept. Matt. 25:5, RSV.

Ellen White's dealing with Bates in 1851 was not the first time she had opposed date setting. As early as 1845 she had repeatedly warned her fellow believers that time was no longer a test and that every passing of a suggested date would weaken the faith of those who had put their hope in it. Even her first vision hinted that the city might be a "great way off." In response to her position on date setting, some charged her "with being with the evil servant that said in his heart, 'My Lord delayeth his coming'" (EW 14, 15, 22).

She was clear that the third angel's message provided a more certain foundation for their faith than date setting. Beyond that, in relating to time setting she consistently pointed the Sabbatarians away from excitement and toward their present duty on earth. That emphasis would, as we shall see, eventually form the rationale for the creation of Adventist institutions that could take Seventh-day Adventism to the far corners of the earth.

Jesus seems to be clear on the topic of date setting in Matthew 24. But if that isn't enough, Ellen White pounds home the problems associated with it.

Yet the Seventh-day Adventist date setters go on and on in their desperate attempt to continue the excitement. I remember 1964. Many were quite sure that Jesus would come that year because the Bible taught that "as it was in the days of Noah, so will it be in the days of the Son of man" (Luke 17:26, RSV). And hadn't Noah preached his message for 120 years before the Flood came? *Voilà!* There you have it. Adventists had been preaching their message for 120 years since 1844. The "proof" was conclusive. Jesus would return in 1964, probably on October 22.

And then there was the year 2,000, the beginning of the seventh millennium, the Sabbath millennium of heavenly rest. People everywhere got excited about that one. About that year a best-selling Adventist book hit the market featuring a clock indicating that it was merely minutes until midnight, "when the Bridegroom cometh."

The sad fact is that Adventists are still high on eschatological excitement and low on "PRESENT DUTY." They, unfortunately, have it just backward from Jesus' message of Matthew 24 and 25.

Help us, Lord, to desire solid food rather than spiritual sugar.

THE ALTERNATIVE TO DATE SETTING—1

His master said to him, "Well done, good and faithful servant; you have been faithful over a little, I will set you over much; enter into the joy of your master." Matt. 25:21, RSV.

Matthew 24, 25 is a strange sermon!
It finds the disciples inquiring of Christ about the destruction of the Temple and asking for a sign regarding His return and the end of the age. To put it bluntly, Jesus' answer must have been frustrating. For one thing, He provided a list of "signs" that occur in every age, such as wars, earthquakes, and famines, and then goes on to say that "the end is not yet," that "all this is but the *beginning* of the birth-pangs" (Matt. 24:6, 8, RSV).

Beyond that, Jesus mixed together events related to the destruction of Jerusalem in A.D. 70 and the Second Advent. And if that wasn't enough, He told them that no one except God knows the time of the event (verse 36). Jesus concludes His presentation on the request for a sign with the admonition to "watch therefore: for ye know not what hour your Lord doth come" (verse 42). He might as well have said, "Don't worry about the time."

At that point in His sermon, Jesus moves beyond signs to what He most needed to tell His end-as-soon-as-possible desiring disciples. Beginning in verse 43 Jesus sets forth five parables that move progressively toward what they most *need* to hear, rather than what they most *want* to hear (i.e., how near the end is).

The first parable (verses 43, 44) merely tells them to watch since they don't know the timing of the Second Advent. The second (verses 45-51) tells them that they have duties while they are watching and waiting, and that time will last longer than expected. The third (Matt. 25:1-13) continues the theme of a delayed coming, but stresses the need to prepare for the event. The fourth parable (verses 14-30) emphasizes how they are to prepare. They are to develop and faithfully utilize their talents. And the climactic parable—the one about the sheep and the goats (verses 31-46)—explicitly states the essential nature of their working while they are waiting and watching.

In other words, Jesus directs the whole discussion away from the excitement over time and toward "PRESENT duty." John Wesley, the founder of Methodism, caught Jesus' point. When someone asked him what he would do today if he knew for sure that Jesus would come tomorrow, he replied that he would do just what he had planned.

Lord, help us to realize that being ready is not excitement, but the responsible doing of Your will as we live in this world.

THE ALTERNATIVE TO DATE SETTING—2

Truly, I say to you, as you did it to one of the least of these my brethren, you did it to me. Matt. 25:40, RSV.

How to be a faithful Adventist? That is the question.

The disciples and the early Adventists (and many in our day also) wanted to spend their wait in emotional excitement. But Jesus sought to direct their attention to the more sober realm of living as a Christian in the daily world.

Yesterday we closed with the parable of the sheep and goats in Matthew 25:31-46. Ellen White caught Jesus' meaning when she wrote: "Thus Christ on the Mount of Olives pictured to His disciples the scene of the great judgment day. And He represented its decision as turning upon one point. When the nations are gathered before Him, there will be but two classes, and their eternal destiny will be determined by what they have done or have neglected to do for Him in the person of the poor and suffering. . . . Those whom Christ commends in the judgment may have known little of theology, but they have cherished His principles. Through the influence of the divine Spirit they have been a blessing to those about them. Even among the heathen are those who have cherished the spirit of kindness; before the words of life had fallen upon their ears, they have befriended the missionaries, even ministering to them at the peril of their own lives. Among the heathen are those who worship God ignorantly, those to whom the light is never brought by human instrumentality, yet they will not perish. Though ignorant of the written law of God, they have heard His voice speaking to them in nature, and have done the things that the law required. Their works are evidence that the Holy Spirit has touched their hearts, and they are recognized as the children of God" (DA 637, 638).

Has the Holy Spirit touched my heart? Where is my focus as an Adventist? Is it on the excitement of the latest preacher who persuades the church on the nearness of the Advent? Or is it on "PRESENT duty" as we wait for that event?

I must admit that excitement by definition is more captivating. But "PRESENT duty" is more Christian.

The true Adventist according to Jesus is not the one who can only think of how close the coming is, but the one who is living the life of God's love while hoping and waiting and watching for that better day.

Today, my friend, Jesus wants each of us to rededicate our life to being Christians in our world as we await the next one.

BECOMING OPEN-DOOR ADVENTISTS—1

Behold, I have set before you an open door, which no one is able to shut. Rev. 3:8, RSV.

Some weeks ago we noted that the early Sabbatarians were shut-door Adventists. Miller had used the phrase "shut door" from Matthew 25:10 to signify the close of probation before the arrival of the Bridegroom, or Christ. Another way of putting it is that Miller believed that every person will have made a decision for or against Christ before He comes again, that there will be no second chances after the Second Advent. That is good Bible teaching.

But Miller's understanding of the shut door had an inbuilt problem. More specifically, he had tied the Second Advent to the end of the 2300 days of Daniel 8:14. Thus he believed up through the end of 1844 that probation had closed by October 22 of that year, that the work of preaching the gospel to sinners had ended, that no more sinners could be converted.

All early Sabbatarian Adventists, without exception, were shut-door believers. However, Bible study, as we saw earlier, soon led them to conclude that the cleansing of the sanctuary was not the Second Advent, but had to do with Christ's ministry in the heavenly temple.

At that point they found themselves holding a theology that no longer fit together. They had changed their interpretation of the cleansing of the sanctuary but had not reinterpreted the timing of the shut door. A transformation in one belief, however, demanded a shift in the other. But that point was not immediately obvious to the Sabbatarians.

It would be the early 1850s before they had worked out a harmonized position on the topic. But the change did not come about because they first saw their mistake in the Bible. To the contrary, they faced another problem that wouldn't go away. Whether they liked it or not, they kept getting converts to their message who had not gone through the Millerite experience. At first they thought that they should refuse to baptize them, since such conversions were "impossible." Such was the case of J. H. Waggoner, who later became a leading minister among the Seventh-day Adventists.

It was the reality of the converts who shouldn't have been that drove the Sabbatarians back to the Bible to restudy the topic. By late 1851 or early 1852 they had realized their mistake. As a result, they concluded that while it was true that probation would close before the Advent, that that event was still future. That insight opened the way for them to spread their message to everyone.

The good news is that God leads us even through our muddles!

GOD USES EVEN OUR MISTAKES

The Lord says, "I will teach you the way you should go; I will instruct you and advise you." Ps. 32:8, TEV.

We serve a gracious God.

If I were dealing with people who could not see their mistakes I would probably either ignore them or let them pay the price for their problems. I certainly wouldn't bless them in spite of their mistakes. We can all be thankful that someone like me is not God. The God we serve blesses us in spite of who we are. He not only helps us solve our problems, but blesses us in the process. The gospel truth is that God even uses our mistakes.

So it was with the shut-door experience. The Sabbatarians had obvious and serious theological error. After all, during the shut-door period of Adventist history they believed that the evangelistic outreach of their movement was restricted to those who had accepted the Millerite message of the 1830s and early 1840s, since the door of mercy had closed for all others.

But God could employ that mistake to the good of the movement. First, He guided the small band of Sabbatarians to use that period of their history to build a solid theological foundation. Thus they spent little of their scarce resources on evangelism until they had a message. Second, after developing their theological identity, they restricted their evangelism between 1848 and 1851 to other Millerites. It was only after they had a solid theological base and a substantial membership core group that they were in a position to reach out to the larger population and eventually to the ends of the earth.

Looking back on the shut-door era of Adventist history, I see it as a necessary stage in the movement's development. God was leading step by step to build a solid platform from which to launch a mission "to every nation, and kindred, and tongue, and people" (Rev. 14:6).

God blesses us anyway. That's gospel, that's good news. And how about you, my friend? Do we bless even the slow to learn? Do you and I have the same spirit? Do we even want it? I challenge each of us today to apply His grace in our daily lives to our wives, husbands, children, and fellow church members.

Help us, our Father, to be a positive blessing, even when people around us make serious mistakes.

BECOMING OPEN-DOOR ADVENTISTS–2

And to the angel of the church in Philadelphia write: "The words of the holy one, the true one, who has the key of David, who opens and no one shall shut, who shuts and no one opens." Rev. 3:7, RSV.

One of the most significant events in Seventh-day Adventist history was its shift from shut-door Adventism to open door in the early 1850s.

Before we examine the new position, we need to summarize the various meanings they had read into the old one. By the late 1840s the shut-door phrase had at least three meanings in their minds: (1) that probation had closed by October 22, 1844, (2) that prophecy had been fulfilled on that date, and (3) that their evangelistic mission after that time was restricted to those who had been Millerites.

Most discussions of the topic center on points 1 and 3, but the second was equally important. When James White referred to the Sabbatarians as the seventh-day shut-door people, he was referring to their two cardinal doctrines—the Sabbath and their understanding that prophecy had indeed been fulfilled in 1844 at the end of the 2300 days. They never changed their understanding of the second meaning.

But, as we noted earlier, the fulfillment of prophecy had obviously not been the Second Advent. Thus probation had not closed. As a result, they eventually realized their error on point 1 and gave up that interpretation of the shut door.

That conclusion led them to change on the third point. Beginning with Ellen White's vision in November 1848 regarding the Advent message going round the world like streams of light, the perception of an open door on mission to the world gradually dawned to the struggling believers. They began to see ever more clearly that they had an end-time message for the entire world, rather than merely to ex-Millerites.

As Ellen White put it in March 1849, "I was shown that . . . the time for the commandments of God to shine out with all their importance . . . was when the door was opened in the most holy place in the heavenly sanctuary, where the ark is." In 1844, according to this view, Jesus rose up and shut the door of the holy place, and opened the door of the Most Holy. "I saw that Jesus had shut the door of the holy place, and no man can open it; and that He had opened the door into the most holy, and no man can shut it" (EW 42). And with that opening came insights on a new message on the Sabbath and related prophetic topics that would eventually drive the Sabbatarians to the far corners of the earth.

In terms of mission, Adventism would never be the same. It faced open-door mission with a message that the world needed to hear before the advent of Jesus in the clouds.

REFINING THE ADVENT MESSAGE

For the Lamb which is in the midst of the throne shall feed them, and shall lead them unto living fountains of waters. Rev. 7:17.

Revisionism was a part of the development of Sabbatarianism in the 1850s as they began to take a second look at some of their understandings and adjust accordingly.

So it was on aspects of the shut-door issue, as we saw yesterday. Thus by early 1852 James White could proclaim: "This OPEN DOOR we teach, and invite those who have an ear to hear, to come to it and find salvation through Jesus Christ. There is an exceeding glory in the view that Jesus has OPENED THE DOOR into the holiest of all. . . . If it be said that we are of the OPEN DOOR and seventh-day Sabbath theory, we shall not object; for this is our faith."

During the early 1850s he and the other Sabbatarians were rejoicing not only in God's progressive leading but in the beauty of their message and in the magnitude of the mission He had set before them.

Their attitude has something vital in it. They were not afraid to admit that they had made a mistake. Not only did they stand firm on those beliefs that held up to careful Bible study, but they were willing to adjust those that time and further study showed to be in error.

Too many of us view truth as static. Some of us even perceive the message of the Seventh-day Adventist Church as something that was born fully developed back in the 1840s.

Nothing could be further from the truth. The Adventist belief system is a dynamic aspect of the movement. As God leads, the denomination has been willing to follow. Thus its understanding of Bible truth and its mission has grown and expanded across time. Building on what has proven solid, including its central pillar doctrines and its understanding of the flow of prophecy between Revelation 12:1 and 14:20, it continues to adjust its belief system to match up to more adequate understandings of the Bible's message and the needs of a sinful world.

And the transformations aren't over yet. God will continue to lead His people up through that day when we see Christ coming in the clouds.

We thank You, our Father, for leading us in the past. And we look forward to Your guidance in the future. Help us to have open minds and ready hearts as You direct us step by step.

REFINING THE SECOND ANGEL'S MESSAGE—1

And another angel, a second one, followed, saying, "Fallen, fallen is Babylon the great, she who has made all the nations drink of the wine of the passion of her immorality." Rev. 14:8, NASB.

To what extent should Seventh-day Adventists cooperate with other Christian denominations? Should Adventist ministers be active in community ministerial associations? Should the church and its members participate with other denominations in community projects? If so, on what basis?

Those are important questions. After all, didn't our earliest believers teach that all other churches were a part of the fallen Babylon of Revelation 14:8 and 18:1-4?

They certainly did. And because of that teaching Adventism still experiences tension among its various subgroups over the question of cooperation with other Christians. Fortunately, Adventist history throws a great deal of light on both the topic of the fall of Babylon and the issues related to it.

As we observed earlier, the earliest Adventist interpretations of Babylon were well in place before the birth of Sabbatarian Adventism. Charles Fitch, we noted, set the stage for the Millerite understanding when he began to proclaim the fall of Babylon in the summer of 1843. For Fitch, Babylon consisted of both Roman Catholics and those Protestants who rejected the Bible's teachings about the Second Advent.

James White ratified that basic understanding in 1859, when he wrote that "we unhesitatingly apply the Babylon of the Apocalypse to all corrupt Christianity." Corruption, as he saw it, involved both a moral fall and the intermingling of Christian teachings with non-Christian philosophies, such as the immortality of the soul. The latter left the churches defenseless against such beliefs as spiritualism. *Babylon, in short, stood for confused churches.*

But as time went on, the Sabbatarian Adventists in the early 1850s began to notice that the Sundaykeeping denominations had some good things about them. They obviously weren't wrong in many areas of their teaching and practice. The world wasn't nearly so black and white as they had first thought. Such thoughts put them on a course that would lead to further insight on the implications of the second angel's message.

Help us, Father, to keep our eyes open to the good in others, even those who are somewhat or even massively confused in their belief system. Give us eyes to see the good, and give us the grace to accept the gift.

REFINING THE SECOND ANGEL'S MESSAGE—2

And after these things I saw another angel come down from heaven, having great power; and the earth was lightened with his glory. And he cried mightily with a strong voice, saying, Babylon the great is fallen, is fallen, and is become the habitation of devils, and the hold of every foul spirit, and a cage of every unclean and hateful bird. Rev. 18:1, 2.

Once Sabbatarian Adventists had given up the teaching that the door of probation had been shut, the way opened for another look at their understanding of the fall of Babylon.

The one important line of development in terms of the second angel's message was to conceive of the fall of Babylon as a two-phase or progressive corruption. Whereas Fitch had seen Revelation 14:8 and 18:1-4 as one event, James White and the Sabbatarians came to interpret those two texts as separate incidents.

White noted that the fall of Babylon described in 14:8 "is in the past" while that set forth in 18:1-4 is present and especially future. As he put it in 1859: "First she falls [14:8]; second, she becomes the habitation of devils, and 'the hold of every foul spirit,' etc.; third, God's people are called out of her; and fourth, her plagues are poured out upon her."

Thus although the Sabbatarians believed that the religious world had made a serious mistake during the early 1840s in rejecting a biblical teaching related to the Second Advent and for persecuting people for holding that belief, that 1840s fall was only the beginning of confusion. Developments before the end of time would lead the churches into much more serious moral and doctrinal turmoil until God would have to finally give up on those hopelessly confused churches that chose to be part of Babylon.

Ellen White agreed with her husband's reinterpretation of the fall of Babylon as being progressive, but she eventually would advance beyond it. To her "the perfect fulfillment of Revelation 14:8 is yet future." As a result, "the great body of Christ's true followers are still" in churches outside of Adventism. Thus Babylon is confused but not totally fallen. Beyond that, the call to leave Babylon will not reach its full force until right before the Advent, when Babylon will have at last completed its ongoing fall. As a result, she claimed, the call to "come out of her, my people," of Revelation 18:1-4 will "constitute the final warning to be given to the inhabitants of the earth" (GC 389, 390, 604).

Lord, not everyone believes just as I do. There may be good reasons for that. Help me today to cultivate an understanding heart that stands for the truth but is gentle with those who do not see things the way I do.

A Foundation for Cooperation—1

I have other sheep, that are not of this fold; I must bring them also, and they will heed my voice. John 10:16, RSV.

W ith their reinterpretations of the shut door and the fall of Babylon, James and Ellen White had created a theological foundation for Adventism's cooperation with other Christian bodies. Such partnership became increasingly more of an issue as Seventh-day Adventists realized that the Second Advent wasn't as close as they had at first expected.

But association with "outsiders" would bring its own strains into the denomination that would divide Adventist thinking into what we might think of as "moderate" and "hardline" orientations. The moderates would come to favor cooperation that did not compromise the theological and ethical integrity of the movement, while the hardliners would have a difficult time working with any group that did not see things exactly as they did.

A case in point is Adventism's relationship to the Women's Christian Temperance Union (WCTU). The movement obviously had some good ideas (i.e., truth). After all, it advocated temperance—a topic in line with Adventism's concerns. As a result, as early as 1877 the Adventists began uniting their efforts with the WCTU,

So far, so good, in terms of the WCTU. They seemed to be nice Christian women. But then in 1887 they muddied the waters by aligning themselves with the National Reform Association in its drive to gain national legislation for Sunday sacredness. That same year the WCTU added a Sabbath (Sunday) Observance Department to its own organization. The next year it supported the national Sunday bill set forth by Senator Blair.

Such steps definitely made the WCTU look more like it was rapidly moving toward a fully developed Babylon in the eyes of some Adventists. While having "the truth" on temperance, it at the same time supported "error" on the Sabbath issue. Some Adventists concluded that if that isn't confusion or Babylon, what is? Such developments continued to cause concern in the Adventist ranks throughout the 1890s.

Those are the facts of the case. Today's assignment: Discuss with others or think about the proper attitude and course of action to take in such a situation.

Why did you make the choice(s) you did? What principles undergirded your decision? How do these issues affect what it means to be a Christian Adventist in today's world?

A FOUNDATION FOR COOPERATION—2

"Teacher," said John, "we saw a man driving out demons in your name and we told him to stop, because he was not one of us." Mark 9:38, NIV.

D o not stop him," Jesus said. "No one who does a miracle in my name can in the next moment say anything bad about me, for whoever is not against us is for us." Mark 9:39, 40, NIV.

Should we as Adventists unite our efforts publicly with those who have some truth along with some serious theological error? That is the question we raised yesterday.

Ellen White and other Adventists during the 1890s were well aware of the Sunday advocacy views of the Women's Christian Temperance Union (WCTU), but they sought to cooperate as much as possible with them throughout the 1890s.

Still other Adventists were not so sure that that was the right position. Alonzo T. Jones, for example, as editor of the *Review and Herald* unleashed a string of editorials suggesting that the WCTU was apostate and hadn't gone far enough in its opposition to religious intolerance.

That black-and-white mentality triggered a series of letters from Ellen White. As one who was willing to work within a certain amount of tension, she counseled Jones not to be so hard and judgmental on those who didn't see things through Adventist eyes. "There are," she wrote, "vital truths upon which they have had very little light." As a result, "they should be dealt with in tenderness, in love, and with respect for their good work. You ought not to handle them as you do" (Lt 62 1900).

She noted that she was not arguing with the "real truth" of his position, but rather with his lack of vision, tact, and kindness. His approach, she claimed, would lead the WCTU members to conclude: "You see, it is impossible to have any union with Seventh-day Adventists; for they will give us no choice to connect with them unless we believe just as they believe" *(ibid.)*.

Thus she distinctly opposed such a black-and-white attitude. Rather, she noted, "we should seek to gain the confidence of the workers of the WCTU, by harmonizing with them as far as possible." They could learn things from us and we from them *(ibid.)*.

By way of contrast, she urged Jones not to represent truth as "so formidable" that others would turn away in despair. She pleaded with him to have "Christlike tenderness" toward those who didn't see things like him *(ibid.)*.

How is my "tolerance quotient"? Does my approach to others who differ from me express "Christlike tenderness"?

Help me, Lord, to be more like You in my relationships with all people.

A FOUNDATION FOR COOPERATION—3

They helped every one his neighbour; and every one said to his brother, Be of good courage. Isa. 41:6.

Redefining the shut door and Babylon laid the foundation for the Sabbatarians to cooperate with those who differed from them theologically. But on what principles?

Once again the Sunday sacredness supporting Women's Christian Temperance Union provides us with a good example. "The light has been given me," Ellen White penned, that "while there is to be no sacrifice of principle on our part, as far as possible we are to unite with them in laboring for temperance reforms. . . .

"I have been shown we are not to shun the WCTU workers. By uniting with them in behalf of total abstinence we do not change our position regarding the observance of the seventh day, and we can show our appreciation of their position regarding the subject of temperance.

"By opening the door, and inviting them to unite with us on the temperance question, we secure their help along temperance lines; and they, by uniting with us, will hear new truths which the Holy Spirit is waiting to impress upon hearts" (RH, June 18, 1908).

It was that same irenic spirit that led Ellen White to suggest that Adventist pastors should become acquainted with other clergy in their district, letting them know that Adventists "are reformers, but not bigots." Her advice was to focus on the "common ground" that Adventism shared with others and "to present the truth as it is in Jesus" rather than to run down other churches. Using such techniques, Adventist pastors could "come near to the ministers of other denominations" (Ev 143, 144, 227, 562).

We need to beware of shooting the "Babylon gun" at everyone who does not view things as we do. Adventist history is informative on that point. The redefinition of Babylon in the 1850s provided a crucial foundation for the participation of Adventism in a world that just won't come to an end.

Such is the fruit of James White's growth in the understanding of the two-stage fall of Babylon in 1859. We need to learn to live in the tension of working with those who differ with us while firmly maintaining and standing for those beautiful and biblical truths that have made us a people. The only alternative is the Adventist cloister.

Help us, Lord, to learn the principles and the necessities of cooperation as we reach out to change our world.

REDEFINING THE FIRST ANGEL'S MESSAGE—1

And I saw another angel fly in the midst of heaven, having the everlasting gospel to preach unto them that dwell on the earth, and to every nation, and kindred, and tongue, and people, saying with a loud voice, Fear God, and give glory to him; for the hour of his judgment is come: and worship him that made heaven, and earth, and the sea, and the fountains of waters. Rev. 14:6, 7.

A powerful message! One that Seventh-day Adventists hear talked about all the time, but one that they probably don't sit down and analyze. So let's do it this morning.

The message has four central teachings. First, the everlasting gospel. For the Millerites the everlasting gospel was more than merely the cross and the resurrection of Jesus. It also included the best of the good news—that Jesus was returning to bring to full reality the blessings made possible by His crucifixion and victory over death. Thus the everlasting gospel included the Second Advent, the resurrection of those who had died in Christ, the translation of those still living to meet Christ in the air, and the kingdom of heaven in its fullness. The everlasting Gospel included all of that and more to Millerites and early Sabbatarians.

The second part of the message stipulated that it would be preached to all the earth. As a result, J. V. Himes sent Millerite literature to every Protestant mission station in the world. The earliest Sabbatarians, by way of contrast, were quite willing to say that the Millerites had fulfilled the commission during the early 1840s. Only gradually would the Sabbatarians take hold of their missiological responsibilities.

The third part, proclaiming the fact that the hour or time of God's judgment had arrived, the Millerites viewed as the Second Advent. For them it was an executive judgment, one in which God passed out the rewards to those who had served Him. Here is a point at which the Sabbatarians would have some fresh ideas, as we will see.

The fourth part, having to do with worshipping the Creator, the Millerites did not especially emphasize. But, as we saw some weeks ago, the Sabbatarians correctly viewed those words as an allusion to the Sabbath as reflected upon in Exodus 20 and Genesis 2:1-3. They linked the Sabbath allusion to Revelation 12:17 and 14:12, verses indicating that God would have a commandment keeping people during the last days. Thus the worship the Creator part of Revelation 14:7 formed a central aspect of Adventist teaching.

The messages of the three angels of Revelation 14 are God's final ones to a dying world. We need to spend more time contemplating their meaning in our day.

REDEFINING THE FIRST ANGEL'S MESSAGE—2

Thrones were placed and one that was ancient of days took his seat. . . . A thousand thousands served him, and ten thousand times ten thousand stood before him; the court sat in judgment, and the books were opened. Dan. 7:9, 10, RSV.

Besides emphasizing the seventh-day Sabbath aspect of Revelation 14:7, the one major change the Sabbatarians would make in the first angel's message focused on the words "the hour of his judgment is come."

The Millerites had identified the judgment scene of Daniel 7, the cleansing of the sanctuary of Daniel 8:14, and the judgment of Revelation 14:7 as the judgment that would take place at the Second Advent. Thus for them it was an executive judgment, a time when God passed out rewards according to what individuals had chosen and done (see Matt. 16:27). Charles Fitch stated that the judgment of Revelation 14:7 referred to the "destruction" of the world.

The Sabbatarians, after years of study for some of them, would come to see the judgment of those texts as a pre-Advent judgment, or what they eventually called an investigative judgment. That new interpretation, however, would cause disruption in their ranks and not all the Sabbatarian leaders would accept the concept until the mid to late 1850s. Some critics in the twentieth century taught that Adventists quickly put the pre-Advent judgment in place soon after 1844 as an apology for the Disappointment. That may sound like a plausible interpretation, but it doesn't match up with the historical facts.

For one thing, the concept of a pre-Advent judgment originated before the October 1844 disappointment. Josiah Litch had developed the idea by the late 1830s. His main point at that time was that the judgment needed to precede the resurrection.

In 1841 he wrote that "no human tribunal would think of executing judgment on a prisoner until after his trial, much less God." Thus God, before the resurrection, would bring every human deed into judgment. At the resurrection He would execute judgment in accordance with His findings. Several Millerites adopted Litch's concept before October 1844. And that wasn't too difficult a task, since the Bible teaching that Christ rewards people when He comes in the clouds of heaven suggests that prior to that time God has decided who will come up in the first resurrection.

We can be thankful that we serve a just God who is not arbitrary, one who relies on evidence and not despotic whim.

REDEFINING THE FIRST ANGEL'S MESSAGE—3

The court shall sit in judgment, and his [the little horn's] dominion shall be taken away. . . . And the kingdom and the dominion . . . shall be given to the people of the saints of the Most High. Dan. 7:26, 27, RSV.

We saw yesterday that beginning in the late 1830s Josiah Litch began to interpret "the hour of his judgment is come" of Revelation 14:7 as something prior to the final day of judgment. Litch himself believed that the trial or pre-Advent judgment had begun in 1798 at the end of the 1260-day prophetic time period of Daniel 7:25, and that it would finish before the Second Advent at the end of the 2300 days.

The idea of a pre-Advent judgment didn't die with the October 1844 disappointment. Non-Sabbatarian Enoch Jacobs, for example, after discussing the breastplate of judgment worn on the Day of Atonement, stated in November 1844 that "unless something as decisive as the setting of the judgment took place on the tenth day [October 22, 1844], the antitype is not yet given," prophecy is not fulfilled, and we are still in darkness. To Jacobs "the judgment sits before the personal appearing of Christ and resurrection of the saints."

Again, in January 1845 Apollos Hale and Joseph Turner called for a deeper understanding of the wedding parables. In particular, they pointed out that the wedding parable of Luke 12 says that people needed to wait until Christ returned *from* the wedding. They went on to note that the wedding parable of Matthew 22 has a judgment scene in which the king examines his guests to determine whether they are wearing a wedding garment.

Turner and Hale linked those wedding parables to Christ's reception of His kingdom in the judgment scene of Daniel 7. They concluded that beginning on October 22 Christ had a new work to perform "in the invisible world." Accordingly, they proclaimed, *"The judgment is here!"*

By March 20, 1845, Miller had equated the judgment of Revelation 14 with the judgment scene of Daniel 7. He pointed out that since 1844 God was in his "judicial character deciding the cases of all the righteous," so that "the angels may know whom to gather" at the Second Coming. "If this is true," Miller added, "who can say God is not already justifying his Sanctuary."

Thank You, Lord, for the logic of Your Word. Thank You that You will eventually remove the selfish forces that have controlled this world and will set up an everlasting kingdom in which righteousness rules.

REDEFINING THE FIRST ANGEL'S MESSAGE—4

When the king came in to look at the guests, he saw there a man who had no wedding garment. Matt. 22:11, RSV.

Yesterday we saw that Enoch Jacobs, Apollos Hale, Joseph Turner, and William Miller had by late 1844 and early 1845 tied the October date and the sanctuary doctrine to the heavenly pre-Advent judgment of Daniel 7. Thus those non-Sabbatarians had begun to see such central Millerite texts as the judgment of Daniel 7 and the arrival of the bridegroom at the wedding as being the coming of Christ to the pre-Advent judgment rather than His return in the clouds of heaven. That same rationale applied to the cleansing of the sanctuary of Daniel 8:14 and the judgment hour of Revelation 14:7.

But what about the Sabbatarian leadership? How did they stand on the teaching of a pre-Advent judgment in the late 1840s?

Joseph Bates was quite positive on the topic. "Respecting 'the hour of God's judgment is come,'" he penned in 1847, "there must be order and time, for God in His judicial character to decide the cases of all the righteous that their names may be registered in the Lamb's Book of Life, and they be fully prepared for that eventful moment of their change from mortality to immortality." And in late 1848 he claimed that "the dead saints are now being judged." Bates was probably the first of the Sabbatarian leaders to teach the pre-Advent judgment.

It appears that by January 5, 1849, Ellen White agreed with him on the topic. Commenting on a vision she had received on that date, she wrote that she "saw that Jesus would not leave the most holy place until every case was decided either for salvation or destruction" (EW 36).

So far so good. Bates and Ellen White seem to be in harmony on the topic. But not James. As late as September 1850 he would openly and aggressively disagree with Bates on the topic of a pre-Advent judgment. In that month he wrote that "many minds have been confused by conflicting views that have been published on the subject of the judgment." "Some [meaning Bates] have contended that the day of judgment was prior to the second advent. This view is certainly without foundation in the word of God."

A side lesson here is that even the Seventh-day Adventist pioneers differed with each other on important topics, yet they still managed to respect each other. We need that spirit in our own day.

REDEFINING THE FIRST ANGEL'S MESSAGE—5

My reward is with me, to give every man according as his work shall be. Rev. 22:12.

Yesterday we left James White publicly thundering at Joseph Bates that the latter was confused regarding the judgment in his belief that it was prior to the Second Advent. Such a teaching, James declared, "is certainly without foundation in the word of God."

For James "the great day of judgment will be one thousand years long" and would begin at the Second Advent. As to a pre-Advent judgment, White had observed that "it is not necessary that the final sentence should be given before the first resurrection, as some have taught; for the names of the saints are written in heaven, and Jesus, and the angels will certainly know who to raise, and gather to the New Jerusalem." Thus as late as September 1850 White opposed his wife and Bates on the topic of a pre-Advent judgment. But that would change—gradually.

Circumstantial evidence for White's shift appears in the *Review* of February 1854, in which he published a piece by J. N. Loughborough that tied the first angel's message to the pre-Advent judgment. Even though Loughborough had not written it for publication, James notes in a short introduction that he had printed it anyway because "it meets inquiries which have been presented to us."

Any questions about James' position were put to rest in January 1857 when he published a full-blown treatment of the pre-Advent judgment under his own name. Both the just and the evil, he penned that month, "will be judged before they are raised from the dead. The investigative judgment of the house, or church, of God will take place before the first resurrection; so will the judgment of the wicked take place during the 1000 years of Rev. 20, and they will be raised at the close of that period."

The terminology of "investigative judgment" had earlier that month found its first use in print in an article by Elon Everts. By 1857 the Sabbatarian Adventists had widely accepted the teaching of a pre-Advent judgment.

The development of the doctrine of the pre-Advent judgment nicely illustrates how God leads the understanding of His followers across time. He is always guiding as His people seek a better grasp of His Word. His task is to provide that Word. Ours is to study it prayerfully as we seek to know God's will and ways ever more fully.

123

JUDGMENT IS GOOD NEWS!

As I watched, this horn was waging war against the holy people and was defeating them, until the Ancient One came and judged in favor of the holy people of the Most High. Then the time arrived for the holy people to take over the kingdom.
Dan. 7:21, 22, NLT.

The judgment is good news! Judgment is gospel!

Is it? Certainly that is not the way many Adventists have viewed the topic.

I remember the first time I attended an Adventist church. Living on a merchant marine ship in San Francisco Bay, I had not the slightest interest in Christianity or the judgment. But I had met a girl who took me to church.

The whole place was rather a shock to my system. But the knockout blow came when an "old" lady (she must have been all of 40) stood up before the youth group and began waving her bony finger at them, letting them know in no uncertain terms that they had better be lying awake at night dredging up and confessing every sin that they had ever committed. After all, no one knew when their name would come before the heavenly judgment. And when it did, if they had one unconfessed sin they would not be spending eternity in their destination of first choice.

Decades of such teaching not only presented Adventists with a "bad news" interpretation of the pre-Advent judgment, but led them to despise the teaching itself. That is unfortunate, because the biblical picture is that for God's people the judgment is good news. In fact, it is the best of news. As God put it to Daniel, the pre-Advent judgment is "for" or "in favor" of the saints. The Bible pictures the divine Judge as being on our side. After all, it is God who sent the Savior. He is not trying to keep people out of heaven, but to get as many in as possible. The Lord wants His house to be full.

But not all accept His offer of salvation and the change of heart that He provides. Some rebel against His ways, mistreat others, and become aggressive and destructive. He can't let that go on forever. So they also come under judgment. For those who choose to live a life of active rebellion against God and His principles the judgment is obviously not good news.

But for Christians it is the best of news. God's judgment is their vindication. Because it is in their favor it is the event that opens to them the doors of the everlasting kingdom. Praise God for His loving judgment.

RETROSPECT ON JUDGMENT

He has fixed a day in which He will judge the world in righteousness through a Man whom He has appointed, having furnished proof to all men by raising Him from the dead. Acts 17:31, NASB.

Judgment. A fearful topic to some. A hopeful one to others. And a complex subject for all. Today we want to stand back and take a look at the breadth of the topic. Most people think of judgment as a single event taking place somewhere near the end of time or for individuals at death. But the early Adventists discovered that it was a process rather than a single event. By 1857 James White had come to regard the final judgment as having four quite discrete phases.

Phase one he saw as the pre-Advent or investigative judgment of those who claimed to be followers of the God of the Bible. The earliest Adventists arrived through Day of Atonement typology at the fact that it would include only God's people. On that day the high priest went into the holy of holies wearing the breastplate of judgment, which had inscribed on it the names of God's people. It was those who he interceded for on the annual judgment day.

The second phase as the Adventists viewed it was an executive judgment that would take place at the Second Advent, when God in His executive role brought blessings to His people (Rev. 22:12; Matt. 16:27).

The third phase is the millennial judgment mentioned in Revelation 20:4. "Then," we read, "I saw thrones, and seated on them were those to whom judgment was committed" (RSV). At this point you may be wondering what is left to be judged. After all, the righteous are in heaven with God, and the wicked are sleeping in their graves. That's true on both counts. But the wicked have not yet faced eternal destruction. And before they do, God gives every person a chance to go over the records of the unjust during the millennium. Wanting no one still to have questions, He provides time for all to realize that He is doing the best thing He can in a bad situation. Thus the millennial phase of the judgment is in a sense an "investigative" judgment of the wicked. But it is even more a judgment on God's righteousness and the adequacy of His decisions.

The final phase of judgment comes at the end of the 1,000 years, when an executive judgment forever removes those who have continued to reject God and His principles (Rev. 20:9, 12-15). That final phase is not a happy one, but God has no choice if He will not force people's wills and if He desires to create a universe in which sin and destructive relationships have no part.

WHEN DOES THE SABBATH BEGIN?—1

From even unto even, shall ye celebrate your Sabbath. Lev. 23:32.

Unlike the pre-Advent judgment, the central leaders of early Adventism had no dispute with each other on when to begin and end the Sabbath.

In spite of the fact that the Seventh Day Baptists, from whom Bates indirectly got the Sabbath, observed it from sunset to sunset, Bates himself argued that it should be kept from 6:00 p.m. Friday to 6:00 p.m. Saturday.

He put forth that position in his 1846 book on the Sabbath, claiming that "history shows that the Jews . . . commenced their days at 6 o'clock in the evening." I don't know what history he was looking at or if he had inferred his conclusion from whatever he was reading, but he was dead wrong.

Bates also set forth theoretical reasons for keeping the Sabbath from 6:00 p.m. to 6:00 p.m. Put simply, he argued that if everyone honored the Sabbath from sunrise to sunrise or sunset to sunset, then people at different latitudes would be keeping the Sabbath at different times. And God certainly didn't want that. Therefore, he concluded, since sunset was 6:00 p.m. at the equator year-round, if everyone kept that time they would all be observing the same Sabbath, just as God wanted it.

This was no matter of small importance to the good captain. After all, he claimed in 1849, "it is just as sinful in the sight of God to willfully reject the Bible light on the commencement of the Sabbath . . . as it would be not to keep it at all."

That's a powerful conviction. And Bates was an enthusiastically powerful and persistent man when convinced about something.

As a result, the church repeatedly got the message that the Sabbath began at 6:00 p.m. Bates managed to sell his interpretation to nearly all the Sabbatarians, including James and Ellen White. Thus, for 10 years they and most other Adventists kept the Sabbath wrongly.

Now, there is a problem! And what is God's attitude to such a mistake? Did He consign them to the spiritual "slammer" because they were wrong?

Obviously not. There is a wideness in God's mercy. In our sincerity He accepts us where we are. But He doesn't stop there. He also gently leads in the path of truth.

WHEN DOES THE SABBATH BEGIN?—2

But at the place which the Lord thy God shall choose to place his name in, there thou shalt sacrifice the passover at even, at the going down of the sun. Deut. 16:6.

Ｈow could God for 10 years let His people live in error on the time to begin the Sabbath? I don't know. But I do know that He did. Perhaps that tells us something about Him.

We should realize that not all Adventists believed that Bates was right in his 6:00 p.m. argument. Some held for sunrise and others for sunset and a few for midnight.

By 1854 the issue had become so troublesome that James White feared "division unless the question could be settled by good testimony." White claimed that he never had been completely satisfied on the 6:00 p.m. time and that the Sabbatarians had never fully investigated it from the Bible. He would later note that Bates' stubborn "stand upon the question, and respect for his years, and his godly life" were undoubtedly reasons why they had "not sooner investigated" the issue from the Bible "as thoroughly as some other points."

In the summer of 1855 White asked young John Nevins Andrews to prepare a study on the topic from the Bible. Andrews was the right man. Thorough to a fault, he went at the task with a vengeance.

Being a firm believer in the 6:00 p.m. time, Andrews was shocked by what he found:

1. "Thou shalt sacrifice the passover *at even, at the going down of the sun*" (Deut. 16:6).
2. "The soul which hath touched any such shall be *unclean until even. . . . and when the sun is down, he shall be clean*" (Lev. 22:6, 7).
3. "And *at even, when the sun did set,* they brought unto him all that were diseased" (Mark 1:32).

Text after text piled up as Andrews set forth the biblical evidence on the Bible definition of "even."

His conclusions: (1) that Scripture offered no evidence for the 6:00 p.m. time and (2) that "the Bible, by several plain statements, establishes the fact that even is at sunset."

He presented those conclusions at a general meeting of Sabbatarians on November 17, 1855, and they moved into line with this "new" biblical light.

Lord, help us to keep our minds open, even when we are convinced that we know the truth.

WHEN DOES THE SABBATH BEGIN?—3

They . . . searched the scriptures daily, whether those things were so. Acts 17:11.

The Bible and searching it diligently were central to early Sabbatarian Adventists. Thus it was, as we saw yesterday, on the time to begin and end the Sabbath.

James White reported that Andrews' Bible study in late 1855 had settled the minds of nearly all of those present that the sunset time was correct. He undoubtedly included himself in that group.

But not everyone agreed with Andrews' conclusions. As White put it, "Bates, and a few others" were at that point out of harmony with the body of believers. Joseph had taught the 6:00 p.m. position for a decade, and he dug in to defend his position.

Here was a problem. Some of the movement's leaders clung to the old position even after Bible study had clearly set forth text after text that the biblical "even" began at sundown and that, therefore, the Sabbath also must of necessity, by Bible definition, commence at sunset. After all, God had plainly taught that "from even unto even, shall ye celebrate your Sabbath" (Lev. 23:32).

But despite the Bible study on the topic, "Bates, and a few others" still sought to justify the old aproach by the "logical" application of their human reason based on stray texts from here and there.

Now, James White doesn't identify who those "few others" were who were standing against the church body on the topic of the time to start the Sabbath. But Uriah Smith tells us who at least one of them was. It was Ellen White.

The tension over the issue, with two of the three founders of the movement being out of harmony with the majority, must have been both serious and apparent to all.

Two days after Andrews presented his study, James later recalled, they "had a special season of prayer" during which "Mrs. W. had a vision, one item of which was that [the] sunset time was correct. That settled the matter with Bro. Bates and others, and general harmony has since prevailed among us upon this point."

Whether we like it or not, those of us in the church still disagree. We can be thankful that God is ever willing to guide His people toward unity.

MOVING TOWARD A DOCTRINE
OF SPIRITUAL GIFTS—1

And God has appointed in the church first apostles, second prophets, third teachers, then workers of miracles, then healers, helpers, administrators, speakers in various kinds of tongues. 1 Cor. 12:28, RSV.

Regarding the new understanding in 1855 on the topic of the time to begin the Sabbath, we have noted a definite sequence of events: (1) disagreement on the topic; (2) a thorough Bible study; (3) general agreement on the findings of the Bible study, with a few exceptions among those still defending the old position; (4) and a vision from Ellen White that confirmed the results of the Bible study and brought unity among the believers.

That sequence of events brings several observations to our minds. James White brought up one of them. "The question naturally arises," he pointed out, "if the visions are given to correct the erring, why did she not sooner see the error of the six o'clock time? For one," he noted, "I have ever been thankful that God corrected the error in his own good time, and did not suffer an unhappy division to exist among us upon the point. . . .

"It does not appear to be the desire of the Lord to teach his people by the gifts of the Spirit on the Bible questions until his servants have diligently searched his word. When this was done upon the subject of [the] time to commence the Sabbath, and most were established, and some were in danger of being out of harmony with the body on this subject, then, yes, then, was the very time for God to magnify his goodness in the manifestation of the gift of his Spirit in the accomplishment of its proper work. The sacred Scriptures are given us as the rule of faith and duty, and we are commanded to search them. . . .

"Let their gifts have their proper place in the church. God has never set them in the very front, and commanded us to look to them to lead us in the path of truth, and the way to Heaven. His word he has magnified. The Scriptures of the Old and New Testament are man's lamp to light up his path to the kingdom. Follow that, but if you err from Bible truth, and are in danger of being lost, it may be that God will in the time of his choice correct you, and bring you back to the Bible."

Thank God for His gifts, including the gift of prophecy through the Holy Spirit. The early believers appreciated the gift but sought to put it in its "proper" place. In their eyes the Bible was central and the gifts pointed them back to God's revelation in Scripture.

MOVING TOWARD A DOCTRINE OF SPIRITUAL GIFTS—2

The entrance of thy words giveth light; it giveth understanding unto the simple. Ps. 119:130.

Yesterday we noted that James White highlighted the supremacy of the Bible as the teacher for Christians of their duties. According to him the function of the gift of prophecy was not only to confirm the truths already gathered from the Bible and to help unify God's people on the Bible's teachings, but also to "bring you back to the Bible" itself.

There is an important point here. One of the proper functions of spiritual gifts is to *bring people back to the Bible*. In making that point, James hit upon a crucial understanding. All too often Adventists have failed to understand the correct role of spiritual gifts. Some have even gone so far as to spend more time and energy studying Ellen White's writings than the Bible.

Such a course flies in the face of the understanding of her work set forth by James and Ellen White and all the other pioneers of Seventh-day Adventism. From Ellen White's perspective, such people have made the "lesser light" into the "greater light" by relegating the Bible to second place.

"The word of God [the Bible]," she penned, "is sufficient to enlighten the most beclouded mind and may be understood by those who have any desire to understand it. But notwithstanding all this, some who profess to make the word of God their study are found living in direct opposition to its plainest teachings. Then, to leave men and women without excuse, God gives plain and pointed testimonies, *bringing them back to the word* that they have neglected to follow" (5T 663; italics supplied).

Again, "Brother J would confuse the mind by seeking to make it appear that the light God has given through the *Testimonies* is an addition to the word of God, but in this he presents the matter in a false light. God has seen fit in this manner to bring the minds of His people to His word" *(ibid.)* "Little heed," Ellen White wrote in another connection, "is given to the Bible, and the Lord has given a lesser light to lead men and women to the greater light" (CM 125).

The Adventist pioneers were consistently assertive in the role of Ellen White as being a pointer to the Bible rather than being the source for doctrine. In fact, one reason I personally believe that she is a true prophet is that she continually directs her readers to Jesus as Savior and to the Bible as *the light*. May we today follow her counsel.

MOVING TOWARD A DOCTRINE OF SPIRITUAL GIFTS—3

He is the one who gave these gifts to the church: the apostles, the prophets. . . .
Their responsibility is to equip God's people to do his work and build up the church,
the body of Christ, until we come to such unity in our faith and knowledge of God's
Son that we will be mature and full grown in the Lord. Eph. 4:11-13, NLT.

B y 1856 Ellen White had come under more and more criticism from her detractors. Thus the Sabbatarians felt a more pressing need to develop a theology of prophetic gifts and to integrate that concept into their entire theological
package.

In February of that year James White wrote an article that set forth his understanding of the topic. He first supplied several texts that indicated that the gifts of
the Spirit (including prophecy) would remain in the church until the Second
Advent.

Then he focused on Joel 2:28-32 with its promise of an outpouring of the gift
of prophecy, noting that Pentecost was only a partial fulfillment and that the real
emphasis of Joel involved a special outpouring of the gift of prophecy on the
"remnant" of verse 32.

White next equated the remnant of Joel 2:32 with the last-day remnant of
Revelation 12:17 who would be keeping the commandments and "have the testimony of Jesus Christ." And "what is the testimony of Jesus Christ?" James asked.
"We will let the angel who addressed John answer this question. He says 'The
Testimony of Jesus is the spirit of prophecy.' Rev. 19:10." In conclusion, White
implied that a special mark of God's last-day church would be a revival of the gift
of prophecy, a gift that he firmly believed his wife possessed.

Thus by 1856 the Sabbatarians had not only rationalized a biblical understanding of the gift of prophecy but had fit it into those apocalyptic passages that supplied their own self-understanding and identity. As a result, the doctrine of
spiritual gifts by the mid-1850s had become one of those Bible teachings (along
with the Sabbath, sanctuary, Second Advent, and state of the dead) that began to
set them apart in the religious world as a unique church body.

But once again in his February 1856 article James pounded home the truth
that a person "is not at liberty to . . . learn his duty through any of the gifts. We
say that the very moment he does, he places the Gifts in a wrong place, and takes
an extremely dangerous position."

Thank You, Lord, for the clarity of the Adventist pioneers on the centrality of
the Bible and the place of the gift of prophecy. Help me to be equally clear.

MEET URIAH SMITH

The gospel must first be published among all nations. Mark 13:10.

U riah Smith (1832-1903) would become one of the foremost Seventh-day Adventists in setting the denomination's message before the world in print. He got off to kind of a rough start. At an early age he had to have his left leg amputated halfway between the thigh and knee. That was bad enough, but the 29-minute operation took place on the family's kitchen table with no anesthesia. All he had for comfort was his mother's hand. Most of us have little concept of what it meant to live in the "good old days."

Uriah's mother became a Millerite, and the young boy was baptized by an Adventist elder in the summer of 1844. The hope of October 1844 deeply impressed him, but when Jesus didn't come he gave up his Adventism and set about educating himself for a good place on earth. The heavenly concerns highlighted by the Adventists receded further and further from his vision.

At age 16 he entered Phillips Academy at Exeter, New Hampshire, one of the most prestigious private secondary schools of its day. Many of the nation's "greats" have walked through its doors as students. The ambitious young Uriah fully intended to enter Harvard College after graduation. He was aiming at a teaching career in one of the nation's highest schools and certainly had the intelligence for the role.

But God had other plans for the young intellectual. And so did his mother. We saw some weeks ago how Uriah's sister, Annie, had been led to Adventism through her mother's prayers, a dream given to both Annie and Joseph Bates, and Bates' aggressive evangelistic activities. Annie joined the Sabbatarians in 1852, and thereafter the talented Uriah also had her influence to contend with.

Finally in September 1852 the 20-year-old agreed to attend an Adventist meeting, at which he heard James and Ellen White explaining the reason for the 1844 disappointment and the adoption of the seventh-day Sabbath. That led to more than two months of intensive study on the topic. The crisis point came in December 1852 with the death of his father. Brought face to face with reality, Uriah gave himself wholeheartedly to the Lord, who would use him mightily.

Lord, how we struggle against full surrender to You. Help me this day to give myself wholly to Your cause. Use me, Lord, to be a blessing this very day.

THE LORD BLESSES URIAH

And he who had received the five talents came forward, bringing five talents more, saying, "Master, you delivered to me five talents; here I have made five talents more." His master said to him, "Well done, good and faithful servant; you have been faithful over a little, I will set you over much." Matt. 25:20, 21, RSV.

Uriah Smith was definitely a five-talent man. He stood near the top of the Adventist heap when it came to abilities. And after his conversion in late 1852 he dedicated himself to the Advent cause for the rest of his life. But that didn't mean that he didn't have professional offers that tempted him into areas in which the financial rewards would have been much greater than anything he could ever hope to earn in church employment. One such opportunity came a month after his conversion. Uriah's mind, however, was already firmly set on another land—"a city which hath foundations, whose builder and maker is God" (Heb. 11:10).

Early in 1853 the young dreamer sent James White a 3,500-line poem entitled "The Warning Voice of Time and Prophecy." It impressed James so much that he published a part of it weekly for five months in the *Review and Herald.* By May 1853 Uriah Smith was serving on the publishing staff of the *Review*, a career he would follow until his death 50 years later.

Working conditions were primitive at best. The entire *Review* staff lived in a house in Rochester, New York, that James rented for $175 per year. Not only was White's home scantily furnished with borrowed and somewhat broken furniture, but it also housed the entire publishing enterprise.

With no salary, the only promise they had is that they wouldn't starve. But in the eyes of some, they came pretty close to it, existing largely on a diet of beans and porridge. But Uriah in his youthful optimism made light of the whole experience, noting after he had been living there a few weeks that "though he had no objection to eating beans 365 days in succession, yet when it came to making them a regular diet, he should protest!"

Yet, though sometimes hungry, all, including the young man with one leg, were willing to sacrifice for the work they loved.

Lord, we thank You today for the talents that You have given to each of us. Help us to use them for You as You open the way, even though it may cost us in earthly things.

URIAH SMITH: ADVENTIST LEADER

He who is faithful in a very little is faithful also in much. Luke 16:10, RSV.

T o say the least, Adventist publishing was primitive when Uriah Smith first signed on to work with James White. One of his first jobs, given the fact that they didn't have a paper cutter, was to trim the edges of new books with his pocketknife.

But that would change. As the century moved on, not only did Adventists develop a state-of-the-art printing establishment, but Uriah Smith would become the editor-in-chief of the denomination's foremost publication, serving in that capacity from 1855-1861, 1864-1869, 1870-1871, 1872-1873, 1877-1880, 1881-1897, and 1901-1903—more than 35 years altogether. In that post he was in a position to shape Adventist thinking on almost every topic during the denomination's formative years.

In addition to holding Adventism's most influential editorial post during a crucial period, Uriah also authored some of the denomination's most important books. Especially influential in shaping Adventist thinking on prophecy were his *Thoughts, Critical and Practical, on the Book of Revelation* (1867) and his *Thoughts, Critical and Practical, on the Book of Daniel* (1873). Later combined as *Daniel and the Revelation,* Smith's seminal work became the standard on the topic for three quarters of a century.

Beyond being an editor and author, Smith also served the church in its second-most weighty administrative post for almost a quarter of a century. He served as secretary of the General Conference 1863-1873, 1874-1876, 1877-1881, and 1883-1888.

And that wasn't all. Not being able to kneel in prayer with his stiff cork leg, he invented an artificial leg with the advantage of bending all the way back at the knee. Other inventions he patented were a school desk that had a folding back and a combination walking cane and camp stool. The royalties from his books and his inventions made him somewhat prosperous in his later years. Smith had given all to the Lord, and the Lord had given back, blessing the one-legged man who had dedicated his talents to His cause.

Of course, like the rest of us, Uriah would have his spiritual challenges. In future readings we will see some of his struggles. But the good news is that God uses less-than-perfect people. And that is truly good news, since all of us have both talents and struggles.

MEET JOHN NEVINS ANDREWS

Do your best to present yourself to God as one approved, a workman who has no need to be ashamed, rightly handling the word of truth. 2 Tim. 2:15, RSV.

John Nevins Andrews was the foremost scholar of the young Seventh-day Adventist Church. More than any other person he had a burden to study to show himself "approved unto God, a workman that needeth not to be ashamed, rightly dividing the word of truth" (2 Tim. 2:15).

Born in 1829 in Poland, Maine, as an adult Andrews could read the Bible in seven languages and claimed the ability to reproduce the New Testament from memory. His was a life of learning up to his untimely death in 1883.

Appropriately, 15-year-old John Nevins Andrews read himself into the Sabbath message when a copy of T. M. Preble's 1845 tract on the seventh day fell into his hands soon after its publication. He along with several other teenagers covenanted to keep God's special day even before their parents knew about the Sabbath, splitting their wood and completing their baking chores on Friday so that they "might not be Sabbath-breakers any longer." Only later did their parents join them in their new faith.

Andrews first met the Whites in September 1849 when the couple rescued some of the adults in his family and community from fanaticism. At that point, seeing the distracting impact of their teachings, he exclaimed, "I would exchange a thousand errors for one truth."

In 1850 John began traveling as a Sabbatarian minister in New England. But within five years he was "utterly prostrated" because of intense study and a heavy program of writing and public speaking. Having lost his voice and injured his eyesight he went to Waukon, Iowa, to work on his parents' farm while he recovered his health. But even in that condition he couldn't stay away from books. By 1861 he had published his monumental *History of the Sabbath and First Day of the Week*.

He would in 1867 become the third General Conference president and in 1869 take a short term as editor of the *Review and Herald*. Then in 1874 Andrews went to Europe as the denomination's first official foreign missionary. At that time Ellen White wrote that they had sent the "ablest man in all our ranks" (Lt 2a, 1878).

There is no limit to how God can use people who dedicate their lives to Him and the study of His Word.

Help me, O Lord, to become "a workman that needeth not to be ashamed" when it comes to Your sacred Bible.

MEET JOHN LOUGHBOROUGH, THE BOY PREACHER

It is good for a man that he bear the yoke in his youth. Lam. 3:27.

John Loughborough (1832-1924) was 16 when he felt the call to preach. For nine weeks he had been suffering with malaria. In desperation he finally cried out, "Lord, break these chills and fever, and I will go out and preach as soon as I can recover enough strength to do so."

The chills ceased that very day. At that point he had no money for travel. After a few weeks of wood cutting he managed to save a dollar above expenses. "That," he noted, "would get me where I wanted to go, but what about clothing? The neighbor for whom I was working gave me a vest and a pair of trousers, partly worn; but as he was a man much taller than I, these garments, after cutting seven inches off the trousers, were far from being a nice fit. As a substitute for a dress coat, my brother had given me a double-breasted overcoat, the skirt of which had been cut off.

"With this curious outfit and the $1.00, I decided to go into some area where I was unknown, and try to preach. If I failed, my friends would not know it; if I succeeded, I would take that as evidence it was my duty to preach."

On his first night out he found the little Baptist church in the village filled to capacity. "I sang," he reported, "prayed, and sang again. I spoke of the fall of man. Instead of being embarrassed as I feared I would be, the blessing of God came upon me and I spoke freely. The next morning I was told that there were seven ministers present the night before.

"The next evening the place was crowded again. I suppose what drew them was curiosity to hear a beardless boy preach. . . . At the close of my sermon the . . . preacher arose and stated the next evening a service of singing classes would begin, so my meetings would have to close. Then a Mr. Thompson stood and said, 'Mr. Loughborough, this singing school has been planned for the purpose of closing your meetings.'" At that point Thompson invited the young preacher to move his meetings to a large schoolhouse at which he served as a trustee. And once again the budding first-day Adventist preacher succeeded where less-adventurous souls would have failed.

It never ceases to amaze me that the God of grace can bless what seems to be even the poorest of offerings when they are put forward in dedication. Most of us excuse ourselves until we are "ready." And ready never comes.

THE BOY PREACHER RIDES AGAIN

Out of the mouth of babes and sucklings thou hast perfected praise. Matt. 21:16.

The young preacher was understandingly fearful of meeting ministers. That dread soon found fulfillment when the minister who had cancelled his meetings decided to visit Loughborough at an informal gathering of those who had been attending his meetings.

"'Well,' said the older pastor, 'you had quite a hearing last evening.'

"'Yes, and they seemed much interested,' I said.

"'They were probably curious to hear a boy preach, but did I understand you to say last night that the soul is not immortal?'

"I answered, 'I said so. . . .'

"He then asked, 'But what do you do with punishment, the death that never dies?'

"I was surprised and said, 'I don't know of any such scripture. Half of your quotation is in the Bible, and the other half is from the Methodist hymnal.'

"With much earnestness, he insisted, 'I tell you what I quoted is in the Bible! It's in the twenty-fifth chapter of Revelation.'

"I replied, 'I guess you mean the twenty-fifth chapter of Matthew. Half your text is there. It says of the wicked that they will go into everlasting punishment.'

"'Oh yes,' he agreed. 'That's all right, but the text I quoted is in the twenty-fifth chapter of Revelation.'

"'Then it is about three chapters outside of the Bible,' I said, 'for there are only twenty-two chapters in Revelation.'

"'Let me take your Bible and I will show it to you,' he said.'" To the astonishment of all he pursued his quest, only to end up in a fuddle. At that point he returned the Bible and excused himself, noting that he had another appointment.

We may smile at that rather homely story, but it reflects the fact that backwoods and frontier religion in nineteenth-century America was often quite primitive. The preachers in rural areas were often self-taught. And that was true for both the Adventists and their detractors. In such a context Bible knowledge often carried the day.

Much has changed since those days. But not the importance of knowing the Bible. God's Word is a special gift from heaven. And yet how many in our more enlightened age are still almost as ignorant of it as the minister in Loughborough's story. There is no better time than today to make regular Bible study a part of our daily life.

J. N. Loughborough Meets J. N. Andrews

The law of the Lord is perfect, converting the soul. Ps. 19:7.

Loughborough had been preaching as a Sundaykeeping Adventist for about three and one half years when he first met a preacher of the seventh-day variety. It was well known in former Millerite circles that many of the shut-door types had fanatical tendencies, and people had told Loughborough that the group he was about to meet not only kept Saturday for Sunday, but when "they get together" they "scream and yell, and have a great noisy fanatical demonstration."

He wasn't overly anxious to encounter such individuals, but a man named Orton of Rochester, New York, approached him, noting that "the seventh-day folks are holding meetings at 124 Mount Hope Avenue" and that they should attend.

Loughborough at first declined the invitation. But, Orton responded, "you have a duty there. Some of your flock have joined the Sabbath Adventists, and you ought to get them out of this heresy. They will give you a chance to speak in their meeting. So get your texts ready, and you can show them in two minutes that the Sabbath has been abolished."

With that challenge ringing in his ears, Loughborough "got his texts together" and with several of his first-day Adventist friends attended the Sabbatarians' meetings.

The young preacher would never be the same. Not only were the gatherings absent of fanaticism and noisy demonstrations, but a minister by the name of J. N. Andrews took up the very texts on the law and the Sabbath that Loughborough had listed and explained each of them. Not only did Andrews treat the same texts, but, claims Loughborough, he did so in the same order. That was too much for him. J. N. Loughborough accepted the Sabbath in September 1852 and immediately began preaching for the Sabbatarian Adventists.

In later years he would pioneer the Seventh-day Adventist Church in California and England, serve as a pastor and administrator in several parts of the United States, and publish the first history of the Seventh-day Adventists in 1892 *(The Rise and Progress of Seventh-day Adventists,* revised in 1905 as *The Great Second Advent Movement).*

Somewhere Ellen White noted that there is no end to the usefulness of persons who dedicate their life to God. Such was the case of J. N. Loughborough. And so it can be for each of our lives.

CENTERING IN BATTLE CREEK

Now in the church at Antioch there were prophets and teachers. . . . While they were worshiping the Lord and fasting, the Holy Spirit said, "Set apart for me Barnabas and Saul for the work to which I have called them." Then after fasting and praying they laid their hands on them and sent them off. Acts 13:1-3, RSV.

Every movement has a center. The early Christian church launched its mission to the Gentiles from Antioch in Syria.

Battle Creek, a small town in Michigan, would become the headquarters of the Seventh-day Adventist Church during the nineteenth century. From it publications and missionaries would eventually spread to the far corners of the earth as Adventism ever more fully grasped its responsibility to preach the three angels' messages to all the earth.

Sabbatarian Adventism first found a rootage in Battle Creek when the ever moving Joseph Bates visited the village of some 2,000 people in 1852. His arrival put him in somewhat of a quandary. Usually he began in a new area by contacting members of the local first-day Adventist congregation. But Battle Creek had none. So Bates, J. N. Loughborough tells us, went to the post office and inquired to the identity of the most honest man in town. The official referred him to David Hewitt on Van Buren Street.

Finding the Hewitts at breakfast, the intrepid evangelist told the head of the family that since people considered him the most honest man in town, he had some truth to share with him. Beginning at breakfast and going to evening, Bates "laid before them the third angel's message and the Sabbath," which they accepted before the sun went down.

Hewitt's baptism was the beginning of the Sabbatarian congregation in Battle Creek. In 1855 four of Bates' converts—Dan Palmer, J. P. Kellogg, Henry Lyon, and Cyrenius Smith—provided funds for the Sabbatarians to build a publishing house in that city. Some of those men even sold their farms to finance the venture.

Battle Creek, Michigan, became the hub of Adventism for the rest of the century. As we shall see, a full range of Adventist institutions would be invented there. And at the center of the community life would be the Dime Tabernacle, built in 1879 by dimes sent from Adventists throughout the denomination. Seating 4,000 people, it provided quite a monument for a denomination of 15,000 members worldwide at the time it was built. The "Tab" would serve as the site for the general meetings of the denomination.

Just as the sacrificial gifts of God's people financed the move to Battle Creek, so have they every advancement of God's church. Without sacrifice there is no progress.

AND WHO WANTS CHURCH ORGANIZATION?

Proclaim liberty throughout all the land unto all the inhabitants thereof. Lev. 25:10.

And who wants church organization?
Certainly not James White and Joseph Bates in the late 1840s. They had both belonged to the Christian Connexion, a religious body in which liberty meant being free from church structures and any form of organization above the local congregation.

One of its leading ministers wrote in the early 1830s that the Connexion had arisen simultaneously in several parts of the United States in the early 1800s "not so much to establish any peculiar and distinctive doctrines, *as to assert, for individuals and churches, more liberty and independence* in relation to matters of faith and practice, *to shake off the authority* of human creeds *and* the *shackles* of prescribed modes and forms, to make the Bible their only guide, claiming *for every man* the right to be his own expositor of it, to judge, for himself, what are its doctrines and requirements, and in practice, to follow more strictly the simplicity of the apostles and primitive Christians."

A historian of the movement in 1873 summarized the fierce independence of the Connexionists in the following manner: "When asked, 'of what sect they were?' the reply was, 'None,' 'What denomination will you join?' 'None,' 'What party name will you take?' 'None,' 'What will you do?' 'We will continue as we have begun—we will be Christians. Christ is our leader, the Bible our only creed, and we will serve God free from the trammels of sectarianism.'"

To put it mildly, the early Christian Connexionists were anti-organizational. They did grant the need for structure at the local level, but they considered "each church" or congregation "an independent body." The glue that held the various strands of Connexionists together was largely their periodicals. It is fitting, therefore, that the movement entitled its first periodical *Herald of Gospel Liberty*. A second strategy for maintaining a loose unity was periodic meetings of like minded-believers.

It was that type of organization that Bates and White brought to the earliest Sabbatarians—periodicals and the Sabbatarian conferences. They saw no need for any further structures.

Now, freedom, we should point out, is a good thing. But, as we shall see, it is not the total Bible picture on the topic. The early Adventists discovered that God leads in all of our endeavors as needs arise.

ORGANIZATION IS BABYLON

And upon her forehead was a name written, MYSTERY, BABYLON THE GREAT, THE MOTHER OF HARLOTS AND ABOMINATIONS OF THE EARTH. Rev. 17:5.

Unlike the Connexionists, most Millerite Adventists had not been anti-organizational in their attitudes during the early years of their movement. On the other hand, they had no desire to form their own church structure. After all, the Lord was coming soon, and there was no need for it. Thus the Millerite believers had sought to remain in their various denominations while they witnessed to their Advent faith and waited for Christ's coming.

That worked well until the summer of 1843, when many congregations began to disfellowship them because of their constant and increasing agitation about the approaching Advent. That aggressive action, as we saw earlier, led Charles Fitch to proclaim the fall of Babylon and the need for believers to come out of the various denominations. The conflict and persecution resulting from the rejection of the Advent message led many to conclude that the churches were indeed acting the part of Babylon—the Old Testament oppressor of God's people.

One Millerite preacher who felt especially impressed to proclaim the message to leave the denominations was George Storrs. He wrote that Babylon "is the *old mother* and all her children [the Protestant denominations] . . . are known by the family likeness, a domineering, lordly spirit; a spirit to suppress a free search after truth, and a free expression of our conviction of what is truth." Individuals needed to abandon the denominations because "we have no right to let any man, or body of men, thus lord it over us. And to remain in such an organized body . . . is to remain in Babylon."

To Storrs the history of organized religion (both Catholic and Protestant) was one of bigotry and persecution. He eventually concluded that "no church can be organized by man's invention but what it becomes Babylon *the moment it is organized."*

That message, along with the believers' painful experiences at the hands of various churches, left an impression on most Millerites that was so strong that all Millerite groups found it next to impossible to organize in the late 1840s and early 1850s.

Such was the case with the Sabbatarians. But they would soon discover that "Babylon" had more than one biblical meaning.

Help us, Lord, to see clearly, even in confusing times.

FREEDOM FROM STRUCTURE IS NOT FREEDOM FROM PROBLEMS

As I urged you when I was going to Macedonia, remain at Ephesus that you may charge certain persons not to teach any different doctrine. 1 Tim. 1:3, RSV.

The earliest Christians may have had little formal structure, but they probably felt no need of it. After all, Jesus would return soon.

But Jesus didn't come as soon as they expected. That resulted in problems in the church that needed to be cared for. Thus by the time Paul wrote his Pastoral Epistles (1 Timothy, 2 Timothy, and Titus) he had to deal with creating mechanisms for maintaining order in the congregations.

Adventism went through a similar experience. As early as September 1849 we find James White arguing for financial support for the movement's traveling preachers and the necessity to "suspend" one woman "from fellowship." Then in March 1850, in the context of remarks concerning an individual whom he believed God had not called to be an itinerant preacher, James wrote of the need to move in "gospel order."

His wife's concerns seem to have paralleled his. In December 1850 she wrote: "I saw that everything in heaven was in perfect order. Said the angel, 'Look ye; Christ is the head; move in order, move in order. Have a meaning to everything.' Said the angel, 'Behold ye, and know how perfect, how beautiful the order in heaven; follow it.'" She went on to speak of fanaticism and of those who had been disfellowshipped because of their improper behavior. Near the conclusion she noted that "if Israel [i.e., the church] moved steadily along, going according to Bible order, they would be terrible as an army with banners" (MS 11 1850).

James and Ellen White's early concerns regarding organization seem to be essentially the same. Both feared disorderly, fanatical, and unauthorized representatives within the budding Sabbatarian movement. Then again, the early 1850s saw rapid growth in the number of individuals attracted by the logic of the Sabbatarians' preaching. In three short years the movement's adherents had zoomed from about 100 to more than 2,000 in 1852.

While that growth was good, it also brought with it new problems and challenges. With no structure above the congregational level, for example, the scattered groups of Sabbatarians became easy prey to fanatics and unauthorized preachers.

Help us, Father, to learn to appreciate the value of structure in Your work, just as we do in our personal lives.

ORDAINING LEADERS

That thou shouldest set in order the things that are wanting, and ordain elders in every city, as I had appointed thee. Titus 1:5.

By 1851 the problems among the growing Sabbatarian congregations led the Whites to believe that the movement required their personal presence from time to time to correct abuses. The next few years would see their reports in the *Review* with such titles as "Our Tour East." During their journeys the Whites repeatedly dealt with fanaticism and church order at the congregational level. At a conference in Medford, Massachusetts, in late 1851, for example, James stated that "the burden of the meeting was Church Order, pointing out the errors of S. Smith, H. W. Allen, and the importance of church action [withdrawing fellowship] as to the course of some brethren."

At various locations on the same tour White reported disfellowshipping one who had "fallen a victim to the bewitching power of spiritualism," of rebuking fanaticism and "opposing spirits," and of speaking about "gospel order and perfect union among the brethren, especially those who preach the Word."

The 1851 eastern tour is also significant since accounts of it provide our first information on the appointment of officers at the local church level. Thus we read that in one meeting "a committee of seven was chosen (see Acts 6) to attend to the wants of the poor."

Earlier that year the Review reported for the first time an ordination in Sabbatarian ranks. In July "Bro. [Washington] Morse was set apart by the laying on of hands, to the administration of the ordinances of God's house. The Holy Ghost witnessed by the gift of tongues, and solemn manifestations of the presence and power of God. The place was awful, yet glorious."

By 1852 the Sabbatarians had come to see themselves less as a "scattered flock" and more as a church. And with a reinterpretation of the shut door they began to recognize that they had a larger mission beyond the realm of Millerism. Such realizations would add their weight in pressing the Sabbatarians toward a more substantial organization.

Lord, day by day as we read and meditate we see Your church gradually waking up to its larger and larger responsibilities. Help us to regard that waking up not only as something that happened 150 years ago, but as an event that needs to take place in our personal lives as You progressively guide us as individuals.

WOLVES AMONG THE SHEEP

I know that after I leave, savage wolves will come in among you and will not spare the flock. Even from your own number men will arise and distort the truth in order to draw away disciples. Acts 20:29, 30, NIV.

The major problem the Sabbatarians faced in the early 1850s was that they had no systematic defense against impostors. Almost anybody who wanted to could preach in Sabbatarian congregations. Large sectors of Adventism had no checks on ministerial orthodoxy or even morality as it faced the crisis of a self-appointed ministry.

That problem had become evident to all of the ex-Millerite denominations before they organized during the late 1850s and early 1860s. One letter to a first-day Adventist paper, for example, complained that the writer's congregation in 1850 had "again been troubled with what we consider to be false teaching. . . . About three weeks since, a man by the name of Joseph Bates arrived here by stage, professing to be an Advent preacher. . . . We had an interview with him, and found his 'message' was the Sabbath, or seventh day, and shut door."

Himes, the editor, replied: "Capt. Bates is an old personal friend of ours, and, so far as we know, is better as a man than most of his associates; but we have no confidence in his teaching.—He should not be tolerated for a moment."

The real problem that all of the ex-Millerite religious bodies faced was that of boundaries. If Bates felt free to do evangelism among first-day congregations, they were more than eager to return the favor. Worse yet were those insincere impostors whose primary aim was to fleece the saints financially.

The year 1853 would see the Sabbatarians take two steps to protect their congregations from "false" brethren. First, the most prominent Sabbatarian ministers adopted a plan whereby approved preachers received a card "recommending them to the fellowship of the Lord's people everywhere." Two recognized leaders signed and dated the cards. The one received by John Loughborough in January 1853 carried the names of James White and Joseph Bates.

The second method utilized by the Sabbatarians to certify their leaders was ordination. By late 1853 they had begun regularly ordaining both traveling preachers (ministers assigned to specific congregations did not yet exist) and deacons, who appear to have been the only local church officers at that early period.

Thank You, Father, for building protective mechanisms into Your church on earth for our safety.

THE CALL FOR GOSPEL ORDER—1

For God is not the author of confusion, but of peace, as in all churches of the saints. 1 Cor. 14:33.

G od is not the author of confusion."
You'd never know it from the condition of some of the Sabbatarian Adventist congregations in 1853. The movement had grown rapidly, but it lacked the structures that could bring order to its ranks.

Even though they had made some progress in the direction of order, they were still quite vulnerable, a reality evident in Ellen White's report of her and James's fall 1853 eastern tour. "This was," she reported, "a laborious and rather discouraging journey. Many had embraced the truth who were unsanctified in heart and life; the elements of strife and rebellion were at work, and it was necessary that a movement should take place to purify the church" (LS 150, 151).

With that state of affairs in mind, it is not difficult to see why she and her husband both issued major calls for "gospel order" in December 1853.

James led the assault for better organization in a *Review* series entitled "Gospel Order." His December 6 article pointed out that it "was a subject of great importance to the early [Christian] church" and "it cannot be of less importance in the last days of peril. . . . . If gospel order was of such vast importance that it was necessary for Paul to dwell much upon it in his epistles to the churches, it should not be overlooked by the people of God at this day. We think that it has been much neglected, and that the attention of the church should be turned to this subject, and vigorous efforts should be put forth to realize as far as possible the order of the gospel. . . .

"It is a lamentable fact that many of our Advent brethren who made a timely escape from the bondage of the different churches, who as a body rejected the Advent doctrine, have since been in a more perfect Babylon than ever before. Gospel order has been too much overlooked by them. . . .

"Many in their zeal to come out of Babylon, partook of a rash, disorderly spirit, and were soon found a perfect Babel of confusion. . . . God has not called any of his people away from the confusion of the churches, designing that they should be without discipline."

Happy mediums are difficult to maintain in a sinful world. Finding a position between oppressive control and uncoordinated freedom is not the least of the difficult balancing acts in church history. But God leads His people not only in doctrine but also in effective governance.

THE CALL FOR GOSPEL ORDER—2

All things should be done decently and in order. 1 Cor. 14:40, RSV.

How to bring order and united action out of a growing herd of highly independent and somewhat opinionated, individualistic believers was the task that faced James White during the early 1850s. Many of the Sabbatarians had come to believe that any sort of restraint from a church body was Babylonish oppression. It is that point that led White to call for gospel order in December 1853. In his first article on the topic he claimed that "to suppose that the church of Christ is free from restraint and discipline, is the wildest fanaticism."

In his second article he urged the believers to look to the methods set forth in the New Testament and emphasized the importance of unity of sentiment and action. "That there may be union and order in the church," he penned, "it is of the highest importance that those who go forth as religious teachers should be in perfect union. . . . The reverse would produce division and confusion among the precious flock. He who enters upon the work of the gospel ministry, must be called of God, a man of experience, a holy man of God."

That declaration set the stage for his third article, which dealt with the selection, qualification, and ordination of ministers, since "in no one thing has the gospel suffered so much as by the influence of false teachers."

"We can say," James wrote, "from the experience of several years, that the cause of present truth has suffered more in consequence of those who have taken upon themselves the work of teaching, whom God never sent, than in any other thing. . . . Brethren shall we still mourn over" the disastrous influences of the self-appointed preachers "and make no effort to prevent them? God forbid." According to the New Testament, the church must take care in the choice and ordination of ministers.

In his fourth and final article in the series, James emphasized the role of the church as a whole in gospel order. "The labor, care and responsibility of this great work," he argued, "does not rest alone upon a few preachers. . . . The whole church should be taught to feel that a portion of the responsibility of good order, and the salvation of souls rests upon her individual members." He especially stressed the necessity of the members supporting its ministers through prayer and finances.

Sometimes we fail to catch the impact of White's last article. I would suggest that if we wait for the clergy to finish the work by themselves, it will be a little more than eternity before it's done. Each of us has a responsibility.

THE CALL FOR GOSPEL ORDER—3

If any one aspires to the office of bishop, he desires a noble task. Now a bishop must be above reproach, the husband of one wife, temperate, sensible, dignified, hospitable, an apt teacher. 1 Tim. 3:1, 2, RSV.

Late in December 1853 Ellen White publicly joined her husband in his plea for gospel order. Basing her sentiments on a vision received during her and James's eastern tour in the fall of 1852, she wrote that "the Lord has shown that gospel order has been too much feared and neglected. Formality should be shunned; but in so doing, order should not be neglected.

"There is order in heaven. There was order in the church when Christ was upon the earth, and after His departure order was strictly observed among His apostles. And now in these last days, while God is bringing His children into the unity of the faith, there is more real need of order than ever before; for, as God unites His children, Satan and his evil angels are very busy to prevent this unity and to destroy it" (EW 97).

She was especially concerned with the appointment of ministers. "Men," she wrote, "whose lives are not holy and who are unqualified to teach the present truth enter the field without being acknowledged by the church or the brethren generally, and confusion and disunion are the result. Some have a theory of the truth, and can present the argument, but lack spirituality, judgment, and experience" (*ibid.*, 97, 98).

Such "self-sent messengers," she expostulated, "are a curse to the cause," especially to those "honest souls [who] put confidence in them," thinking that they are in harmony with the church. Because of problematic self-appointed clergy, "it is much more wearing to the spirits of God's messengers to go into places where those have been who have exerted this wrong influence than to enter new fields" (*ibid.*, 99).

Because of the problems, she urged that "the church should feel their responsibility and should look carefully and attentively at the lives, qualifications, and general course of those who profess to be teachers." The solution, she added, included going to God's Word to discover the biblical principles of gospel order and to "lay hands upon" only "those who have given full proof that they have received their commission of God" (*ibid.*, 100, 101).

Church leadership is a fearful responsibility. We need to take it seriously in both its qualifications and in its practice.

May God help His church as it seeks its way in a broken world.

SCHISM IN THE CAMP

You are aware that all who are in Asia turned away from me, and among them Phygelus and Hermogenes. 2 Tim. 1:15, RSV.

James and Ellen White's minds were quite settled by the beginning of 1854 on the need for more order and structure among Sabbatarians. James not only considered it important, he also believed that the movement wouldn't see much progress without it. Thus he could write in March that God "is waiting for his people to get right, and in gospel order, and hold the standard of piety high, before he adds many more to our numbers."

The fact that Sabbatarian Adventism also faced its first organized schisms at that time undoubtedly reinforced James's convictions on the topic. By early 1854 two ministers, H. S. Case and C. P. Russell, had turned against the Whites. During the fall of that year they began their own publication, the *Messenger of Truth,* which they hoped would not only rival the *Review and Herald* but would also bring a significant number of Sabbatarians under their influence.

Concurrent with the rise of the Messenger Party was the defection of two of the four Sabbatarian preachers in Wisconsin. J. M. Stephenson and D. P. Hall began to promote a temporal millennium and age-to-come view that proposed a second chance at conversion during the millennium. Before long the two Wisconsin ministers joined forces with the Messengers in their opposition to the leadership of the Whites.

With so many unruly individuals in their midst, it is little wonder that the Sabbatarians during the second half of the 1850s increasingly penned articles reflecting a developing understanding of Bible principles related to church order and the ordination of approved leaders. God is good!

He even helps His people learn from schism and problems in their midst. It was so in the early Christian church. As a result, we have Paul's great pastoral letters to Timothy and Titus that outline biblical principles of organization. In addition, the epistles penned by Paul, James, Peter, Jude, and John rebutted the false teachings of schismatics. Without God's guidance through the problems that such false teachers continue to raise, the church would be poorer in every age.

Help us, Father, to realize more clearly how You use even problematic situations to grow Your church.

CONGREGATIONALISM THE WAY TO GO?

The churches of Asia send greetings. Aquila and Prisca, together with the church in their house, send you hearty greetings in the Lord. 1 Cor. 16:19, RSV.

Joseph Bates joined the Whites in their concern for gospel order. And in harmony with the restorationist roots of his Connexionist background, he claimed that biblical church order must be restored before the Second Advent.

He argued that during the Middle Ages the "law breakers" "deranged" such essential elements of Christianity as the Sabbath and biblical church order. God had used the Sabbatarian Adventists to restore the seventh-day Sabbath and it was "perfectly clear" to his mind "that God will employ law-keepers as instruments to restore . . . a 'glorious church, not having spot or wrinkle.' . . . This unity of the faith, and perfect church order, never existed since the days of the apostles. It is very clear that it must exist prior to the second advent of Jesus . . . in restoration of all things."

While Bates indicated that he believed in the recovery of the apostolic order of the church, he made no room for any element of organization not found in the New Testament.

James White at this early period shared a similar opinion. Thus he could write in 1854 that "by gospel, or church order we mean that order in church association and discipline taught in the gospel of Jesus Christ by the writers of the New Testament."

A few months later he spoke of the "perfect system of order, set forth in the New Testament, by inspiration of God. . . . The Scriptures present a perfect system."

White, Bates, and others were quite certain that every aspect of church order needed to be explicitly spelled out in the Bible. Thus it was that J. B. Frisbie even argued against any church name except the one given by God in the Bible. As he put it, "THE CHURCH OF GOD . . . IS THE ONLY NAME THAT God has seen fit to give his church."

With that extremely literalistic view, it is not surprising to see early Adventist leaders discussing the duties of deacons and elders as set forth by Paul, but it is a little more puzzling to find them defining "CHURCH" as signifying "a particular congregation of believers," given the implications of Acts 15 and the overseer function of Paul and his associates. But so it was. Congregationalism was the structure favored by the Sabbatarians in the mid-1850s.

Thank You, Lord, for our local congregations. Help us never to forget the important place they hold in Your work.

CONGREGATIONALISM NOT ENOUGH!

As they went on their way through the cities, they delivered to them for observance the decisions which had been reached by the apostles and elders who were at Jerusalem. Acts 16:4, RSV.

The early Christian church discovered that some issues transcended the local congregation and thus needed a ruling from a larger coordinating body. In the council of Acts 15 the elders and apostles met to decide in part how to bring the Jewish and Gentile congregations into a working relationship. The assembly made decisions for the body of congregations.

The early Adventists also found that they could not handle all issues at the level of the local congregation. If the first half of the 1850s saw the Sabbatarians establishing structures and offices in the local congregations, the second half focused on what it meant for congregations to be "united together."

At least four issues would force leaders such as James White to look at church organization more globally. The first had to do with the legal ownership of property—especially the publishing house and church buildings. The last thing he wanted was the responsibility of owning the printing house property in his own name.

A second issue driving his thinking was the problem of paying preachers. That was an especially difficult situation since Sabbatarian preachers in those days did not serve specific local congregations but traveled from church to church somewhat like itinerant evangelists. The support of preachers was complicated by the fact that Adventists had no tithing procedure or any other way of collecting money to pay them.

A third issue driving White to a broader form of church organization involved the assignment of preachers. In 1859 James wrote that whereas such communities as Battle Creek often had several preachers on hand, others remained "destitute, not having heard a discourse for three months." Whether anybody liked it or not, by 1859 James White was *acting* the part of superintendent in the assignment and paying of preachers, but without any official structure to undergird his efforts. Such a system left him open to criticism regarding mismanagement and misappropriation of funds,

A fourth problem concerned the transfer of membership between congregations, especially when a person had been disfellowshipped by one congregation and desired fellowship in another.

The churches needed system and order if they were to move forward unitedly. They still exist in a less than perfect world with less-than-perfect people.

CRISIS IN THE MINISTRY

The Lord has ordered that those who preach the gospel should get their living from it. 1 Cor. 9:14, TEV.

Ministers may deal with heavenly things but even they need earthly food. And food costs money.

How to pay the ministers in the budding denomination reached a crisis point during the mid-1850s. A case in point is young John Nevins Andrews, a man who later served the church as its leading scholar, its first official foreign missionary, and as General Conference president. But in the mid-1850s exhaustion and deprivation had forced him into retiring from the ministry while only in his mid-20s. The fall of 1856 found him becoming a clerk in his uncle's store in Waukon, Iowa.

Waukon, in fact, was rapidly becoming a colony of apathetic Sabbatarian Adventists. Another leading minister who fled to Waukon in 1856 was John N. Loughborough, who had become, as he put it, "somewhat discouraged as to finances."

The Whites temporarily averted a crisis in the Adventist ministry by making a danger-filled midwinter journey to Waukon to wake up the sleeping Sabbatarian community and to reclaim the dropout ministers. Both Andrews and Loughborough saw the hand of God in the visit and rededicated their lives to preaching.

But that did not change financial realities. For example, for his first three months' labor after leaving Waukon, Loughborough received room and board, a buffalo skin coat worth about $10, and $10 in cash. The problem was far from solved. At least Mrs. Loughborough must have reached that conclusion.

"I am tired," James White penned, "of seeing statements of want among our preachers and appeals for funds in the *Review*. I am tired of writing them. Those general appeals to everybody, and nobody in particular, do not amount to much besides filling up the paper, and paining the reader. These things hurt the *Review* and are a blot on the cause."

Christian workers may not live by bread alone, but they still need bread. At least their wives or husbands and children do. Paul is clear that "those who preach the gospel should get their living from it."

But from where?

The obvious answer is from each of us.

As we provide funds for their support we enter into the blessing of their ministry.

HOW TO RAISE THE MONEY?

On the first day of every week, each of you is to put something aside and store it up, as he may prosper. 1 Cor. 16:2, RSV.

Raising funds needed for the work of the Sabbatarians was a central issue in the mid-1850s. Samuel H. Rhodes of Brookfield, New York, unwittingly became the catalyst to ignite dialog on a giving plan when in December 1856 he sent $2 to the *Review,* telling James White that he believed 1 Corinthians 16:2 defined his duty as setting aside money for the Lord's cause each Sunday.

White was excited with the possibilities of the plan. "We recommend to all Christians," he exuded, "a careful consideration of this text. It is evidently an individual work which 'everyone' should attend to in the fear of God." If every Adventist did as Rhodes, "the Lord's treasury would be full of means to advance the precious cause of truth."

Three weeks later another individual mailed money to the *Review* office, citing the same text. White noted that "no better plan can be devised than the one introduced by the apostle." "Take hold of it," he challenged his readers. But as my friend Brian Strayer points out, they "did not take hold." As a result, in April 1858, White wrote that "repeated discouragements are saddening and discouraging our preachers." Some "moved out expecting to be sustained by their brethren . . . but their brethren have often failed to do their duty." Thus several ministers "are sunken down under poverty, broken-down health and discouragement."

At that point the somewhat desperate James White came up with a second plan to alleviate the problem, urging believers to send an amount equal to their yearly state taxes. "But," notes Strayer, "if Adventists had proved reluctant to adopt the 1 Corinthians 16 plan, they seemed even more hesitant to respond to a church tax plan." Three weeks later White noted that Satan "exults" because of the lack of a successful program to finance the church.

In the throes of a problem that wouldn't stop, the Battle Creek, Michigan, congregation formed a study group in the spring of 1858 to search the Bible for a plan to support the ministry. Under the leadership of J. N. Andrews, the group developed a concept that would be accepted in early 1859.

Sometimes we forget how our forebears wrestled with issues that never trouble us. The plain fact is that we stand on their shoulders, daily benefiting from their trials and solutions. And we can learn from their struggles.

SISTER BETSY

Each man should give what he has decided in his heart to give, not reluctantly or under compulsion, for God loves a cheerful giver. 2 Cor. 9:7, NIV.

I n February 1859 James White gladly announced the results of the committee that had been studying how to finance the work of the church. He presented a concept known as Systematic Benevolence, which would provide a way for every member to give regularly to sustain the church.

Quite convinced that the plan was from God, White emphasized 1 Corinthians 16:2 to justify a weekly offering and texts such as 2 Corinthians 9:5-7, which set forth the principles of reaping as we sow and the fact that God loves a cheerful giver.

White not only announced the new plan of Systematic Benevolence, but he set forth guidelines. Males 18-60 years should give from 5 to 25 cents weekly, while females in the same age group should donate 2 through 10 cents, and both groups should add 1 through 5 cents more for every $100 worth of property they owned.

Following the example of 1 Corinthians 16:2, the Systematic Benevolence funds were collected on Sunday morning when treasurers visited each member's home with their offering containers and Systematic Benevolence record books in hand.

Such a process, as you might guess, did not meet with exuberant enthusiasm from all. Yet James White, two years later, put an encouraging face on the situation when he wrote that "all expect" the treasurer "and all get ready for him and meet him with open hands and benevolent feelings." "No one," he penned, "feels poorer, but all feel happier after casting their small sums into the treasury."

But what to do with the funds became an issue. White at first suggested that each congregation could dispose of them as it saw fit. Later he proposed that each church keep at least $5 on hand to assist visiting preachers and then send the rest to Michigan tent evangelism.

Systematic Benevolence, or what many later thought of as Sister Betsy, was a step forward, but it fell far short of the needs of the church. And beyond that, the Sabbatarians in 1859 still lacked any systematic way to utilize the funds or to pay ministers.

Most of us today are thankful that the church treasurer does not show up on our porch every Sunday morning with record book in hand. God has led us to a better way that is less intrusive and more adequate to fund His church.

TITHING—A BETTER WAY

Bring ye all the tithes into the storehouse, that there may be meat in mine house, and prove me now herewith, saith the Lord of hosts, if I will not open you the windows of heaven, and pour you out a blessing, that there shall not be room enough to receive it. Mal. 3:10.

Interestingly, the early discussions of Systematic Benevolence did not utilize Malachi 3:8-10, nor did writers in the *Review* emphasize the blessings of faithful giving.

What they did stress was the fact that Systematic Benevolence was painless and nonsacrificial in nature. It was, in fact, so painless and nonsacrificial that it failed to support the needs of the growing church adequately.

Only gradually did the Sabbatarians come to an acceptance of Bible tithing. Some had apparently thought of it in 1859, but James White was quite certain that what Adventists had in Systematic Benevolence was superior to the "Israelitish tithing system."

Things began to change when in February 1876 Dudley M. Canright published a series of articles in the *Review* stressing Malachi 3:8-11. Setting forth tithing as the Bible plan for supporting the ministers, he was emphatic that "God requires that a *tithe,* or *one tenth,* of *all* the *income* of his people shall be given to support his servants in their labors." He went on to note that "the Lord does not say you should give me a tenth, but he says one tenth is the Lord's." Since the tithe was already God's, believers merely returned it to Him. Canright also emphasized the blessings and rewards of tithing. "I am thoroughly satisfied," he wrote, "that the special blessing of God does attend those who are prompt and liberal in paying" their tithe.

Beyond personal blessing, the tithing system would succeed in supporting the church, whereas Systematic Benevolence had failed. At the 1876 General Conference session Canright estimated that if all members paid a faithful tithe, the General Conference treasury would receive $150,000 yearly instead of only $40,000.

Canright went on to urge that the General Conference approve the tithing system, which it did in October 1876. From that point on biblical tithing increasingly became the way that Adventism supported its ministers. And, of course, by that time it had an organizational structure that could serve as the "storehouse" of Malachi 3 to both collect and disperse funds.

Lord, we are thankful for Your guidance in even the financial matters of the church. And we appreciate Your blessings for faithfulness to those who follow the biblical plan of tithe and offerings.

REDEFINING BABYLON

Therefore its name was called Babel, because there the Lord confused the language of all the earth. Gen. 11:9, RSV.

By the middle of 1859 James White was ready to launch the final drive for formal denominational organization. *"We lack system,"* he cried out on July 21. "Many of our brethren are in a scattered state. They observe the Sabbath, read with some interest the REVIEW: but beyond this *they are doing but little or nothing for want of some method of united action among them."* To meet the situation, he called for regular meetings in each state to give guidance to the activities of Sabbatarians in that region.

"We are aware," he wrote, "that these suggestions will not meet the minds of all. Bro. Overcautious will be frightened, and will be ready to warn his brethren to be careful and not venture out too far; while Bro. Confusion will cry out, 'Oh, this looks just like Babylon! Following the fallen church!' Bro. Dolittle will say, 'The cause is the Lord's, and we had better leave it in his hands, he will take care of it.' 'Amen,' says Love-this-world, Slothful, Selfish, and Stingy, 'if God calls men to preach, let them go out and preach, he will take care of them, . . .'; while Korah, Dathan, and Abiram are ready to rebel against those who feel the weight of the cause [e.g., James White] and who watch for souls as those who must give an account, and raise the cry, 'You take too much upon you.'"

White let it be known in the most descriptive language that he was sick and tired of hearing the cry of Babylon every time that anyone mentioned organization. "Bro. confusion," he wrote, "makes a most egregious blunder in calling system, which is in harmony with the Bible and good sense, Babylon. *As Babylon signifies confusion, our erring brother has the very word stamped upon his own forehead. And we venture to say that there is not another people under heaven more worthy of the brand of Babylon than those professing the Advent faith who reject Bible order."*

By this time James's concerns for the health of the Sabbatarian movement had reached a high pitch. In his strident call for organization, we should note, he redefined Babylon from "oppression" to "confusion," a word aptly describing the situation in 1859.

Sometimes it is important to stand up and emphasize our biblical convictions. God still uses men and women of balance and pious conviction, just as he did James White, to help His church get back on course. May God grant us courage to speak up at the proper time.

THINKING BIG

Where there is no vision, the people perish. Prov. 29:18.

Small thinking leads to small results. Most Sabbatarian Adventists in the 1850s thought small. But James White's strategic place in Adventism had given him a scope of vision that not only separated him from the reasoning processes of many of his fellow believers but had transformed his own thinking.

Beyond his pointing out the confused, Babylonish state of Sabbatarian Adventism that demanded structure and his growing understanding of the immensity of Adventist mission, by 1859 White had discarded the biblical literalism of his earlier days when he believed that the Bible must explicitly spell out each aspect of church organization. He now argued that "we should not be afraid of that system which is not opposed to the Bible, and is approved by sound sense."

Thus he had come to a new hermeneutic. James had shifted from a principle of Bible interpretation that held that the only things Scripture allowed were those it explicitly mentioned to a hermeneutic that approved of anything that did not contradict the Bible.

That transformation in thinking was essential to the creative steps in church organization that he would advocate in the 1860s.

That revised hermeneutic, however, put him in opposition to those who maintained a literalistic approach to the Bible that demanded that it explicitly spell something out before the church could accept it.

To answer that mentality, White noted that nowhere in the Bible did it say that Christians should have a weekly periodical, a steam-powered press, build places of worship, or publish books. He went on to say that the "living church of God" needed to move forward with prayer and common sense.

James White was a big thinker. He may not have started out that way, but as he grasped the task ahead of the church, his vision forced him to think large and creatively.

For that we can praise God. Without great thinkers such as James White, Seventh-day Adventism would have never advanced beyond the northeastern corner of the United States.

God is still calling for big thinkers to spur His work on. And He is asking each of us to think bigger thoughts of what we can do for His work on earth.

Choosing a Name

A good name is better than precious ointment. Eccl. 7:1.

It is difficult to understand how a growing movement could exist for almost two decades without a name. But so it was for Sabbatarian Adventism. To choose a name, thought some, was to be like the other churches. Beyond that, where in the Bible did it tell churches to have a name at all?

That latter point is true enough, but what the Bible didn't command, the government did when a church holding property had to incorporate. The naming crisis resulted from the need to incorporate the Adventist publishing house in Battle Creek, Michigan. By early 1860 James White had come to the place at which he refused to continue to take personal responsibility for the financial aspects of the institution. The Sabbatarians needed to make arrangements to hold church property in a "proper manner."

That suggestion brought forth a vigorous reaction. Even though he recognized that a church could not incorporate unless it had a name, R. F. Cottrell still wrote that he believed that "it would be wrong to 'make us a name,' since that lies at the foundation of Babylon."

James went ballistic over Cottrell's suggestion that the Lord would take care of the church's property, declaring that "it is dangerous to leave with the Lord what he has left with us." And he again argued the crucial point that "every Christian duty is not given in the Scriptures."

In 1860 a conference of Sabbatarians voted to incorporate the publishing house, have local churches so "organize as to hold their church property," and select a denominational name.

Many favored "Church of God," but too many groups, the leadership decided, already used that one. Eventually David Hewitt suggested the name Seventh-day Adventists. His motion carried, many delegates recognizing that it was "expressive of our faith and [doctrinal] position."

Ellen White had remained silent during the debate, but she would later express her exuberant opinion. "The name Seventh-day Adventist," she declared after the meetings, "carries the true features of our faith in front. . . . Like an arrow from the Lord's quiver, it will wound the transgressors of God's law, and will lead to repentance toward God and faith in our Lord Jesus Christ" (1T 224).

Such is the value of a "good name."

ORGANIZED AT LAST

And when they had appointed elders for them in every church, with prayer and fasting, they committed them to the Lord in whom they believed. Acts 14:23, RSV.

Although the concept of church structure that provides order across congregations is far from absent in the New Testament, it was not a favorite topic of many Adventists.

But the time had come. In April 1861 the Sabbatarians established a committee that recommended the formation of district or state conferences to oversee church activities in their respective regions.

Reactions were forceful, especially in the Eastern states. James White reported in August that "the brethren in Pennsylvania voted down organization, and the cause in Ohio has been dreadfully shaken." He summed up the situation by writing that "on our eastern tour thus far we seem to be wading through the influence of a stupid uncertainty upon the subject of organization. . . . We are in many places but little better than broken fragments, still scattering and growing weaker."

Ellen White shared his opinion, declaring that same month that she was "shown that some have feared that our churches would become Babylon if they should organize; but those in central New York have been perfect Babylon, confusion. And now unless the churches are so organized that they can carry out and enforce order, they have nothing to hope for in the future; they must scatter into fragments." She deplored the lack of "moral courage" and the abundance of "cowardly silence" on the part of those ministers who believed in organization but had remained silent. Her words left no doubt that the time had come to "stand together" on the issue (1T 270-272).

The moment for action had arrived.

In the general meeting of the believers in October 1861 the first item of business was "the proper manner of organizing churches." And one of the central contributions of the session was the "recommendation" to the churches in the state of Michigan that they unite under the name of the Michigan Conference of Seventh-day Adventists.

James White was elated. To him it was "a sign of better days."

The next year saw seven more local conferences established.

The devil likes nothing better than to sow confusion. And he can do that more successfully in an unorganized group. Unfortunately, the value of organization is not fully appreciated until it is gone.

Thank You, Lord, for what You have given us.

THE GENERAL CONFERENCE

There is one body, and one Spirit, even as ye are called in one hope of your calling. Eph. 4:4.

While the formation of state conferences was helpful, they did not solve all of the administrative problems. Who, for example, would coordinate their work or assign ministers to different areas? J. H. Waggoner raised that issue to consciousness in a forceful manner in June 1862. "I do not believe," he wrote, "that we shall ever fully realize the benefits of organization till this matter" of a general or umbrella conference "is acted upon." Several readers of the *Review* responded to Waggoner's proposition with hearty affirmations during the summer of 1862.

Without a general overarching structure to represent the whole body of believers, J. N. Andrews argued, "we shall be thrown into confusion every time that concert of action is especially necessary. The work of organization, wherever it has been entered into in a proper manner, has borne good fruit; and hence I desire to see it *completed* in such a manner as shall secure its full benefits, not only to each church, but to the whole body of brethren and to the cause of truth."

B. F. Snook noted that already sectional feelings had developed in the young denomination and that the only way to bring unity into the movement was through a "general conference."

James White, as you might guess, enthused with such talk. As he saw it, the proposed General Conference must be "the great regulator" of the state conferences if they were to secure "united, systematic action in the entire body of believers." The duty of the General Conference would be "to mark out the general course to be pursued by the State Conferences." Thus "if General Conference is not higher in authority than State Conferences, we see but little use for it." Its function would be to coordinate the work of the church across its entire geographic range.

The General Conference of Seventh-day Adventists organized at a meeting called for that purpose in Battle Creek from May 20 to May 23, 1863. That momentous step opened the way for a unified church to eventually take the message of the three angels of Revelation 14 to the far corners of the earth. The extent of the Adventist mission program could never have been accomplished by a collection of disjointed churches or conferences each with its own goals.

Thank You, Lord, for the unity and strength that comes from organization.

Retrospect on Organization—1

We are to grow up in every way into him who is the head, into Christ, from whom the whole body, joined and knit together by every joint with which it is supplied, when each part is working properly, makes bodily growth and upbuilds itself in love. Eph. 4:15, 16, RSV.

The organization of the General Conference marked the end of an era in Adventist history. Sabbatarian Adventism had moved from a virtually unstructured beginning to a mildly hierarchical form.

Both of the Whites, as the "unofficial" leaders of the church, were quite pleased with the new organization. They had experienced enough of the chaotic condition of Adventism during the late 1840s and the 1850s that they would never cease to uphold *properly exercised* church authority.

Ellen White penned one of her strongest statements on the value of organization in 1892. Looking back, she reminisced: "We had a hard struggle in establishing organization. Notwithstanding that the Lord gave testimony after testimony upon this point, the opposition was strong, and it had to be met again and again. But we knew that the Lord God of Israel was leading us, and guiding by his providence. We engaged in the work of organization, and marked prosperity attend[ed] this advance movement. . . .

"The system of organization has proved a grand success. . . . *Let none entertain the thought . . . that we can dispense with organization.* It has cost us much study, and many prayers for wisdom that we know that God has answered, to erect this structure. It has been built up by his direction. . . . *Let none of our brethren be so deceived as to attempt to tear it down,* for you will thus bring in a condition of things that you do not dream of. In the name of the Lord, I declare to you that it is to stand, strengthened, established, and settled. . . . *Let everyone be exceedingly careful not to unsettle minds in regard to those things that God has ordained for our prosperity and success in advancing his cause*" (Lt 32a 1892; italics supplied).

God believes in organization. So do I. Taking the everlasting gospel and the other teachings of Revelation 14 to all the world did not happen by accident. Adventists developed organization to forward the denomination's mission. And it has done so. The success of the decision to establish the General Conference as a coordinating body back in May 1863 would absolutely astound those who voted it in.

RETROSPECT ON ORGANIZATION—2

Keep watch over yourselves and all the flock of which the Holy Spirit has made you overseers. Acts 20:28, NIV.

The impelling force behind the drive for organization was an integrated complex of interrelated ideas. One of the most important was a growing biblically based understanding of the church's mission. By 1861 some denominational leaders had concluded that they had a world to win, and by 1863 the newly formed General Conference executive committee began to discuss sending a missionary overseas. A broader vision of mission led to a more extensive recognition of the necessity of developing an adequate organization to support that mission. In short, James White and others gradually came to realize that no significant mission outreach could exist without a rational and effective support system.

A second reality that helped James and his fellow believers broaden their concept of church structure was the need to maintain doctrinal unity. In 1864 he contrasted the good fruits of Seventh-day Adventist organization with the "miserably confused condition of those who reject organization."

G. I. Butler developed that line of thought a bit further in 1873 when he wrote that "we are a thoroughly organized people, and our organization is not based on mere appearances, but upon a solid foundation. Having struggled against all kinds of influences, within and without, and being now a unit, speaking the same thing from ocean to ocean, it is not a very easy thing to shake us to pieces."

The doctrinal issue, of course, had close ties to mission. Because they were unified in doctrine, they were willing to unite in mission to the far corners of the United States and eventually to the rest of the world.

In the end it was the mission of the church that demanded an adequate church structure. As James White repeatedly noted, "it was not ambition to build up a denomination that suggested organization, but the sheer necessities of the case."

While for James in 1871 the stamp of an adequate system was that "the machinery works well," the early Adventists also sought to base their organizational structures on a foundation that was in harmony with the Bible's teaching on the principles that should undergird the nature and mission of the church. In the long run, organization was a by-product of a scriptural understanding of the church and its end-time role of warning the world before the Second Advent.

NINETEENTH-CENTURY HEALTH: THE GOOD OLD DAYS WERE TERRIBLE—1

Is there no balm in Gilead? Is there no physician there? Jer. 8:22, NASB.

C. P. Snow once wrote that "no one in his senses would choose to have been born in a previous age unless he could be certain that he would have been born into a prosperous family, that he would have enjoyed extremely good health, and that he could have accepted stoically the death of the majority of his children."

To put it bluntly, the good old days weren't nearly as wonderful as nostalgia would make them. Average life expectancy at birth was 32 in 1800, 41 by 1850, 50 by 1900, and 67 by 1950. Currently life expectancy for women in the United States is about 80, even though it is somewhat lower for men.

Why the change? you might be thinking. The answer is fairly straightforward—better health habits, sanitation, and medical care.

The health habits of nearly everyone in the early nineteenth century left much to be desired. Not only did those with money gobble down large quantities of food at a rapid rate, but much of what they ate was unhealthful. Fruits and vegetables were largely avoided by many who believed that the deadly cholera epidemic of 1832 had been brought about by fruit. And many had suspicions that fruits and vegetables especially harmed children. The basic facts of nutrition were unknown. In addition, even good food was generally in poor condition because of unsanitary processing and lack of refrigeration.

Diet, of course, was merely a part of the personal health problem. Bathing habits, for example, also were unsatisfactory. Most people seldom took a bath, and some authorities claim that average Americans of the 1830s never took a bath during their entire life. Even as late as 1855 New York City had only 1,361 bathtubs for its 629,904 residents. And in 1882 only an estimated 2 percent of the homes in New York had water connections.

Advocacy of the Saturday night bath was no joke. In 1872 when Ellen White recommended that "persons in health" should "bathe as often as twice a week" (3T 70) she was on the cutting edge of an aspect of personal health care.

Most people today have no idea how unhealthy life was in the mid-nineteenth century. When we read the writings of Ellen White and other health reformers of her day, we need to evaluate them against the times of ignorance, sickness, and death in which they lived.

When it comes to health, we can praise the Lord that we live in a better day.

NINETEENTH-CENTURY HEALTH: THE GOOD OLD DAYS WERE TERRIBLE—2

You shall have a place outside the camp and you shall go out to it; and you shall have a stick with your weapons; and when you sit down outside, you shall dig a hole with it, and turn back and cover up your excrement. Deut. 23:12, 13, RSV.

You may think this a strange devotional text, but God cares about every aspect of our lives. If people would have followed the biblical injunctions on community health down through history, it would have saved countless millions of lives from disease and epidemics. Should those lives have been those of your spouse or children, you would be jumping up and down praising the Lord for such texts as Deuteronomy 23:12, 13.

Sanitation was one aspect of the health problem in nineteenth-century America. Even middle- and often upper-class homes generally still had outdoor privies at midcentury. New York City, for example, had only 10,388 water closets (indoor toilets) in 1855. And the seepage of massed privies made for some interesting bacteriological conditions in well water.

As to garbage, cities had no system for processing it. Most of it ended up in the street for free-running hogs to root in. New York City of the 1840s had thousands of unchaperoned hogs to help care for the problem.

Of course, the omnipresent horse droppings oozed in the generally unpaved streets in wet weather and were pulverized to highly flavored dust that blew everywhere in dry weather. On New York City streets in 1900 horses deposited an estimated 2.5 million pounds of manure and 60,000 gallons of urine daily. H. L. Menken described an American city as one "solid stink." And rural life wasn't much healthier, most homes being surrounded by "an expanse of muck and manure."

And then there was spitting. In the days before the popularity of the cigarette, Americans deposited chewing tobacco sputum everywhere, both inside and out, although the more sophisticated didn't spit on the table.

The "good old days" were times of ignorance—ignorance that took a high toll in human lives. The Memphis, Tennessee, yellow fever epidemic of 1878, for example, killed 5,150 out of a population of 38,500. That same year New Orleans lost an estimated 3,977. But that was only half as many deaths as the city's 1853 epidemic, which cost 7,848 lives. People attributed yellow fever and other epidemics to bad air—what the authorities called "miasma." Thus people often slept in poorly ventilated or unventilated rooms to preserve their health.

Thank You, God, for the simple things of life, such as clean water and pure air.

NINETEENTH-CENTURY HEALTH:
THE GOOD OLD DAYS WERE TERRIBLE—3

And there was a woman in the crowd who had had a hemorrhage for twelve years. She had spent everything she had on doctors and still could find no cure. Luke 8:43, NLT.

If you would have gotten sick in most of the nineteenth century you certainly wouldn't want to visit a hospital. A trip there tended to be a death sentence in an era before the knowledge of germs. Epidemics were regular visitors to those unhygienic institutions originally founded for the poor. A hospital in the 1840s was a place of last resort—somewhere to go to die. People with money had physicians treat them at home.

Unfortunately, home medical practice wasn't all that sophisticated. The common view of disease was that the bodily "humors" must be out of balance. The cure: rebalance them. A first step in that process often involved bleeding off some of the excess blood, often a pint or two. Purging the body generally followed bloodletting. Physicians did that through the administration of powerful drugs, often compounded partly from mercury and strychnine, substances that we now know to be extremely poisonous.

But in an age that believed that fever, diarrhea, and vomiting were symptoms of recovery, such drugs had the desired effect of rapidly and violently emptying the body of excess fluids. No wonder they called it the age of "heroic" medicine.

Surgery, meanwhile, was no less heroic when one considers that it involved no anesthesia. One only has to recall young Uriah Smith getting his leg amputated on the kitchen table with no anesthetic but his mother's hand. And even after the surgery, one's prospects were poor given the fact of the unsanitary conditions caused by a lack of knowledge of germs.

And what did it take to become a physician? Not much. Four to eight months in one of the diploma mills would earn a medical degree, even if a person hadn't gone to high school.

It is little wonder that Oliver Wendell Homes declared that "if the whole materia medica as now used could be sunk to the bottom of the sea, it would be all the better for mankind, and all the worse for the fishes."

Ellen White's son Edson had one of those M.D. degrees. He quipped of his experience that the physician in charge "is a villain—the Hygieo-Therapeutic Clinic is a humbug, and the Old Doctor Mill ought to be tipped into the Delaware" River.

Error is a killer.

Truth sets us free—even in the physical realm.

ENTER THE HEALTH REFORMERS

You will know the truth, and the truth will make you free. John 8:32, RSV.

It was in the context of the ignorance about health that we find the rise of the American health reform movement during the 1830s. One of the most influential and representative reformers was Sylvester Graham. We can catch a glimpse of his ideas from an 1837 article in *The Graham Journal*. According to him, (1) "the chief food should be vegetables and fruit"; (2) bread should be made of unrefined flour; (3) "good cream may be used instead of butter"; (4) food should be thoroughly chewed; (5) "flesh-meat and fish . . . had better be omitted"; (6) one should avoid fat, rich gravies, and spicy condiments; (7) "all stimulants, of every sort and kind, as tea, coffee, wine, tobacco (in all its forms), cider, beer, etc., are prohibited"; (8) "pure soft water" is the preferred drink; (9) "the last meal of the day should be light" and taken three or four hours before going to bed; (10) "not a particle of food should be taken except at meals"; (11) avoid eating too much; (12) "abstinence should always be preferred to taking medicine"; (13) one should sleep about seven hours a day in "properly ventilated rooms"; (14) always avoid tight clothing; (15) "bathing [even daily] in warm or cold water is highly recommended"; (16) "exercise in the open air is very necessary"; and (17) "bread must not be eaten till 12 to 24 hours old."

To religious health reformers the laws of health were divine. Thus Theodore Dwight Weld could assert that "these are *God's* laws as really as 'Love the Lord with all thy heart' and 'Love thy neighbor as thyself.'" Obeying them meant a healthy body, while disobeying brought disease. The choice, Weld suggested, was "between *obeying God* and *resisting him, preserving life* and *destroying it, keeping* the *sixth commandment* and *committing suicide.*"

Clearly related to the health reform movement and quite compatible with it was the rise of forms of medical practice that opposed the drugging and bleeding techniques of the standard medicine of the day. One of them, hydrotherapy, recommended the internal and external applications of water as a therapeutic system. The water-cure physicians generally adopted the Graham health system.

Sometimes we Adventists think that the health reform program originated with us.

Not so! God loves all people, and He moves upon the hearts of many to alleviate the woes of a sick planet. Praise God for the broadness of His mercy.

ELLEN WHITE AND THE HEALTH REFORMERS

God be merciful unto us, and bless us; and cause his face to shine upon us. . . . That thy way may be known upon earth, thy saving health among all nations. Ps. 67:1, 2.

Those with a knowledge of Ellen White's counsels on health will recognize that she was in harmony with most of the reforming views of the health reformers. Thus she stood in good company when she rejected the "use of poisonous drugs," "which, in place of helping nature, paralyzes her powers" (MH 126; MM 224).

In a more positive line, Ellen White supported the reformers in her recommendation of natural remedies: "pure air, sunlight, abstemiousness, rest, exercise, proper diet, the use of water, trust in divine power" (MH 127).

The early Adventists were aware of both Ellen White's agreement with the health reformers of her day and her specifically Adventist contributions. Thus J. H. Waggoner could write in 1866 that "we do not profess to be pioneers in the general principles of health reform. The facts on which this movement is based have been elaborated, in a great measure, by reformers, physicians, and writers on physiology and hygiene, and so may be found scattered through the land. But we do claim that by the method of God's choice [Ellen White's counsel] it has been more clearly and powerfully unfolded, and is thereby producing an effect which we could not have looked for from any other source.

"As mere physiological and hygienic truths, they might be studied by some at their leisure, and by others laid aside as of little consequence; but when placed on a level with the great truths of the third angel's message by the sanction and authority of God's Spirit, and so declared to be the means whereby a weak people may be made strong to overcome, and our diseased body cleansed and fitted for translation, then it comes to us as an essential part of present truth."

While Ellen White largely agreed with the health reformers of her day, one of her contributions in the area of health was to integrate the message of health reform into Adventist theology.

From the time that she first began to write on the topic in 1863 to the present, Seventh-day Adventists have had a distinctive lifestyle. It has resulted in healthier bodies and longer lives. That longevity has been a demonstration to the world, as illustrated recently in the *National Geographic* magazine and other places. The witness of the church should be that of health in all areas of life.

ADVENTISTS WEREN'T ALWAYS HEALTH REFORMERS

I have yet many things to say unto you, but ye cannot bear them now. John 16:12.

Adventists weren't always health reformers.

Take unclean meats, for example. In November 1850 James White noted that a few of the Sabbatarians were "troubled in regard to eating swine's flesh" and some abstained from its use. He had no objections to such a practice, but stated that he did "not, by any means, believe that the Bible teaches that its proper use, in the gospel dispensation, is sinful," What he really objected to was individuals distracting others from the center of their message—the Sabbath in end-time perspective.

Some years later, after his wife penned a letter to a woman named Curtis that the use of swine's flesh was not a religious test, James wrote on the back: "That you may know how we stand on this question, I would say that we have just put down a two hundred pound porker."

Again, in 1859 Ellen White counseled S. N. Haskell and others that his "views concerning swine's flesh would prove no injury if you" keep "them to yourselves; but in your judgment and opinion you have made this question a test, and your actions have plainly shown your faith in this matter" (1T 206, 207).

She went on to add that "if God requires His people to abstain from swine's flesh, He will convict them on the matter. . . . If it is the duty of the church to abstain from swine's flesh, God will discover it to more than two or three. He will teach His church their duty.

"God is leading out a people, not a few separate individuals here and there, one believing this thing, another that. . . . The third angel is leading out and purifying a people, and they should move with Him unitedly. Some run ahead of the angels that are leading this people. . . .

"I saw that the angels of God would lead His people no faster than they could receive and act upon the important truths that are communicated to them. But some restless spirits, . . . get in haste for something new, and rush on . . . , and thus bring confusion and discord into the ranks. They do not speak or act in harmony with the body" (*ibid.*, 207).

Ellen White held the firm conviction throughout her long ministry that God was forming a people, and that as they united on one issue (but not before then) He would guide them to the next step. The progress up to 1863 had been clear. First they united on doctrine, and then on organization. Only then were they ready for His leading on health reform and other lifestyle issues.

God's leading always has a logic to it.

BUT THERE WAS ONE HEALTH REFORMER

And the Lord will take away from you all sickness. Deut. 7:15, RSV.

Joseph Bates, as in so many other areas of Sabbatarian Adventism, was the movement's pioneer health reformer. As a sea captain in 1821 he had abandoned hard drink when he realized that he looked forward to his daily dram more than he did food. Soon he discarded wine in 1822, tobacco in 1823, and all other forms of alcohol in 1824. Then in 1831 he swore off tea and coffee because "it is poison." "It had such an effect upon my whole system," he wrote, "that I could not rest nor sleep until after midnight."

Next to go were flesh foods. "In February 1843," he recalled, "I resolved to eat no more meat. In a few months after, I ceased using butter, grease, cheese, pies, and rich cakes."

He had first become alerted to the advantages of a vegetarian diet in 1820 when he discovered that two potato-eating Irish laborers could outwork seven or eight of his meat-eating men. Later such writers as Sylvester Graham led him further toward a complete vegetarian diet.

Bates' life was a good advertisement for the benefits of health reform. In contrast to most of the other early Sabbatarian leaders, he had exceptional health. From the time that he left the sea in the late 1820s, he was ill only two times that we know of. And both episodes were apparently malaria.

In his seventy-ninth year he testified to a health convention regarding his early health reform experiences and on the excellent health that had resulted. "Contrary to my former convictions, that if I was ever permitted to live to my present age, I should be a suffering cripple from my early exposure in following the sea, thanks be to God . . . , whose rich blessing ever follows every personal effort to reform, that I am entirely free from aches and pains, with the gladdening, cheering prospect that if I continue to reform, and forsake every wrong, I shall, with the redeemed followers of the Lamb, 'stand without fault before the throne of God.'"

Before the early 1860s however, Bates was a silent health reformer. When asked why he did not use certain foods, his usual reply was "I have eaten my share of them." James White reports that "he did not mention his views of proper diet in public at that time, nor in private, unless questioned upon the subject."

That would change in 1863.

But before moving on, we should reflect on the connecting link between healthful living and vigorous health. The relationship was not accidental in Bates' life. And it isn't in ours, either.

THE HEALTH REFORM VISION

Do you not know that your body is a temple of the Holy Spirit within you, which you have from God? 1 Cor. 6:19, RSV.

A few days ago we noted that truth is progressive and that God leads His people step by step. It was thus with health reform. Once the doctrinal and organizational steps were in place, lifestyle issues (including health reform) became the next stage in the development of Adventism and present truth.

On June 6, 1863, a mere 15 days after the formation of the General Conference of Seventh-day Adventists, Ellen White had one of the most influential visions of her entire ministry. Later that day, she wrote that "I saw that now we [she and James] should take special care of the health God has given us, for our work was not yet done. . . . I saw that we should encourage a cheerful, hopeful, peaceful frame of mind, for our health depends on our doing this. . . . *The more perfect our health, the more perfect will be our labor.*

"We must not leave the care of ourselves to God to see to and to take care of that which He has left for us to watch and care for. It is not safe nor pleasing to God to violate the laws of health and then ask Him to take care of our health and keep us from disease when we are living directly contrary to our prayers.

"I saw that it was a sacred duty to attend to our health, and arouse others to their duty. . . . We have a duty to speak, to come out against intemperance of every kind—intemperance in working, in eating, in drinking, and in drugging—and then point them to God's great medicine, water, pure soft water, for diseases, for health, for cleanliness, and for a luxury" (MS 1, 1863).

While this was personal counsel for James and Ellen, it also applied to the church at large. "I saw," she penned, "that we should not be silent upon the subject of health but should wake up minds to the subject" (*ibid.*).

And seek to wake up people she did. From that point on, her writing ministry focused to a considerable extent on the need and duty to preserve health and on how to do so.

And it didn't come any too soon. Her husband was on the verge of the crippling stroke that would hinder his ministry for the rest of his life, they had recently lost two of their four children to disease, and much of the leadership of the church struggled with chronic illness.

There was nothing so much needed at that time than the blessing of good health. And that is still true.

JUNE 11

A SECOND HEALTH REFORM VISION

You are not your own; you were bought with a price. So glorify God in your body.
1 Cor. 6:19, 20, RSV.

I n the vision given me in Rochester, New York, December 25, 1865, I was shown that our Sabbathkeeping people have been negligent in acting upon the light which God has given in regard to health reform, that there is yet a great work before us, and that as a people we have been too backward to follow in God's opening providence as He has chosen to lead us" (1T 485).

Her 1865 vision indicated that health reform for Seventh-day Adventists was not just a personal thing, but had social and missiological implications. That vision called for Adventists to establish their own health-care institution.

Such an institution, according to Ellen White, would have a twofold missiological impact. First, it would affect the lives of Adventist believers by preparing them for "the loud cry of the third angel" through fitting them for translation (*ibid.*, 486). Of course, improved health would also enable believers to be better communicators of their message to others.

A second missiological aspect of their new health institution would be direct outreach to non-Adventists. "As unbelievers," Ellen White penned, "shall resort to an institution devoted to the successful treatment of disease and conducted by Sabbathkeeping physicians, they will be brought directly under the influence of the truth. By becoming acquainted with our people and our real faith, their prejudice will be overcome and they will be favorably impressed. By thus being placed under the influence of truth, some will not only obtain relief from bodily infirmities, but will find a healing balm for their sin-sick souls. . . . One such precious soul saved will be worth more than all the means needed to establish such an institution" (*ibid.*, 493).

There in a nutshell is Ellen White's philosophy for operating health-care institutions. Their missiological function stood at the center of her thinking. The church was to establish institutions that would not only aid its own members but be agencies in spreading the message of the third angel to those outside denominational membership. Such institutions would not only speak to the physical needs of individuals, but also to their spiritual and moral.

We live in a broken world, and God wants all of us to find wholeness in every way. As Adventists, we still have the privilege of not only living a healthy life but of sharing a healthy lifestyle with others.

UNBALANCED BALANCERS

The Lord is the strength of my life. Ps. 27:1.

E llen White's December 25, 1865, health reform vision not only set the tone for the missiological purpose of Adventist health-care institutions—it also integrated health reform with Adventist theology, indicating that "the health reform . . . is a part of the third angel's message and is just as closely connected with it as are the arm and hand with the human body" (1T 486).

That insight was both helpful to individual Adventists and crucial in making the connection evident between the lifestyle issue of health and the denomination's end-time theology, indicating that just as our bodies are unified in their physical, mental, and spiritual aspects, so is the Adventist belief system an integrated whole rather than a "herd" of disconnected ideas.

Adventists soon came to think of the health message as "the right arm of the message." That was good. But some preachers and other Adventist believers must have gotten carried away with enthusiasm for it.

Thus a few months later Mrs. White carefully corrected any wrong impressions she may have given by writing that "the health reform is closely connected with the work of the third message, yet it is not the message. Our preachers should teach the health reform, yet they should not make this the leading theme in the place of the message. Its place is among those subjects which set forth the preparatory work to meet the events brought to view by the message; among these it is prominent. We should take hold of every reform with zeal, yet should avoid giving the impression that we are vacillating and subject to fanaticism" (*ibid.*, 559).

Unfortunately, balance for many in health reform has been difficult to achieve. Some, James White pointed out, moved too fast on the topic, fell into fanaticism, and brought reproach on both the church and the topic itself. Others failed to advance at all.

For her part, Ellen White struggled over the years with those who "select statements made in regard to some articles of diet that are presented as objectionable—statements written in warning and instruction to certain individuals who were entering or had entered on an evil path. They dwell on these things and make them as strong as possible, weaving their own peculiar, objectionable traits of character in with these statements . . . , thus making them a test, and driving them where they do only harm" (3SM 285).

Lord, give us balance in every aspect of our lives. Amen.

SPREADING THE WORD ON HEALTH—1

Jesus Christ maketh thee whole. Acts 9:34.

F our months after her second major health reform vision Ellen White had opportunity to present her views before the young denomination at the fourth General Conference session in May 1866. In vigorous tones she put before the leading ministers the principles of health reform and the importance of both accepting and teaching those principles.

She asserted that such reform had "scarcely been entered upon yet" and that the church had "a much greater work" in this line than anyone had yet comprehended, climaxing her appeal with the call that Seventh-day Adventists "should have an institution of their own" for health and healing (1T 486, 487, 492).

In response, the General Conference session passed several resolutions. One acknowledged the importance of health reform "as part of the work of God incumbent on us at this time; and that we pledge ourselves to live in accordance with these principles, and that we will use our best endeavors to impress their importance upon others."

A second resolution requested Dr. Horatio S. Lay (probably the only Seventh-day Adventist physician at the time) "to furnish through the *Review* a series of articles on the health reform."

A new day had come. The resolutions reflect a profound conviction that the light on health reform was of great importance.

Now it is frequently the case that people are stronger in their resolutions than in subsequent actions. But in this case it was the opposite. While people might look in vain for the proposed series of articles on health reform by H. S. Lay, they will find something better yet—the announcement of Dr. Lay as the editor of a monthly 16-page periodical called *The Health Reformer.*

In his prospectus for *The Health Reformer* Dr. Lay stated that its purpose was "to aid in the great work of reforming, as far as possible, the false habits of life so prevalent at the present day." It would advocate the cure of disease through the "use of nature's own remedies—air, light, heat, exercise, food, sleep, recreation," and so on.

These early Adventists were serious about sharing their new vision. Because so many of them at the time were suffering from poor health, they valued such new understandings all the more. They could rejoice that God was leading them in a better path.

SPREADING THE WORD ON HEALTH—2

I shall yet praise him, who is the health of my countenance, and my God. Ps. 42:11.

The denomination didn't waste any time getting out the *Health Reformer*. The first issue appeared in August 1866, three months after the General conference session.

That initial issue had articles from a bevy of ministers, Dr. Lay, and one from Ellen White. She urged that "men and women should inform themselves in regard to the philosophy of health," and concluded by stating that "ignorance upon this important subject is sin; the light is now beaming upon us, and we are without excuse if we do not cherish the light and become intelligent in regard to these things, which it is our highest earthly interest to understand" (HR, Aug. 1866).

With so many ministers writing for the periodical, Lay in the second issue wrote a note for the benefit of those who might think that "nobody can talk on health but an M.D., and nobody on theology but a D.D." He pointed out that many of his nonmedical contributors had experienced health reform in the practical realm and all of the articles had been "examined professionally and endorsed before they are laid before the reader."

The testimonials to transformed health were many. G. W. Amadon, for example, reported that *"every day my heart dilates with joy as I realize the blessings of the Health Question,* as lived out by its sincere converts. . . . As an individual, I can say that I am a hundredfold better off than when I was living in such gross violation of the laws of our beings. Today, instead of aches and rheums, with congested brain, and a numerous train of mental and bodily ailments, I am, to a great extent, entirely free. Blessed be God for all this!"

Isaac Sanborn observed that because of health reform "I am entirely well of the rheumatism, which I used to have so bad by spells that I could not walk a step for days" and that even though he often was in poor weather and in ill-ventilated speaking venues that exposed him to disease he had not had a bad cold for more than two years.

Then there was the tidbit from one individual that "if he were to offer a burnt offering to the devil, he should choose a pig stuffed with tobacco."

Our hearts should dilate with joy when we consider the alternatives to good health. It is all too easy to forget the days of ignorance and the heartfelt blessing of good health.

RETROSPECT ON HEALTH REFORM

May the God of hope fill you with all joy. Rom. 15:13, NIV.

My heart is still warm from the statement we read yesterday from the early Adventist who declared that his heart dilated with joy when he realized the blessings of health reform.

That thought brings me to the first evangelistic series I presented. The venue was Corsicanna, Texas, a town of about 26,000 people in 1968 with an Adventist church of 12 members. And of those 12 nearly all were in their 70s and only one was male.

Now, I have nothing against old people. After all, I am getting to be one. And I have nothing against females. My mother is one. But a young preacher wants a full house of all ages and sexes. The good news was that I had a good crowd every night, with one non-Adventist woman bringing five professional people to each meeting. But on the way out one evening she said, "Brother Knight, I'm not coming tomorrow night, and I'm not bringing my friends."

"Why?" I inquired.

"I don't like your sermon title. You are going to tell me what I can't do."

I thought my title was cute if not strikingly brilliant—"Why I Don't Eat Rats, Snakes, and Snails."

Caught almost speechless, I told her and her friends to return the next evening, and when they left they would say it was the best sermon yet. The only problem was that I had no sermon prepared yet and didn't know how I was going to rescue my promise.

A sleepless night. But about 4:00 or 5:00 in the morning it all came together.

God loves you!

And because He loves you He wants you to be happy.

And He knows you're not happy when you are sick.

Therefore He has given us a few ideas on how to be happier.

On her way out that evening with her friends she stopped and declared, "Brother Knight, that was the best sermon yet."

If it was good for her, it was even better for me. It moved me from preaching in a negative direction toward a positive.

And what is more positive and joyful than good health.

Thank You, Father, for that special blessing. Our hearts also dilate with joy.

A HEALTH REFORM INSTITUTE OF THEIR OWN

And when was it that we saw you sick . . . ? And the king will answer them,
"Truly I tell you, just as you did it to one of the least of these who are members of
my family, you did it to me." Matt. 25:39, 40, NRSV.

Healing played a large part in Christ's earthly ministry. The same is true of Adventism. Today it sponsors a system of nearly 800 health-related institutions worldwide.

That massive system experienced its genesis in Ellen White's December 1865 health reform vision and her call for an Adventist health reform institute in May 1866. As with the *Health Reformer,* the response by the church was immediate and forceful. The Adventists opened their Health Reform Institute in Battle Creek, Michigan, on September 5, just four months after the General Conference session.

Of course, its inauguration wasn't all that impressive, "with two doctors, two bath attendants, one nurse (untrained), three or four helpers, one patient, any amount of inconveniences, and a great deal of faith in the future of the institution and the principles on which it was founded."

A note from James White published on the back page of the September 11 *Review* rejoiced in the rapid response of the church and its members. "We have only to look back to our conference in May last, less than four short months ago, for the time when this matter first began to take practical shape among our people.

"Now we behold an elegant site secured, buildings ready for operation, a competent corps of assistants on the ground, two numbers of a health journal already issued, with a subscription list that has doubled within the past few weeks, a sum bordering on eleven thousand dollars already subscribed for stock in the enterprise, and the institute opened and operations actually commenced. In no enterprise ever undertaken by this people has the hand of the Lord been more evidently manifested than in this thing."

That little institution may have had a rather humble beginning, but during the next 35 years it would grow into one of the world's premier health-care institutions as J. H. Kellogg transformed it into the Battle Creek Sanitarium.

Meanwhile, its very existence witnessed to a broadening sense of mission among the Adventist people. And it should be so. The message of the parable of Matthew 25:31-46 is that God wants his people to be socially concerned with the needs of others.

ENTER JOHN HARVEY KELLOGG

I will restore health unto thee, and I will heal thee of thy wounds. Jer. 30:17.

D ynamic, forceful, and visionary are the best words to describe the young 23-year-old John Harvey Kellogg who assumed the leadership of the Battle Creek Sanitarium in 1876. He was only five feet three inches tall, but what he lacked in stature he made up for in sheer exuberance in every task he undertook.

Early on he had had no desire to become a physician. He really wanted to be a teacher. But when James White sponsored him, along with Edson and Willie White, for six months of training at Dr. Trall's Hygieo-Therapeutic College in 1872 he not only received an M.D. degree but a desire to study further.

Again with financial backing from the Whites, he spent a year studying medicine at the University of Michigan and a final year at New York's Bellevue Hospital Medical School, then perhaps the most advanced medical college in the nation. Upon completion of his program in 1875 he told Willie White that "I feel more than 50 pounds bigger since getting a certain piece of sheepskin about two feet square. It's *bona fide* sheep too, by the way, none of your bogus paper concerns like the hygeio-therapeutic document."

In the summer of 1875 he returned to Battle Creek and was soon working at the Health Reform Institute, the next year becoming its director, on his conditional request that his term would last only one year. Little did he realize that he would head the institution 67 years.

When he took over in 1876, the institute had 20 patients, but six departed with the previous administrator, and two others left after one look at the boyish physician. But Kellogg wasn't concerned.

Within a few months he had twice the usual number of patients, and by 1877 he had to add a new building. That was the beginning of a building program that by the turn of the century would make what had become the Battle Creek Sanitarium into one of the largest and most well-known hospitals in the United States.

Meanwhile Kellogg in his spare time wrote some 50 books, invented cornflakes and the cold cereal industry, developed cutting-edge medical technology, and became a world-famous surgeon.

God had blessed the little giant more than anyone could have imagined. He always blesses those who are willing to grow.

ADVENTISM IN TIME OF WAR—1

Thou shalt not kill. Ex. 20:13.

Seventh-day Adventism was in the midst of its birth as an organized denomination when a civil war devastated the United States between 1861 and 1865. It would take more lives from the nation's relatively small population than the Revolutionary War, the War of 1812, the Mexican American War, the Spanish American War, World Wars I and II, the Korean War, and the Vietnam War combined. Yet Adventism was sending no soldiers into this most important of all conflicts, one that would determine if the United States would continue to exist as a unified nation and that would eventually do away with slavery.

Why? What was wrong with the Adventists? Why were they holding back?

That is the question that James White set out to answer in the *Review and Herald* of August 12, 1861. His first points had to do with the fact that Adventists were loyal citizens of the United States, noting that "slavery is pointed out in the prophetic word as the darkest and most damning sin upon this nation," that many Adventist publications because of their anti-slavery teachings "had been positively forbidden in the slave states," and that "those of our people who voted at all at the last presidential election, to a man voted for Abraham Lincoln." "We know," White concluded, "of not one man among Seventh-day Adventists who has the least sympathy for secession."

Having established that Adventists were loyal citizens, he went on to explain why they were as a church providing no soldiers. Standing firmly on the Ten Commandments, he wrote that "the position which our people have taken relative to the perpetuity and sacredness of the law of God contained in the ten commandments, is not in harmony with all the requirements of war. The fourth precept of that law says, 'Remember the Sabbath day to keep it holy'; the sixth says, 'Thou shalt not kill.'" His position was clear enough. Adventists couldn't volunteer for military service because it would put them in a place where they chose to voluntarily break at least two of God's commandments.

White had begun to solve the problem even though he wasn't yet finished. But he had raised an issue that would affect tens of thousands of young Adventist lives. Not all moral issues are clear-cut in a world of sin. The church needs divine guidance in such times.

Give us wisdom, Lord, as we as a church continue to wrestle with important issues relating to our duty to both You and earthly governments.

ADVENTISM IN TIME OF WAR—2

Render therefore to Caesar the things that are Caesar's, and to God the things that are God's. Matt. 22:21, RSV.

How should a Christian relate to the military? That was the issue James White had raised on August 12, 1861. His first response was straightforward enough: Adventists could not volunteer for military service because such an act would place them in a position in which they made a choice to break at least two of the Ten Commandments.

But what about if the government drafted a person? What if that individual has no choice, but is merely following the laws of the nation? To those questions James White put forth an unexpected and controversial suggestion. "In the case of drafting," he penned, "the government assumes the responsibility of the violation of the law of God, and it would be madness to resist. He who would resist until, in the administration of military law he was shot down, goes too far, we think, in taking the responsibility of suicide. . . . For us to attempt to resist the laws of the best government under heaven, which is now struggling to put down the most hellish rebellion since that of Satan and his angels, we repeat it, would be madness."

So there we have James's answer to the complex issue of how Adventists can render to both God and the government. In a nutshell:

1. Adventists are loyal citizens.
2. Adventists can't volunteer because that would place them where they chose to break God's law.
3. But if they were drafted, the breaking of the law became the government's responsibility, and Adventists should submit to taking up arms and killing, even on the Sabbath day.

How do you feel about his arguments? What biblical evidence can you marshal for and/or against his logic? How are we to act if the commands of the government conflict with the commands of God?

Now, we should remember that at this time the United States had not yet passed a draft law. It was merely a possibility. But it was one that the young Adventist Church, still in 1862 without a General Conference to represent it to the government, had to contemplate seriously, as the "meat grinder" of a vicious conflict continued to destroy lives.

As Christians we are citizens of two kingdoms. We all face the challenge of how to be faithful to both.

ADVENTISM IN TIME OF WAR—3

Let every person be subject to the governing authorities. For there is no authority except from God, and those that exist have been instituted by God. Therefore he who resists the authorities resists what God has appointed, and those who resist will incur judgment. Rom. 13:1, 2, RSV.

Adolf Hitler's favorite text! He stipulated that it or its companion in 1 Peter 2:13 be read at least once a year in every church in the Third Reich.

Romans 13 leaves no doubt that Christians are to obey the government. But what, we ask again, should we do if God's appointed agency (the government) tells us to perform things that put us in a position of disobeying some of God's other teachings? That was the question troubling the Adventists during the American Civil War—the first war they had had to face as a church.

James's August 12, 1862, article in the *Review* stirred up quite a bit of heat on the question. As he put it on August 26, "Several brethren refer to our re-marks . . . two weeks since, in a rather feverish style. . . . This is no time for Christian gentlemen to give way to feelings of prejudice, and virtually charge us with teaching Sabbath-breaking and murder. . . . If any of you are drafted, and choose to have a clinch with Uncle Sam rather than obey, you can try it. We shall not contend with you, lest some of you nonresistants get up a little war be-fore you are called upon to fight for your country."

At that point White significantly added that "any well-written articles, calcu-lated to shed light upon our duty as a people in reference to the present war, will receive prompt attention."

That invitation prompted a tidal wave of responses for the next three months as Adventists argued publicly through the pages of the *Review* regarding the du-ties of Christians in their conflicting roles as citizens of both the kingdom of heaven and a particular nation here on earth, with each having its own laws—sometimes in conflict.

One theme that surfaces in the discussions is that we should study such con-troversial yet important questions during periods of peace when emotions are calm and there is time to do a proper job.

Such wasn't the case here, though. They were struggling to find an answer in the midst of an emotion-fraught crisis. But the idea of thinking through impor-tant issues before a crisis is important.

Help us, Father, to use the times of peace in our individual and our collective lives as a church to come to You in study and prayer so that we might more fully discern Your will.

ADVENTISM IN TIME OF WAR—4

Peter and the other apostles replied: "We must obey God rather than men!"
Acts 5:29, NIV.

S uch were the words and the conclusions of the apostles when they came
face to face with a conflict in commands between God and earthly government.

But what the implications of that truth were for Adventists in the face of military service was not all that clear to church members in 1862.

James White's invitation to submit articles on the topic of the proper position
of the church on military service brought in not only a high volume of responses
but also a complete range across the spectrum of possible options.

On one end were the total pacifists, who believed that Christians should avoid
military service altogether. It was probably such an orientation of members in
Iowa whose aggressive pacifist agitation had triggered charges that Adventism was
not patriotic that brought about the publication of White's initial thoughts on the
topic.

At the other end were the crusaders for full participation in the war, such as
Joseph Clarke. "I have," he wrote, "been very anxious to know duty respecting
the war, not so much for fear of the draft, as because I want to see treason receive
its just deserts.

"Consequently, I have written to Bro. White, to know if it would be allow-
able for us to go into the ranks. I have had my fancy full of Gideons, Jephthaths,
and fighting Davids. . . .

"I have wished sometimes that I had it where Joab had Absalom, and almost
fancied that the time might come when a regiment of Sabbathkeepers would strike
this rebellion a staggering blow, in the strength of Him who always helped his
valiant people when they kept his statutes.

"Last winter I had the war fever so high, that it injured me somewhat."

In another article Clarke wrote, "Was there not war in heaven?" "Is it murder to hang or shoot a traitor? No! no! . . . Were Joshua and David murderers?
Let us lay aside fanaticism and act like men."

So the debate went, until at long last White called for an end to it as far as
Review articles went, since someone had adequately represented every perspective.

The whole debate indicates a refreshing openness in early Adventism, one
that over time would help them move toward a consensus on controverted issues.

ADVENTISM IN TIME OF WAR—5

It is lawful to do good on the Sabbath. Matt. 12:12, NKJV.

So said Jesus in regard to acts of mercy on the Sabbath.
That principle would eventually unlock the answer to the Adventist quandary over how to serve both God and an earthly government during times of war.

Meanwhile, we should remember that no draft law existed in the United States until March 1863. Also we should note that no nation at that time had noncombatant options for military service. A person in the military was automatically a combatant who would carry arms and kill when commanded to do so.

The conscription law passed on March 3, 1863, let draftees find substitutes if they could pay a fee to use in procuring one. The Adventist Church aided its members to raise the fee. But July 4, 1864, saw a revision of the draft law stating that only those "conscientiously opposed to bearing arms" could be exempted by paying the fee.

At that point the recently established General Conference of Seventh-day Adventists went on record as being a noncombatant denomination. On August 3 the state of Michigan granted the new denomination noncombatant status. Other states soon followed. Then the church sent J. N. Andrews with letters from the various state governors to apply for noncombatant status from the federal government in Washington, D.C. Thus it was that in September 1864 the United States government recognized Adventism as a noncombatant church.

Theoretically that meant that if its members did get drafted they would not have to bear arms or kill enemies. But in practice noncombatant draftees often met with opposition and threats. On a more positive note, by the end of the war noncombatants could serve as medics both on the battlefront and in hospitals.

Adventists were happy with that arrangement, since it freed them from taking the lives of others and it was lawful to do good to others on the Sabbath.

From that time forward the noncombatant medic role became the standard for Seventh-day Adventist draftees. But the denomination still frowned on volunteer service. In fact, several volunteers during the latter days of the civil war were disfellowshipped, even though some (probably including Ellen White) weren't so sure that was the proper course.

God leads His people not merely in things strictly spiritual, but also in their dealings with issues related specifically to this world. For His guidance in all things we can rejoice.

RETROSPECT ON ADVENTISM IN TIMES OF WAR

Love your enemies. Matt. 5:44.

I personally find it impossible to love enemies and set out to take their lives at the same time.

Thus it was that in the summer of 1961, in the midst of the Berlin Wall crisis, I faced the threat of a court-martial.

The circumstance was that I was a trained infantry soldier who had up to that time been a confirmed agnostic. But throughout the first half of the year I had become interested in Adventism and had come to the conviction that I should no longer carry arms or drill on Sabbath. I had begun to appreciate the biblical logic undergirding the denomination's position even though I had not yet become a church member.

But, we need to ask, how is it that a young person who had only a brief and tenuous relationship with Adventism even knew about the church's position on military service? The answer is as simple as it is straightforward—the church had aggressively and consistently publicized its position and advised its pastors and young people on the topic.

Not only had the General Conference assigned special pastors to the local conferences to help draftees attain noncombatant rights, but the church made large numbers of publications on the topic available to its youth. And then there was the Medical Cadet Corps, sponsored by Adventist colleges and academies that specifically prepared Adventists to fill noncombatant roles when drafted.

In addition, there circulated stories of the many young Adventists around the world who had been imprisoned and even at times martyred for their refusal to bear arms or work on Sabbath. And if that wasn't enough there was the ubiquitous medic Desmond T. Doss who received the Medal of Honor for having saved the lives of at least 75 wounded men in one battle in Okinawa.

But then the draft ended, the publicity stopped, and Adventism neglected the topic and eventually forgot its history. As of 2007 the United States military had some 7,500 Adventist volunteers, virtually all of them (except chaplains) having enlisted as combatants.

Sometimes a church loses its history and needs to remember what it stands for.

That also happens in our personal lives. May God grant us the willpower to do so honestly.

EDUCATION IN THE GOOD OLD DAYS

Canst thou speak Greek? Acts 21:37.

While that might not seem a very good text for a devotional thought, it does raise an important issue.

The good old days in education weren't very good. Society did not consider anyone educated unless they were well learned in ancient Greek and Latin and the literature in those languages. Traditional education focused on the ancient classics.

Such an education, of course, had no meaning for the masses who had to work for a living. But that didn't make much difference, since there was no provision for even their elementary and secondary education. To put it in stark terms, formal education in schools for most of history was not open to most people, even in its most rudimentary forms. Schooling was the province of the upper classes, those relatively few who came from moneyed backgrounds and never found themselves forced to earn a living.

As in health care, the good old days in education were terrible. For more than 2,000 years education in the West had focused on ancient languages, words, ideas, and the "great books" of its heritage. The very prestige and longevity of this tradition made it difficult for educators to envision alternative approaches.

But reform would come, climaxing in the nineteenth century at the very time Adventism was rising.

At the cutting edge of the educational reforms in the 1830s were such people as Horace Mann, who led the battle for quality public elementary education for every child. Mann and his friends sought not only to make education available, but also to make it practical and healthy. They knew that it did little good to educate the mind if children's bodies were diseased.

On the higher education front was Oberlin College, an institution that in the 1830s displaced the Latin and Greek classics in the curriculum, centralized the worldview of the Bible, and developed a manual labor study program to help people acquire useful skills in addition to book learning, thus ensuring a balance between the mental and the physical.

"The system of education in this institute," read the prospectus for Oberlin, "will provide for the *body and heart* as well as the *intellect,* for it aims at the best education of the whole man."

Adventism's educational ideas didn't arise in a vacuum. We can always, even today, learn from the larger culture as we evaluate traditions and practices from the perspective of the biblical worldview.

IN SEARCH OF PROPER EDUCATION—1

Surely I come quickly. Amen. Even so, come Lord Jesus. Rev. 22:20.

To Adventists living in the twenty-first century it may seem that Christian education has been central to their church from its inception. That, however, is far from the truth. Formal education, in fact, was the last major institutional development within the denomination. The establishment of a rigorous publishing program in 1849, a centralized church organization in 1863, and a health-care outreach in 1866 had all preceded it. By way of contrast, the Adventist Church established its first school in 1872 (28 years after the Millerite disappointment) and did not have a widespread elementary system until nearly 1900.

While the tardy development of Adventist schooling might come as a surprise to present-day Adventists, it had its roots in the very logic of their spiritual forebears, who, above everything else, believed in the *immediate return of Jesus.* Religious groups focusing on the nearness of the end of the world have generally not felt much need for educating their children beyond the essential concepts of their religious persuasion and the skills needed to earn a living in the short interim.

That was true of the early Christian church, and it was also the case of early Seventh-day Adventism. Why send children to school, so the logic runs, if the world is soon to end and they will never grow up to use their hard-earned learning? Some might interpret providing a formal education for one's children as a lack of faith in the immediacy of the Advent. Such attitudes were widespread among Seventh-day Adventists.

As late as 1862 a church member wrote James White asking if it was "right and consistent for us who believe with all our hearts in the immediate coming of the Lord, to seek to give our children an education? If so, should we send them to a district school, where they learn twice as much evil as good?"

White replied that "the fact that Christ is very soon coming is no reason why the mind should not be improved. A well-disciplined and informed mind can best receive and cherish the sublime truths of the Second Advent."

With that statement he set the stage for the development of an Adventist system of schooling.

God wants us to develop all of our talents as we await Jesus to return.

ENTER GOODLOE HARPER BELL

Train up a child in the way he should go: and when he is old, he will not depart from it. Prov. 22:6.

A flash of concern for Adventist education occurred during the 1850s. James White wrote that you couldn't just take children from school and "let them run at large with the children in the streets. 'An empty brain is the devil's workshop.'"

Attempts at Adventist schooling sprang up in such places as Buck's Bridge, New York, and Battle Creek, Michigan. But all failed. Thoroughly discouraged on the topic of schooling, James wrote in 1861 that "we have had a thorough trial of a school at Battle Creek, under most favorable circumstances, and have given up."

For another seven years it looked as if schooling was a dead issue in Adventism. Then came Goodloe Harper Bell.

Bell first went to Battle Creek in the winter of 1866-1867 at the age of 34, when he accompanied a friend to the recently established Health Reform Institute. It must have impressed him because the next year when Bell needed treatment himself he returned.

That was good enough, but Bell got stuck in a room with an Adventist by the name of Osborne. Night after night he heard Osborne, who thought Bell had gone to sleep, praying out loud for him. The man's utter sincerity so affected Bell that the educator joined the church.

Part of his treatment was physical work in the fresh air. Accordingly, Willie White tells us, someone gave Bell a handsaw and put him to the task of sawing wood for the nearby Adventist publishing house.

It was there that Edson White, James's oldest living son, met him. Finding out he was a teacher, Edson mentioned how much he hated grammar. To that Bell replied that properly taught, grammar was one of the most interesting studies.

That chance contact led in the next few months to Bell being employed by the Battle Creek church. In 1872 the General Conference took over the school. Thus it was that his little institution became the first one of a worldwide system that in 2006 counted 5,362 elementary schools, 1,462 secondary schools, and 106 colleges and universities.

God even uses strange Adventists like Brother Osborne to do special things for His work. If He can use Osborne, he can use you and me if we let Him guide our hearts and minds.

IN SEARCH OF PROPER EDUCATION–2

And these words which I command you this day shall be upon your heart; and you shall teach them diligently to your children. Deut. 6:6, 7, RSV.

The first 28 years of Ellen White's prophetic ministry produced no articles on schooling or formal education, although she had written on home education and the responsibility of parents as early as 1854.

But that would radically change in 1872, when Bell's private school became the first denomination-sponsored educational institution. For it she wrote "Proper Education," one of her most important and comprehensive statements on education.

"Proper Education" has been influential among Adventist educators because they have correctly perceived it as a mandate concerning the ideal nature of Christian education. It left no doubt that Adventists were to be educational "reformers" (FE 44). Part of that reform ideal involved moving beyond an overemphasis on books and toward a balanced education that emphasized "the physical, mental, moral, and religious education of children" (*ibid.*, 15). The concept of a balanced education that treated the whole person would become a hallmark of Ellen White's writings on education during the next 40 years.

"Proper Education" falls into three basic sections. The first part sets forth true education as the development of self control. Whereas people may train animals, human beings are to be educated as individuals to make responsible moral decisions. Thus we must enlist their will on the side of right.

The second section, comprising 25 pages of the 31-page document, treats physical health and useful manual labor in relation to education within both the home and school. She stressed practicality, usefulness, and the physical aspects of education again and again. It was in this section that she highlighted the fact that Adventists are educational reformers.

The third segment briefly discussed the teaching of the Bible and the "common branches" of knowledge for those preparing for the ministry.

She had no doubt about the importance of education. After all, "ignorance will not increase the humility or spirituality" of Christians and "Christ can be best glorified by those who serve Him intelligently. The great object of education is to enable us to use the powers which God has given us in such a manner as will best represent the religion of the Bible and promote the glory of God" (*ibid.*, 45).

IN SEARCH OF PROPER EDUCATION—3

I will instruct you and teach you in the way which you should go. Ps. 32:8, NASB.

Seventh-day Adventists had taken an important step forward in the adoption of Bell's school in 1872 as the first official denominational school. But the leadership knew that they had to do more. If for no other reason, they required some way to prepare ministers. Up into the early 1870s a young person desiring to become a minister merely watched how the older ministers did things and went out to do the same.

By 1873 James White, the spark plug for every Adventist advance, realized that the denomination needed to do something toward the training of leadership. "Probably there is no branch of this work," he told the 1873 General Conference session, "that suffers so much at the present time as the proper education of men and women to proclaim the third angel's message." The situation demanded "more sanctified education in the ministry! My heart rejoices to know that the Spirit of God is moving upon men of education to come into our midst to take hold of the [educational] work."

But it wasn't only the preparation of ministers that called for a larger educational vision. The denomination was also being eased into the realm of foreign missions. Thus J. N. Andrews could write in 1873 that "the calls that come from every quarter, from men speaking other languages, must be answered by us. We cannot do this in our present circumstances. But we can do it if the Lord bless our effort" in upgrading the Battle Creek school. "We have delayed this effort too long. The time past cannot be improved, but the time still remaining can be improved. . . . Men of other nationalities desire to be instructed concerning" the Second Advent.

The leadership had come to see that they must establish a college, which they would do in 1874. Just before the opening of that institution, General Conference president George I. Butler penned that "we see a great work before us. . . . We see the time coming when scores and hundreds of missionaries will go from this land to other lands to sound forth the message of warning." To that end the proposed college needed to educate not only ministers, but translators, editors, and others who could forward the message of the third angel.

Vision is never static. God leads His people one step at a time. When we grasp one level of need, He pushes us to see the next. So it is in every aspect of lives lived for Him.

IN SEARCH OF PROPER EDUCATION—4

Come now, and let us reason together, saith the Lord. Isa. 1:18.

The founders of Battle Creek College in 1874 were extremely clear on what they wanted in their new school. They desired an institution that would teach the Bible, prepare ministers and missionaries, and develop in its students the ability to reason with God. They knew why they were establishing their college.

But then there was the faculty. Even more basic yet was the question of where the budding denomination could even find teachers and staff.

Fortunately, they had at least one university graduate in their midst. Sidney Brownsberger had completed the classical studies program of the University of Michigan in 1869 and would soon receive an M.A. from the same institution in 1875. Given the needs of the church and Brownsberger's education and dedication to Adventism, he was the obvious choice to head up the new college.

But his appointment had only one drawback. While he was excellent in academics, he had next to no understanding of how to implement the goals of the founders.

At one of the first meetings of the college board, Willie White tells us, his mother "read to them the testimony on proper education. All listened with deep interest. They recognized it as timely. They also admitted that it called for a broader work than they had planned, and that their beautiful location" on the edge of Battle Creek "so convenient and near did not provide for all that was called for.

"One said, 'Well, Brother Brownsberger, what can we do?'

"He answered, 'I do not know anything about the conducting of such a school. . . .'

"Then it was agreed that the work of the school should be organized on the ordinary lines and that the matter of the industries should be studied with a view to their [later] introduction. But no definite steps were taken regarding the industries till many years had passed."

The young educational leader did what he knew best. The school that he developed in the mid 1870s had as its ideal curricular core a traditional liberal arts course focusing on Latin, classical Greek, and the literatures of those languages. It was hardly a "reform" institution.

But God used it anyway. And therein is the good news. That God uses us in spite of ourselves, in spite of our shortcomings. *Thank You, Lord!*

IN SEARCH OF PROPER EDUCATION—5

How much better is it to get wisdom than gold! Prov. 16:16.

B attle Creek College, as we saw yesterday, failed to meet the expectations of its founders. Not only did it have the classical languages and literatures at its center, but Bible study and religion found scant place in the school's offerings. In fact, it had no regular religion courses, let alone required ones. While it is true that Uriah Smith hobbled over on his one real leg to provide some dusty elective lectures on Bible prophecy, it appears that he didn't have a large number of takers.

The college catalogues advertised that "there is nothing in the courses of study, or in the rules and practices of discipline, that is in the least denominational or sectarian. The Bible courses are before a class of only those who attend them from choice." Again, "the managers of this college have no disposition to *urge* upon students sectarian views, or to give such views any prominence in their school work." Such was the birth of Seventh-day Adventist higher education.

But it got worse. Brownsberger resigned in 1881 and the school replaced him with Alexander McLearn, who arrived in Battle Creek with the advantage of having an exalted Doctor of Divinity degree, but the disadvantage of not being an Adventist or of being a recent convert.

Brownsberger may not have understood the needs of a genuinely Adventist education, but McLearn didn't even understand Adventism. He may have been an excellent academic, but under his leadership things went from bad to worse.

The institution closed its doors for the 1882-1883 school year with no certainty that it would reopen. So much for the first attempt at Adventist higher education. One of the Battle Creek newspapers characterized the Adventists debacle as "the west end circus."

It was into the mess of the McLearn leadership that Ellen White waded with a testimony entitled "Our College," a paper read in College Hall in December 1881 before the combined ecclesiastical and educational leadership of the denomination. And she didn't mince any words. "There is danger," she began, "that our college will be turned away from its original design" (5T 21).

This sad history can teach us something important. It is all too easy for us to think that the church has run continually downhill from its founding. Not so. The church has always had problems. It always will. But God didn't give up on it. That's the way He is. He works with less-than-perfect people and less-than-ideal institutions. God continues on even after we are willing to give up.

IN SEARCH OF PROPER EDUCATION—6

A new heart also will I give you, and a new spirit will I put within you. Eze. 36:26.

It's not only individuals that need new hearts. Sometimes it's institutions also. So it was with Adventist education during the 1870s and 1880s as it searched for its proper role in the church.

Yesterday we ended with Ellen White's powerful call for reform in the tottering Battle Creek College of December 1881. She feared that it was being "turned away from its original design. . . . For one or two years past there has been an effort to mold our school after other colleges. . . . The moral and religious influences should not be put in the background" (5T 21).

"If a worldly influence is to bear sway in our school, then sell it out to worldlings and let them take the entire control; and those who have invested their means in that institution will establish another school, to be conducted, not upon the plan of popular schools, nor according to the desires of principal and teachers, but upon the plan which God has specified. . . .

"God has declared His purpose to have one college in the land where the Bible shall have its proper place in the education of the youth" (*ibid.*, 25, 26).

In her hard-hitting presentation Ellen White especially emphasized the role of the Bible and the need to get back on track with the goals of the founders.

"Too little attention," she proclaimed, "has been given to the education of young men for the ministry. This was the primary object to be secured in the establishment of the college" (*ibid.*, 22).

She was not against the arts and sciences. To the contrary, she advocated the study of the broader field of knowledge, but "at the same time to learn the requirements of His word" (*ibid.*, 21). It was the "mere" study of books that she objected to. Such an "education can be obtained at any college in the land" (*ibid.*, 22). Ellen White encouraged a more comprehensive learning, one that saw everything from the biblical perspective. "As an educating power the Bible is without a rival," as it challenges students "to grapple with difficult problems" and stretch the comprehension of their minds (*ibid.*, 24). Hers was a call to put Adventist education back on track.

Thank You, Father, for the prophetic voice in our past history. Help us to hear that same voice as we move through this day.

IN SEARCH OF PROPER EDUCATION—7

There is hope for a tree: If it is cut down, it will sprout again, and its new shoots will not fail. Job 14:7, NIV.

In the spring of 1882 the young tree of Adventist education had not just been pruned. It had been cut down.

But the drastic step had not been in vain. From the stump would sprout shoots in several directions that would vitalize the system and help it immensely in its search for proper education. Battle Creek College itself would reopen in the fall of 1883 with a resolve to be more faithful to its mission. And it would make significant progress in that direction during the 1880s.

But perhaps even more important was the fact that the former leaders of the Battle Creek school had scattered across the country. Both had learned lessons that would help them in the future as they strengthened Adventist education.

Goodloe Harper Bell set up camp in Massachusetts, where he established South Lancaster Academy in the spring of 1882, which eventually evolved into Atlantic Union College.

Sidney Brownsberger, meanwhile, headed west, where in April 1882 he founded Healdsburg Academy, an institution that became Healdsburg College and eventually Pacific Union College. Brownsberger vowed not to make the same mistakes twice. He began his tenure at Healdsburg with a very different educational frame of mind than that with which he had commenced his work in Battle Creek. After his experience in Michigan, he had resolved "never again to enter [denominational employment] except on the basis of the *Testimonies.*"

Prominently featured in the Healdsburg announcements and catalogues during the Brownsberger years was the fact that the school sought to give a balanced education between the bookish and the practical, the mental and the physical. In short, besides academics it would prepare its graduates for the world of work. Beyond that, the school was designed "to provide instruction especially adapted to the work of young men and women desiring to prepare themselves to enter the ministry." A modified reform institution itself, Healdsburg College would have a good influence on the one in Battle Creek.

"Old dogs can learn new tricks." And with God's help institutions and people can reform to more closely approximate His ideals. A start had been made, but the real revolution in Adventist education would come during the 1890s.

THOUGHTS ON LIFESTYLE AND DOCTRINE–1

Show me Your ways, O Lord;
Teach me Your paths. Ps. 25:4, NKJV.

You may have noted in our readings during the past few months that Ellen White took a larger role in the area of Adventist lifestyle practices than she did in the formation of doctrine. In doctrinal formation the procedure consisted of Bible study until a general consensus developed. At that point she sometimes received a vision that reaffirmed the consensus and helped those who still had questions to accept the correctness of the biblically derived conclusions of the group. Thus we can best think of Mrs. White's involvement in the formation of doctrine as one of confirmation rather than initiation.

The same does not hold true for her part in the area of Adventist lifestyle. But before moving on with that topic, we should recognize some differences between the realm of lifestyle and that of doctrine.

Even though twenty-first-century Adventists tend to see doctrinal and lifestyle issues as being of equal magnitude, that was not the position of the denomination's founders. Whereas they hammered out the basic doctrines through intense Bible study and held conferences to bring about consensus, lifestyle development followed a somewhat different pattern.

Perhaps the difference revolved around the fact that doctrines define a denomination. Doctrine among early Sabbatarian Adventists, therefore, was a crucial issue and received a great deal of attention. Lifestyle items, on the other hand, tend to be second-order concerns. Many lifestyle issues are not so much basic determiners of a denomination's identity as they are ways of life that facilitate its mission in spreading its doctrinal message.

From this perspective, health reform enables people to become better witnesses and missionaries and enables healed people to reach the place where they can better understand the gospel. Similarly, Christian education facilitates the development of both individual church members and gospel preachers. Again, tithing and sacrificial giving not only enable people to reflect the character of the one who so loved that He gave His only Son, but also forward God's mission on earth.

Lord, we appreciate both the doctrinal package and the lifestyle issues that have made Seventh-day Adventism a unique people. Help us to understand better their roles in our individual and collective lives.

THOUGHTS ON LIFESTYLE AND DOCTRINE—2

Walk as children of light. Eph. 5:8.

When it comes right down to it, there are only two ways to walk—in the light or in darkness. The Bible is clear on that point.

But what is light?

Many of us act as if correct doctrine or even biblical lifestyle is the light. Wrong! Christ is the light, and religion centers on our relationship to Him. Encompassed in that center is the problem of sin and God's solution to it in the cross of Christ.

Both doctrine and lifestyle are secondary issues. After all, you can believe all the right doctrines and live the right lifestyle and still be lost. Salvation has to do with your relationship to God through Jesus. Doctrine is not an end in itself, but is rather a means to understanding God better so that we can love Him more effectively. Lifestyle is a means even further from the center of the faith. Health reform, for example, enables us to have clearer minds so that we can understand doctrine and thus God better, and have sweeter personalities in order that we might be able to love our neighbors and God more fully.

At any rate, in the minds of Adventism's founders the realm of lifestyle and doctrine were not equal. Thus they put forth a great deal of effort to state their doctrines precisely, while basically neglecting most lifestyle issues until necessity and crisis forced them to take a position.

Adventists filled the resulting lifestyle void in various ways. Sometimes they formed a position through Bible study and conferences as a crisis arose, but at other times Ellen White took the lead in raising the issue, pointing to the solution, and indicating how that solution fit into the larger picture of the three angels' messages. That latter course was evident in such areas as health reform, while the former, as we have seen, predominated in such aspects as military service and tithing.

Because Ellen White often applied biblical principles to the everyday life of the church and its individual members, through the years her counsel has come increasingly to the center of discussions of Adventist lifestyle.

As we view the development of early Adventism we need to recognize that Ellen White had a dual role, with less activity in the realm of doctrinal formation and more in lifestyle development.

Guide us, Father, in helping us understand how the various parts of our religious faith package relate to each other and our lives.

RISE OF THE CAMP MEETING—1

For seven days you shall keep the feast to the Lord your God at the place which the Lord will choose. Deut. 16:15, RSV.

T he ancient Israelites punctuated the religious year with a series of festivals during which the people left their homes and journeyed to meet together for several days of religious edification.

While we have no exact parallel to the Jewish feasts in the Christian Era, the camp meeting had many of their attributes. Camp meetings had played a large role in the revivals of early nineteenth-century North America and in the Methodist and Millerite movements, but the first one specifically called by Seventh-day Adventists would take place in Wright, Michigan, in September 1868.

The *Review* announcement for it on August 18 stated that "this meeting has not been appointed for the purpose of spending a few days in recreation and vanity. Nor has it been appointed as a novelty, for the purpose of calling out the idle and the curious who might not otherwise be reached. Nor do we by this means merely seek to gather a large concourse of people, that we may thereby make a display of our strength. We have a very different object in view.

"We desire to call out as many of our brethren, both preachers and people, as we can, and also as many of our unconverted fellowmen as we may be able to interest in this meeting, that we may do them good.

"We want all who shall come to this meeting to come for the purpose of seeking God. We want our brethren to come for the purpose of seeking a new conversion. We want our preachers to set them in this an example worthy of imitation.

"We desire also to see many of our fellowmen who have no interest in Christ, or at least no knowledge of the present truth, converted to the Lord, and rejoicing in the light of His truth."

There we have it.

The purpose of the camp meeting was for the edification and instruction of the saints, the conversion of those church members who needed it, and to introduce the third angel's message to those who hadn't accepted it or even heard it.

In short, the camp meeting was to be a spiritual feast of the first order, put on by the Adventists for the entire community.

RISE OF THE CAMP MEETING—2

Now [Jesus] parents went to Jerusalem every year at the feast of the Passover.
Luke 2:41, RSV.

C amp meeting in early Adventism came to be an exciting time. People heard good preaching, they got to meet old friends, they broke their daily routine, they bought Adventist publications, and they received a spiritual blessing. The annual camp meeting was a mountaintop experience for those who attended.

The first official camp meeting in Wright, Michigan, from September 1-7, 1868, set the pattern for those to follow. Two round 60-foot tents housed general meetings while the people lived in smaller ones. Without a local K-Mart or Wal-Mart in which to purchase a cheap tent, the *Review* editors offered instruction on the construction of simple tents to serve families and churches.

Altogether there were 22 church tents, often with sleeping quarters divided off by hanging blankets or quilts so that the various families could have a bit of privacy. Other tents had a rope running down the middle on which attendees could hang blankets for the separation of the sexes.

Families and friends did their cooking on open fires, and the log circles on which they sat for meals offered excellent opportunities for fellowship. It must have been a great time for kids, but it was also the high point of the year for adults.

Yes, things weren't quite as comfortable as at home. And yes, one could have used a bit more privacy. And then again, they did demand a financial sacrifice, given the expenses of travel and downtime on the job. But the early Adventists thought such convocations were worth it in spite of the costs and inconveniences.

The annual camp meeting caught on after the one at Wright. The next year seven states held one. And after that they were everywhere in the Adventist world.

They are still around. Quite vigorous in some places and languishing in others, but always a blessing. If you haven't attended one lately, make the effort, especially to spend a few days and nights on the grounds. You will be blessed. Adventism would be better off today if it could have a revival of the yearly blessing.

Help us, Lord, to appreciate more fully each and every opportunity that You provide for blessing throughout the day, week, and year.

RISE OF THE CAMP MEETING—3

In this mountain shall the Lord of hosts make unto all people a feast of fat things.
Isa. 25:6.

F at things" in the Bible are good things, spiritual blessings, the fulfillment of God's promises. Not only did God speak of feasts of fat things in the Old Testament, but also of the great heavenly feast of the redeemed at the end of time. In the interim, as the early Adventists saw it, the camp meeting was a feast of fat things.

At the one back in 1868 Ellen White gave what we might think of as the keynote address. She spoke on the needs of the Advent people and got the attendees mentally prepared for the spiritual feast to come. As Uriah Smith phrased it, she "put the brethren upon the right train of thought at the very commencement." And "those who before had not seen the need of such a gathering, if any such there were, must have seen it, when its objects were thus clearly set forth."

Or as Joseph Clarke reported, "Sister White's testimony was such as to cause us to feel somewhat as the disciples when they queried 'Lord, is it I?' It was full of warning," urging the people of the possibilities in the meetings, and "to speak of heavenly things" rather than earthly.

The preaching services were central at Wright, James speaking six times, Ellen five, J. N. Andrews four, and Nathan Fuller one. Smith reported of the messages that they were "all aglow with the fire of present truth."

Afterward all the states wanted James and Ellen each year. They did their best to comply, sacrificing most of August through October for that purpose for years.

That Wright camp meeting saw some 300 people tented on the grounds, with several hundred staying in nearby homes, making up to 1,000 in attendance during the week. The weekend, of course, spiked the attendance figures, which soared to 2,000 and probably would have reached 3,000 except for the extremely heavy rain.

Later camp meetings often convened within easy traveling distance from the cities for the benefit of the large numbers of non-Adventists that they hoped would attend to hear the third angel's message and related truths. The most successful may have been the camp meeting held in Groveland, Massachusetts, when an estimated 20,000 persons gathered on Sunday to hear Ellen White speak on temperance.

What an opportunity! What a blessing!

THINKING ABOUT MISSIONS

Let it be known to you then that this salvation of God has been sent to the Gentiles; they will listen. Acts 28:28, RSV.

The plain fact is that the earliest Seventh-day Adventists didn't think much about missions. Believing that the end-time commissions to take the gospel to all the world in Matthew 24:14 and Revelation 10:11 and 14:6 had been fulfilled by the Protestants in the early nineteenth century and by the Millerites in the early 1840s, they had a shut-door belief toward both foreign and home missions. Their rather limited mission was to other disappointed Millerites, who needed to be comforted and led from the first and second angels' messages to the third.

While it is true that Ellen White had a vision in 1848 regarding one portion of the Adventist work being like streams of light that went clear around the world and a couple of other visions that pointed to extensive mission, the shut door Sabbatarians had no understanding or seeming interest in the implications.

Their shut-door phase ended about 1852 when they realized that they had been wrong on the close of probation. From that point on, James White proclaimed that they had an "open door" to preach the Sabbath and third angel's message to everyone, whether they had been in the Millerite movement or not.

The door to mission had cracked open a bit, but not very far. It would still be nearly a quarter of a century (1874) before Seventh-day Adventists would dispatch their first overseas missionary. Meanwhile, the Sabbatarian approach to missions moved with the speed of evolution rather than with that of revolution.

While some calls to mission emerged during the 1850s, there were also many suggestions as to why the church should not send overseas missionaries.

One of the more fascinating solutions to the mission issue came from Uriah Smith in 1859. The delay of the Advent was leading some to raise missiological questions. One *Review* reader inquired if the third angel's message needed to go outside of the United States.

Editor Smith replied that that might not be necessary since the United States consisted of people from all nations. Thus if the message reached one representative from each language group, that might be enough to say that it had gone to all tongues and nations.

Lord, how patient You are as You guide us step by step through a shortsighted existence.

MEET MICHAEL BELINA CZECHOWSKI

Jesus said to him, ". . . go and proclaim the kingdom of God." Luke 9:60, NIV.

Sabbatarian Adventist foreign mission happened in spite of the attitudes of the Adventists. The circulation of Adventist publications offered one avenue, as immigrants sent them back home and others mailed or shipped them to friends living in other countries.

As a result, Adventists in America were aware of converts in Ireland in the early 1860s. And by 1864 Africa had at least two believers in the third angel's message, and one of those would soon take the message to Australia.

Whether it liked it or not, the newly organized Seventh-day Adventist Church was being faced with the challenge of worldwide mission. Not only were there converts, but the converts kept requesting missionaries to visit their lands.

As on so many other occasions, James White was at the forefront of those who envisioned a larger mission for the denomination. A month before the organization of the General Conference in May 1863, he wrote in the *Review* that "ours is a worldwide message." And a few months before that, he had pointed out the need for sending a missionary to Europe. Then in June the *Review* reported that "the General Conference Executive Committee may send [B. F. Snook] a missionary to Europe before the close of 1863."

While the organization was so short on personnel that it couldn't release Snook from his current duties, it did have a minister who was more than eager to make the trip.

In 1858 Michael Belina Czechowski (an ex-Roman Catholic Polish priest who had converted to Sabbatarian Adventism in America in 1857) wrote: "How I would love to visit my own native country across the big waters, and tell them all about Jesus' coming and the glorious restitution, and how they must keep the commandments of God and the faith of Jesus."

But Czechowski was new to the faith and perceived by some to have personality instabilities. As a result, the Seventh-day people refused to send him. In frustration, the creative Pole requested the first-day Adventists to sponsor him. They did. But when he got to Europe he preached the seventh-day message.

The church is full of interesting people. But God manages to use all of us, in spite of our obvious lacks. Thanks be to the Father for His enabling grace.

CZECHOWSKI'S EUROPEAN MISSION

As my Father hath sent me, even so send I you. John 20:21.

M. B. Czechowski was an interesting Adventist to say the least. After gaining a mission sponsorship from a first-day Adventist group, he sailed to Italy where he preached Sabbatarian Adventist doctrines. His departure date was May 14, 1864, a full 10 years before the Seventh-day Adventists would send their first overseas missionary.

For 14 months he worked in the Waldensian villages in the Italian Alps. There he baptized several believers and formed the first Sabbatarian Adventist company outside of North America.

But overwhelming opposition eventually forced him in 1865 to move to Switzerland, where he visited house to house, preached in public halls, printed and sold tracts, and issued a periodical named *L'Evangile Eternal* ("The Everlasting Gospel"). When he departed Switzerland in 1868, he left behind about 40 baptized believers worshipping in several groups.

Not knowing exactly what he was teaching, but assuming that he had been "thrown off" by the Seventh-day Adventists, his first-day Adventist sponsors waxed eloquent on his virtues and continued to raise money for him, "saying with one voice, Go, and God be with you."

And go he did, preaching the Sabbatarian message in Romania, Hungary, and other parts of Europe. By the time of his death in Austria in 1876 he had laid the foundations for future Seventh-day Adventist activity throughout much of eastern and southern Europe.

By late 1869 the Seventh-day Adventist Church had discovered the nature of his European mission and saw God's providence in what Czechowski had done. At the 1870 General Conference session the denominational leaders specifically acknowledged God's hand in his mission. "In consequence of our fears to trust money with Bro. Czechowski, and our lack of care to patiently counsel him as to its proper use, God used our decided opponents to carry forward the work. . . . We acknowledge the hand of God in this."

As we will see in the days to come, Czechowski's mission would directly lead to the sending of J. N. Andrews, the first "official" Seventh-day Adventist missionary, in 1874.

Gradually and reluctantly the seventh-day people were waking up to the extent of their mission. But they didn't seem to be in much of a hurry.

MISSION TO FAR-OFF CALIFORNIA

Pray the Lord of the harvest to send out laborers into His harvest. Matt. 9:38, NKJV.

The first mission of the Seventh-day Adventist Church outside of the northeastern United States was to far-off California—a state separated from the rest of the republic by more than 1,500 miles of desert, forest, and mountains. The intervening wilderness between the two parts of the nation was not only great in distance but also difficult (and at times dangerous) to travel.

In the nineteenth century individual Adventists or denominational printed matter generally arrived in a locale long before the church had any formal activity there. Such was the situation in California. In 1859 Merritt G. Kellogg (older half brother to J. H. Kellogg) arrived in San Francisco after a difficult six-month trip across the country by railroad, wagon, and oxcart. He was probably the first Adventist in the state.

Two years later Kellogg (a lay believer) preached a series of meetings in San Francisco and baptized 14. Four years later the group of believers there decided to send $133 in gold to Battle Creek to pay the travel expenses of a minister. But the church had no one to send.

Then in 1867 Kellogg returned to the East for a few months to earn an M.D. degree at Trall's Hygieo-Therapeutic College. While in the East he attended the 1868 General Conference session, where he appealed for a missionary for California. But who should go? James White asked.

In response, J. N. Loughborough related dreams and told of strong impressions he had had relative to holding tent meetings in California. The leadership soon agreed that he should go. But should he venture alone? After all, James noted, Christ sent them out two by two. At that point D. T. Bourdeau arose and stated that he had felt convicted that it was time for a move, and that he and his wife had come to the session with everything they had already packed. They were ready to go wherever the church directed.

So it was that the two Adventist preachers arrived in San Francisco in July 1868. There they found a letter from Ellen White telling them not to be miserly in their work in California. "You cannot labor in California," she wrote, "as you did in New England. Such strict economy would be considered 'penny-wise' by Californians." That was good counsel. But where should they pitch their evangelistic tent? Rental for a lot in San Francisco was more than they could even think about. They prayed, and God would answer.

The dedication of those early believers astounds me. How many of us would attend a General Conference session with everything we have ready to move as the Lord directed? How is our "dedication quotient" today?

DREAMERS OF CALIFORNIA DREAMS

He shall send his angel before thee. Gen. 24:7.

God works in mysterious ways. Several weeks prior to the arrival of Loughborough and Bourdeau in San Francisco a New York newspaper reached California containing an item that two evangelists were about to sail for California to hold religious meetings in a large tent.

The article came to the attention of a group of Christians in Petaluma, a village about 40 miles north of San Francisco, who prayed that the Lord would bless the evangelists.

Among the Petaluma believers was a Mr. Wolf, who dreamed that he saw two men kindling a fire that made a brilliant light, but that the local ministers would seek to extinguish the flames. But their attempts only made the fire burn more brightly. Wolf learned in his dream that the two men were the same two mentioned in the New York newspaper, and that the Petaluma believers needed to help them. Thus it was that they sent one of their company to search for the preachers in booming San Francisco. With 150,000 people in the city, he wasn't quite sure where to start. So he went to the wharf, asked if anyone had recently delivered a large tent, and got the address. Within an hour he found the two evangelists.

Without telling Loughborough and Bourdeau about the dream he invited them to Petaluma, where they could dine with Mr. Wolf, who would be able to tell the group there if these were the same men he had seen in his dream. They were. As a result, the Petaluma group arranged for tent meetings. Some 40 persons attended. But the number rapidly swelled to 200 and then to 400. Soon it was necessary to roll up the walls of the tent so those outside could hear the sermons.

Before long the opposition predicted in the dream began as local ministers and even the leaders of the group of believers who had brought them to Petaluma began to work against the Adventist evangelists, especially after the Sabbath doctrine came up.

But the meetings closed with 20 accepting the teachings and a company of believers being organized. Within a short time they had another eight or nine groups organized in Santa Rosa and other parts of Sonoma County.

God had worked in a mysterious way. And He still does. He operates in ways that we have no knowledge of. We are not alone in our labors for Him here on earth. The Lord still sends His angels before us.

CZECHOWSKI'S FOLLOWERS
DISCOVER THE *REVIEW*

Come over to Macedonia and help us. Acts 16:9, RSV.

Paul's dream of the Macedonian call for missionaries finds itself reflected countless times in Adventist history. It would be so with Czechowski's European converts.

That interesting man, who did so much to establish the Adventist presence in Europe, never told his converts about the Seventh-day Adventist Church in North America. When asked where he had learned what he was teaching, his answer was "from the Bible." As far as they knew, his converts were the only people in the world who believed the teachings of the Bible as they did. But that ignorance didn't last forever. Eventually Albert Vuilleumier, one of the Swiss believers, found a copy of the *Review and Herald* in a room that Czechowski had occupied during a recent visit. Vuilleumier's English wasn't perfect, but he could understand enough to grasp the fact that there existed in America a religious group that taught the same views as Czechowski.

That discovery led to a letter to Uriah Smith, editor of the *Review*. The surprised leaders in Battle Creek responded with an invitation to the Swiss believers to send a representative to the 1869 General Conference session. So it was that James Erzberger came to America.

Erzberger himself was a recent convert. He had been a theological student studying for the ministry when he first encountered the Swiss Sabbathkeepers. Examining their beliefs to see if they were true, he soon became convinced.

Although Erzberger arrived in Battle Creek too late for the session, he remained for 15 months, living most of the time in the home of James and Ellen White. His stay was one of study as he perfected his English and explored more fully the Adventist message. When he returned to Switzerland, he went as the first officially ordained Seventh-day Adventist minister in Europe.

Meanwhile, Czechowski had become quite disturbed over the contact of his Swiss converts with the American church. He soon left for Romania, where he founded the first Sabbathkeeping groups in that country.

The Swiss experience had two other major results. First, it prompted a heightened discussion of mission among the Adventists in America. And, second, it led to the persistent call for a missionary to go to Europe.

The calls from Macedonia still come. And God still needs people who will respond.

ALIVE TO FOREIGN MISSION—1

All the ends of the world shall remember and turn unto the Lord. Ps. 22:27.

The contact from Switzerland changed Adventism forever. The once-anti-foreign-mission people soon found themselves on a path that would eventually take them to the ends of the earth.

Even though Erzberger failed to arrive in time for the 1869 General Conference session, the implications of his visit were pregnant with meaning.

That session saw the creation of a Seventh-day Adventist Missionary Society. "The object of this society," read the action that created it, "shall be to send the truths of the third angel's message to foreign lands, and to distant parts of our own country, by means of missionaries, papers, books, tracts, etc." In introducing the resolution, James White noted that the church was receiving "almost daily applications to send publications to other lands."

A few months later Andrews noted the providence of God in the work of Czechowski. And in 1871 the General Conference session voted to "do what lies in our power to assist the spread of the truth" to the countries of Europe.

Meanwhile, Ellen White did her part to encourage the denomination's missionary outreach. In December 1871 she had a vision that showed her that the Seventh-day Adventists had "truths of vital importance" that were "to test the world." Thus young Adventists should qualify themselves in "other languages, that God may use them as mediums to communicate His saving truth to those of other nations" (LS 203, 204).

Not only was the denomination to send its publications to foreign peoples, but "living preachers" as well. "Missionaries," she asserted, "are needed to go to other nations to preach the truth." The Adventist "message of warning" was to "go to all nations" that the light of its truth might test them. "We have not one moment to lose," she penned. "If we have been careless in this matter, it is high time we were now in earnest to redeem the time, lest the blood of souls be found on our garments." "This will be attended with considerable expense, but expense should in no case hinder the performance of this work" (*ibid.,* 205, 206).

Adventism was being transformed again. This time it involved the opening of their missiological eyes. The God who always leads His people was still guiding them step by step.

ALIVE TO FOREIGN MISSION–2

The earth shall be full of the knowledge of the Lord, as the waters cover the sea. Isa. 11:9.

I n spite of the fact that some leading Adventist ministers still preached as late as 1872 that the taking of the gospel to all the world referred to in Matthew 24:14 had seen its fulfillment, the momentum for mission continued to gain force among Adventists. But where to get the educated personnel was the problem, one that led to moves in 1873 and 1874 toward founding the denomination's first college.

By the summer of 1873 James White was not only requesting a college, but urging that J. N. Andrews go to Switzerland that autumn in answer to the request for a missionary from the Swiss Adventists. That November saw White summon a special session of the General Conference to discuss a missionary. But still nothing happened.

It is significant that White's featured sermon at the November 1873 session was an exposition of Revelation 10 in connection with foreign missions. Earlier in the year he had applied the imperative of Revelation 14:6 to preach the everlasting gospel to all the world and the command of Revelation 10:11 to "prophesy again before many peoples, and nations, and tongues, and kings" to the worldwide commission of the Seventh-day Adventist Church in the wake of the Millerite disappointment. Those two texts, along with Matthew 24:14, would eventually impel Adventist missions to every corner of the earth as the denomination sought to fulfill what it came to see as its prophetic role in history.

In January 1874 White established the *True Missionary*. Adventism's first missionary periodical's pages urged the sending of foreign missionaries. Ellen White shared the broader vision of her husband. During April 1874 she had an "impressive dream" that helped overcome the remaining opposition to missions. "You are entertaining too limited ideas of the work for this time," the angelic messenger told her. "Your house is the world. . . . The message will go in power to all parts of the world, to Oregon, to Europe, to Australia, to the islands of the sea, to all nations, tongues, and peoples." She "was shown" that the mission work was far more extensive "than our people have imagined, or ever contemplated or planned." As a result, she called for a larger faith that would express itself through action (LS 208-210).

"Larger faith." That was the need then. It is the need now.

Increase our faith, Father, that we might see Your will, even in our lives.

J. N. Andrews Goes to Europe

And when they had fasted and prayed, and laid their hands on them, they sent [Barnabas and Saul] away. Acts 13:3.

When things finally move they can do so rapidly. So it was with Adventist mission. In August 1874 the General Conference voted that J. N. Andrews should go to Europe "as soon as practicable." A month later he sailed for Switzerland as the first "official" Seventh-day Adventist foreign missionary. He arrived on October 16.

In Switzerland Andrews found several small congregations of Sabbathkeepers already in existence—the work of Czechowski and Erzberger. Andrews more fully indoctrinated those believers during his first meetings with them. Beyond that, within two months of his arrival he had heard of congregations of believers in Prussia and Russia and had become convinced that "there are Sabbathkeeping Christians in most of the countries of Europe." His plan was to develop those already-existing core groups.

But how could he locate them? To answer that question he utilized what seems to me to be an unlikely plan. He hoped to reach them by advertising his desire to correspond with them "in the most widely circulated papers of Europe." Surprise of surprises. The "want ad" approach to mission worked with a fair degree of success. Within a short time Seventh-day Adventists had missions in England, Scandinavia, and Germany, as well as in Switzerland. From those bases the Adventist message would reach other European nations.

Those operating the new missions often consisted of first-generation European immigrants who had converted to Adventism in the United States and had then been encouraged to return to their native countries. Such nationals had the advantage of not only knowing the language and culture, but they also nearly always had a group of acquaintances with whom to begin their ministry.

As we have repeatedly noted, God leads His people step by step. The first stage (1844-1850) in Adventist mission development provided time for the building of a doctrinal platform. The second (1850-1874) allowed for the emergence of a power base in North America for the support of a foreign mission program. And the third (1874-1889) would create further development in Europe and other parts of the "civilized" world so that Adventism would be prepared to take its message to "all the world" in the years following 1890.

A MATURING MISSION

What is the kingdom of God like? And to what shall I compare it? It is like a grain of mustard seed which a man took and sowed in his garden; and it grew and became a tree. Luke 13:18, 19, RSV.

By the early 1880s the European mission had reached its adolescent stage. Several factors indicate the mission's increasing importance to the denomination.

One of them was a series of visits by prominent Adventist leaders sent by the General Conference to tour the various European missions between 1882 and 1887. The first was S. N. Haskell in 1882. Haskell recommended publishing in more languages and helped the Europeans develop a more functional organizational structure.

More important, however, were the tours by G. I. Butler (president of the General Conference) in 1884 and of Ellen White and her son (W. C. White) from 1885 through 1887. Such visits not only strengthened the Seventh-day Adventist Church in Europe—they demonstrated the denomination's interest in its mission program. Slowly but surely Adventism was becoming a world church.

A second set of indicators regarding the growing maturation of the European mission were organizational developments. Foremost was the first general meeting of workers from the different Seventh-day Adventist missions in Europe in 1882 "for consultation concerning the general wants of the cause." Closely related to the development of the European Council of Seventh-day Adventists was the commencement of publication of German, Italian, and Romanian periodicals in 1884. One in French had existed since 1879.

Outside of the European mission, the Adventists established General Conference-sponsored missions among the European Protestants of Australia and New Zealand in 1885 and of South Africa in 1887. It is of interest to note that all of those countries had had lay members prior to the arrival of official missionaries.

And those new missions would soon join North America and Europe as home bases for the sending of missionaries to other nations for the next phase of Adventist mission development—the taking of the three angels' messages to *every* nation throughout the world. That phase, beginning about 1889, was a logical outgrowth of the developing Adventist interpretation of the to-every-kindred-tongue-and-people passages of Revelation 14:6, Revelation 10:11, and Matthew 24:14.

The hope of Adventism is a completed mission. *Come, Lord Jesus,* the early Adventists prayed. *Come, Lord Jesus, and come quickly* is still the Adventist daily prayer.

AND WHY EUROPE?

These twelve Jesus sent forth, and commanded them, saying, Go not into the way of the Gentiles. Matt. 10:5.

The question has often been asked why Seventh-day Adventism should have chosen Central Europe . . . as the first field for their foreign mission operations," B. L. Whitney stated in 1886 in the first paragraph of *Historical Sketches of the Foreign Missions of the Seventh-day Adventists,* the first Adventist book on overseas missions. Part of the answer has to do with "Czechowski's preparatory mission," but there is more to it than that.

J. N. Andrews provides us with a crucial insight into Whitney's query in his first letter home after arriving in Europe. He wrote that "I firmly believe that God has much people in Europe who are ready to obey his holy law and to reverence the Sabbath, and to wait for his Son from heaven. I came here to give my life to the proclamation of these sacred truths concerning the near advent of Christ and the observance of the Sabbath."

In other words, Andrews believed that his task was to present the Adventist doctrines to those who were already Christian. His was not a mission of general Christianity to pagans. Responsibility to the latter would remain outside the scope of Adventist missiology until the 1890s.

Borge Schantz accurately summarizes the Adventist attitude between 1874 and 1890 when he observes that "mission to non-Christians was approved of and praised" by the Adventists, but "it was regarded as the task that other evangelical mission societies could take care of. When they had brought people to Christ, the SDAs were committed to bringing them the last warning" and the distinctive Adventist doctrines.

Such an approach grew out of the Adventists' understanding that they were to call people "out of Babylon." James White had earlier expressed that viewpoint explicitly when he wrote that Adventists needed a missionary spirit, "not to send the gospel to the heathen, but to extend the warning throughout the realms of corrupted Christianity."

With that perspective in mind, it is not surprising that the denomination began its mission work in the heartland of Christian Europe. It echoed the early missionary labors of Paul, who preached to the Jews first, and only later to the Gentiles.

Thank You, God, for light. As You have given Your church a wider vision across time, we pray that in the same way You will widen and deepen our own personal visions.

THE WAY THINGS WORKED:
THE CASE OF J. G. MATTESON

Each one should use whatever gift he has received to serve others, faithfully administering God's grace in its various forms. 1 Peter 4:10, NIV.

Sometimes things actually do work well. Sometimes everything does seem to come out as God would have it. Such was the case of John Gottlieb Matteson. Born in Denmark in 1835, he immigrated with his parents to Wisconsin in 1854, bringing with him a good education but also the skepticism of so many of his native land. Considering himself a freethinker, one of his enjoyable pastimes was to bait preachers with questions they couldn't answer.

But open-minded baiters can meet their Waterloo. So it was when Matteson heard a preacher talk enthusiastically about the beauty of heaven. Having been raised in the atmosphere of the "dead state churches of old Europe," he "had never known a living religion." That experience led to a chain of events in which, he recalls, "in the forest alone I found Jesus as my personal Saviour" in 1859. Soon after his conversion he felt called to preach. And preach he did, even though he didn't know his Bible very well. God blessed from the beginning as people responded to his obvious sincerity. In 1860 he entered the Baptist theological seminary in Chicago and in 1862 was ordained a Baptist pastor.

So far so good. But it got better. In 1863 he accepted the Seventh-day Adventist message. His congregation requested that he preach his new faith to them, which he happily did. For six months he presented a series of sermons on Adventist beliefs, with the result that all joined the Seventh-day Adventist Church except one family.

An effective preacher, Matteson developed Danish-Norwegian churches across the Midwestern states. Then in 1872 he got the idea to publish a periodical in the language of his converts. The *Advent Tidende* became the first Seventh-day Adventist periodical in a language other than English.

Copies soon found their way back to Scandinavia to make converts. In a pattern that would repeat itself in many lands, the new believers soon wrote to America requesting a missionary. Matteson accepted the call in 1877 and the next 11 years he established churches in Denmark, Norway, and Sweden. While there he organized the first conference outside of North America (Denmark in 1880) and founded the first publishing house outside the United States. During his ministry he would lead some 2,000 people into the faith he loved.

Matteson's life illustrates the way things should work.

Thank You, Father, for such blessings in the past. We pray for them in the present.

THE WAY THINGS DIDN'T WORK: THE CASE OF HANNAH MORE

I was a stranger, and ye took me not in. Matt. 25:43.

As we saw yesterday, events in the Adventist life of J. G. Matteson worked out the way they should. On the opposite side of the ledger is the case of Hannah More.

Like Matteson, More had an excellent education for the times. And like Matteson, she had excellent potential to make a contribution to Adventism.

An avid Bible student, she had committed the entire New Testament to memory. She had a broad Christian work experience as a teacher, school administrator, missionary of the American Board of Commissioners of Foreign Missions to the displaced Cherokee and Choctaw tribes in Oklahoma, and missionary to West Africa under the sponsorship of the American Missionary Association.

In 1862 she met S. N. Haskell, who loaded her down with good Adventist books, including J. N. Andrews' *History of the Sabbath*. Returning to Africa, she read herself into Adventism. That's the good part of her story.

Rejected by her former community because of her Adventism, she traveled to Battle Creek, Michigan, in the spring of 1867, hoping to find comfort and work among fellow believers. That is where the bad part of the story begins.

Arriving in Battle Creek when the Whites were on a travel itinerary, she was unable to find either a job or a place to live among church members. Rejected by the Adventists, she eventually found a home with a former mission colleague in northern Michigan.

Remarkably, given the way the Adventist community treated her, she did not give up her faith. The Whites, realizing the tragedy, began corresponding with Hannah, pledging to help her relocate in Battle Creek in the spring. But such was not to be. Hannah More became ill in February and passed to her rest on March 2, 1868. From Ellen White's perspective, "she died a martyr to the selfishness and covetousness of professed commandment keepers" (1T 674).

Years later, as the Adventists were trying to get started in foreign missions she wrote, "Oh, how much we need Hannah More to aid us at this time in reaching other nations! Her extensive knowledge of missionary fields would give us access to those of other tongues whom we cannot now approach. God brought this gift . . . ; but we prized not the gift." She went on to deplore the loss of what Hannah could have contributed to Adventist mission (3T 407, 408).

Forgive us, our Father. Help us to have a heart like Yours.

FAMILY AND MISSION

In thee shall all families of the earth be blessed. Gen. 12:3.

Our text in some ways reminds me of the "other" James Bond. His brother Seth became one of the first Adventists in California in 1872 through the ministry of J. N. Loughborough. Jamming his pockets full of tracts, his first missionary target was James, a farmer in California's central valley.

Finding the man plowing with a 10-mule team, he lost no time in beginning his mission. He talked his new faith in the field, followed it up in the barn, and continued on into the house. James' wife, Sarah, a devout Baptist, stood for this for a few days, until her patience gave out. But finally, after telling Seth that they appreciated his visits, she noted that if he didn't stop talking about this Sabbath business he had better move on.

"Sarah," he replied, "if you can show me just one text in the New Testament that implies we are obliged to keep the first day of the week, I'll say no more."

"That's easy," she answered.

Getting James to halt his plowing until they found the passage, they read the New Testament together. Four days later they arrived at the last verse of Revelation, but without their text.

Saturday morning James Bond went out and fed and harnessed his mules, preparing to plow. Coming back into the house, he ate breakfast, led family worship, and returned to the barn. About nine o'clock his wife saw the plow standing idle in the field. Fearing he had been hurt, she rushed out, only to discover that he was sitting on a box reading Sabbath tracts. At that point both became Sabbatarians.

Later, under Ellen White's urging, this father of 11 became a medical doctor. Five of his sons became ministers and seven of his children became foreign missionaries.

Two of them, Frank Starr Bond and Walter Guy Bond, pioneered the Adventist mission in Spain in 1903. Walter would give his life there 11 years later at the age of 35, apparently a victim of poisoning. Both of them experienced the trials of Paul as they were stoned and forcefully driven out of villages.

I have a personal interest in this story because my wife (Elizabeth, or "Bonnie," Bond) is the granddaughter of Frank and the great-granddaughter of James.

Families make a difference! How our children relate to the Lord, the church, and to service is shaped to a large extent by fathers and mothers in the faith.

A DIFFERENT KIND OF MISSIONARY: THE CASE OF GEORGE KING

For as the rain and the snow come down from heaven, and return not thither but water the earth, . . . so shall my word be that goes forth from my mouth; it shall not return to me empty, but it shall accomplish that which I purpose, and prosper in the thing for which I sent it. Isa. 55:10, 11, RSV.

George King wanted to be a preacher. He had only one problem—he couldn't preach. His stumbling speech and lack of education convinced James White that he had no gift for preaching. But Ellen White, with her mother's heart, convinced Richard Godsmark, a farmer near Battle Creek, to take him in for the winter so that he could have a trial run in the spring.

With Godsmark's encouragement, young King spent his spare time preaching to the empty chairs in the parlor. Then came the time for the trial sermon in public. "Disaster" is the only word for the experience. At that point Godsmark suggested to King that he preach in a different sort of way—by selling books door to door. As a result, he began peddling small books and subscriptions to *Signs of the Times.* His first week, with sales totaling 62 cents, wasn't exactly a shining success. But King liked the work.

On the other hand, this colporteur who wanted to preach desired to see the entire three angels' messages placed before the people. Thus in the fall of 1880 he convinced the managers of the Adventist publishing house in Battle Creek to bind Uriah Smith's books on Daniel and Revelation in one volume so that he could sell them. If such a volume included dramatic illustrations of the beasts and the other symbols that it treated, he was sure he could easily market the book.

The managers weren't so sure, but they bound up a few copies. King's success astounded everyone. The next year the publishing house put out a handsomely illustrated new edition of *Daniel and the Revelation.*

Given King's growing success and his enthusiastic recruiting abilities, soon others entered the field. And with that a new Adventist career came into being.

Colporteuring became one more way that God's last-day message began to reach people around the world. They bought the books, read them, and joined the church. Truly God's promise to Isaiah was being fulfilled. As He sent the rain to bless the crops and feed earth's peoples, so the printed word went out and converted the minds and hearts of people around the world. Before closing, I should note that I bought my very first Christian book from a colporteur.

The moral of the George King story? Just because we can't preach doesn't mean that God can't use all of us.

THE ADVENTIST QUADRILATERAL: A DESIGN FOR MISSION

Now may the God of peace make you holy in every way, and may your whole spirit and soul and body be kept blameless until the day when our Lord Jesus Christ comes again. 1 Thess. 5:23, NLT.

The biblical view of human beings is interested in their total health. Scripture is not merely concerned with people's spiritual lives, but also their mental and physical ones. Thus the healing and teaching aspects of Jesus' ministry.

The missiological corollary of such a theology leads to a program that not only touches people's spiritual nature but also seeks to meet their mental and physical needs. As a result, there eventually developed what I would like to call the Adventist missiological quadrilateral.

The quadrilateral found its birth in Battle Creek, where the church established its publishing ministry in the early 1850s, its conference structure in 1861, its initial medical institution in 1866, and its first educational institution in 1872. Adventist leadership may not have been completely conscious of what they were doing at the time, but those institutions provided an approach to mission that reached the needs of the whole person. Thus it provided a model for mission.

With that in mind, we should not see it as accidental that Adventists exported the quadrilateral to California, the denomination's first "overseas" mission field. Things got under way in a more formal way when in February 1873 the 238 believers from seven churches organized the California Conference.

The next step took place in 1874 and 1875 with the publishing of *Signs of the Times* and the formation of the Pacific Seventh-day Adventist Publishing Association (Pacific Press today) in Oakland. Then in 1878 came the Rural Health Retreat (St. Helena Hospital today) in the northern part of the state. Finally they established in 1882 what became Healdsburg College and eventually Pacific Union College.

The European mission followed the same pattern during the 1870s and 1880s. Beginning in the 1890s the quadrilateral would spread around the world as Seventh-day Adventism sought to better the lives of people in every way.

God has a message for earth's people. And that message is not merely theological. It concerns healthier living, better thinking, and social responsibility.

We thank You, Lord, for a balanced message and a balanced mission. Help me to live a balanced life this very day.

WHAT IS THE AUTHORITY OF THE GENERAL CONFERENCE?—1

By what authority are you doing these things, or who gave you authority to do them? Mark 11:28, RSV.

By what authority?

A good question. One that we ought to ask and think through, not only in relationship to Christ but to the leadership of His church on earth.

Not everyone was happy with the newly formed General Conference of Seventh-day Adventists in the 1860s. The most active objectors were the first president and secretary of the recently organized Iowa Conference—B. F. Snook and W. H. Brinkerhoff.

They opposed a strong church organization and conducted a campaign of criticism and disaffection against the general leadership of the church, especially James and Ellen White. In July 1865 the Iowa Conference constituency replaced Snook with George I. Butler. Subsequently Snook and Brinkerhoff left the denomination, taking some of the members with them to form the Marion Party. Unlike most offshoots from Seventh-day Adventism, the Marion Party did not disappear. Today we know it as the Church of God (Seventh Day).

While not all were happy with the 1861/1863 organization, it seems to have been serving its purpose during the years after the establishment of the system. The Marion rebellion would be the last significant schism in the denomination until early in the twentieth century.

Ten years after the founding of the General Conference, James White continued to praise the results of organization: "When we consider the small beginning, and in how obscure a manner this work commenced, the rapidity and soundness of our growth, the perfection of and efficiency of our organization, the great work it has already accomplished. . . . When we look at all these things, and see how God has prospered us, we that are connected with this work can say, 'What hath God wrought!'"

Yet, in spite of the accolades, all was not well. Tensions existed in the Adventist camp over the nature and extent of the authority of the General Conference, especially in relation to the state conferences. Those tensions came to a head in 1873.

And they have not disappeared more than 130 years later. It therefore behooves us to take a look at the topic in Adventist history.

Thank You, Lord, for wills to serve and for heads to think and for hearts to care. Help us to use all of them to their full capacity as we relate to You and the church.

WHAT IS THE AUTHORITY OF
THE GENERAL CONFERENCE?–2

He called his twelve disciples together, and gave them power and authority.
Luke 9:1.

N o Bible-believing Christian doubts the fact that Christ gave authority to His 12 disciples. But we have a bit more difficulty with authority issues in our day.

The tensions in Adventism on the topic became evident in 1873, when James White faced the issue head-on. First, he stated his positive convictions. While noting the belief that "we unhesitatingly express our firm conviction that organization with us was by the direct providence of God" and that God's "guiding hand" could be seen in leading them to an organization that after a "lapse of more than ten years has not revealed defects which have demanded changes," White also sounded a defensive note in discussing the role of the General Conference.

In particular, he wrote that it is "simply an insult to our system of organization" to let the president (George I. Butler) and other members of the General Conference Executive Committee do all the work at the state camp meetings and then "not show proper regard for their position and judgment in the important business of the State Conferences."

In that mode, White observed that "our General Conference is the highest earthly authority with our people, and is designed to take charge of the entire work in this and in all other countries." Thus "the officers of our State Conferences and, also, those of our institutions . . . are expected to respect our General Conference Committee as the men appointed to take the general supervision of the cause in all its branches and interests."

White went on to claim that General Conference representatives should be present at each business convocation of the state conferences. To disregard the proper role of the General Conference leaders, he told his readers, "is an insult to God's providential dealings with us, and a sin of no small magnitude."

We should keep in mind that James White said quite a bit when he stated that the "General Conference is the highest earthly authority" in Adventism, reflecting his wife's earlier sentiments.

Now, we know that the immediate context of that statement relates to the local conferences. But what are the implications for the life of the church and even my personal life? The larger question for each of us is How should I relate to my church? That is an especially important issue since God is a Diety of order rather than confusion.

WHAT IS THE AUTHORITY OF THE GENERAL CONFERENCE?—3

Christ is the head of the church. Eph. 5:23, RSV.

C larification often comes through give-and-take discussion. That was certainly the case as the church wrestled with the issue of the authority of the General Conference.

Possibly taking his cue from James White's pronouncements on the topic, George I. Butler, president of the General Conference since 1871, also decided to write on the power of the General Conference president.

"There never was any great movement in this world without a leader; and in the very nature of things there cannot be," he asserted in his address on leadership to the November 1873 General Conference session. While Christ is head of the church, he argued, it is "no small thing" to hinder an individual when God has called him to the leadership of His cause. Butler had no doubt that James White had played a role akin to that of Moses, and that in all matters of expediency in the Adventist cause it was right "to give [White's] judgment the preference."

While Butler was ostensibly writing to support James White as the true leader of the Adventist church, undoubtedly he was at the same time seeking to strengthen his own position.

In response, the General Conference session delegates resolved "that we fully endorse the position taken in the paper read by Eld. Butler on Leadership. And we express our firm conviction, that our failure to appreciate the guiding hand of God in the selection of his instruments to lead out in this work has resulted in serious injury to the prosperity of the cause, and in spiritual loss to ourselves." The resolution concluded with a commitment by the delegates to "faithfully . . . regard" the principles that Butler had set forth.

The far-reaching claims regarding individual leadership made by Butler left both of the Whites distinctly uncomfortable—not only because Butler had cast them in the role of Moses, but because they saw dangers in his glorification of human leaders.

James felt that he had to meet Butler's claims publicly in the *Signs* and the *Review*. He left no doubt in anyone's mind that Christ is the head of the church and that He had never appointed one particular disciple to direct the affairs of His church.

Lord, as both members and leaders in Your church, help us never to lose sight of the Christ who is ultimately in charge.

WHAT IS THE AUTHORITY OF THE GENERAL CONFERENCE?—4

And he has put all things under his feet and has made him the head over all things for the church, which is his body. Eph. 1:22, 23, RSV.

I t is easy to take either too high or too low a view of church leadership. Butler, we noted yesterday, erred on the side of too high.

Ellen White joined her husband in opposing Butler's perspective. Asserting that he, in defense of his independent style of leadership and rather highhanded manner, had developed his ideas of leadership for his "own benefit," she went on to deny the validity of his principle of one-man leadership.

On the other hand, while rejecting the authority of any one person as leader, she upheld the prerogative of the General Conference as a body. "You," she penned to Butler, "did not seem to have a true sense of the power that God has given His church in the voice of the General Conference. . . . When this power which God has placed in the church is accredited to one man, and he is invested with the authority to be judgment for other minds, then the true Bible order is changed. . . . Your position on leadership is correct, if you give to the highest organized authority in the church what you have given to one man. God never designed that His work should bear the stamp of one man's mind and one man's judgment" (3T 492, 493).

Acknowledging that James of necessity had led during the early days of the church, Ellen went on to say that once Adventists had established organization, "it was the proper time for my husband to cease to act longer as one man to stand under the responsibilities and carry the heavy burdens" (3T 501).

In a pamphlet containing her letter to Butler, James attached a section on leadership in which he noted that he had "never professed to be a leader in any other sense than that which makes all of Christ's ministers leaders."

Thus James and Ellen White both stood firmly for the power of the General Conference as a body and against the type of individualistic power proposed by Butler.

Most modern Seventh-day Adventists don't give much thought to the question of church authority. We merely speak out about what we like or don't care for in leadership.

But this topic is of crucial importance in both the Bible and in our history. We do well in taking a look at what is church authority and how it should impact our lives.

WHAT IS THE AUTHORITY OF THE GENERAL CONFERENCE?—5

We will hold to the truth in love, becoming more and more in every way like Christ, who is the head of his body, the church. Eph. 4:15, NLT.

Sometimes we learn only after we have been fairly well beat down. Thus it was with General Conference president George I. Butler. With both of the Whites, whom he highly respected, opposing him on the idea of individualistic leadership, he repented of his actions, resigned from the presidency, bought up and burned every obtainable copy of his *Leadership* booklet (some 960), and at the 1875 General Conference session proposed a resolution rescinding the endorsement of his leadership ideas.

But instead of rushing through an action on such an important topic, the convocation appointed a committee to study the matter. The 1877 session, acting on the committee's report, voted to rescind approval for all portions of Butler's *Leadership* tract that taught "that the leadership of the body is confined to any one man." The 1877 meeting further voted that "the highest authority under God among Seventh-day Adventists is found in the will of the body of that people, as expressed in the decisions of the General Conference when acting within its proper jurisdiction, and that such decisions should be submitted to by all without exception, unless they can be shown to conflict with the word of God and the rights of individual conscience."

Thus by 1877 Butler and James White, who alternated in holding the General Conference presidency from 1869 to 1888 (White, 1869-1871, 1874-1880; Butler, 1871-1874, 1880-1888), were in general outward agreement on the authority of the General Conference as a body.

Unfortunately, albeit unavoidably, the General Conference delegation from the local conferences met with each other for only a few weeks each year. That resulted quite naturally in Adventists looking to the president of the General Conference and the members of its small executive committee for leadership. That was especially true when forceful individuals such as Butler and White held the presidency. Both men had a tendency to take too much authority into their own hands and thus leaned more toward Butler's one-person leadership style in practice than in theory.

We find an important lesson here that affects all of us, whether our leadership be in the conference office, the local church, or even the family. No matter what we believe in our heads about leadership, nearly all of us find ourselves tempted to "take over."

Help us, Father, as we deal with our natural inclinations. Make us better leaders.

WHAT IS THE AUTHORITY OF THE GENERAL CONFERENCE?—6

He who has an ear, let him hear what the Spirit says to the churches. Rev. 2:29, RSV.

Some of us are just plain hard of hearing. General Conference president Butler seemed to have that affliction. Ellen White repeatedly counseled both him and her husband on the dangers of their one-person leadership style.

Her frustration with Butler came to a head about the time of the 1888 General Conference session. Soon after the meetings she wrote that "Elder Butler . . . has been in office three years too long and now all humility and lowliness of mind have departed from him. He thinks his position gives him such power that his voice is infallible" (Lt 82, 1888).

Looking back after another three years, she stated: "I hope there will never be the slightest encouragement given to our people to put such wonderful confidence in finite, erring man as has been placed in Elder Butler, for ministers are not as God, and too much reliance has been placed upon Elder Butler in the past. . . . It is because men have been encouraged to look to one man to think for them, to be conscience for them, that they are now so inefficient, and unable to stand at their post of duty as faithful sentinels for God" (Lt 14, 1891).

It was easier for Butler to refine his ideas on the "great men" theory of church leadership verbally than to stop actually practicing them. Given human nature, that is a perennial problem that those in leadership positions have continued to struggle with across time.

That unfortunate fact of life also led Ellen White to make some statements regarding the authority of the General Conference in the 1890s. Several times during the decade she raised the issue. In 1891, for example, she wrote that "I was obliged to take the position that there was not the voice of God in the General Conference management and decisions. Methods and plans would be devised that God did not sanction, and yet Elder Olsen [General Conference president from 1888 to 1897] made it appear that the decisions of the General Conference were as the voice of God. Many of the positions taken, going forth as the voice of the General Conference, have been the voice of one, two, or three men who were misleading the Conference" (MS 33, 1891).

Ears are hard things to come by if you don't have ones that work. We may tend to be critical of the administrators that Ellen White had to confront, but in the process, let's remember our own lack of ears in so many things that the Spirit is trying to say to us personally.

WHAT IS THE AUTHORITY OF THE GENERAL CONFERENCE?—7

Obey your leaders and submit to their authority. They keep watch over you as men who must give an account. Heb. 13:17, NIV.

And what is their proper authority?

Yesterday we heard Ellen White complain about the management style of the General Conference when it actually represented only the authority of the president. Five years later she commented that "the sacred character of the cause of God is no longer realized at the center of the work. The voice from Battle Creek, which has been regarded as authority in counseling how the work should be done, is no longer the voice of God" (Lt 4, 1896). Careful analysis of such statements indicates that they refer to accusations related to when the General Conference did not act as a representative body, when its decision-making authority was centralized in a person or a few people, or when the General Conference had not been following sound principles.

Such a conclusion lines up with Ellen White's statements across time. In fact, she specifically spoke to the point in a manuscript read before the delegates of the 1909 General Conference session, in which she responded to the schismatic activities of A. T. Jones, who was working to destroy the authority of the General Conference in a drive to revert back to congregational forms of church government.

"At times," she told the delegates, "when a small group of men entrusted with the general management of the work have, in the name of the General Conference, sought to carry out unwise plans and to restrict God's work, I have said that I could no longer regard the voice of the General Conference, represented by these few men, as the voice of God. But this is not saying that the decisions of a General Conference composed of an assembly of duly appointed, representative men from all parts of the field should not be respected. God has ordained that the representatives of His church from all parts of the earth, when assembled in a General Conference, shall have authority. The error that some are in danger of committing is in giving to the mind and judgment of one man, or of a small group of men, the full measure of authority and influence that God has vested in His church in the judgment and voice of the General Conference assembled to plan for the prosperity and advancement of His work" (9T 260, 261).

In the counsel of many there is wisdom. And, we should add, the balance of counsel of those from several perspectives and geographical regions also leads to well-considered decisions. The decisions of a world church have inbuilt protections that are not available to individuals and congregations.

RETROSPECT ON CHURCH AUTHORITY

I will give you the keys of the kingdom of heaven; and whatever you bind on earth shall have been bound in heaven, and whatever you loose on earth shall have been loosed in heaven. Matt. 16:19, NASB.

Those were the words of Christ as He set up His church on earth. But people have translated and interpreted them in various ways. The King James Version, for example, renders it "whatsoever thou shalt bind on earth shall be bound in heaven," making it appear that heaven ratifies whatever the church decides here on earth. *The New American Bible* takes that line of thought even further when it renders the passage as "whatever you declare bound on earth shall be bound in heaven; whatever you declare loosed on earth shall be loosed in heaven."

Such interpretations miss what Jesus was actually saying. The Greek tense clearly indicates that we should translate the verb as "will [or shall] have been bound." Thus Jesus is saying that "it is the church on earth carrying out heaven's decisions, not heaven ratifying the church's decision." That is no subtle difference. And the two translations have led in church history to two different views on church authority.

The *Seventh-day Adventist Bible Commentary* correctly reads the text when it notes that "to extend the meaning of 'bind' and 'loose' to the authority to dictate what members of the church may believe and what they may do, in matters of faith and practice, is to read into these words of Christ more than He meant by them, and more than the disciples understood by them. Such a claim God does not sanction.

"Christ's representatives on earth have the right and the responsibility to 'bind' whatever has been 'bound in heaven' and to 'loose' whatever has been 'loosed in heaven,' that is, to require or to prohibit whatever Inspiration clearly reveals. But to go beyond this is to substitute human authority for the authority of Christ . . . , a tendency that Heaven will not tolerate in those who have been appointed to the oversight of the citizens of the kingdom of heaven on earth."

We have spent quite a few days meditating about church authority because it is an important biblical topic that affects us all and because most of us give it very little thought.

Rather than merely to accept or reject the church's authority, we need to understand both its theological base and its limitations and purpose.

We can be thankful that as Christians we are not on our own. We belong to a church that gives guidance within the framework of the Bible. Balanced church authority is one more thing we can praise God for.

THE RISE OF BLACK ADVENTISM

From one man he created all the nations throughout the whole earth. Acts 17:26, NLT.

Adventist outreach to African-Americans got off to a slow start, partly because Adventism was a Northern church in a nation bitterly divided over slavery and race. Nearly all Blacks in the middle decades of the nineteenth century lived in the South, and even the denomination's evangelism among the Whites in that region did not have much momentum until the late 1870s and early 1880s.

It wasn't that early Seventh-day Adventism had no concern over the plight of African-Americans. To the contrary, the new church was abolitionist at its birth, holding that African slavery was America's greatest sin. Ellen White had counseled disobedience to the federally enacted Fugitive Slave Law, even if it meant going to prison. And such Sabbatarian leaders as J. P. Kellogg (father of John Harvey and Merritt G.) and John Byington (first president of the General Conference) had operated stations of the Underground Railroad on their farms to aid slaves fleeing the South to reach freedom in Canada.

After the freeing of the slaves during the Civil War the General Conference in 1865 recognized that "a field is now opened in the South for labor among the colored people and should be entered upon according to our ability." Unfortunately, the ability of the denomination in terms of both finances and personnel was very limited.

The first Black Seventh-day Adventists were probably in the North, but we know little about their identity. It wasn't until the denomination began entering the South that it encountered Blacks in any number, and then in a segregated situation.

During the 1870s several individual Adventists made efforts to help the former slaves receive a basic education. A major step forward came when R. M. Kilgore arrived in Texas to help organize churches in the racially inflamed area. Several times he faced threats of lynching, and on one occasion someone burned his tent down.

How even to preach to the people in the divided South was problematic. One approach involved speaking to both Whites and Blacks from a doorway that separated their respective rooms. The General conference sessions of 1877 and 1885 debated the question of whether to create separate churches for the two races, with most speakers believing that to do so would be less than Christian. But when evangelists attempted to preach to mixed groups in the South, Whites and sometimes Blacks boycotted the meetings. What to do?

Lord, we humans have made a real mess of the race issue. Help us to realize that we are one people. And help us as Christians to move beyond the prejudices of our cultures.

MEET CHARLES M. KINNY

There is neither Jew nor Greek, there is neither slave nor free, there is neither male nor female; for you are all one in Christ Jesus. Gal. 3:28, RSV.

C harles M. Kinny (or Kinney) would become the first Afro-American or-dained as a Seventh-day Adventist minister. Born as a slave in Virginia in 1855, after the Civil War as a boy of 10 or 11 he drifted west with a group of ex-slaves who hoped to find better opportunities in the newly opened territories. And Kinny did exactly that.

The turning point in his life came in 1878 when he attended a series of evan-gelistic meetings conducted by J. N. Loughborough in Reno, Nevada. At its con-clusion Kinny, presumably the only Black, became one of the seven charter members of the new Reno congregation.

While Loughborough's series was still in progress, Ellen White visited Reno, and on July 30 she preached to a crowd of 400 on the words of John: "Behold, what manner of love the Father hath bestowed upon us, that we should be called sons of God." That text and the sermon that filled out its implications provided Kinny with an assurance and a courage that allowed him to push forward in his life.

His life as a slave and as a transient had been uncertain, but in Adventism he found a nurturing family. The Reno members, sensing his dedication, elected Kinny their first church clerk. But better things were soon to follow. The California Conference offered him the position of secretary of the Nevada Tract and Missionary Society. After he succeeded in that, the California Conference en-tered into an agreement in 1883 with the Reno church members to sponsor Kinny for study at the recently established Healdsburg College.

At the end of two years of study, church leadership sent him to Topeka, Kansas, in 1885 to begin work among the growing Black population of that city. In 1889 the General Conference assigned him to Louisville, Kentucky, ordaining him to the ministry that same year. For more than two decades Kinny labored across the upper South, organizing Black churches and becoming the first major Adventist spokesperson of Afro-American aspirations.

Like so many things in Adventism, the 1890s would witness the Black work take a giant step forward through the ingenuity of Edson White and the founding of a school at Oakwood.

Lord, we are impressed with what You did with the life of Charles M. Kinny. Take our lives today and enable us to be a blessing to others. Amen.

TEMPERANCE CRUSADERS

Who hath woe? Who hath sorrow? Who hath contentions? Who hath babbling? Who hath wounds without cause? Who hath redness of eyes? They that tarry long at the wine. Prov. 23:29, 30.

One of the great crusades of nineteenth-century America was the temperance movement, which had as its goal the outlawing of the use and sale of alcoholic beverages. Lyman Beecher, one of the nation's most influential preachers, started the movement in 1825. "Intemperance," he thundered, "is the sin of our land, . . . and if anything shall defeat the hopes of the world, . . . it is that river of fire." Beecher went on to call for a national remedy through the banning of strong drinks as an item of commerce.

By the time Adventism had reached its adolescence in the 1870s the general temperance campaign had broadened to include the abolition and all alcoholic beverages. The young church actively advocated voting for temperance candidates, and Ellen White was so concerned with the issue that she even suggested the unprecedented step of going to the polls and voting on Sabbath for temperance proponents.

Across the United States and eventually around the world, Adventism offered its speakers and its properties to aid the anti-alcohol crusade. In 1874, for example, the Adventists lent their two large evangelistic tents to a series of meetings aimed at closing the 135 saloons in Oakland, California, home of Adventism's publishing program on the West Coast. Such cooperation brought the Adventists into working relationship with the "city mayor, several clergymen, one of the daily papers, and several of the leading citizens and businessmen. . . . Having thoroughly organized, the executive committee planned for a series of mass meetings, which were held in our large and commodious tents. They worked night and day, until the whole city was roused to action."

The result was a "glorious victory" for which the Adventists got partial credit in the newspaper headlines.

Ellen White was at the forefront of the Adventists in temperance, often speaking to large non-Adventist audiences in America, Europe, and Australia. By 1879 the Seventh-day Adventists had formed the American Health and Temperance Association under the leadership of John Harvey Kellogg.

The temperance crusade was one avenue that God used to open the way for the church to have a larger impact on the culture of its day. What reform movements should we (or I) be involved in today?

The End of an Era

All flesh is like grass
and all its glory like the flower of grass.
The grass withers,
and the flower falls,
but the word of the Lord endures forever. 1 Peter 1:24, 25, NRSV.

B etween 1872 and 1881 the Seventh-day Adventist Church would see two of its three founders laid to rest. The first was Joseph Bates, who died at the Health Reform Institute in Battle Creek on March 19, 1872, shortly before his eightieth birthday. The old health reformer had kept a strong program going until near the end. The year before his death he held at least 100 public meetings besides those at his local church and the conferences that he attended.

The aged warrior attended one of his last General Conference sessions a year before his death. "The annual meeting," he exuberantly reported, "was one of deep, stirring interest to the cause. It was encouraging to hear what has been accomplished the past year, and to learn of the wide openings for missionary work and the urgent and pressing calls for ministerial labor throughout the wide harvest field." Bates desperately desired to answer the call, but couldn't.

He attended his last session two months before his passing, closing with a prayer: "O Lord, in Jesus' dear name, help us, with this dear people, to fulfill our sacred promise, and may all thy remnant, waiting people also enter into covenant with thee."

Whereas Bates was in good health right up to the end, the same cannot be said of James White. Overwork had triggered a series of debilitating strokes beginning in the mid-1860s. Given his health condition, it is absolutely amazing how much he continued to accomplish. He would die two days after his sixtieth birthday on August 6, 1881.

Ellen was shattered. "I am fully of the opinion," she penned to her son Willie, "that my life was so intertwined or interwoven with my husband's that it is about impossible for me to be of any great account without him" (Lt 17, 1881).

Sixteen years later she wrote: "How I miss him! How I long for his words of counsel and wisdom! How I long to hear his prayers blending with my prayers for light and guidance, for wisdom to know how to plan and lay out the work!" (2SM 259).

That's where the Advent hope comes in. Along with Ellen we also await the greeting on that resurrection morning of not only her husband and Bates, but our own beloved ones.

NEW BEGINNINGS

Let us search and examine our ways, and turn back to the Lord. Lam. 3:40, NKJV.

T he period running from 1885 to 1900 would be one of the great turning points in Adventist history. The denomination would face massive changes in almost every aspect of its identity, so much so that by the beginning of the new century it almost looked like something different from what it had been before.

Heading the list was the massive ground shift in Adventist theology eventually flowing out of the 1888 General Conference session in Minneapolis, Minnesota. It prompted a call for a more Christ-centered preaching, put Christ at the focal point of Adventist preaching as He never had been before, and led to an emphasis on salvation by grace through faith, what the church came to see as righteousness by faith. The older emphasis on the law did not disappear, but was reoriented to its proper place in the plan of salvation.

The new focus on Christ and His righteousness would also see new personalities rise to the fore in Adventism. Of particular importance were Alonzo T. Jones, Ellet J. Waggoner, and W. W. Prescott. Jones and Waggoner would become the foremost Adventist preachers in the 1890s, dominating, for example, the pulpit at each of the six General Conference sessions from 1889 to 1899. And by the end of the decade Jones would be editor of the *Review and Herald,* one of the most influential positions in the church at that time.

The decade of the 1890s would also witness the beginning of a transformation in Adventist views of the Godhead. After all, whenever you begin to talk about salvation through Christ, you have to have a Savior and a Holy Spirit adequate for the job.

Accompanying the reformation in Adventist theology would be an explosion in the denomination's mission program that would finally send it into "every" nation. By 1900 the Seventh-day Adventist Church would truly be worldwide.

Another area of massive change would be the educational. Theological reformation and mission explosion would lead to a transformation in the denominational educational system in both its orientation and in its relative importance in the church.

Change, some discovered, could be painful. But it was also essential.

Give us open minds, O God, as we glimpse the transformations of the past and as You move us into the future.

NEW ISSUES—1

For by grace you have been saved through faith; and this is not your own doing, it is the gift of God. Eph. 2:8, RSV.

B y 1850 the Sabbatarian Adventists were excited about the new truths they had found. They never ceased to talk, write, and preach about those doctrines that set them off as a distinctive people—the literal, visual, pre-millennial Second Advent, the two-phase ministry of Christ in the heavenly sanctuary, the seventh-day Sabbath in its end-time context, and conditional immortality. When viewed through the prism of the three angels' messages of Revelation 14, such doctrines formed a powerful theological package. One worth shouting about!

At this point we need to realize that the Adventists were really holding two sets of beliefs. The first category included doctrines that they *shared* with other Christians, such as salvation by grace alone through faith, the importance of the Bible as the only determiner of doctrinal truth, the historic role of Jesus as the world's Savior, the power of intercessory prayer, and so on.

The second doctrinal category consisted of those beliefs that made them a distinct group of people, beliefs that *separated* them from other Christians, such as the Sabbath and the teaching on the heavenly sanctuary.

Since nineteenth-century Adventists lived in a largely Christian culture, they tended not to emphasize what they shared with other Christians. After all, why preach saving grace to Baptists or the importance of prayer to Methodists when they already believed those teachings.

The important thing, as they saw it, was to present those distinctively Adventist truths that others needed to hear and accept.

As a result, when they entered a new village or town they would locate the best meeting place, often a school auditorium, and then challenge the foremost area preacher to a public debate on Which day is the Sabbath? Or What happens to a person at death?

I have a question for you.

Have you ever thought about your own belief system and how it fits together? Or even if it is valid biblically?

You should. Each of us is responsible to know why we are Christians and why we are Adventists. I challenge you today to deeper personal Bible study.

NEW ISSUES—2

Simon Peter answered, "You are the Christ, the Son of the living God."
Matt. 16:16, NASB.

Yesterday we noted that the early Adventist preachers felt that they needed to focus on those points, such as the seventh-day Sabbath, that made them distinctive rather than those doctrines that they shared with other Christians.

Their method of entering a community and challenging a prominent minister to a public debate seemed to work. After all, without television sets, the best show in a small town might be two preachers getting into an argument over how long people suffer in hell. At any rate, the Adventist evangelists seem to have had no difficulty getting a crowd to hear their message.

But 40 years of stressing the distinctive Adventist truths in a debating atmosphere, to the neglect of the general Christian doctrines, had two detrimental effects. For one, it developed some pretty combative Adventists, a personality trait that would trouble the denomination in events surrounding the 1888 meetings.

Beyond that, four decades of overemphasizing the distinctive teachings and neglecting the shared doctrines led to a disjunction between Adventism and basic Christianity. By the mid-1880s the issue had grown to problematic proportions. The church had done an excellent job at preaching what was Adventist in Adventism, but had lost sight of the larger package that made Adventism Christian.

Adventism needed a course correction. Two relatively young men from the western part of the United States—A. T. Jones and E. J. Waggoner would begin that correction. At first Jones and Waggoner seemed to be making a doctrinal adjustment by giving a larger place to Christ and faith in Adventist theology and a less prominent role to the law.

But the denominational leaders—G. I. Butler and Uriah Smith—viewed such a "correction" as a major theological earthquake. They saw the new teachings as an overthrow of historic Adventism with its emphasis on law and works.

As a result, they fought it with all their might, which was not small, given the fact that they had a direct influence over the preachers of a denomination that still had only about 25,000 members worldwide.

Lord, help us learn from our history the lessons of theological balance in our walk with You.

NEW ISSUES—3

As cold waters to a thirsty soul, so is good news. Prov. 25:25.

By 1886 the sides in the oncoming Adventist theological struggle were quite visible. On one hand was G. I. Butler, the General Conference president, and Uriah Smith, secretary of the General Conference. On the other were the two up-start editors from the West—A. T. Jones and E. J. Waggoner.

It appears that the only leading female participant in the conflict sought to remain neutral so that she might work with both sides. But by early 1887 Ellen White began to conclude not only that the younger men were being wrongly treated in an unequal struggle, but that they had something to teach that the Seventh-day Adventist Church desperately needed to hear. Thus by April 1887 she had dedicated herself to making sure that Jones and Waggoner would get a hearing at the 1888 General Conference session.

In the end it would be Ellen White who would come out the clearest on the real significance of Jones and Waggoner's 1888 message. Her major theme would center on a reinterpretation of part of Revelation 14:12: "Here is the patience of the saints: here are they that keep the commandments of God, and the faith of Jesus."

That passage is the central text in Adventist history. It contains the last message God would give to the world before the Second Advent, which is pictured as taking place in verses 14-20.

The interesting thing is that both sides in the Adventist struggle surrounding 1888 would focus on Revelation 14:12. But they would emphasize different parts of the verse. The traditionalists would uplift "the commandments of God," while the reformers stressed "the faith of Jesus." Out of the Minneapolis meetings would flow a new interpretation of Revelation 14:12, one that would forever change the shape of Adventist theology.

Ellen White would suffer for her support of Jones and Waggoner. In December 1888 she would look back at the recently closed General Conference session and declare, "My testimony was ignored, and never in my life . . . was I treated as at that conference" (Lt 7 1888).

Some of us think that in the "good old days" everything went well in the church. Not so! As then, so today. Good people get upset with each other, and need to pray to God for forgiveness.

NEW FACES: MEET E. J. WAGGONER

This is my blood of the covenant, which is poured out for many. Mark 14:24, RSV.

Ellet J. Waggoner was the youngest of the major participants at the 1888 General Conference session. Born in 1855, he was the son of Elder J. H. Waggoner, whom we have already met.

Ellet earned an M.D. degree in New York City in 1878, but never found the fulfillment he desired in medical practice. As a result, he entered the ministry and received an invitation to the assistant editorship of *Signs of the Times* in 1884.

The major theological turning point in young Waggoner's life took place at a camp meeting at Healdsburg, California, in October 1882. During a sermon he experienced what he called an "extra-biblical revelation."

"Suddenly," he reported, "a light shone round me, and the tent was, for me, far more brilliantly lighted than if the noonday sun had been shining, and I saw Christ hanging on the cross, *crucified for me*. In that moment I had my first positive knowledge, which came like an overwhelming flood, that God loved *me*, and that Christ died *for me*."

Waggoner "knew that this light . . . was a revelation direct from heaven." He therefore resolved then and there that he would "study the Bible in the light of that revelation," in order that he might "help others to see the same truth." Because of that plan, he noted, "wherever I have turned in the Sacred Book, I have found Christ set forth as the power of God, to the salvation of individuals, and I have never found anything else."

It was Waggoner's "vision" that eventually led him into an in-depth study of the book of Galatians. Thus, given his starting point, it is little wonder that he found the gospel in Galatians. That discovery would bring him to prominence in Adventism during the late 1880s. It would also set him up for direct confrontation with the leaders of the General Conference—G. I. Butler and Uriah Smith—at the 1888 General Conference session.

As we will see, E. J. Waggoner was the gentlest of the men who participated in the events that swirled around the new teachings in the 1888 era.

Waggoner's experience shaped his life. A "vision" of Christ's righteousness always transforms our thinking and the way we act. Every day we need to ask if our Adventism has been baptized by the light of the cross.

NEW FACES: MEET A. T. JONES

Though an army should encamp against me, My heart shall not fear. Ps. 27:3, NKJV.

D ead to the world, and alive to thee, O my God!"
With those words and upraised hands Sergeant Alonzo T. Jones arose from the watery baptismal grave in Walla Walla, Washington Territory, August 8, 1874. For weeks he had been "earnestly seeking the Lord," and a few days earlier he had received "bright evidence of sins forgiven." Charismatic, forceful, dramatic, handsome, and tending to extremes, Jones became a leading figure in Adventist circles during the 1890s.

Jones was proud of his military past. Any claim to military glory came from his participation in the Modoc war of northern California in 1873, during which he asserts that he and his squad "poured a hail of bullets" toward the enemy in an effort to protect a wounded officer.

The fearless Jones would spend the rest of his life pouring "a hail of bullets" at whichever target he perceived to be the enemy.

His personality and confrontational style did much to antagonize his opponents. Ellen White would repeatedly warn him against his hard comments, but Jones found it almost impossible to distinguish between frankness and harshness. He made that point clear in 1901 when some challenged his candidacy for the presidency of the California Conference because his "directness and plainness of speech . . . hurt folks." Jones confessed to the charge, but, he noted, "I cannot repent of it, because it is simple Christianity."

His abrasiveness did much to set the tone for the Minneapolis meetings when he blurted out to the delegation that he should not be held responsible for Uriah Smith's ignorance of certain historical points about Daniel 7. Having done his homework, Jones knew that he was correct, and drove his point home.

While such assertiveness toward a denominational patriarch did little for his cause, his fearless forcefulness undoubtedly aided him in the halls of the United States Congress and elsewhere as he fought against impending Sunday laws. Jones was a man who thrived in the heat of battle.

But God used him mightily anyway!

I find something important here for me. With all of my faults, God can still use me (and you). While it is true that He desires to change us if we will let Him, He starts with us just where we are.

OLD FACES: MEET G. I. BUTLER

A just man falleth seven times, and riseth up again: but the wicked shall fall into mischief. Prov. 24:16.

S ome people are just tougher than others.

Such was the case of George I. Butler, president of the General Conference in 1888. In his better moments he could be quite honest about himself. Perhaps he made his most accurate and perceptive self-analysis in 1886 when he wrote: "I . . . naturally [have] . . . too much iron in my nature" and not enough of the love of Jesus. "The school in which I have had to be trained to meet every kind of influence," he added, "has been very favorable to keep the iron in me and make me stiff."

That last remark may help us understand the "toughness" of many of the nineteenth-century Adventist leaders. It was not easy to lead a small and despised movement that provided no earthly security and had virtually no institutions to lend prestige in an era when the Millerite disappointment was still a vivid memory among the general population. Only strong-willed individuals could succeed when Butler began his early administrative posts. An iron will was a necessity for most Adventist pioneers before Adventism became a more "comfortable" and respectable religion.

Butler had what took to survive in such an era, but the price to pay had been the "iron." Thus he described himself in 1886 as being "a little on the fighting order." Sensing early in his controversy with Waggoner over Galatians that he was too belligerent, he penned to Ellen White that "he wanted to be like Jesus—wise, patient, kind, tender-hearted, [and] frank," with "a love of justice and fairness to all." He lamented the fact "that there is considerable human nature left in me" and that "I have great struggles with the old man." Butler wanted his old nature "to die, WHOLLY DIE."

Such a wish, however, was slow of fulfillment. With him, as with most of us, the process of sanctification was truly the work of a lifetime. Writing to J. H. Kellogg in 1905, the elderly Butler noted: "I am a pretty tough old customer, think for myself. You hit it pretty well once when you said, 'You might as well reason with a post as to reason with Elder Butler, when he gets his stakes set.'"

My Father, I'm afraid there is a little of Butler in me. Help me today to WHOLLY DIE.

OLD FACES: MEET URIAH SMITH AGAIN

Take my yoke upon you, and learn of me; for I am meek and lowly in heart: and ye shall find rest unto your souls. Matt. 11:29.

By 1888 Uriah Smith, Butler's accomplice in power, had been secretary of the General Conference for all but three years since its beginning in 1863. Beyond that, Smith had been associated with Adventism's semiofficial periodical (the *Review and Herald*) since the 1850s, and by 1888 he had served for nearly 25 years as its editor-in-chief.

In addition, he was the denomination's unrivaled authority on prophetic interpretation. His *Thoughts on Daniel and the Revelation* was an Adventist bestseller among both church members and nonmembers alike. One of the Minneapolis-St. Paul newspapers noted in announcing his arrival for the 1888 meetings that "Elder Uriah Smith . . . has the reputation of being one of the ablest writers and speakers in the conference, and is, moreover, a profound scholar."

Like Butler, Smith viewed himself as a guardian of denominational orthodoxy. He succinctly stated his editorial policy in regard to some of the new ideas of A. T. Jones in 1892: "Having by long study, and years of observation in the work, become settled on certain principles, I am not prepared to flop over at the suggestion of every novice." That had certainly been his position in the face of Jones and Waggoner's "new theology" in 1888. Neither Smith nor Butler had the slightest inclination to "flop over" in the face of the teachings of the younger men from California. In fact, the exact opposite proved to be the case.

As we have noted, certain characteristics of Jones and Waggoner didn't help matters. Ellen White wrote a letter to them in early 1887 that sought to tone down their aggressiveness. "Elder [J. H.] Waggoner," she said, "has loved discussions and contention. I fear that E. J. [Waggoner] has cultivated a love for the same. We need now good humble religion. E. J. W. needs humility, meekness, and Brother Jones can be a power for good if he will constantly cultivate practical godliness" (Lt 37, 1887).

Don't we all need humility? It is one thing to sing for the Lord to make us humble and meek. But it is quite another to accept the gift. *Lord, help us.*

ENTERING THE YEAR 1888

Then I saw another beast which rose out of the earth; it had two horns like a lamb and it spoke like a dragon. Rev. 13:11, RSV.

W e turn our eyes to the future," Uriah Smith wrote in his opening *Review* editorial for 1888. "The prospect, year by year, grows clearer, the evidence surer, that we have not followed cunningly devised fables in making known the soon coming of the Lord. Prophecies are converging to their fulfillment. Events are moving with accelerated velocity. The word of God is demonstrating its claims to truthfulness, and comforting every humble believer with the thought that the hope that is built thereon can never fail."

General Conference president G. I. Butler shared similar perspectives with Smith. "We have much reason to thank God and take courage as we enter the year 1888," he penned in January. Noting that Seventh-day Adventists had "never taken a stand upon Bible exegesis which they have been compelled to surrender," he pointed out that "every year we have more and more evidence that we are right in our interpretation of the great prophetic themes which distinguish us as a people."

January 1888 also saw A. T. Jones, coeditor of the *Signs of the Times,* take the position that events then occurring in the uniting of religion and state in America were in "direct course of the fulfillment of Rev. 13:11-17" with its teaching on the formation of the image of the beast.

Seventh-day Adventists everywhere were excited about the Second Advent in early 1888 as happenings on every side indicated that they would soon see the long-predicted national Sunday law become a reality.

The Adventist interpretation of Revelation 13 predicted a last-day showdown between those who honored the true Sabbath and those who symbolically followed the beast. As a result, Seventh-day Adventists had been publicly predicting since the late 1840s that they would eventually endure persecution for their faithfulness to the biblical Sabbath.

In that historical and theological context it is not too difficult to see why Revelation 14:12 ("Here is the patience of the saints: here are they that keep the commandments of God, and the faith of Jesus") was their flagship text, printed in full under the masthead of the *Review* for nearly a century. Given their emphasis, it is easy to see why they were sensitive to Sunday legislation.

We thank You, Lord, for the prophecies of Daniel and Revelation. Help me to study them more faithfully.

Sunday Persecution on Every Hand

Blessed are they which are persecuted for righteousness' sake; for theirs is the kingdom of heaven. Matt. 5:10.

Throughout the 1880s Sunday legislation and persecution grew in strength and scope. The problem surfaced in an explosive way in California in 1882, when the Sunday question became a major issue in the state's elections. The consequences hit Adventists when the local authorities arrested W. C. White for operating the Pacific Press on Sunday.

Although California soon repealed its Sunday law, the threat of similar legislation across the nation spurred Seventh-day Adventists to action. Perhaps their most important move was to establish what became the *American Sentinel of Religious Liberty* (now called *Liberty*) in 1884 to spearhead the struggle against Sunday legislation.

The scene of action shifted to Arkansas in 1885. Between 1885 and 1887 the state had 21 cases related to Sunday desecration. All but two had involved Sabbathkeepers, and the authorities had released the defendants in those two instances without bail and dismissed their cases. For the Adventists, however, bail ranged from $110 to $500 each—a stiff fine in an era when a laboring male earned about $1 a day.

A. T. Jones concluded that "there could be no clearer demonstration that the law was used only as a means to vent religious spite against a class of citizens guiltless of any crime, but only of professing a religion different from that of the majority."

By late 1885 the focal point for Sunday legislation would shift to Tennessee, where authorities would arrest a number of Adventists during the late 1880s and early 1890s. Some, including ministers, served on chain gangs as common criminals.

The Adventists' eschatological excitement intensified in 1888 when Roman Catholic cardinal James Gibbons joined hands with Protestants by endorsing a petition to Congress on behalf of national Sunday legislation. The Protestants were more than willing to accept such help. "Whenever they [the Roman Catholics] are willing to cooperate in resisting the progress of political atheism," proclaimed the *Christian Statesman*, "we will gladly join hands with them."

Religious liberty is a precious gift. We need to appreciate it and use it while we still have it.

THE NATIONAL SUNDAY BILL

[The lamblike beast] exercises all the authority of the first beast in its presence, and makes the earth and its inhabitants worship the first beast, whose mortal wound was healed. Rev. 13:12, RSV.

The high-water mark in the Sunday issue came on May 21, 1888, when New Hampshire's senator H. L. Blair introduced a bill into the United States Senate for the promotion of the observance of "the Lord's day" "as a day of religious worship."

Blair's national Sunday bill was the first such legislation to go before Congress since the establishment of the Adventist movement in the 1840s. Four days later he submitted a proposed amendment to the United States Constitution that would Christianize the nation's public school system.

Seventh-day Adventists did not miss the prophetic significance of the Blair bills. The eschatological excitement of the Sunday law movement served as one factor contributing to heightened tensions in the period leading up to the 1888 General Conference session.

That eschatological crisis created an emotional atmosphere directly related to two other issues that would surface at the Minneapolis meetings. The first concerned the interpretation of prophecy—especially in the book of Daniel. The second involved the kind of righteousness needed for salvation. That second issue would bring the function of God's law in the plan of salvation into focus as Adventists struggled over its role in the book of Galatians.

It is impossible to understand the high emotional pitch of the participants at the 1888 meetings without grasping the fact that Adventists felt, because of the Sunday crisis, that they already faced the end of time.

S. N. Haskell wrote shortly before the beginning of the session that their liberty as Sabbath observers would quickly be taken away, and that they might soon be bearing their testimony in courts and prisons.

With that in mind, it is not difficult to see why some of the Adventist leaders reacted violently and emotionally when Jones and Waggoner began to question the validity of aspects of the denomination's interpretation of prophecy and its theology of the law. Such questions, they reasoned, threatened the very core of Adventist identity in a time of utmost crisis.

Reacting and overreacting to issues are often close neighbors. May the Lord help us to not only know the difference but to practice the healthier way in both our life in the church and in our private lives.

TEN HORNS EXPLOSION

And behold, a fourth beast. . . . And it was different from all the beasts that were before it, and it had ten horns. Dan. 7:7, NASB.

Well, you may be thinking, *that's not much of a text for my daily devotion.*

You're right. But it has a story behind it that shook Adventism in the 1880s. It all began when the 1884 General Conference session asked A. T. Jones to gather historical information on the fulfillment of prophecy, including the 10 horns of Daniel 7.

Uriah Smith was overjoyed that Jones had time to do it. But his pleasure disappeared when the younger man differed from him on the identity of one of the horns, thereby suggesting that the traditional list was wrong. Things got worse when Jones published his findings in the *Signs*. Smith rebutted him in the *Review* as the "discussion" went from cool to hot.

And why so much concern over such a small topic?

Let Smith answer. If, he noted, we changed from what we had preached for 40 years, people would notice and would say, "Oh! now you find that you are mistaken on what you have considered one of your clearest points; and so if we give you time enough, you will probably come to acknowledge finally that you are mistaken on everything!" And with that stroke the entire prophetic understanding that included the national Sunday law would collapse. Or so Smith argued.

Jones also fought on the basis of the Sunday issue, noting that "the real battle of the truth and for the truth has not yet begun." But the emergence of the Sunday laws would change all that. Seventh-day Adventist beliefs in the end-time crisis would "become the principal subject of discussion. . . . Then our views are going to be noticed by the high in the land. Then every point is going to be analyzed and challenged. . . . We shall then . . . have to present some better reason for our faith than 'it has been preached for forty years' or that Bishop Chandler says so."

It was the Sunday crisis that made such a seemingly unimportant topic as the identity of one of the 10 horns explosive. To Smith and Butler it hardly seemed to be a good time to be publicly tinkering with a long-standing interpretation of prophecy.

One of the facts of Adventist history is that even a *small topic* could set the stage for *big battles* as the minds and spirits of individuals heated up for an unedifying clash.

Help us, Father, to gain proper perspective as we read Your Word and deal with one another.

LAW IN GALATIANS EXPLOSION—1

The law was our custodian until Christ came, that we might be justified by faith. But now that faith has come, we are no longer under a custodian. Gal. 3:24, 25, RSV.

I t's a little easier to see how this passage could cause an Adventist explosion than the 10 horns of Daniel 7, especially if one reads the text to imply that there was no need at all for the law after the coming of Christ rather than that the law always points out our sins and beyond them to the Savior.

Butler and his friends undoubtedly feared the first option. And that would be serious if the law was the Ten Commandments. They got around that problem by interpreting the law in Galatians as the ceremonial regulations. Thus as they saw it, the ceremonial law pointed them to Christ, but after He came we no longer needed it.

And then comes Waggoner in 1884 with his view that the law in Galatians is the Ten Commandments. The Butler forces viewed that interpretation as a threat to the very heart of Adventist theology—the continuing sacredness of the seventh-day Sabbath embedded in the moral law. Thus the church leadership perceived Jones and Waggoner as endangering one of Adventism's central pillars.

For more than 30 years the church had held to the ceremonial law interpretation. And then in the midst of the Sunday law crisis Waggoner had to raise a teaching that, as Butler and Smith saw it, undermined the very basis of their reason for keeping the Sabbath, thus providing "great aid and comfort" to the Adventists' anti-law enemies.

Butler viewed the new teaching as "the opening wedge" by which a "deluge" of doctrinal and prophetic changes might be "let in" to the Adventist Church.

Smith was one in heart and mind with Butler. For him, "next to the death of Brother White, the greatest calamity that ever befell our cause was when Dr. Waggoner put his articles on the book of Galatians through the *Signs*." If the denomination ever changed its position on Galatians, he flatly stated, "they may count me out," because "I am not yet prepared to renounce Seventh-day Adventism."

Sometimes fear drives our theology more than careful Bible reading. When it does, we overreact and lose our ability to read the text clearly.

Father, help us to read Your Word with both eyes open and our emotions in place.

LAW IN GALATIANS EXPLOSION–2

In Christ you are all sons of God, through faith. Gal. 3:26, RSV.

The fact that Ellen White had had a vision in which she had identified the Galatians law in the 1850s further complicated the controversy. Butler and Smith asserted that she had specified it as the ceremonial law. She replied that she remembered the vision, but had no written record of it, couldn't recall what she had said, and that the whole issue should be dropped as it wasn't important. To her it was a "mere mote" of a problem. Her burden was not the law but "to present Jesus and His love before my brethren, for I saw marked evidences that many had not the spirit of Christ" (MS 24, 1888).

Such talk further inflamed Butler and Smith, who now charged Ellen White with changing her mind. And no true prophet, they implied, could do such a thing. Thus her prophetic gift had also come under fire from the leadership of the denomination in an already tense time.

But it wasn't the first time in the 1880s that Smith had been upset with the Adventist prophet. In 1882 he had become stirred up over a testimony that faulted him in his handling of Goodloe Harper Bell at Battle Creek College. At that time he had concluded that everything that she wrote wasn't from God. Her counsel was only inspired if she said "I saw." Thus her letters to him, unless she said "I saw," were merely good advice. Or bad advice as Smith regarded it in the case of Bell.

By the mid-1880s, in the midst of the Galatians controversy, Butler had come to join Smith in his jaundiced view of Ellen White's bad advice.

Ellen White, of course, had her own opinion on the topic: "If the preconceived opinions or particular ideas of some are crossed in being reproved by testimonies, they have a burden at once to make plain their position to discriminate between the testimonies, defining what is Sister White's human judgment, and what is the word of the Lord. Everything that sustains their cherished ideas is divine, and the testimonies to correct their errors are human—Sister White's opinions. They make of none effect the counsel of God by their tradition" (MS 16, 1889).

Protect us, O God, from ourselves.

SOUNDS OF BATTLE IN 1886

A sound of battle is in the land. Jer. 50:22, NKJV.

Butler was out to settle the struggles over the law in Galatians and the 10 horns of Daniel 7 by the end of 1886. First, he wrote a series of letters to get Ellen White on his side. Second, he prepared a "brief comment" on Galatians that in fact was an 85-page book entitled *The Law in the Book of Galatians* that took aim at Waggoner's position.

Third, he sought to use the 1886 General Conference session to put Jones and Waggoner and their "false teachings" in their proper place and thus get the denomination back on track. The General Conference president provided every attendee with a copy of his *Law in the Book of Galatians.* More important, he organized a theological committee to settle the debated issues once and for all.

But Butler's hope for a creedal statement that would establish the truth on the controverted points for all time met with frustration. The nine-member committee split five to four. "We had an argument of several hours," Butler reported, "but neither side was convinced." The next question, he noted, "was whether we should take this into the conference and have a big public fight over it." Being an astute politician, he realized that such a move would only cause more trouble.

Both Butler and Ellen White would look back on the 1886 General Conference session as that "terrible conference." While he noted that the meeting was one of the saddest he had ever attended, she pointed out that "Jesus was grieved and bruised in the person of his saints." She especially felt disturbed about the "harshness," "disrespect, and want of sympathetic love in brother toward brother" (Lt 21, 1888; MS 21, 1888). The dynamics of the Minneapolis meetings were already in place.

The most serious casualty of the 1886 meeting was D. M. Canright, a firm supporter of Butler's position on the law. Apparently he saw that Adventism's traditional position had problems. He had recognized that Butler and his friends were "exalting the law above Christ." But instead of adopting Waggoner's view of the Ten Commandments as leading individuals to Christ, Canright dropped both Adventism and the law and would become the denomination's most aggressive antagonist.

There is no more important topic than uplifting Jesus.

Guide us, Lord, as we meditate through Adventist history on the place of Christ in our life.

ELLEN WHITE SEEKS TO BALANCE THINGS

Blessed are the meek, for they shall inherit the earth. Matt. 5:5, RSV.

E llen White was becoming ever more deeply concerned about her church and where it was heading. She put some of her thoughts and fears in a letter to Jones and Waggoner on February 18, 1887. "There is danger," she emphasized, "of our ministers dwelling too much on doctrines, preaching altogether too many discourses on argumentative subjects when their own soul needs practical godliness. . . . The wonders of redemption are dwelt upon altogether too lightly. We need these matters presented more fully and continuously. . . . There is danger of keeping the discourses and the articles in the paper like Cain's offering, Christless" (Lt 37, 1887).

Part of her letter was a rebuke to Jones and Waggoner for making divisive issues public in a time of crisis and for certain of their undesirable character traits. Both men replied positively, humbly apologizing for their public and private faults.

A copy of the letter reproving Jones and Waggoner went to Butler. Ecstatic with its contents, he mistakenly interpreted it as confirmation of his position on the law. In his euphoria he wrote to Ellen White that he had really come to "love" the two young men, noting that he felt sorry for them. "I always pity those who suffer keen disappointment." Despite his "pity," Butler joyfully published an aggressive article in the *Review* of March 22 promoting his position on the two laws.

To put it mildly, Butler's use of her letter to Jones and Waggoner upset Mrs. White. On April 5, 1887, she fired off an epistle to Butler and Smith, claiming that the only reason that she had sent them a copy of her letter to the younger men was that they needed to follow the same cautions in bringing disagreements into public. But now that Butler had reopened the battle publicly, it was only just to give Waggoner a chance to present his view.

As Ellen White began to see the issues more clearly, she became more aggressive toward the high-handed methods of the General Conference leadership. "We must work as Christians," she wrote. Always yielding to Bible truth, "we want to be filled with all the fullness of God, and have the meekness and lowliness of Christ" (Lt 13, 1887).

That is still needed by each of us.

Help us, Lord, to have Your humility and Your spirit, even in times of theological controversy.

THE SPIRIT OF THE PHARISEES

It is honorable to refrain from strife. Prov. 20:3, NRSV.

E llen White "discerned at the very commencement of the meeting [at Minneapolis] a spirit that burdened" her, an attitude that she had never seen previously among her fellow leaders and ministers. It bothered her that it was "so unlike the spirit of Jesus, so contrary to the spirit that should be exercised toward each other" (MS 24, 1888). She would come to think of that hostility as the "spirit of Minneapolis" or the "spirit of the Pharisees." An understanding of the attitude displayed at Minneapolis is essential if we are to grasp the dynamics of the 1888 meetings and subsequent Adventist history.

A composite description of the spirit of Minneapolis, as Mrs. White portrayed it, would have the following characteristics. First, it displayed sarcasm and jesting toward the denomination's reform element. Some, for example, referred to Waggoner as "Sister White's pet." Second, it led to criticism. Third, many manifested evil surmisings, hatred, and jealousy. Fourth, the Minneapolis spirit prompted "sharp feelings" and attitudes. Fifth, its possessors were "intoxicated with the spirit of resistance" to the voice of the Spirit. Sixth, it drove those having it to speak in a manner calculated to inflame one another regarding those who held opposing doctrinal views. Seventh, it bread contention and doctrinal debate in place of the spirit of Jesus. Eighth, it generated an attitude that led to "playing upon words" and "quibbling upon words" in doctrinal discussions. In short, the spirit manifested "was uncourteous, ungentlemanly, and not Christlike."

One of the most noteworthy things about the Minneapolis spirit is that it resulted from a desire to protect Adventism's old doctrinal "landmarks." Ellen White deplored the fact that "a difference in the application of some few scriptural passages makes men forget their religious principles" (MS 30, 1889). "God deliver me from your ideas . . . ," she declared, "if the receiving of these ideas would make me so unchristian in my spirit, words, and works" (MS 55, 1890).

The tragedy of Minneapolis was that in seeking to preserve Adventism's doctrinal purity and its traditional scriptural interpretations, the Battle Creek leadership had lost its Christianity.

Save us, O Lord, from the spirit of the Pharisees. Fill us with the spirit of Jesus in all that we do this day.

ADVENTISM'S GREATEST NEED

Blessed are they which do hunger and thirst after righteousness: for they shall be filled. Matt. 5:6.

A revival of true godliness among us," Ellen White penned in 1887, "is the greatest and most urgent of all our needs. To seek this should be our first work." But, she noted, many Adventists were not prepared to receive God's blessing, and many needed to be converted. "There is nothing that Satan fears so much as that the people of God shall clear the way by removing every hindrance, so the Lord can pour out His Spirit upon a languishing church and an impenitent congregation" (RH, Mar. 22, 1887).

By the late 1880s Ellen White had become deeply concerned about the condition of Adventism. Too many leaders and members had a theory of the truth, but were failing to grasp the truth itself.

That burden was not new to her writing. In 1879 she had written that "it would be well to spend a thoughtful hour each day reviewing the life of Christ from the manger to Calvary. . . . By thus contemplating His teachings and sufferings, and the infinite sacrifice made by Him for the redemption of the race, we may strengthen our faith, quicken our love, and become more deeply imbued with the spirit which sustained our Saviour. If we would be saved at last we must all learn the lesson of penitence and faith at the foot of the cross." She went on to say that she longed "to see our ministers dwell more upon the cross of Christ" (4T 374, 375).

The same emphasis rang true at the 1883 General Conference session, at which Mrs. White told the assembled ministers that "we must learn in the school of Christ. Nothing but His righteousness can entitle us to one of the blessings of the covenant of grace. We have long desired and tried to obtain these blessings, but have not received them because we have cherished the idea that we could do something to make ourselves worthy of them. We have not looked away from ourselves, believing that Jesus is a living Saviour" (1SM 351).

Again, she penned on the eve of the Minneapolis meetings, "the burden of our message should be the mission and life of Jesus" (RH, Sept. 11, 1888).

The greatest lack of Adventism in the 1880s was that of Jesus and His love. It is still the greatest lack.

POINTING OUT THE PROBLEM

Do your best to present yourself to God as one approved, a workman who has no need to be ashamed, rightly handling the word of truth. 2 Tim. 2:15, RSV.

On August 5, 1888, two months before the beginning of the General conference meetings, Ellen White wrote a powerful letter to the "Dear Brethren Who Shall Assemble in General Conference" that put a finger on the problems at the heart of the theological standoff. Listen carefully to her burdens and her themes.

"In humility of mind, with the Spirit of Christ, search the scriptures carefully to see what is truth. The truth can lose nothing by close investigation. Let the Word of God speak for itself, let it be its own interpreter. . . .

"There is a most wonderful [i.e., amazing] laziness that is indulged in by a large class of our ministers who are willing others [i.e., Smith and Butler] should search the scriptures for them; and they take the truth from their lips as a positive fact, but they do not know it to be Bible truth, through their own individual research, and by the deep convictions of the Spirit of God upon their hearts and minds. . . .

"Our people individually must understand Bible truth more thoroughly, for they certainly will be called before councils; they will be criticized by keen and critical minds. It is one thing to give assent to the truth, and another thing, through close examination as Bible students, to know what is truth. . . .

"Many, many will be lost because they have not studied their Bibles upon their knees, with earnest prayer to God that the entrance of the Word of God might give light to their understanding. . . .

"One of the greatest hindrances to our spiritual success is the great want of love and respect evidenced for one another. . . . It is the work of the enemy to create a party spirit, and to have party feelings, and some feel that they are doing the work of God in strengthening prejudice and jealousies among brethren. . . .

"The Word of God is the great detector of error; to it we believe everything must be brought. The Bible must be our standard for every doctrine and practice. We must study it reverentially. We are to receive no one's opinion without comparing it with the scriptures. Here is divine authority which is supreme in matters of faith" (Lt 20, 1888).

In such thoughts we find our marching orders for today.

THE "CALIFORNIA CONSPIRACY"

Jesus knew what they were thinking and asked, "Why are you thinking these things in your hearts?" Luke 5:22, NIV.

Thinking *can* be a good thing.

But it is not necessarily good. That is especially true when it is fueled with conspiracy theories.

It was just such thinking that overwhelmed Butler and his friends on the eve of the 1888 General Conference session. The match that set the conspiracy blaze aflame was a late September letter from California pastor William H. Healey to George I. Butler that suggested that the Western leaders (Jones, Waggoner, W. C. White, and Ellen White) of the church had developed a scheme to change the denomination's theology.

Before the arrival of Healey's letter, Butler appears to have been emotionally stable. He didn't like the thought of the controverted points on Daniel and Galatians coming up, but the August letters of W. C. and Ellen White had convinced him of the necessity of permitting it.

However, it devastated the already-tense General Conference president when he received what appeared to him to be news of an organized conspiracy just a few days before the opening of the Minneapolis session. Suddenly the events of the past two years all seemed to make sense to him. The reason the Whites had pushed so hard to get a hearing for Jones and Waggoner's new theology was that they were all in it together. Certainly, Butler concluded, here was a conspiracy of the most dangerous type and a threat to Adventism's time-tested beliefs.

That reasoning led Butler into a spurt of last-minute frenzied activity as he organized his forces to resist what he saw as the Western coalition by sending off a series of telegrams and letters to the delegates, warning them of the conspiracy and urging them to "stand by the old landmarks."

Meanwhile, the Whites, Waggoner, and Jones, and the other California delegates remained ignorant of the fact that the Battle Creek forces viewed them as conspirators. As W. C. White put it, he was "innocent as a goose" about the misunderstanding, an unawareness that soon led the Westerners to play unwittingly into the hands of the conspiracy theory advocates.

Correct thinking is difficult enough. But when it is tainted with conspiracy theories it becomes emotionally impossible. We still need to be aware of such thinking and pray for God's grace to be free from it.

A CONFUSED LEADER

For where envy and self-seeking exist, confusion and every evil thing will be there. James 3:16, NKJV.

Talk about *confusion.*

That very word describes the mind of General Conference president George I. Butler on the eve of the 1888 General Conference session. Influenced by thoughts of the "California conspiracy," he fired off a 42-page typewritten letter to Ellen White on October 1, just a few days before the meetings, that at the very best reveals an utterly confused mental state.

After stating that he was suffering from "nervous exhaustion" and that because of his "nerve force having given out" he "should drop out of all positions of responsibility in the cause," he laid into Ellen White, telling her that she was the cause of his "present condition more than any one thing."

Butler was especially incensed about her seeming reversal on the nature of the law in Galatians. He was, to say the least, obsessed with the topic.

"The opening up of this question as it has been on the Pacific Coast during the last four years," he wrote, "is fraught with evil and only evil. I firmly believe it will be found to be the cause of unsettling of the minds of many of our people, and breaking down their faith in the work as a unity, and that souls will be lost and give up the truth because of this, and that it will open a wide door for other innovations to come in and break down our old positions of faith.

"And the way it has been managed will tend to break the confidence of our people in the testimonies themselves. And this whole matter I believe will do more to break down confidence in your work than any thing which has occurred since this cause has had an existence. . . . It will break the faith of many of our leading workers in the testimonies."

He went on to blame W. C White for a great deal of the problem and claimed that Jones and Waggoner needed to be "publicly rebuked."

Butler believed that he had been "slaughtered in the house of his friends." Broken in mind and health, he would not attend the 1888 session.

And all over an issue that Ellen White told him wasn't important.

Such are the facts of history.

We may be shocked at Butler. But how many of us have stewed upon the theological edges of the Bible till we find ourselves in a similar state of spiritual and mental ill health. May we have God's grace not to major in minors but to focus on the great central themes of Scripture.

THE 1888 MESSAGE–1

And I, if I be lifted up from the earth, will draw all men unto me. John 12:32.

We hear a lot these days about the 1888 message. What was it? What is it? Perhaps the best summary appeared in a letter that Ellen White wrote a few years after the Minneapolis meetings. Read on and listen with the ears of your heart.

"The Lord in His great mercy sent a most precious message to His people through Elders Waggoner and Jones. This message was to bring more prominently before the world the *uplifted Saviour,* the *sacrifice* for the sins of the whole world. It presented *justification through faith* in the Surety; it invited the people to receive the *righteousness of Christ,* which is made manifest in obedience to all the commandments of God. *Many had lost sight of Jesus.* They needed to have their eyes directed to His *divine person,* His merits, and His changeless love for the human family. All power is given into His hands, that He may dispense rich gifts unto men, imparting the priceless *gift* of His own *righteousness* to the helpless human agent. *This is the message that God commanded to be given to the world.* It is the third angel's message, which is to be proclaimed with a loud voice, and attended with the outpouring of His Spirit in a large measure.

"The *uplifted Saviour* is to appear in His efficacious work as the Lamb slain, sitting upon the throne, to dispense the priceless covenant blessings, the benefits He died to purchase for every soul *who should believe on Him.* John could not express that love in words; it was too deep, too broad; he calls upon the human family to behold it. Christ is pleading for the church in the heavenly courts above, pleading for those for whom He paid the redemption price of His own lifeblood. Centuries, ages, can never diminish the efficacy of this atoning sacrifice" (TM 91, 92; italics supplied).

What a message!

Adventists had uplifted the Sabbath, the sanctuary, the state of the dead, the Second Advent, *but* they had failed to uplift sufficiently the only Person who made everything else even meaningful.

To say the least, Ellen White joined Jones and Waggoner in a call for Adventism to shift its focus. Have you? If not, why not?

THE 1888 MESSAGE–2

They are justified by his grace as a gift, through the redemption which is in Christ Jesus. Rom. 3:24, RSV.

We continue on from where we left off yesterday in what is undoubtedly the very best summary of the significance of Jones and Waggoner's 1888 message.

"The message of *the gospel of His grace* was to be given to the church in clear and distinct lines, *that the world should no longer say that Seventh-day Adventists talk the law, the law, but do not teach or believe Christ.*

"The efficacy of the *blood of Christ* was to be presented to the people with freshness and power, that their *faith* might lay hold upon its merits. As the high priest sprinkled the warm blood upon the mercy seat, while the fragrant cloud of incense ascended before God, so while we confess our sins and plead the efficacy of Christ's *atoning blood,* our prayers are to ascend to heaven, fragrant with the merits of our Saviour's character. Notwithstanding our unworthiness, we are ever to bear in mind that *there is One that can take away sin and save the sinner.* Every sin acknowledged before God with a contrite heart, He will remove. *This faith is the life of the church.* . . .

"Unless he makes it his life business to behold the uplifted Saviour, and by faith to accept the merits which it is his privilege to claim, the sinner can no more be saved than Peter could walk upon the water unless he kept his eyes fixed steadily upon Jesus. Now, it has been Satan's determined purpose to eclipse the view of Jesus and lead men to look to man, and trust to man, and be educated to expect help from man. For years the church has been looking to man and expecting much from man, but *not looking to Jesus, in whom our hopes of eternal life are centered.* Therefore God gave to His servants a testimony that presented *the truth as it is in Jesus,* which is the third angel's message, in clear, distinct lines. . . . This is the testimony that must go throughout the length and breadth of the world. It presents the law and the gospel, binding up the two in a perfect whole" (TM 92-94; italics supplied).

The overwhelming thought of the 1888 message was to uplift Jesus. That is something we can never overdo. Uphold Him today in your work, your family, your play, your all. Let Him truly be Savior and Lord of your life.

THE 1888 MESSAGE—3

By this all men will know that you are my disciples, if you have love for one another.
John 13:35, RSV.

For the past two days we have been examining the core of the 1888 message from a letter written in 1895. Today we want to look at it from a diary entry Ellen White penned in February 1891.

"Many of our ministers," she mused, "have merely sermonized, presenting subjects in an argumentative way, and scarcely mentioning the saving power of the Redeemer. Not having themselves partaken of the living bread from heaven, their testimony was destitute of nourishment, destitute of the saving blood of Jesus Christ, which cleanseth from all sin. Their offering resembled the offering of Cain. . . .

"Why is not He presented to the people as the living Bread? Because He is not abiding in the hearts of many of those who think it their duty to preach the law. . . . The church has been starving for the Bread of life.

"Of all professed Christians, Seventh-day Adventists should be foremost in uplifting Christ before the world. . . . The law and the gospel, blended, will convict of sin. God's law, while condemning sin, points to the gospel, revealing Jesus Christ. . . . In no discourse are [the law and the gospel] to be divorced. . . .

"Why, then, is there manifested in the church so great a lack of love . . . ? It is because Christ is not constantly brought before the people. His attributes of character are not brought into the practical life. . . .

"There is danger of presenting the truth in such a way that the intellect is exalted, leaving the souls of the hearers unsatisfied. A correct theory of the truth may be presented, and yet there may not be manifested the warmth of affection that the God of truth requires. . . .

"The religion of many is very much like an icicle—freezingly cold. . . . They can not touch the hearts of others, because their own hearts are not surcharged with the blessed love that flows from the heart of Christ. There are others who speak of religion as a matter of the will. They dwell upon stern duty as if it were a master ruling with a scepter of iron,—a master stern, inflexible, all-powerful, devoid of the sweet, melting love and tender compassion of Christ" (MS 21, 1891).

Help us, Father, to get the picture of what the gospel is all about and what it is to do in our lives. Amen.

AT THE GENERAL CONFERENCE SESSION—1

A brother offended is harder to be won than a strong city: and their contentions are like the bars of a castle. Prov. 18:19.

N ot all meetings of the church are equally pleasant. The Minneapolis meetings, unfortunately, fell on the negative side of the ledger.

The Minneapolis *Journal* of October 13 trumpeted the Adventists as "A Peculiar People Who Keep Saturday as Sunday, Revere a Prophetess, and Believe the End of the World Is Nigh."

The October 19 *Journal* reported that the Adventists "tackle difficult problems in theology with about the same industry that an earnest man would assail a cord of wood." The newspaper might have added that they were just about as gentle with each other in their theological dialogue. The aggressive spirit evidenced was just what Ellen White had feared might happen.

The 1888 General Conference session convened in the newly constructed Adventist church in Minneapolis, Minnesota, from October 17 through November 4. A ministerial meeting lasting from the tenth of October through the seventeenth preceded the formal conference session. While the business items were restricted to the formal session, the theological debates extended through both meetings. Waggoner noted near the close of the session that the three main theological items on the agenda had been the 10 kingdoms of Daniel 7, the Papacy and the proposed Sunday law, and "the law and the gospel in their various relations, coming under the general head of justification by faith."

Of those three, the only one that did not divide the Adventist leadership at Minneapolis was the religious liberty issue. All agreed that the proposed National Sunday law represented an ominous sign of prophetic history related to Revelation 13 and 14. As a result, no one questioned A. T. Jones's sermons on religious liberty.

The session took three actions regarding the Sunday issue: to publish Jones's sermons on the topic, to sponsor him on a speaking tour to present the topic, and to have him lead a delegation of three to testify before the appropriate United States Senate committee.

Thus by the end of the conference Jones was well on his way to becoming a full-time religious liberty advocate—a position in which he would make some of his most important contributions to the Adventist Church.

Father, fill us, especially in difficult times, with Your spirit that we might learn to work with each other in more effective ways.

AT THE GENERAL CONFERENCE SESSION–2

The law has become our tutor to lead us to Christ, so that we may be justified by faith. Gal. 3:24, NASB.

Not much theological light came from the debate over the 10 horns of Daniel 7 at Minneapolis. Its main contribution was tension as Smith uttered that even discussing the topic was "utterly unnecessary" and was a "tearing up of old truth." Jones proclaimed that he should not be held responsible for Smith's ignorance on certain topics, and Ellen White responded, "Not so sharp, Brother Jones, not so sharp."

On the other hand, genuine theological progress did take place in the area of coming to an understanding of justification by faith. One of the interesting facts of the 1888 meetings is that even though the contending sides entered the meetings with the issue of the law in Galatians at the forefront of their minds, the main outcome of the meetings was a new emphasis on righteousness by faith. How that happened has been a mystery to many.

Waggoner should receive credit for the new direction on the topic. He made a strategic decision not merely to debate the issue of the law in Galatians, but to raise the larger issue of salvation in terms of law and gospel, and then to discuss the book of Galatians in that context.

Thus even though Waggoner made at least nine presentations on gospel/law topics, the first five or six centered on righteousness by faith. Only after that did he deal more specifically with Galatians. That put the Galatians issue into the background and pushed the salvation topic to the front.

According to Waggoner's theology, the ten-commandment/schoolmaster law brings us "unto Christ, *that we might be justified by faith.*" Ellen White backed him on that point. She told the delegates, "I see the beauty of truth in the presentation of the righteousness of Christ in relation to the law as the doctor has placed it before us. . . . [It] harmonizes perfectly with the light which God has been pleased to give me during all the years of my experience" (MS 15, 1888).

In that passage Ellen White highlighted what she considered to be one of Waggoner's most important contributions to Adventist theology. He had built a bridge between law and gospel by making explicit the gospel function of the ten-commandment law.

The law still functions that way in our lives. It not only holds up God's ideal, but it leads individuals who have fallen short of that ideal to Christ for forgiveness and justification.

DOING THEOLOGY:
APPEALS TO HUMAN AUTHORITY—1

What saith the scripture? Rom. 4:3.

What does the Bible have to say on the topic? That was the query of Paul as he thought about righteousness by faith in the book of Romans. It had also been the question of the early Sabbatarian Adventists. A people radically committed to the Bible, they had refused to use tradition, church authority, academic expertise, or any other form of religious authority to settle their theological inquiries. They were a people of one Book.

Things had changed among the Adventist leadership by the late 1880s. In the Minneapolis era they would seek to use at least four forms of human authority to settle the theological controversies troubling the church.

The first centered on authoritative position. The iron-willed Butler particularly found himself susceptible to that approach. His concept of leaders having "clearer views" and more important positions than followers, set him up for authoritative abuses. Ellen White chided him in October 1888 for favoring those who agreed with him, while looking with suspicion on those who "do not feel obliged to receive their impressions and ideas from human beings, [acting] only as they act, [talking] only as they talk, [thinking] only as they think, and in fact, [making] themselves little less than machines" (Lt 21, 1888).

The General Conference president's approach in encouraging Adventists "to look to one man to think for them, to be conscience for them" had in the eyes of Mrs. White created too many weaklings who were "unable to stand at their post of duty" (Lt 14, 1891).

Denigrating authoritative position in doctrinal and biblical issues, Ellen White pointed out in December 1888 that "we should not consider that either Elder Butler or Elder Smith are the guardians of the doctrines for Seventh-day Adventists, and that no one may dare to express an idea that differs from theirs. My cry has been: *Investigate the Scriptures for yourselves.* . . . *No man is to be authority for us*" (Lt 7, 1888; italics supplied).

And so it is. God's Word as found in the Bible is the authority for every Christian. It was so in 1888. And it is still so today. With that in mind, we with the apostle Paul need to begin each day with a "What saith the Scripture?"

Doing Theology:
Appeals to Human Authority—2

Man does not live by bread alone, but that man lives by everything that proceeds out of the mouth of the Lord. Deut. 8:3, RSV.

While we all agree that the Bible is important, it is terribly difficult not to attempt to solve our theological problems by citing the opinions of the "experts." Both Uriah Smith and G. I. Butler made such appeals in the 1888 era. While the majority of Adventist ministers may have agreed with the leadership, Adventism's reform element raised a chorus of objections.

E. J. Waggoner was as lucid as anyone on the topic. In refuting Butler's use of expert opinion to settle the Galatians issue, he met the older man at his most vulnerable spot. *"I care nothing,"* Waggoner argued, *"for what a man says. I want to know what God says.* We do not teach for doctrine the word of men, but the word of God. I am verily convinced that you would not quote Greenfield if you could find scripture argument instead."

If Adventists were to begin relying on authoritative opinion, Waggoner asserted, "we might as well turn Papists at once; for to pin one's faith to the opinion of man is the very essence of the Papacy." Seventh-day Adventists, he asserted, "should be Protestants indeed, testing everything by the Bible alone."

Not only did Adventists face the temptation to call upon the standard Christian authors to support various positions, but they also had their own well-established authors, such as Uriah Smith.

W. C. White pointed out that some Adventist ministers gave "equal importance to the quotations of Scripture, and to Eld. Smith's comments," because Ellen White had commended his *Daniel and the Revelation.* After all, some ministers argued, didn't she say that Smith "had the help of heavenly angels in his work"?

Now, here is an interesting argument from Adventist history. Again and again people have argued for accepting some person's authority because Ellen White commended their writings or said they had the truth.

Such was not the position of the reformers at Minneapolis, including Ellen White herself. All of them would say that no matter how much truth someone might have, the only way to validate any particular teaching of theirs would be to go to the Bible and thoroughly check it out.

That's still good advice. Or as I like to say it, the eleventh commandment is "never trust a theologian." All ideas are to be verified by the Bible.

DOING THEOLOGY:
APPEALS TO HUMAN AUTHORITY–3

You leave the commandment of God, and hold fast the tradition of men.
Mark 7:8, RSV.

A third invalid use of human authority during the 1888 era concerned reliance upon Adventist tradition to settle a point. Both Smith and Butler used the argument repeatedly that since the Adventist positions on Galatians and Daniel had stood for 40 years, they should not be changed. Smith even went so far as to claim that if the traditional understandings were wrong he would be forced to renounce Adventism.

E. J. Waggoner and A. T. Jones, of course, rejected the appeal to Adventist tradition. J. H. Waggoner backed up his son. "I have long believed," he penned, "it to be a serious error which was growing up among us, that an individual, or even a publishing house, should send forth their views and hold the denomination bound to that view because it chanced to be published by them. . . . Expositions of Scriptures cannot rest on" the authority of tradition. "They can be settled only by calm investigation, and just reasoning, and then all must have an equal right to express their opinions."

Ellen White, as usual, was in the reformers' corner. "As a people," she warned, "we are certainly in great danger, if we are not constantly guarded, of considering our ideas, because long cherished, to be Bible doctrines and in every point infallible, and measuring everyone by the rule of our interpretation of Bible truth. This is our danger, and this would be the greatest evil that could ever come to us as a people" (MS 37, 1890).

Tradition is an interesting topic. Every red-blooded Adventist can see that other Christians are wrong in relying upon their tradition. After all, those traditions in some cases are obviously erroneous. They should, we affirm, go to the Bible

But *Adventist tradition* often gets viewed in a different light. Didn't, the logic runs, our pioneers have the truth?

Yes, we might reply, but it wasn't all the truth without error. The only genuine test of tradition or any other source of authority is to compare a teaching with the biblical position on the topic.

In short, Adventist tradition by itself is no better than that of any other religious group. It is always to the Bible that we must appeal.

Doing Theology:
Appeals to Human Authority—4

I felt the necessity to write to you appealing that you contend earnestly for the faith which was once for all handed down to the saints. Jude 3, NASB.

Contending for the faith was not one of the shortcomings of the Adventist leaders in the 1880s. Their problem wasn't contending, but doing so on a correct basis.

A final category of human authority employed by the Smith-Butler group in their attempt to maintain traditional Adventism was their drive for a voted creed-like statement that would set the pre-1888 theology in concrete and thus render it exempt from change in the future.

The General Conference leadership had attempted a voted statement at the 1886 General Conference session, but had failed when they couldn't get their theological committee to line up on the "right side" of the issues related to Galatians and Daniel 7.

One of the problems with voted creeds is they have tended to set marginal issues of current interest firmly next to the fundamental doctrines of the Bible as landmarks of the faith. Such new landmarks, once established in a creed, become almost impossible to overturn in the future, since people interpret any change as destroying the faith of the fathers.

The Minneapolis meetings witnessed attempts at creedlike resolutions on both the 10 horns and the law in Galatians. On October 17, for example, G. B. Starr called for a vote on the 10 horns. "'I'd like,' he said, 'to put an everlasting settler on this question so it would not come up for argument again.'" The audience responded with "cries of 'amen,' 'amen.'"

Waggoner and the Whites, however, successfully resisted such a move. Mrs. White wrote on the last day of the meetings that she and "Willie . . . had to watch at every point lest there should be moves made, resolutions passed, that would prove detrimental to the future work" (Lt 82, 1888).

She noted in 1892 that "the church may pass resolution upon resolution to put down all disagreement of opinions, but we cannot force the mind and will, and thus root out disagreement. These resolutions may conceal the discord, but they cannot quench it and establish perfect agreement." As a result, she suggested that some "Christlike forbearance" of variation of belief was necessary. On the other hand, "the great truths of the Word of God are so clearly stated that none need make a mistake in understanding them." The problem comes with those who magnified "mere molehills . . . into mountains and . . . made barriers between brethren" (MS 24, 1892).

Help me, Father, not to be a molehill specialist.

Doing Theology:
Appeals to Ellen White's Authority–1

The grass withereth, and the flower thereof falleth away: But the word of the Lord endureth for ever. 1 Peter 1:24, 25.

The General Conference leadership had failed in attempting to solve the theological issues facing the church through the use of human authority. But they felt that a "testimony" from Ellen White on the disputed points would be even better. After all, were not her writings from God?

Butler was particularly excited about the possibilities inherent in that type of decision. Between June 1886 and October 1888 he wrote a series of letters that indicate an increasing degree of pressure as he sought to force Ellen White to provide the authoritative interpretation he needed to settle the Galatians issue. Had he been more successful, he could have written a book entitled *How to Push a Prophet*.

Employing good psychology, he began in a mild manner to elicit a response from her. On June 20, 1886, he wrote to her complaining of Jones and Waggoner's teachings about the law in Galatians being the moral law—a point, he emphasized, that was out of harmony with traditional Adventist teaching.

Butler then slid into his appeal by gently nudging her toward the proper answer: "I heard it intimated years ago that you had light concerning the added law, to the effect that it related to the remedial system rather than the moral law. I think this question ought in some way to be set at rest. It would be a most bitter pill to many of our leading brethren to be compelled to see the idea taught generally, that the law which was added . . . was the moral law itself."

On August 23 the General Conference president came a little more out in the open on the topic. After noting that the subject was creating controversy, he became quite specific about the situation in the 1850s when the Adventist leadership had adopted the ceremonial law interpretation. He suggested that he might write a tract on the topic. And, finally, he hinted that he knew very little of her opinion, thereby providing Mrs. White with an opportunity to rubber-stamp the "true" view that he had just finished outlining to her.

Now here was a problem for Butler. Just how do you force, maneuver, convince, or urge a prophet to do anything?

Good question. We will see a bit more of the answer tomorrow.

Meanwhile we need to begin to think deeply about the relation of the modern gift of prophecy to the Bible.

Doing Theology:
Appeals to Ellen White's Authority–2

Whatever was written in former days was written for our instruction, that by steadfastness and by the encouragement of the scriptures we might have hope. Rom. 15:4, RSV.

We left President Butler yesterday in his attempt to try to maneuver Ellen White to "produce" a testimony to solve the Galatians controversy. He hadn't gotten very far by August 23, 1886. By December 16 his patience with the silent prophet had rapidly deteriorated. His plan to have the issue settled by creedal resolution at the 1886 General Conference session had failed, and he was beginning to feel desperate regarding her lack of cooperation. "We have been waiting for years to hear from you on the subject [of Galatians]," he blurted out, "knowing that its agitation would end only in debate." Twelve days later he flatly told her that "nothing short of a testimony from heaven" would change his mind.

March 1887 found Butler in somewhat better spirits, having received Ellen White's rebuke of Waggoner and Jones for making their controversial views public. Interpreting some of her remarks to indicate that she was on his side in the Galatians controversy, and believing that she would say the correct things, he therefore reminded her that he had repeatedly written to her on the subject, "but got no reply."

While claiming that he was not urging her to make a statement, he ominously hinted that he felt "certain that after all the stir over this question it will make constant trouble till your opinion is known." "If our people knew that you had light that the moral law was not the added law, the question would be settled in short order. That is precisely what our people are waiting with much anxiety to know."

Positive that she would now come out in public for his side, Butler was both hurt and shocked when she wrote to him in April 1887 that her letter rebuking the younger men did not mean that his position was correct.

After that "betrayal," he did not waste any more ink asking for her opinion on the topic. Rather, specters of theological disaster, prophetic betrayal, and conspiracy began to grow in his mind, eventually leading to a nervous breakdown and the massive October 1, 1888, letter in which he finally attacked her for not coming up with the correct answer.

And that all in the face of her repeated counsel that the issue was of no importance and should be dropped.

Here is a question for each of us. How much of our own agenda dominates our thinking as we approach the Bible and Ellen White's counsels? Think about it! Be honest!

DOING THEOLOGY:
APPEALS TO ELLEN WHITE'S AUTHORITY—3

Seek and read from the book of the Lord. Isa. 34:16, RSV.

As we have noted the past couple of days, president G. I. Butler of the General conference had been seeking to maneuver Ellen White into giving the authoritative answer to his biblical/theological issues, since he didn't have enough evidence from "the book of the Lord" to carry his point.

The entire sequence of the Butler letters is of great interest, given the way many Adventists view the work of Ellen White. Many have both silently and verbally wished that she were still alive in our day so that they could ask her the "real" meaning of a particular scriptural passage. In the Butler sequence we find her answer to such an approach—silence, frustrating silence. The General Conference leaders wanted her to function as a theological policewoman or an exegetical referee. That, significantly enough, is exactly what she refused to do.

Not only did Ellen White decline to settle the biblical issue through appeal to her writings, but she went so far as to infer to the delegates at the Minneapolis meetings on October 24 that it was providential that she had lost the testimony to J. H. Waggoner in which she had purportedly resolved the law in Galatians issue once and for all in the 1850s. *"God has a purpose in this. He wants us to go to the Bible and get the Scripture evidence"* (MS 9, 1888; italics supplied).

In other words, she was more interested in what the Bible had to say on the subject than in what she had written. For her, the testimonies were not to become the authoritative last word on Bible topics. Nor were they to take the place of the Bible. She would emphasize that point forcefully in early 1889 in the publication of *Testimony 33,* which has an extensive section on the role of her writings. We need to become familiar with that section. Why not read it today or this coming Sabbath (see 5T 654-691)?

Ellen White made it explicit that her writings were to bring people "back to the word" (*ibid.,* 663) and to aid them in understanding biblical principles, but she never held them up as a divine commentary on Scripture. But that was not always obvious to her fellow Adventists. And many even today have not grasped it.

Ellen White never ceased directing people to "the book of the Lord" and to Jesus. She did not point to herself or to her writings as the authority. That is the best witness we have to the validity of her gift.

DOING THEOLOGY:
APPEALS TO ELLEN WHITE'S AUTHORITY—4

They welcomed the message very eagerly and examined the scriptures every day to see whether these things were so. Acts 17:11, NRSV.

The faithful Bereans studied the scriptures faithfully to uncover the truth. That is exactly what Ellen White was seeking to get the Adventist leadership to do in the late 1880s. But too many of them were looking to her writings to solve their biblical issues instead of doing their homework in the Bible. It was just that problem that she tried to head off. Her misguided "followers" may have failed in getting her to "produce" a testimony on the Galatians issue, but they could at least feel a wave of thankfulness that they at least had her published writings on the topic, especially since she had seemingly identified the law in Galatians in her *Sketches From the Life of Paul* (1883). From diary entries we know exactly what pages certain individuals read at the 1888 session.

On October 24 J. H. Morrison utilized *Sketches* in his attempt to demonstrate the validity of the ceremonial law interpretation. Turning to page 193, he read to the delegates: "He [Paul] describes the visit which he made to Jerusalem to secure a settlement of the very questions which are now agitating the churches of Galatia, as to whether the Gentiles should submit to circumcision and keep the ceremonial law." Next Morrison quoted from her discussion of the nature of the Galatians problem on page 188: "Having gained this point, they [the judaizing Christians] induced them [the Christians at Galatia] to return to the observance of the ceremonial law as essential to salvation. Faith in Christ, and obedience to the law of ten commandments were regarded as of minor importance." Morrison also read from page 68, in which Mrs. White spoke on the yoke of bondage mentioned in both Acts 15:10 and Galatians 5:1: "This yoke was not the law of ten commandments, as those who oppose the binding claim of the law assert; but Peter referred to the law of ceremonies."

Having submitted this evidence, Morrison sat down and the traditionalists must have believed they had clinched the argument. After all, they had a quotation from Ellen White. Thus they were right and Waggoner and Jones were wrong on the basis of her commentary on the Bible.

That position, as we will see tomorrow, was not the one Ellen White took.

Guide us, Father, as we contemplate the important question of religious authority and the relationship of the gifts of the Spirit to the Bible.

Doing Theology:
Appeals to Ellen White's Authority—5

The ears of all the people were attentive unto the book of the law. Neh. 8:3.

Yesterday we left off with J. H. Morrison having read from Ellen White's *Sketches From the Life of Paul* in order to clinch the argument that the law in Galatians was the ceremonial rather than the moral law. The quotations he cited certainly appear to teach that position. Morrison and his friends were convinced they had proved their point on the basis of Ellen White's "divine commentary" on Scripture.

But that was *not* the position that Mrs. White assumed. That very morning (before Morrison's presentation) in addressing the Galatians issue, she had said: "I cannot take my position on either side until I have studied the question" (MS 9, 1888). It was in that context that she noted that it was providential that she could not find her testimony to J. H. Waggoner on the topic. Some would have mis-used it to keep people from exploring God's Word.

Ellen White had light for the General Conference delegates on the subject of Galatians, but that light, as she repeatedly asserted, was that they needed to study the Bible and not rely on any other form of authority as they sought the meaning of Scripture. She would hammer that message home in her last recorded message at Minneapolis—"A Call to a Deeper Study of the Word."

Apparently Morrison's use of *Sketches* to prove his point did not impress her. We have no indication that she considered the matter settled by that method, nor did she quote her own writings at Minneapolis to decide any of the theological, historical, or biblical issues. Her writings had their purposes, but one of them was not to take a superior position to the Bible by providing an infallible commentary.

Mrs. White would reflect that same attitude 20 years later in the controversy over the "daily" of Daniel 8, a struggle once again based on her comments. And once again she told people not to use her writings that way.

In fact, to keep people from misusing her writings on the law in Galatians, she had the statements removed when she revised *Sketches* into *The Acts of the Apostles* in 1911. She meant what she said about people going to the Bible to find out its meaning rather than relying upon her writings.

The issue of authority is a most important one. May God help us daily as we study His Word to discover His truth and His will for our lives.

DOING THEOLOGY:
THE AUTHORITY OF THE BIBLE

All Scripture is inspired by God and is useful to teach us what is true and to make us realize what is wrong in our lives. It straightens us out and teaches us to do what is right. 2 Tim. 3:16, NLT.

Waggoner, Jones, and the Whites stood in harmony with each other on the proper way to resolve theological issues. All held that the Bible is the only determiner of Christian belief. As a result, they were united against the attempts of the traditionalists to utilize any other form of authority to settle biblical issues.

Ellen White was particularly insistent on the need for Bible study in dealing with theological disputes. In April 1887, for example, she wrote to Butler and Smith that "we want Bible evidence for every point we advance. We do not want to tide over points as Elder Canright has done with assertions" (Lt 13, 1887). In July 1888 she set forth her position with the greatest clarity when she published in the *Review* that *"the Bible is the only rule of faith and doctrine"* (RH, July 17, 1888; italics supplied).

And on August 5, 1888, she told her readers to "search the Scriptures carefully to see what is truth," adding that "the truth can lose nothing by close investigation. Let the Word of God speak for itself, let it be its own interpreter." "The Word of God is the great detector of error; to it we believe everything must be brought. *The Bible must be our standard for every doctrine and practice. . . . We are to receive no one's opinion without comparing it with the Scriptures. Here is divine authority which is supreme in matters of faith. It is the word of the living God that is to decide all controversies"* (Lt 20, 1888; italics supplied).

Ellen White also drummed home that message during her last presentation at Minneapolis: "The Scriptures must be your study, then you will know that you have the truth. . . . You should not believe any doctrine simply because another says it is truth. You should not believe it because Elder Smith, or Elder Kilgore, or Elder Van Horn, or Elder Haskell says it is truth, but because God's voice has declared it in His living oracles" (MS 15, 1888). She could have as easily added her own name to that list, given the position that she had taken during the meetings.

Thank You, Lord, for Your Word in the Bible. Today we want to recommit our lives to the daily study of it with more persistence and energy.

VICTORY AT MINNEAPOLIS
ON THE AUTHORITY ISSUE

[All Scripture] is God's way of preparing us in every way, fully equipped for every good thing God wants us to do. 2 Tim. 3:17, NLT.

Quite a number of the ministers took to heart Ellen White's plea at Minneapolis for personal Bible study. "Many go from this meeting." W. C White wrote on November 2, 1888, "determined to study the Bible as never before, and this will result in clearer preaching."

R. DeWitt Hottel jotted down in his diary that one of his first activities after returning home from Minneapolis "was reading in Brother Butler's book on Galatians and also Bro. Waggoner's reply. Also read in the Bible." Hottel was apparently testing the conclusions of both men by the scriptures.

Another success story was that of J. O. Corliss, who had been examining God's Word with gratifying results. "I never had such floods of light in the same length of time," he declared, "and the truth never looked so good to me as it does now. All alone by myself, I have studied the subjects of the covenants, and the law in Galatians. I came to my conclusions without consulting any one but the Lord and His Holy Word. I think now that I have the matter straight in my mind, and I can see the beauty and harmony of the Dr's [Waggoner's] position on the Galatians law."

Apparently not everyone had tuned out Ellen White at Minneapolis. During the 1889 General Conference session she could write that she was "thankful to see with our ministering brethren a disposition to search the scriptures for themselves" (MS 10, 1889).

During the early 1890s the General Conference sponsored annual schools for the ministers as a response to the call at Minneapolis for the Adventist clergy to become better Bible students. The 1888 meetings had highlighted their inability to interact with the Bible. The domineering G. I. Butler was no longer president of the General Conference, and O. A. Olson's administration did what it could to enable the denomination's ministers to become better students of Scripture.

Given the importance of the Bible, one of the wonders of the twenty-first-century church is that we don't spend more time with it. Most of us pass more time before the TV than before an open Bible.

Today is the day to change that pattern.

FAILURE AT MINNEAPOLIS
ON THE AUTHORITY ISSUE

Thy words were found, and I did eat them; and thy word was unto me the joy and rejoicing of mine heart. Jer. 15:16.

It's good to eat the words of God. But sometimes we would rather partake of those of other people.

That thought brings us back to the issue of authority at Minneapolis. While the aftermath of the conference had its successes, it also had its failures. Perhaps the most obvious one was the continuing temptation to rely on human opinions. By 1894, however, it was no longer the authoritative words of Butler and Smith, but those of Jones that were causing the problem. Ellen White's repeated endorsement of him and Waggoner at Minneapolis and beyond had undoubtedly prepared the minds of many to accept whatever they said or wrote. Because of their uplifting of Christ and the power of the forces in Adventism lined up against them she had to "shout loud" her endorsement of them to get them a hearing.

Her voice did not go unheard. By 1894 S. N. Haskell felt compelled to observe to her that it had been "absolutely necessary" for her to "uphold Eld. Waggoner and A. T. Jones for these number of years." "But," he added, "the whole country has been silenced against criticizing them to any extent. That battle has been fought, and the victory gained."

The denomination, he told her, now faced the opposite problem—the people and church leaders "were taking everything they [Jones and W. W. Prescott] said as being almost inspired of God." F. M. Wilcox had come to a similar conclusion. Writing from Battle Creek, he noted that "there was a time when many of the principles that Brother Jones has brought out were opposed, but lately the great mass of our people have hung on his words almost as though they were the words of God."

Thus by 1894 Adventists had created a new crisis of authority. "Some of our brethren," Ellen White commented, "have looked to these ministers, and have placed them where God should be. They have received every word from their lips, without carefully seeking the counsel of God for themselves" (Lt 27, 1894).

Will we ever learn?

One of the great lessons of the 1888 General Conference session involves authority—that God's Word is the supreme authority, and that we need to move away from trusting the words of human beings and reading the Bible through their eyes.

God, help us!

THE PROPHET AND THE MESSENGERS

Get Mark and bring him with you; for he is very useful in serving me.
2 Tim. 4:11, RSV.

The biblical prophets and apostles from time to time recommended individuals who would be a special blessing to the church. Ellen White wasn't different in that regard. The most repeated endorsement she made during her ministry was that involving Waggoner and Jones. Again and again she upheld them for their Christ-centered message.

But did her repeated recommendation mean that she agreed with all they taught—even in relation to the law and the gospel?

Let's let her answer for herself. Early in the Minneapolis meetings she wrote of her angelic "guide" who "stretched out his arms toward Dr. Waggoner and to you, Elder Butler, and said in substance as follows: 'Neither [has] all the light upon the law; neither position is perfect.'" While the context of that statement is the 1886 General Conference session, she still held the same position in 1888 (Lt 21, 1888).

In early November she told the delegates at Minneapolis that some of the things that Waggoner had presented on the law in Galatians "do not harmonize with the understanding I have had of this subject." Later in the same talk she claimed that "some interpretations of Scripture given by Dr. Waggoner I do not regard as correct" (MS 15, 1888).

W. C. White substantiates his mother's position. He wrote to his wife from Minneapolis that "much that Dr. W. teaches is in line with what" his mother had "seen in vision." That had led some to the conclusion "that she endorses all his views, [and that no] part of his teaching disagrees [with Mother] and with her Testimonies. . . . I could prove all this to be [false]."

Constantly Ellen White validated the central core of what Jones and Waggoner presented on the righteousness of Christ. But an examination of their writings reflects a number of significant theological issues on which she differed from them.

They were, however, pointing in the right direction as they sought to uplift Christ and righteousness through faith rather than through keeping the law.

As with any prophetic pointing, there are no flawless targets. All must be evaluated in the light of the Bible.

TWO KINDS OF RIGHTEOUSNESS—1

"Teacher, what good deed must I do, to have eternal life?". . . "If you would enter life, keep the commandments." Matt. 19:16, 17, RSV.

A dventists through the years have heard a great deal about righteousness by faith at the 1888 General Conference session. But what were Jones and Waggoner actually teaching? And what positions of Smith and Butler needed correcting? We will spend several days looking at the answers to those questions.

Perhaps the best way into the subject is through Uriah Smith's *Review* editorials in January 1888. In a January 3 piece entitled "The Main Point" he asserted that the aim of the Adventist pioneers was to herald the last proclamation of the Second Advent and "to lead souls to Christ through obedience to this closing testing truth. This was the one objective point of all their efforts; and the end sought was not considered gained unless souls were converted to God, and led to seek through an enlightened obedience to all his commands, a preparation from the Lord from heaven." Smith tied "The Main Point" to the third angel's message by underscoring the word "keep" when he quoted Revelation 14:12: "'Here are they that *keep* the commandments of God, and the faith of Jesus.'"

We need to stop here for a moment. Think about it. How do people come to Christ? Through obedience as Smith asserts? Or by some other method?

His emphasis appears again in his last editorial of January 1888—"Conditions of Everlasting Life." He based his comments on the question of the rich young ruler to Christ: "'Good Master, what good thing shall I do, that I may have eternal life?'" The Bible answer, Smith proclaimed, could be summed up in one proposition as "repent, believe, obey, and live." That, he claimed, was Jesus' response. After all, didn't He say to the young ruler, "'If thou wilt enter into life, keep the commandments'"?

Smith continued on to note that "the trouble with the righteousness of the Pharisees" was that they had not reached an acceptable degree of "moral character" in relation to the "moral law."

Following the false lead of Joseph Bates on the meaning of the story of the rich young ruler, Smith and his associates were mired in legalism. They had not yet discovered the New Testament relationship of law and gospel.

Some of us, and I include myself, have struggled mightily with the same issue. But hold on. That's what 1888 is all about.

TWO KINDS OF RIGHTEOUSNESS—2

Was not Abraham our father justified by works . . . ? James 2:21, RSV.

The relationship between faith and obedience is at the heart of righteousness and justification. Yesterday we found Uriah Smith arguing in early 1888 that obedience was the key to salvation. His primary illustration was the rich young ruler. What Smith failed to notice was that even though the young ruler had kept the commandments he still went away from Christ quite lost.

Smith and his colleagues, of course, believed in justification by faith. They had to, since it's in the Bible. But they based their understanding on the King James Version's misleading translation of Romans 3:25, which claims Christ's "righteousness for the remission of sins that are *past.*" Thus J. F. Ballenger could write: "To make satisfaction for past sins, faith is *everything.* Precious indeed is that blood that blots out all our sins and makes a clean record of the past. Faith only can make the promises of God our own. But present duty is ours to perform. . . . Obey the voice of God and live, or disobey and die."

One result of their belief that justification by faith dealt with past sins was that Smith, Butler, and their friends taught that maintaining justification after conversion was a matter of "justification by works." After all, Ballenger later wrote in quoting James, "was not Abraham our father *justified by works . . . ?*" "When we obey, that act, coupled with our faith secures our justification."

Thus for these Adventists justification was not by faith alone, as Paul repeatedly asserts (even of Abraham; see Rom. 3:20-25; 4:1-5; Eph. 2:5, 8; Gal. 2:16), but faith + works.

It was precisely that theology that Waggoner and Jones disagreed with. In a January 1888 editorial in the *Signs* entitled "Different Kinds of Righteousness," Waggoner, in contending with Smith, noted that a person could not improve on the moral righteousness of the scribes and Pharisees because "they trusted to their own works, and did not submit to the righteousness of God." In fact, he asserted, their righteousness was not "real righteousness at all." They had simply tried "to cover up one filthy, ragged garment by putting on some more filthy rags."

How are we saved? And how do works relate to that salvation? That was the essence of the struggle at Minneapolis. It was also the conflict between Paul and his adversaries in Romans and Galatians.

Give us understanding of this crucial topic, Father, as we reflect upon it day by day.

TWO KINDS OF RIGHTEOUSNESS—3

All our righteousnesses [or "righteous deeds," RSV] are as filthy rags. Isa. 64:6.

Are they?
That is the position Waggoner took in the face of the emphasis by Smith and his friends on justification by works. "Human righteousness," Waggoner penned, "is of no more value after a man is justified than it was before." The justified Christian "'shall live by faith.'" Therefore, "the one who has the most faith will live the most upright life." That is true because Christ is "'THE LORD OUR RIGHTEOUSNESS.'" For Waggoner, faith was everything and the equation of faith + works = justification found its roots in "the spirit of the antichrist."

Jones stood firmly with Waggoner. In May 1889, for example, he told his hearers that the law was *not* the place to seek righteousness. All "our righteousness is as *filthy rags.*"

Smith took exception to such comments. A month later he fired off a broadside at Jones in the *Review* entitled "Our righteousness." He noted that some of the correspondents of the *Review* were playing into the hands of those who would do away with the law by making remarks about our righteousness being "filthy rags." The *Review* editor went on to say that "perfect obedience to the [law] will develop perfect righteousness, and that is the only way any one can attain righteousness." "We are not," he asserted, "to rest on the stool of do-nothing, as a mass of inertia in the hands of the Redeemer. . . . 'Our righteousness' . . . comes from being in harmony with the law of God. . . . And 'our righteousness' cannot in this case be filthy rages." There is, he concluded, a righteousness that is "to be secured by doing and teaching the commandments."

When that article came out, Ellen White was preaching that faith must come before works at camp meeting in Rome, New York. When the people couldn't harmonize what she was saying with Smith's article, her response was that Brother Smith "doesn't know what he is talking about; he sees trees as men walking." She pointed out that just because Jesus and His righteousness are central in salvation, that does not mean that we discard God's law (MS 5, 1889). To Smith she wrote that he was on a path that would bring him to a precipice and that he was "walking like a blind man" (Lt 55, 1889).

How is our spiritual eyesight? Are we clear on the relation of faith and works, law and grace? Maybe not. But that's what the 1888 emphasis is all about. Answers will come as we follow God's leading through this bit of Adventist history.

TWO KINDS OF RIGHTEOUSNESS—4

No human being will be justified in his sight by works of the law, since through the law comes knowledge of sin. Rom. 3:20, RSV.

That Bible teaching seems to be clear enough. The law's function is to hold up God's ideal and to point out our sin when we fail to meet that ideal. The law, Romans 3:20 plainly states, has absolutely no power to save.

That is all true. But! But if I really believe that justification is by grace through faith without works of law, then what happens to the law?

Good question!

It was the fear that a downplaying of the law would end up doing away with the Sabbath that motivated the Smith and Butler forces in the 1888 era.

Let's listen to Butler on the topic. In an article titled "The Righteousness of the Law Fulfilled by Us" he noted that "there is a sentiment prevailing almost everywhere" that is pleasant but dangerous: "'Only believe in Christ, and you will be all right.' . . . Jesus does it all." That teaching, he proclaimed, "is one of the most dangerous heresies in the world." The whole point of the third angel's message, he emphasized, is "the necessity of obedience to the law of God. 'Here are they that *keep the commandments of God,* and the faith of Jesus.'" The Christian world, Butler added, was rapidly losing that truth, and Adventists needed to uplift it.

There we have it. Too much of Christ and His righteousness, some feared, would do away with the law, obedience, and the need for human righteousness.

That fear was at the heart of the reaction to Jones and Waggoner's teachings at Minneapolis.

The two sides had two vastly different perspectives. For the reformers the key words and phrases were "Christ," "faith," "justification by faith," and terms related to Christ's righteousness. The Smith/Butler group, on the other hand, emphasized "human effort," "works," "obedience," "law," "commandments," "our righteousness," and "justification by works."

Those two emphases are still quite distinct in Adventism 120 years after Minneapolis.

Do they have to be mutually exclusive? Why or why not?

How do you line up on these issues? Think it through. Discuss it with your family and friends.

HOW DID WAGGONER VIEW SALVATION?—1

For by grace you have been saved through faith, and this is not your own doing; it is the gift of God, not a result of works, so that no one may boast. Eph. 2:8, 9, ESV.

The first thing to note in Waggoner's theology is that human beings can do nothing to earn salvation. "Our salvation," he penned, "is wholly due to the infinite mercy of God through the merits of Christ." God "does not wait for sinners to desire pardon, before he makes an effort to save them." That is good news indeed, but it is a gospel far removed from Uriah Smith's view that obedience leads men and women to God. To the contrary, according to Waggoner the God of grace searches out the undeserving lost. The Lord takes the initiative in salvation.

A second pillar in Waggoner's theology is that no person can become good by obeying the law, because "the law has not a particle of righteousness to bestow upon any man." He held that *a man cannot do good until he first becomes good.* Therefore, deeds done by a sinful person have no effect whatever to make him righteous, but, on the contrary, coming from an evil heart, they are evil, and so add to the sum of his sinfulness." Yet, he noted, "the Pharisees are not extinct; there are many in our days who expect to gain righteousness by their own good deeds."

As Waggoner saw it, God never presented the law as an avenue by which to achieve heaven. Both Waggoner and Jones believed that *the function of the law was not only "to give the knowledge of sin," but "to bring people to Christ, that they might be justified by faith."*

"Since the best efforts of a sinful man," he claimed, "have not the least effect toward producing righteousness, it is evident that the only way it can come to him is as a gift." Our own attempts at attaining righteousness are like trying to cover our naked bodies with "filthy garments." But "we find that when Christ covers us with the robe of His own righteousness, He does not furnish a cloak for sin, but takes sin away." In effect, when we accept Christ's righteousness, our "sin has been canceled."

Thank You, Lord, for Christ's robe. Having tried by ourselves fruitlessly for years, we are finally ready to surrender and fully accept Your gift. Amen.

HOW DID WAGGONER VIEW SALVATION?—2

But to all who received him, who believed in his name, he gave power to become children of God; who were born, not of blood nor of the will of the flesh nor of the will of man, but of God. John 1:12, 13, RSV.

At the point where an individual accepts Christ's righteousness by faith, Waggoner asserted, that person becomes a part of the family of God. "Note," he penned, "that it is by being justified by His grace that we are made heirs. . . . *Faith in Christ Jesus makes us children of God;* therefore we know that whoever has been justified by God's grace—has been forgiven—is an heir of God."

But justification and adoption into the family of God are not the sum total of salvation for Waggoner. Far from it, "God does not adopt us as His children because we are good, but in order to make us good."

At the very time that God justifies and adopts individuals into the family of God, He transforms them into new beings. Such persons, Waggoner adds, are not only no longer under condemnation, but they "are now new creatures in Christ and must henceforth walk in newness of life, no longer 'under the law,' but 'under grace.'" At the time of justification God gives the converted sinner "a new heart." Thus "it is proper to say that he is saved."

Here it is important to note that Waggoner often talked of justification by faith and the new birth in the same breath. That is quite appropriate, since they take place at the same moment. In other words, at the very point in time that a person is justified, he or she is also born anew by the Holy Spirit. Thus both being accounted righteous (being justified) and having one's nature changed happen simultaneously.

As a result, being accounted righteous, according to Waggoner, is not a legal fiction. Justified individuals think differently and desire to act differently under the guidance of God. But, of course, when they fail and confess that failure His grace is there to forgive them anew.

Being adopted into God's family as individuals who were born outside of that family (see Eph. 2:1-5) is a beautiful promise.

Thank You, Lord, that we can be a part of the family of God.

HOW DID WAGGONER VIEW SALVATION?–3

If any man be in Christ, he is a new creature: old things are passed away; behold, all things are become new. 2 Cor. 5:17.

Ｎew "creature" (KJV) or new "creation" (RSV) in Christ is a powerful teaching. It runs throughout the New Testament, but finds special expression in the writings of Paul.

Waggoner picked up on that theme, noting that at the very point that persons are justified they are also born again as new beings and adopted into the family of God.

In Waggoner's words, "the difference between a righteous man and a sinner is much more than a mere difference of belief. It is more than a mere arbitrary reckoning on the part of God. It is a real difference. . . . God never declares a person righteous simply because he makes an acknowledgment of the truth. There is an actual, literal change from a state of sin to righteousness, which justifies God in making the declaration." To put it simply, the justified person will live differently than a sinner, because God has made him or her into a new creature at the time of justification.

For Waggoner, justification, new birth, and adoption were the beginning of the Christian walk. Opposing the holiness teachers who held to a form of sanctification "without any change of habit on the part of the individual," *he viewed "holiness" without life-changing obedience to the law to be a "delusion."*

The saved person, according to Waggoner, will live the life of God's law. He wrote, that "a person can no more love God and fail to manifest it by deeds, than he can live without breathing." Victory over sin comes from the indwelling power of the Holy Spirit in a Christian's life. Only those who gain victory over sin, he held, will be in the eternal kingdom.

Waggoner, as we can see, was not against the law and obedience. But he was dead set against the law and obedience being at the center of one's experience. No! That place was for Christ and His righteousness alone.

But within the realm of Christ's righteousness the newborn person will of necessity desire to walk with God and keep His law.

The order is crucial. First comes salvation. Then comes obedience. Put it backwards and you have legalism.

WHAT ABOUT THE COVENANT?—1

The days will come, says the Lord, when I will establish a new covenant with the house of Israel. . . . I will put my laws into their minds, and write them on their hearts. Heb. 8:8-10, RSV.

A religious covenant is an agreement between God and individuals in which God pledges to bless those who accept and commit themselves to Him.

That is a good definition. But what exactly does it mean? What are its implications? Such questions divided the Adventist community back in the 1880s.

Smith and Butler had their answer to the covenant issue. It was simple: "Obey and live." Those who obeyed would have eternal life. Thus their emphasis on the law, obedience, and personal righteousness.

But Waggoner stood the "obey and live" equation on its head. First, he claimed, came justification and life in Christ, and only then obedience. Thus we might state his formula as "live [in Christ] and [then] obey."

The crucial problem of the old covenant, from Waggoner's perspective, was that "it made no provision for forgiveness of sins." But the new covenant had righteousness by faith in Jesus at its very center. It was a covenant of grace in which born again Christians have the law of God in their hearts. "Walking in the law," Waggoner asserted, will be a natural way of life for those who have been born into the family of God and have the indwelling law in their inner being.

The Adventists of 1888 were concerned with the covenant. And they should have been. After all, what is more important than salvation?

Nothing! Compared to salvation, a new car, better house, or even earthly life itself has no significance.

We should not fault those Adventists of more than a century ago for their excitement when someone challenged their idea of salvation and the mission of the church. Each of us ought to be deeply concerned about the same issues. We live in a messed-up world of sickness and death. Is there anything better? Will this mess go on forever and ever? On what basis can God save problematic people in a problematic world? These are the questions of religious belief.

Their answers stimulated the formation of the Adventist Church and they will be related to its final destiny.

Help us, Father, to learn to think Your thoughts. Help us to understand the most important issues in the Bible and in life.

WHAT ABOUT THE COVENANT?—2

The days are coming, says the Lord, when I will make a new covenant with the house of Israel. . . . I will forgive their iniquity, and I will remember their sin no more. Jer. 31:31-34, RSV.

E llen White and Waggoner were in essential harmony on the covenants. Her treatment of the two covenants, penned in the late 1880s, provides a nice summary of their view on the topic.

"The terms of the 'old covenant,'" she writes, "were, Obey and live. . . . The 'new covenant' was established upon 'better promises'—*the promise of forgiveness of sins and of the grace of God to renew the heart and bring it into harmony with the principles of God's law.* 'This shall be the covenant that I will make with the house of Israel; After those days, saith the Lord, I will put my law in their inward parts, and *write it in their hearts.* . . . I will forgive their iniquity, and I will remember their sin no more.' Jeremiah 31:33, 34.

"The same law that was engraved upon the tables of stone is written by the Holy Spirit upon the tables of the heart. Instead of going about to establish our own righteousness we accept the righteousness of Christ. His blood atones for our sins. His obedience is accepted for us. Then the heart renewed by the Holy Spirit will bring forth 'the fruits of the Spirit.' Through the grace of Christ we shall live in obedience to the law of God written upon our hearts. Having the Spirit of Christ, we shall walk even as He walked" (PP 372).

It was the concept of a covenant of grace that shook so many of the old-line Adventists, with their old covenant emphasis on the primacy of obedience, to their very roots. Waggoner's focus on faith in Christ undermined their law-oriented theology, even though, as we have seen, Waggoner, Jones, and Ellen White had a prominent place for the law and obedience in their theology. *But for them obedience flowed out of a saving relationship to Jesus rather than leading to such a relationship.*

Which way is the "flow" going in your life? It is my impression that all too many Adventists are concerned about their performance—in how they are doing—rather than being primarily interested in Christ and what He has done for them.

Today is the best day in the rest of your life to get your "flow" turned around and to begin a new covenant walk with God.

THE RELATIONSHIP BETWEEN
DOCTRINE AND CHRISTIAN LOVE

Beloved, if God so loved us, we also ought to love one another. . . . If we love one another, God abides in us, and His love is perfected in us. 1 John 4:11, 12, NASB.

I suppose that if we could earn salvation under our own steam we might have reason to be proud of our accomplishments and even treat other "lesser beings" with a bit of disgust since they hadn't managed to reach our high level of accomplishment.

But that's not the way it happens. All have failed and continue to do so. It is only the love of God that rescues us. Given that fact, the only possible response is love to Him and to our fellow beings. Love is the only proper response to a God who has saved us in spite of ourselves.

It's not that doctrine isn't important. Ellen White, for example, had a profound interest in the correct understanding of the Bible and Christian doctrine. Yet she was even more concerned that Bible study and doctrinal discussion take place in the context of Christian love.

Back in 1887, when she saw the cruel spirit of Minneapolis on the horizon, she had written that "there is danger of our ministers dwelling too much on doctrines, . . . when their own soul needs practical godliness" (Lt 37, 1887).

Again in 1890, D. T. Jones (secretary of the General Conference) wrote to W. C. White that "your mother and Dr. Waggoner both say that the points of doctrine are not the matters at issue at all, but it is the spirit shown by our people in opposition to these questions which they object to. I am perfectly free to acknowledge that the spirit has not been the Spirit of Christ. It has not been so in my case, and I think I can discern enough to be safe in saying that it has not been so in the case of others. I have often thought over the matter and wondered why it was that such unimportant matters, practically, should cause such a disturbance, such a division. . . . The point in your mother's mind and in the mind of Dr. Waggoner was not to bring in these questions and force them upon all, but to bring in the doctrine of justification by faith and the Spirit of Christ, and try to get the people converted to God."

There's the crucial point! Let's face it—when our "Christianity" makes us unloving we obviously don't have the real thing, even if we are correct on all the doctrines. But when we realize that Christ, through the grace of God, has truly rescued us from the pit of sin, our response will be love. A lack of it indicates that we have yet to be rescued ourselves.

Help me, Father, to accept Your saving grace so that I might become a channel of Your love.

ELLEN WHITE AT MINNEAPOLIS: LET JESUS COME IN—1

For this reason I bow my knees before the Father, . . . [that you might] know the love of Christ which surpasses knowledge, that you may be filled with all the fullness of God. Eph. 3:14-19, RSV.

Ellen White's emphasis at Minneapolis was not some new teaching on some aspect of Adventist theology, but rather a call for Adventism to uplift and practice basic Christianity. "My burden during the meeting," she wrote, "was to present Jesus and His love before my brethren, for I saw marked evidences that many had not the spirit of Christ" (MS 24, 1888).

"Faith in Christ as the sinner's only hope," she noted, "has been largely left out, not only of the discourses given but of the religious experience of very many who claim to believe the third angel's message. At this meeting I bore testimony that the most precious light had been shining forth from the Scriptures in the presentation of the great subject of the righteousness of Christ connected with the law, which should be constantly kept before the sinner as his only hope of salvation. . . .

"The standard by which to measure character is the royal law. The law is the sin detector. By the law is the knowledge of sin. But the sinner is constantly being drawn to Jesus by the wonderful manifestation of His love in that He humiliated Himself to die a shameful death upon the cross. What a study is this! Angels have striven, earnestly longed, to look into the wonderful mystery. It is a study that can tax the highest human intelligence, that man, fallen, deceived by Satan, taking Satan's side of the question, can be conformed to the image of the Son of the infinite God. That man shall be like Him, that, because of the righteousness of Christ given to man, God will love man—fallen but redeemed—even as He loved His Son. . . .

"This is the mystery of godliness. This picture is of the highest value to be placed in every discourse, to be hung in memory's hall, to be uttered by human lips, to be traced by human beings who have tasted and known that the Lord is good, to be meditated upon, to be the groundwork of every discourse" (*ibid.*).

Let Jesus come in. If Ellen White could only give us one piece of advice from the 1888 meetings, that would be it.

Let's choose to let Him in right now before we rise from this reading.

ELLEN WHITE AT MINNEAPOLIS:
LET JESUS COME IN—2

Be imitators of God, therefore, as dearly beloved children and live a life of love, just as Christ loved us and gave himself up for us. Eph. 5:1, 2, NIV.

There have been dry theories presented and precious souls are starving for the bread of life. This is not the preaching that is required or that the God of heaven will accept, for it is Christless. The divine picture of Christ must be kept before the people. . . .

"He is to be lifted up before men. When this is kept before the people, creature merit sinks into insignificance. The more the eye looks upon Him, the more His life, His lessons, His perfection of character are studied, the more sinful and abhorrent will sin appear. By beholding, man can but admire and become more attracted to Him, more charmed, and more desirous to be like Jesus until he assimilates to His image and has the mind of Christ. Like Enoch he walks with God. His mind is full of thoughts of Jesus. He is his best Friend. . . .

"Study Christ. Study His character, feature by feature. He is our Pattern that we are required to copy in our lives and our characters, else we fail to represent Jesus, but present to the world a spurious copy. Do not imitate any man, for men are defective in habits, in speech, in manners, in character.

"I present before you the Man Christ Jesus. You must individually know Him as your Saviour before you can study Him as your pattern and your example. . . .

"All who claim to be followers of Christ are under obligation to walk in His footsteps, to be imbued with His Spirit, and thus to present to the world Jesus Christ, who came to our world to represent the Father. . . .

"Holding up Christ as our only source of strength, presenting His matchless love in having the guilt of the sins of men charged to His account and His own righteousness imputed to man, in no case does away with the law or detracts from its dignity. Rather, it places it where the correct light shines upon and glorifies it. . . . The law is complete and full in the great plan of salvation, only as it is presented in the light shining from the crucified and risen Saviour" (MS 24, 1888).

To hear Ellen White talk, you'd think we couldn't get enough of Jesus. That's true. He is the one thing in the world that you can be intemperate in desiring.

ELLEN WHITE AT MINNEAPOLIS: REFLECTING JESUS—1

I have given you an example, that ye should do as I have done to you. John 13:15.

The humble, loving Jesus. An example worthy of following, but not one that "normal" humans are tempted to emulate. That's where transforming grace and the new birth comes in. God wants to take normal humans and make them into new creatures—into Christians who reflect His character of love.

That was another of Ellen White's preaching themes at Minneapolis. On October 20 she presented a sermon that the Minneapolis *Tribune* noted moved many to tears and that she herself claimed brought forth many heartfelt testimonies from her hearers.

"You cannot," she told her audience, "be a fruitful Christian and have knowledge of our Lord and Saviour Jesus Christ unless you are a practical Christian, unless you are making progress all the time in divine life. This is all important. Many seem to think that as soon as they go down into the water and receive baptism, and their names are entered upon the church book, then the work is all done."

To the contrary, "if they do not bring into their households practical religion, they will soon lose it all. . . . It is important that we keep all the time adding grace to grace, and if we will work upon the plan of addition, God will work on the plan of multiplication" as He develops His "moral image" in His followers.

"All the universe of heaven was interested in the great work" of Christ. "Every world that God has created is watching to see how the battle between the Lord of light and glory and the powers of darkness will end. Here is Satan, who has been seeking with all his power to shut out the true character of God, so that the world could not understand it, and under a garb of righteousness he works upon many who profess to be Christians, but they represent the character of Satan instead of the character of Jesus Christ. They misrepresent my Lord. They misrepresent the character of Jesus every time that they lack mercy, every time that they lack humility" (MS 8, 1888).

"God is love" (1 John 4:8). Christ came to demonstrate that love in His life and death. And He wants us to be like Him, to let Him develop His "moral image" in us.

Take me today, Lord. Help me to not only desire Your gift but to accept it and live it in my daily life.

ELLEN WHITE AT MINNEAPOLIS:
REFLECTING JESUS—2

We know that we have passed from death unto life, because we love the brethren.
1 John 3:14.

D o we really love our fellow believers? Especially the disgusting ones? Loving fellow church members was a central problem in the Adventism of the 1888 era.

"Those who truly love God," Ellen White told the General Conference delegates on October 21, "must manifest loving-kindness of heart, judgment, and righteousness to all with whom they come in contact; for these are the works of God. There is nothing Christ needs so much as agents who feel the necessity of representing Him. Evil speaking and evil thinking are ruinous to the soul. This has been current in this conference. *There is nothing the church lacks so much as the manifestation of Christlike love.* As the members of the church unite together in sanctified association, cooperating with Christ, He lives and works in them.

"Our eyes need the anointing with the heavenly eyesalve, that we may see what we are, and what we ought to be, and that power is provided in Christ sufficient to enable us to reach the high standard of Christian perfection.

"We must keep Jesus our pattern ever before us. This is and ever will be present truth. It was by beholding Jesus and appreciating the virtues of His character that John became one with his Master in spirit. . . . And to him was committed the work of telling of the Saviour's love and the love His children should manifest for one another. 'This is the message that ye heard from the beginning,' he writes, 'that we should love one another. . . . We know that we have passed from death unto life, because we love the brethren. . . .'

"The Lord has plain words for those who, like the Pharisees, make great boast of their piety but whose hearts are destitute of the love of God. The Pharisees refused to know God and Jesus Christ whom He had sent. Are we not in danger of doing the same thing as did the Pharisees and scribes?" (MS 8a, 1888; italics supplied).

It is no accident that Christ (Matt. 5:43-48; 19:21) and Ellen White (COL 67-69, 316, 384) repeatedly tie the concept of perfection and love together. Reflecting the moral character of God is not what you eat or even what you believe. It is being like the God who is love.

Ellen White at Minneapolis: Reflecting Jesus—3

Since we have these promises, beloved, let us cleanse ourselves from every defilement of body and spirit, and make holiness perfect in the fear of God. 2 Cor. 7:1, RSV.

The worst thing—the most grievous—is the want of love and the want of compassion for one another. That," Mrs. White told the delegates, "is what God presented in such a light before me, and I wanted to say to you that if ever there was time when we should humble ourselves before God, it is now. . . .

"It has been Satan's studied work to keep the love of Christ out of our hearts. . . . There is a great lot of ceremony and form. What we want is the love of Christ, to love God supremely and our neighbor as ourselves. When we have this, there will be a breaking down as with the walls of Jericho before the children of Israel. But there is such an amount of selfishness and desire of supremacy in our ranks. . . .

"The lower we lie at the foot of the cross the more clear will be our view of Christ. . . ."

"What are God and Jesus doing? . . . They are cleansing the sanctuary. Well, we should be with [them] in this work and be cleansing the sanctuary of our souls of all unrighteousness, that our names may be written in the Lamb's book of life, that our sins may be blotted out when the times of refreshing shall come from the presence of the Lord. . . .

"You have no time to be exalting self, but [only to] lift Jesus up. Oh, lift Him up! How can we do this? . . . May the God of heaven let His power come upon your hearts that we may have right characters and pure hearts and know how to labor for the sick [and] suffering. . . .

"Just as soon as we love God with all our hearts and our neighbor as ourselves, God will work through us. How shall we stand in the time of the latter rain?" Only if we have His love.

"The love of Christ in the heart will do more to convert sinners than all the sermons you can preach. What we need is to get the love of Christ, that we may study the Bible and know what saith the scriptures. . . . Now, brethren, we might as well tear away the rubbish from the doors of our hearts now, . . . for we have no time to waste" (MS 26, 1888; italics supplied).

And that's the truth. Today is the day of our salvation. To your knees, O Israel!

Father in heaven, these past few days I have realized as never before the absolute centrality of love in genuine Christianity. Help me this very day to be a more fruitful channel of Your love in my family, in my workplace, in . . . .

ELLEN WHITE AT MINNEAPOLIS: THE LAW AND THE GOSPEL

A man is not justified by works of the law but through faith in Jesus Christ, . . . by works of the law shall no one be justified. Gal. 2:16, RSV.

As we have seen in the past few days, Mrs. White was a bit upset with the Adventism of the 1888 era. And with good reason. In their focus on correct doctrine, Adventist tradition, and being good Adventists, they had too often forgotten what the gospel was all about in both theory and practice. Emulating the Pharisees of old, they could be unchristlike to each other, even as they debated the law of God and other good Adventist teachings.

Crying from her heart, on October 24 she told the delegates again that "we want the truth as it is in Jesus. But when anything shall come in to shut down the gate that the waves of truth [about Jesus] shall not come in, you will hear my voice wherever it is, if it is in California or in Europe, or wherever I am, because God has given me light and I mean to let it shine.

"And I have seen that precious souls who would have embraced the truth [of Adventism] have been turned away from it because of the manner in which the truth has been handled, because Jesus was not in it. *And this is what I have been pleading with you for all the time—we want Jesus"* (MS 9, 1888; italics supplied).

Eighteen months later she was still struggling with the Adventist ministry to "open their hearts and let the Savior in." She told those assembled for the General Conference Bible school for ministers that when they left the meetings they should "be so full of the message" of the gospel that it would be like fire shut up in their bones until they would not be able to hold their peace. If they did express their feelings, however, she told them that "men will say, 'You are too excited; you are making too much of this matter, and you do not think enough of the law; now, you must think more of the law; don't be all the time reaching for this righteousness of Christ, but build up the law.'"

To such "good" Adventist sentiments she replied: "Let the law take care of itself. We have been at work on the law until we get as dry as the hills of Gilboa, without dew or rain. Let us trust in the merits of Jesus Christ of Nazareth. May God help us that our eyes may be anointed with eyesalve, that we may see" (MS 10, 1889).

There are some things good to get excited about—if we can do it in the right spirit.

Righteousness by Faith
and the Third Angel's Message–1

Here is the patience of the saints; here are those who keep the commandments of God and the faith of Jesus. Rev. 14:12, NKJV.

As we have seen, by 1888 the disjunction between Adventism and the evangelical understanding of salvation had become problematic. Adventists were strong on the distinctive Adventist beliefs but weak on the great gospel teachings that their founders had shared with other Christians. Ellen White saw Jones and Waggoner as a corrective to that difficulty.

Contrary to some works-oriented leaders of the day, Waggoner realized that his church had departed from the historic doctrine of salvation. Ellen White spoke to the same truth in expressing her surprise that some found Jones and Waggoner's teaching to be a "strange doctrine," when their "message" was "not a new truth, but the very same that Paul taught, that Christ himself taught" (MS 27, 1889).

Waggoner's comment that his interpretation of law and gospel reflected that of Paul, Luther, and Wesley became even more profound and insightful when he added that it "was a step closer to the heart of the third angel's message." Ellen White came to the same viewpoint. Observing that some had "expressed fears that we shall dwell too much upon the subject of justification by faith," she indicated that several had written to her, "inquiring if the message of justification by faith is the third angel's message." She replied that "'it is the third angel's message in verity [i.e., truth]'" (RH, Apr. 1, 1890).

That statement has mystified some. What exactly did she mean? We will examine that topic the next few days.

Meanwhile, we should recall that Revelation 14:12 is the central text in Adventist history. "Here is the patience of the saints: here are they that keep the commandments of God, and the faith of Jesus."

Recognizing the implications of the Adventists' use of that text as a description of their denomination, a reporter for the Minneapolis *Journal* pointed out that "it is either monstrous egotism or sublime faith which leads them to apply this text to themselves."

The Adventists, of course, considered it "sublime faith." And both sides in the 1888 crisis came to realize ever more clearly as time passed that their differences at Minneapolis centered on the meaning of Revelation 14:12.

By the way, that is a good text to memorize as we meditate upon its meaning and implications.

RIGHTEOUSNESS BY FAITH AND THE THIRD ANGEL'S MESSAGE–2

Blessed are they that do his commandments, that they may have right to the tree of life, and may enter in through the gates into the city. Rev. 22:14.

E arly Adventists were great doers of the commandments—sometimes for good reasons and sometimes for not so good.

The doing aspect of the Adventist belief system would play heavily into pre-1888 understandings of Revelation 14:12: "Here is the patience of the saints: here are they that keep the commandments of God, and the faith of Jesus."

The Adventist interpretation of that verse had been quite consistent before 1888. James White provided a model for that understanding in April 1850. He indicated that the verse had three major points of identification.

It indicated (1) a people who were to be patient, despite the disappointment of the 1840s, in waiting for the coming of Jesus; (2) a people who had got " 'the victory over the beast, and his image, and over his MARK' and are sealed with the seal of the living God by keeping 'the commandments of God' "; and (3) a people who "kept the 'faith' " as a body of beliefs in such things as "repentance, faith, baptism, Lord's supper, washing the saints' feet," and so on. A part of keeping the faith, he emphasized, was "KEEPING THE COMMANDMENTS Of GOD." Note that White managed to squeeze obedience to God's law into two of the three parts of the verse.

Two years later he was even more precise: "The faith of Jesus is to be kept, as well as the commandments of God. . . . This not only shows the distinction between the commandments of the Father and the faith of the Son, but also shows that the faith of Jesus to be kept necessarily embraces the sayings of Christ and the apostles. It embraces all the requirements and doctrines of the New Testament."

J. N. Andrews was of the same mind, claiming that "the faith of Jesus . . . is spoken of as being kept in the same manner that the commandments of God are kept."

And R. F. Cottrell wrote that the faith of Jesus "is something that can be obeyed or kept. Therefore we conclude that all that we are required to do in order to be saved from sin belongs to the faith of Jesus."

As we noted earlier, doing is important. But is it true that "all that we are required to do in order to be saved from sin belongs to the faith of Jesus"?

Think about it. Discuss it. Pray about it.

RIGHTEOUSNESS BY FAITH
AND THE THIRD ANGEL'S MESSAGE–3

Here is the perseverance of the saints who keep the commandments of God and their faith in Jesus. Rev. 14:12, NASB.

Nearly all Adventist interpreters of Revelation 14:12 before 1888 saw "the faith of Jesus" as a body of truth that one should believe and keep. Most often, however, Adventists didn't spend much time on that part of the verse. It was the part about obedience to the commandments that got the most attention. Thus, as we noted earlier, Uriah Smith underlined the word "keep" when commenting on the text in January 1888, and G. I. Butler did the same for *"keep the commandments of God"* in May 1889.

Such an emphasis followed from their view that the Sabbath truth, in the context of the mark of the beast, would be God's last message to a world ripe for the Second Coming. It is slight wonder that such an interpretation and emphasis often led traditional Adventism into the realm of legalism. Such implications lay at the foundation of the vocabulary of their belief. Words such as "keep," "do," "obey," "law," and "commandments" spelled in their minds the significance of the Adventist distinctive contribution to Christianity.

It was that interpretation of Revelation 14:12 that came under fire in 1888. *Out of Minneapolis would flow a new understanding of the central text in Seventh-day Adventist history.*

Jones hinted at the new interpretation in December 1887. "The only way in which they can ever attain to harmony with the righteous law of God," he wrote, "is through the righteousness of God, which is by *faith of Jesus Christ*. . . . In the third angel's message is embodied the supreme truth and the supreme righteousness."

Note what Jones had done. He had equated "the supreme truth" with "the commandments of God" and "the supreme righteousness" with "the faith of Jesus," which he implied was *faith in Jesus.*

At this point we should merely note that the Greek phrase at the end of Revelation 14:12 can be translated as either faith *of* Jesus or faith *in* Jesus, as represented in the translation of today's text from the *New American Standard Bible* and many other versions.

Thought question for today: What are the implications of faith *in* Jesus versus faith *of* Jesus? What difference could those implications make in your life?

RIGHTEOUSNESS BY FAITH
AND THE THIRD ANGEL'S MESSAGE—4

For I am not ashamed of the gospel: it is the power of God for salvation to every one who has faith. Rom. 1:16, RSV.

A. T. Jones may have hinted at a new understanding of the "faith of Jesus" in 1887, but Ellen White would be even more specific.

"The message," she wrote, "that was given to the people" in the Minneapolis "meetings presented in clear lines not alone the commandments of God—a part of the third angel's message—but the faith of Jesus, which comprehends more than is generally supposed. And it will be well for the third angel's message to be proclaimed in all its parts, for the people need every jot and tittle of it. If we proclaim the commandments of God and leave the other half scarcely touched the message is marred in our hands. . . .

"The present message that God has made it the duty of His servants to give to the people is no new or novel thing. It is an old truth that has been lost sight of, just as Satan made his masterly efforts that it should be.

"The Lord has a work for every one of His loyal people to do to bring the faith of Jesus into the right place where it belongs—in the third angel's message. The law has its important position but it is powerless unless the righteousness of Christ is placed beside the law to give its glory to the whole royal standard of righteousness. . . .

"A thorough and complete trust in Jesus will give the right quality to religious experience. Aside from this the experience is nothing. The service is like the offering of Cain—Christless. God is glorified by living faith in a personal, all sufficient Saviour. Faith views Christ as He is—the sinner's only hope. Faith takes hold of Christ, trusts Him. It says, 'He loves me; He died for me. I accept the sacrifice and Christ shall not have died for me in vain.'

"We have not only lost much to our souls, but as ministers have neglected the most solemn part of our work in not dwelling upon the blood of Jesus Christ as the sinner's only hope for eternal life. Tell the story of Christ. . . . Tell the sinners, 'look and live'" (MS 30, 1889).

Faith in Christ as Savior is the core of the gospel. And it is also the core of the third angel's message, the heart of the 1888 message.

Help us, Father, to grasp the relationship of law and gospel in fuller richness as we contemplate the implications of Revelation 14:12.

Righteousness by Faith
and the Third Angel's Message—5

Christ redeemed us from the curse of the law, having become a curse for us—
for it is written, "Cursed be everyone who hangs on a tree." Gal. 3:13, RSV.

Uplifting faith in Christ as the heart of the third angel's message became central to Ellen White's message at the 1888 General Conference session and beyond.

Soon after the Minneapolis meetings she made one of her most power statements on Revelation 14:12 and the core meaning of the 1888 message. "The third angel's message," she penned, "is the proclamation of the commandments of God and the faith of Jesus Christ. *The commandments of God have been proclaimed, but the faith of Jesus has not been proclaimed by Seventh-day Adventists as of equal importance, the law and the gospel going hand in hand.* I cannot find language to express this subject in its fullness.

"'*The faith of Jesus.*' It is talked of, but not understood. What constitutes the faith of Jesus, that belongs to the third angel's message? *Jesus becoming our sin-bearer that He might become our sin-pardoning Saviour.* He was treated as we deserve to be treated. He came to our world and took our sins that we might take His righteousness. And *faith in the ability of Christ to save us amply and fully and entirely is the faith of Jesus.* . . .

"There is salvation for the sinner in the blood of Jesus Christ alone, which cleanseth us from all sin. The man with a cultivated intellect may have vast stores of knowledge, he may engage in theological speculations, he may be great and honored of men and be considered the repository of knowledge, but unless he has a saving knowledge of Christ crucified for him, and by faith lays hold on the righteousness of Christ, he is lost. Christ 'was wounded for our transgressions, he was bruised for our iniquities: the chastisement of our peace was upon him; and with his stripes we are healed.' Isa. 53:5. 'Saved by the blood of Jesus Christ' will be our only hope for time and our song throughout eternity" (MS 24, 1888; italics supplied).

Are you getting the message? We need to. It is the most crucial thing that we can ever hear—that Christ died for us, and that we can be saved only through having a vital faith in His sacrifice. That is at the core of the faith of Jesus and Revelation 14:12. It is the core of what it means to be a Seventh-day Adventist. And it is the core of what it means to be a Christian. With only the commandments of God we might be "Adventists" [i.e., church members], but not Christians.

RIGHTEOUSNESS BY FAITH
AND THE THIRD ANGEL'S MESSAGE—6

And I looked, and behold a white cloud, and upon the cloud one sat like unto the Son of man, having on his head a golden crown, and in his hand a sharp sickle. Rev. 14:14.

I dare say that Ellen White could get excited about a few topics. But her enthusiasm was never greater than that which she had for the plan of salvation in Christ.

Reflecting on the recently completed 1888 General Conference session, she noted that "Elder E. J. Waggoner had the privilege granted him of speaking plainly and presenting his views upon justification by faith and the righteousness of Christ in relation to the law. This was no new light, but it was old light placed where it should be in the third angel's message.

"What is the burden of that message? John sees a people. He says, 'Here is the patience of the saints: here are they that keep the commandments of God, and the faith of Jesus.' Rev. 14:12. This people John beholds just before he sees the Son of man 'having on his head a golden crown, and in his hand a sharp sickle.' Verse 14.

"The faith of Jesus has been overlooked and treated in an indifferent, careless manner. It has not occupied the prominent position in which it was revealed to John. Faith in Christ as the sinner's only hope has been largely left out, not only of the discourses given but of the religious experience of very many who claim to believe the third angel's message.

"At this meeting I bore testimony that the most precious light had been shining forth from the Scriptures in the presentation of the great subject of the righteousness of Christ connected with the law, which should be constantly kept before the sinner as his only hope of salvation.

"This was not new light to me for it had come to me from higher authority for the last forty-four years, and I had presented it to our people by pen and voice in the testimonies of His Spirit. But very few had responded. . . . There was altogether too little spoken and written upon this great question. The discourses given of some might be correctly represented as like the offering of Cain—Christless. The standard by which to measure character is the royal law. The law is the sin detector. By the law is the knowledge of sin. But the sinner is constantly being drawn to Jesus" who died for each individual's sins on the cross (MS 24, 1888).

Meditate upon Him today and what He has done for you. Such thoughts will not only comfort your soul, but will invigorate your life and transform your actions.

RIGHTEOUSNESS BY FAITH
AND THE THIRD ANGEL'S MESSAGE—7

The just shall live by faith. Rom. 1:17.

Of special interest in what we read yesterday is the fact that Ellen White noted more than once that the truth on righteousness by faith that Waggoner had been preaching was not new light—that she herself had been proclaiming it for 44 years. That idea agreed with Waggoner, himself, who noted that the message he was teaching had been that proclaimed "by all the eminent reformers" "from the days of Paul to the days of Luther and Wesley."

In other words, according to Waggoner, what he presented was a recapturing of the evangelical viewpoint of justification by faith.

That was also Ellen White's understanding of at least a part of the contribution of Jones and Waggoner. In August 1889 she wrote that the doctrine of "justification by faith" had been "long hidden under the rubbish of error." That error, she pointed out, had been exhibited by "the Holiness people" who had preached faith in Christ, but had also advocated "away with the law" (RH, Aug. 13, 1889). From that perspective, the teaching of justification by faith had been in the "companionship of error" (MS 8a, 1888).

On the other hand were the Adventists, who had maintained the sanctity of the law but had "lost sight of" the "doctrine of justification by faith." In that context, she notes that "God has raised up men [Jones and Waggoner] to meet the necessity of this time. . . . Their work is not only to proclaim the law, but to preach the truth for this time—the Lord our righteousness."

The Adventists, she points out, had been doing a good job on the law, while the holiness people had been preaching faith in Christ. But both parties had error. The Adventists neglected faith, while the holiness people denigrated the law. The accomplishment of Jones and Waggoner was to get rid of the errors of each group while combining their truths.

In the process, they gave Adventism an understanding of the complete three angel's messages which it had been lacking (*ibid.*).

As a result, Ellen White could state that through Jones and Waggoner's emphasis on justification by faith "God has rescued these truths from the companionship of error [antinomianism], and has placed them in their proper framework [the third angel's message]" (MS 8a, 1888).

What a message! God doesn't want unbalanced law-oriented Adventists or unbalanced faith-oriented Adventists. He wants a people who have put both in proper perspective.

RIGHTEOUSNESS BY FAITH AND THE LOUD CRY

After this I saw another angel coming down from heaven, having great authority; and the earth was made bright with his splendor. And he called out with a mighty voice, "Fallen, fallen is Babylon the great! . . . Come out of her, my people. Rev. 18:1-4, RSV.

We observed yesterday that one aspect of Waggoner and Jones' 1888 message that excited Ellen White was that they had combined the two halves of Revelation 14:12. They not only preached the commandments of God but also faith in Jesus as Lord and Savior. Thus they had rescued the truths of justification by faith "from the companionship of [antinomian] error" and "placed them in their proper framework"—the third angel's message (MS 8a, 1888).

From her perspective, the importance of the 1888 message was not some special Adventist doctrine developed by Jones and Waggoner. Rather, it was the reuniting of Adventism with basic Christianity. It uplifted Jesus Christ as the central pillar of all Christian living and thinking, proclaimed justification through faith, and taught sanctification as reflected in obedience to God's law through the power of the Holy Spirit.

Once we grasp that the heart of Waggoner and Jones' contribution was the putting together of the various parts of the third angel's message, it is possible to understand her intriguing statement regarding the beginning of the loud cry in 1888. In the *Review* of November 22, 1892, we read: "The time of test is just upon us, for the loud cry of the third angel has already begun in the revelation of the righteousness of Christ, the sin-pardoning Redeemer. This is the beginning of the light of the angel whose glory shall fill the whole earth. For [because] it is the work of every one to whom the message of warning has come . . . to lift up Jesus."

Jones, confusing the latter rain (an outpouring of the Holy Spirit—a person) with the loud cry (a message), made a great deal of the 1892 loud cry statement, proclaiming that the latter rain had begun. But he needed to read more carefully. It was the loud cry and not the latter rain that had begun at Minneapolis.

The powerful point that Ellen White made in 1892 was that at last in 1888 the Seventh-day Adventists finally had the complete last message of mercy to preach to the world before the Second Advent. The loud cry message would proclaim the continuing importance of the Ten Commandments in the context of a firm faith in Jesus as Lord and Savior, all set within an expectancy in the Second Advent (Rev. 14:12).

What a message!

And God wants us to be faithful to all three of its parts.

WHAT ABOUT THE TRINITY?—1

Go therefore and make disciples of all nations, baptizing them in the name of the Father and the Son and the Holy Spirit. Matt. 28:19, NASB.

I t comes as a surprise to many present-day Seventh-day Adventists that most of the founders of the denomination could not join the church today if they had to agree to the 28 fundamental beliefs. To be more specific, they would have rejected belief number 2, on the Trinity, because they were antitrinitarian; they would have spurned number 4, on the Son, because they held that the Son was not eternal; and they would have denied number 5, on the Holy Spirit, because to them the Spirit was a force rather than a person.

To a large extent the Christian Connexion had shaped their understanding of these points. In 1835 Joshua V. Himes, a leading minister of the Connexionists, wrote that "at first they [the Connexion believers] were generally Trinitarian," but they had moved away from that belief when they came to see it as "unscriptural." Himes noted that only the Father is "unoriginated, independent, and eternal." Thus of necessity Christ was originated, dependent, and brought into existence by the Father. The Connexionists also tended to view the Holy Spirit as the "power and energy of God, that holy influence of God."

Joseph Bates, James White, and other Connexion adherents brought those views into Sabbatarian Adventism. White, for example, referred to the Trinity in 1846 as that "old unscriptural Trinitarian creed" and in 1852 as that "old Trinitarian absurdity."

J. N. Andrews shared White's views. In 1869 he penned that "the Son of God . . . had God for his Father, and did, at some point in the eternity of the past, have a beginning of days."

Uriah Smith also rejected the Trinity, arguing in 1865 that Christ was "the first created being" and in 1898 that God alone is without beginning.

Here we have kind of a Sabbatarian Adventist Who's Who on the Trinity. Only one name, you may have noted, is missing—that of Ellen White. Its not that she didn't have anything to say on the topic. Rather, it is impossible to tell exactly what she believed from what she said, at least in the early decades of the movement.

How could most of the early Adventist leaders have been wrong on so important a subject?

Here is part of an answer. God leads His people step by step, and as they progress their vision becomes clearer and clearer. In the next few days we will see a transformation take place in Adventist thinking on the Trinity.

WHAT ABOUT THE TRINITY?—2

In the beginning was the Word, and the Word was with God, and the Word was God. John 1:1.

If the old line leadership of Seventh-day Adventism appear to have been almost unanimously antitrinitarian, what about the reformers at Minneapolis?

Here, interestingly enough, is a theological point on which E. J. Waggoner could agree with Uriah Smith. "There was a time," Waggoner wrote in his 1890 book entitled *Christ and His Righteousness,* "when Christ proceeded forth and came from God, . . . but that time was so far back in the days of eternity that to finite comprehension it is practically without beginning."

His statement remarkably parallels one that Smith made that same decade: "God alone is without beginning. At the earliest epoch when a beginning could be—a period so remote that to finite minds it is essentially eternity—appeared the Word."

Now, if Smith and Waggoner were on the same side in regard to the Trinity, we need to ask, Where did the stimulus for change come from?

Here is where one of the other 1888 reformers comes in. The 1888 experience literally transformed Ellen White's writing ministry. It was in the events surrounding that General Conference session that she fully realized the ignorance of the Adventist ministry and laity on the plan of salvation and the centrality of Christ.

The years following would see the publication of her most important books on those topics.

- 1892 her classic *Steps to Christ.*
- 1896 *Thoughts From the Mount of Blessing,* which treated the Sermon on the Mount.
- 1898 *The Desire of Ages,* her book on the life of Christ.
- 1900 *Christ's Object Lessons,* a volume on the parables.
- 1905 *Ministry of Healing,* in which the opening chapters focus on the healing ministry of Jesus.

Nowhere in any of those books did Ellen White offer a chapter or even a paragraph on the Trinity or the full divinity of Christ, but they set forth phrases and words that would drive Adventists back to the Bible to restudy the topic. That Bible study would eventually transform Adventism on the Trinity and related issues.

Thank You, Lord, for Your gentle guidance. You take Your church forward only as fast as it can absorb what You have for it.

WHAT ABOUT THE TRINITY?–3

*But Peter said, "Ananias, why has Satan filled your heart to lie to the Holy Spirit. . . ?
You have not lied to man but to God." Acts 5:3, 4, RSV.*

In spite of the Bible's clarity on the topic, early Adventism had failed to recognize the personhood and the full divinity of the Holy Spirit. That would have disastrous consequences for the denomination by the end of the nineteenth century.

But first we need to recognize that the 1890s saw more written about the Holy Spirit and Christ than perhaps any decade in Adventist history. That was only natural once they began to talk about righteousness by faith and the centrality of Christ in salvation. After all, if Christ does the saving, then it is important to have a Christ adequate for the task. And if the Holy Spirit is a key player in the process, one should expect to speak of His function. It is no accident that discussion of the Godhead erupted in Adventism in the 1890s.

But Adventists weren't the only people then talking about the Holy Spirit. The Wesleyan holiness denominations with their emphasis on faith healing and victorious living emerged during those years, and the turn of the new century would see the rise of modern Pentecostalism. Both movements had a great deal to say about the work of the Spirit in people's lives and in the church. At the other end of the theological spectrum, liberal Christians had begun developing a renewed interest in such spirit-related theories as the immanence of God and the ideas of such Eastern religions as Hinduism, with its pantheistic perspective that everything that exists is God.

Adventism, with its lack of a correct understanding on such topics, would be deeply affected by the movements in the larger religious world. On the one hand, at the turn of the century it would have its own Pentecostal outbreak in the Holy Flesh movement, which proclaimed that even your missing teeth would grow back before Christ returned so that you could have *perfect flesh*. On the other hand, Waggoner and J. H. Kellogg would get caught up in Pantheism, Waggoner claiming to the General Conference sessions of 1897 and 1899, for example, that Christ "appeared as a tree" and that "a man can get righteousness in bathing, when he knows where the water comes from."

Talk about confusion.

It is into that context that God led Adventism into its next step in the progressive pathway of present truth.

God had a message for His people on the Godhead. But they needed to study their Bibles to discover it.

WHAT ABOUT THE TRINITY?—4

But of the Son he says, "Thy throne, O God, is for ever and ever". Heb. 1:8, RSV.

E ven though the Bible has no problem calling Jesus God, the early Adventists did, undoubtedly from an anti-Middle Ages bias that held that the doctrine of the Trinity was a product of a church in apostasy. But that attitude would change.

And at the forefront of those pointing the church in new directions was Ellen White. While she never used the word "Trinity," her writings in the 1888 era and beyond are full of Trinitarian phrases and concepts. She noted, for example, that "there are three living persons of the heavenly trio, . . . the Father, the Son, and the Holy Spirit" (Ev 615). And in 1901 she wrote of "the eternal heavenly dignitaries—God, and Christ, and the Holy Spirit" (*ibid.,* 616). Repeatedly she referred to the Holy Spirit as the "third person of the Godhead" (*ibid.,* 617; DA 671). And she had no doubt "that the Holy Spirit . . . is as much a person as God is a person" (Ev 616).

In regard to Christ, Ellen White moved infinitely beyond Waggoner, Smith, and most other Adventists of her day when she described Jesus as not only being "equal with God" but as being "the pre-existent, self-existent Son of God" (*ibid.,* 615). He had been with the Father "from all eternity" (RH, Apr. 5, 1906).

Perhaps Mrs. White's most controversial and surprising statement for Adventists in the 1890s was a sentence in her book on the life of Jesus in which she noted that *"in Christ is life, original, unborrowed, underived"* (DA 530; italics supplied). That statement caught the denomination off guard, and some wondered if she hadn't left the faith.

We cannot have the slightest doubt that Ellen White was at the very forefront of those who sought to Christianize Adventism in its approach to the Godhead.

But, it is crucial to note, she never solved any problems and she never developed a theology of the Trinity. Rather, she sprinkled her writings with statements that led the ministers and church members to turn to their Bibles to restudy the topic for themselves.

Father in heaven, we are thankful today for a Christ sufficient to save and a Holy Spirit adequate for His redemptive task.

WHAT ABOUT THE TRINITY?–5

For to us a child is born,
to us a son is given;
and the government will be upon his shoulder,
and his name will be called
"Wonderful Counselor, Mighty God." Isa. 9:6, RSV.

Yesterday we saw a few of Ellen White's distinctively Trinitarian statements that appeared in the 1888 era. Especially problematic for many was her statement in *The Desire of Ages* that "in Christ is life, original, unborrowed, underived" (p. 530).

The forcefulness of that sentence caught many off guard. One was a young preacher by the name of M. L. Andreasen. He was convinced that she really hadn't written that statement, that her editors and assistants must have altered it. As a result, he asked to read her handwritten book manuscript. She gladly gave him access to her document files. Later he recalled that "I had with me a number of quotations that I wanted to see if they were in the original in her own handwriting. I remember how astonished we were when *The Desire of Ages* was first published, for it contained some things that we considered unbelievable, among others the doctrine of the Trinity, which was not then generally accepted by the Adventists."

Staying in California for several months, Andreasen had adequate time to check out his suspicions. He was especially "interested in the statement in *The Desire of Ages* which at one time caused great concern to the denomination theologically: 'In Christ is life, original, unborrowed, underived.' . . . That statement may not seem very revolutionary to you," he told his audience in 1948, "but to us it was. We could hardly believe it. . . . I was sure Sister White had never written" the passage. "But now I found it in her own handwriting just as it had been published."

Some people still don't believe it. The past 15 years has seen a revival of anti-Trinitarianism among some Adventists. Like Andreasen, they think the editors changed her thoughts.

That certainly doesn't say much of their knowledge of Ellen White. She knew what she believed and could hold her own in any disagreement with editors or even General Conference administrators, as we saw in 1888. Her assistants could modify her exact words by supplying synonyms, but not her thoughts.

The recovery of the Trinity was one more step in God's progressive leading of Adventism into a fuller understanding of Scripture.

RETROSPECT ON THE TRINITY

The grace of the Lord Jesus Christ, and the love of God, and the communion of the Holy Spirit be with you all. Amen. 2 Cor. 13:14, NKJV.

S uch were the final words of Paul in his Second Letter to the Corinthians, a statement that flashes to all Bible readers the identity of the members of the Godhead—the Father, the Son, and the Holy Spirit.

Between the 1880s and the mid-twentieth century Adventism went through a revolution on the Trinity and the divine natures and personhoods of the Son and the Spirit. Ellen White, as we noted, pointed Adventism in the new direction. But her statements did not create the revolution. Rather, they encouraged other Adventists to explore the Bible for themselves on those topics.

But even then change did not come quickly. In fact, it would take decades. A case in point is the 1919 General Conference-sponsored Bible Conference, which had an open discussion of the Trinity that made some nervous. One leading minister declared: "I have not been able to accept the so-called Trinitarian doctrine. . . . I cannot believe that two persons of the Godhead are equal, the Father and the Son. . . . I cannot believe the so-called Trinitarian doctrine of the three persons always existing."

General Conference president A. G. Daniells sought to calm things down by indicating that "we are not going to take a vote on trinitarianism or arianism." He also claimed that he had had the scales knocked from his eyes by the publication of *The Desire of Ages* and had turned to the Bible on the topic.

The year 1931 saw the denomination's first statement of fundamental beliefs take a Trinitarian position. That doesn't mean that all were agreed. Pockets of anti-Trinitarianism remained up into the 1940s, but by the 1950s the church was of one voice on the Trinity.

For that reason, it has been somewhat surprising to see a revival in anti-Trinitarianism. Some of the apostles of that doctrine caught me in a "dark alley" at the Toronto General Conference session in 2000. I asked them why they believed their position was truth. Because, they responded, it was the position of our founders. Such logic would lead us to eating pork and keeping the Sabbath from 6:00 p.m. to 6:00 p.m. Tradition, I responded, is a good position for a medieval church, but not for a Bible-based movement. That was settled back in the 1840s and reiterated in the 1888 era.

The only tradition that counts is that Adventism is a people of the BOOK.

THE POST-MINNEAPOLIS YEARS—1

And we bring you the good news that what God promised to the fathers, this he has fulfilled . . . by raising Jesus. Acts 13:32, 33, RSV.

Spreading the "good news" or the "glad tidings" (as the King James Version puts it) was the task for the 1888 reformers after the close of the General Conference session.

Ellen White left Minneapolis discouraged with the ministerial leadership of the denomination, but she still had hope in the Adventist people as a whole. Before the close of the conference she had told the assembled ministers that if they would not accept the light, she wanted to "give the people a chance; perhaps they may receive it" (MS 9, 1888). They certainly needed it. In September 1889 she would remark that "there is not one in one hundred" who really understood what it meant to be justified by faith, what it meant that "Christ should be . . . the only hope and salvation" (RH, Sept. 3, 1889).

Up through the fall of 1891 she, Jones, and Waggoner would tour the nation, preaching righteousness by faith to "the people" and to the ministry. After she left for Australia in 1891 and Waggoner had gone to England, Jones and W. W. Prescott continued to present the message in the United States. All through this period and beyond it, Ellen White emphasized that God had chosen Jones and Waggoner to bear a special message to the Adventist church, and she published widely on the topic of righteousness by faith herself.

The new General Conference administrations of O. A. Olsen (1888-1897) and G. A. Irwin (1897-1901) responded positively by giving Jones and Waggoner exposure throughout the 1890s. The two men had access to the people through the churches, the Sabbath school lessons, the colleges, the in-service schools regularly held for the ministry, and the denomination's publishing houses.

Especially important was the fact that during each General Conference session from 1889 to 1897 Jones and Waggoner received the leading role in the study of the Bible and theology. Beyond that, Jones by 1897 had assumed the powerful position of *Review and Herald* editor.

It would have been hard to conceive of a program that could have given the reformers more prominence during the 1890s.

Truly the "glad tidings" were being taken to "the people." And they still are. Christ is still the center attraction in biblically oriented Adventist preaching.

THE POST-MINNEAPOLIS YEARS–2

How beautiful are the feet of those who preach good news! Rom. 10:15, RSV.

The months following Minneapolis were strenuous for Ellen White, Jones, and Waggoner as they preached Christ and His love to Adventist ministry and laity across the nation in 1889. While the results were far from those desired, some confessions regarding a wrong attitude at Minneapolis did occur as well as a fair amount of rejoicing over newly found freedom in Christ's righteousness. Mrs. White joyfully wrote during the 1889 General Conference session that they were "having most excellent meetings. The spirit that was in the meeting at Minneapolis is not here." Many of the delegates testified that the past year had "been the best of their life; the light shining forth from the Word of God has been clear and distinct—justification by faith, Christ our righteousness" (3SM 160).

The good news is that progress was being made. And it would continue throughout the 1890s, even though some did hold back.

By 1899 Waggoner told the delegates at the General Conference session that the principles that he and Jones had preached at Minneapolis "have been accepted, to a considerable extent, since that time."

Four days later Jones noted in the *Review* that not only had the church largely accepted the message, but "I am afraid that there has been a tendency to go over to the other end now, and preach the faith of Jesus without the commandments." He went on to argue proper balance in presenting the various parts of Revelation 14:12.

A third witness to the theological acceptance of the 1888 message was Ellen White. On February 6, 1896, she advised the discontinuation of the three- to five-month ministerial institutes set up in the wake of the Minneapolis crisis to educate the ministry. "There was a time when this work was made necessary, because our own people opposed the work of God by refusing the light of truth on the righteousness of Christ" but such effort was no longer required (TM 401).

Praise the Lord! The denomination had made progress. But such a thing is never universal nor totally lasting. Reformation is a constant mandate of the church. We need more of Christ today, but we also need an ongoing balance as we seek to present both saving faith and the commandments of God in their proper relationship.

WHAT HAPPENED TO BUTLER?—1

Thou hast left thy first love. Rev. 2:4.

N ot all the journeys after Minneapolis were happy ones. G. I Butler, feeling that he had been "slaughtered" in the house of his friends, gave up the General Conference presidency at the conclusion of the 1888 session. Soon after, he and his wife moved to Florida to grow oranges. Six days before his departure for the South in mid-December, Ellen White sent him a letter in which she called him an enemy of the Testimonies and an unconverted man. She closed with an appeal to his heart to change his ways.

That was the first of many letters to Butler. But he was not up to confessions. Looking back at his early Florida period from the perspective of 1905, he wrote: "Some people find it very hard to make a confession. . . . She used to write me, over and over, about the Minneapolis meeting, and things of that kind, and I invariably wrote right back to her that it was utterly useless for me to go to making confessions I did not believe were called for. I stood my ground on that." He would, he claimed, never make the mistake of claiming peace when it did not exist.

To outward appearances Butler's frustration had reached its peak in early 1893 when he asked that the denomination not renew his ministerial credentials. But in actuality Butler was probably not requesting to resign as a minister as much as he was raising a question that he needed to have answered—"Am I still needed?"

About that same time he preached for the first time in four years. Meanwhile, the church renewed his credentials. Overjoyed with his acceptance, Butler de- clared that he was almost ready to exclaim that "the dear brethren have entered into a conspiracy to kill the old sinner with kindness."

But, being a complex person, as all of us are, he still couldn't believe "that God led Waggoner to deluge the denomination with the Galatians controversy." On the other hand, he was now at least willing to admit that God had brought good out of it—especially in terms of the increased prominence of justification by faith and the righteousness of Christ.

Lord, we want to thank You for Your longsuffering with rebellious humans. We each have a little of George I. Butler in us, and we need help. More than that, we want help. Thank You for staying in our lives in spite of who we are.

WHAT HAPPENED TO BUTLER?—2

They still bring forth fruit in old age. Psalm 92:14, RSV.

Brother Butler was a tough old customer, but God loved him anyway. That's good news for most of us.

He did have his repentant moments. In 1893, for example, he wrote to Ellen White that "the past few years" had "pretty effectually broken my back, but that is a small matter compared with the progress of the work." And by the autumn of 1894 Butler was even inviting A. T. Jones to help him at the Florida camp meeting.

In 1901, after his wife's death, Butler came out of his semiretirement to become president of the Florida Conference. Between 1902 and 1907 he served as president of the Southern Union Conference.

Ellen White rejoiced to see the aged pioneer back in a position of leadership. "I have known," she told the delegates at the 1903 General Conference session, "that the time would come when he would again take his place in the work. I want you to appreciate the trials he has passed through. . . . God desires the gray-haired pioneers" who had a part in early Adventism "to stand in their place in His work today. They are not to drop out of sight" (1903 GCB 205).

The new Butler, she wrote in 1902, was not the same man he had been in 1888. Not only was he "strong in physical and spiritual health," but "the Lord has proved and tested and tried him, as he did Job and as he did Moses. I see in Elder Butler one who has humbled his soul before God. He has another spirit than the Elder Butler of younger years. He has been learning his lesson at the feet of Jesus" (Lt 77, 1902).

Such a bill of health did not mean that Butler was straight on the issues of 1888. He told General Conference president A. G. Daniells in 1909 that "he never could see light" in the messages of Jones and Waggoner. His motto was still "obey and live."

Despite his problems, Ellen White wrote of him, "Though he may make some mistakes, yet he is a servant of the living God, and I shall do all I possibly can to sustain him in his work" (Lt 293, 1905). Butler would remain surprisingly active in the church until his death in 1918 at the age of 84.

God uses even less-than-perfect people. And it's a good thing. Otherwise He would have nobody to use.

Take us today, Lord, with all of our defects, and use us to Your glory. Amen.

WHAT HAPPENED TO SMITH?

Everyone who falls on that stone will be broken. Luke 20:18, NIV.

Like Butler, Uriah Smith underwent a traumatic experience at the Minneapolis meetings. Deeply disappointed and upset by the session, he resigned from his long-held position as General Conference secretary in November 1888, but held on to the editorship of the *Review*.

He would maintain that post until 1897, sparring with A. T. Jones for much of the time about prophetic interpretation and other issues. His editorship during those years, however, was a downhill battle in the face of the popularity of the charismatic Jones, who by late 1892 had become the most listened-to ministerial voice in Adventism. In 1897 Smith received his ultimate humiliation when the denomination appointed Jones as *Review* editor with Smith as his associate.

Smith in the post-1888 years found it next to impossible to come to grips with the fact that Waggoner had preached the ten-commandment view of the law in Galatians and that Ellen White had backed Waggoner on the relation of law and gospel. For the next few years after the Minneapolis meetings, Smith would be a ringleader in casting doubt upon Ellen White's work.

But she didn't give up on him. She wrote him letter after letter calling for repentance, but to no avail. Then in January 1891 he confessed his errors at Minneapolis. As Mrs. White put it: "He had fallen on the Rock and was broken."

Smith's falling on the Rock, however, did not mean that he was altogether on the Rock. His law-oriented theology still caused problems.

But in 1901 church leadership reappointed him as *Review* editor. Ellen White was overjoyed, expressing her pleasure that his name was once again at the "head of the list of editors; for thus it should be. . . . When, some years ago, his name was placed second [to Jones's], I felt hurt. When it was again placed first, I wept, and said, 'Thank God'" (Lt 17, 1902).

But he still had some of the same old Smith left. Not long after he became editor he reopened the Galatians war and again had to be sacked. He never recovered from the shock. The same *Review* that announced the change in editorship noted that he was seriously ill. He passed to his rest in 1903 at the age of 70.

Lord, help us this day with our willful selves. Help us to surrender all to You, even our most cherished ideas and ways.

WHAT HAPPENED TO JONES AND WAGGONER?

Hold fast what you have, so that no one will take your crown. Rev. 3:11, NASB.

I mmediately after the Minneapolis event Jones and Waggoner found it difficult to get a hearing in the church. But that situation did not persist. Through the aid of the new General Conference president, O. A. Olsen, Ellen White, and others, they became the leading speakers in the denomination.

We can perhaps best gauge the magnitude of the General Conference support from the central role the two men had as featured speakers on Bible topics at the General Conference sessions in the post-Minneapolis period.

- In 1889 Jones had a series on justification by faith. The people, Ellen White noted, "are being fed with large morsels from the Lord's table," and "great interest is manifested" (MS 10, 1889).
- The 1891 session (after 1889 they convened every second year) featured Waggoner and his 16 sermons uplifting Jesus Christ and the everlasting gospel in Romans.
- Jones led the Bible study sessions in 1893, with 24 sermons on the third angel's message. Ten sermons on the promise of the Holy Spirit by W. W. Prescott—Jones's closest colleague in the United States from 1892 until the end of the century—complemented his work.
- The 1895 meetings again saw Jones as the leading Bible expositor, with 26 sermons on the third angel's message, besides other presentations.
- Waggoner's 18 studies on Hebrews were the focal point of Bible study in 1897. In addition, Jones made 11 presentations.

The Minneapolis reformers had in the long run become the "victors" in the battle with Smith and Butler. Unfortunately, however, their victory was not lasting. Both would leave the church in the early 1900s—Waggoner over his pantheism and a woman who was not his wife, and Jones over a power struggle in which he failed to gain the leadership of the General Conference. By 1907 Jones would become a bitter enemy of both Ellen White and the denomination.

Paradox of paradoxes. The eventual "victors" at Minneapolis became the losers. "Hold fast what you have, so that no one will take your crown." That is needed counsel for all of us in a world of sin. We must keep our eyes focused on Jesus at every step of our journey.

RETROSPECT ON MINNEAPOLIS

Thou shalt call his name Jesus: for he shall save his people from their sins. Matt. 1:21.

The 1888 General Conference session was one of the great turning points in Seventh-day Adventist history.

We cannot have the slightest doubt about its accomplishments. It directed the church back to the Bible as the only source of authority in both doctrine and practice, it uplifted Jesus and placed salvation by grace through faith at the center of Adventist theology, it contexted the proper role of the law within the gospel of grace, and it led to a restudying of the topics of the Trinity, the full divinity of Christ, and the personhood of the Holy Spirit.

And perhaps most important, it gave Adventism a fuller understanding of the third angel's message in Revelation 14:12—the central text in Seventh-day Adventist self-understanding. Not only did that passage identify them as Adventists as they patiently waited for their Lord while keeping all of God's commandments, but it also set before them the gospel message in the fact that God's last message to the world before the Second Advent (verses 14-20) would center on having faith *in* Jesus.

In short, the 1888 message transformed the way Adventists thought about their message. That's the good news.

The bad news is that the devil is always out to make sure that we forget or neglect the good news. Thus it is that some Adventists in the 1890s and beyond continued to focus on the law rather than the gospel, while others used the message of Jones and Waggoner as a new gate into the old legalism and human perfectionism that they had been raised up to stand against.

The whole story of the Minneapolis saga brings to mind two of the greatest facts on earth. First, the utter perversity of human beings. Second, the unbounded grace of God. Looking back on the history of the church in the Minneapolis era, what comes to my mind are the words of John Newton's great hymn: "Amazing grace! How sweet the sound, that saved a wretch like me!"

"Amazing grace" is the only kind there is. Those two words sum up the message and meaning of the 1888 event.

MEET W. W. PRESCOTT

Those whom I love, I reprove and chasten; so be zealous and repent. Rev. 3:19, RSV.

One of the most forceful leaders of late-nineteenth-century Adventism was William Warren Prescott. But forceful individuals are not always spiritual leaders. So it was with the early Prescott, who had become president of Battle Creek College in 1885.

The turning point in his life came in late 1890, when he read a special testimony entitled "Be Zealous and Repent" before the Battle Creek Tabernacle. "The Lord," it said, "has seen our backslidings. . . . Because the Lord has, in former days, blessed and honored" the Adventist Church, "they flatter themselves that they are chosen and true, and do not need warning and instruction and reproof."

But, "the True Witness says, 'As many as I love, I rebuke and chasten: be zealous therefore, and repent'" or else "'I will come unto thee quickly, and will remove thy candlestick out of his place.' . . . The displeasure of the Lord is against his people. In their present condition it is impossible for them to represent the character of Christ. And when the True Witness has sent them counsel, reproof, and warnings because he loves them, they have refused to receive the message. . . . What does it mean that such amazing grace does not soften our hard hearts? . . .

"There is to be in the churches a wonderful manifestation of the power of God, but it will not move upon those who have not humbled themselves before the Lord, and opened the door of the heart by confession and repentance. . . . Talent, long experience, will not make men channels of light, unless they place themselves under the bright beams of the Sun of Righteousness. . . .

"Light is to shine forth from God's people in clear, distinct rays, bringing Jesus before the churches and before the world. . . . One interest will prevail, one subject will swallow up every other—Christ our righteousness. . . . All who venture to have their own way, who do not join the angels who are sent from heaven with a message to fill the whole earth with its glory will be passed by. The work will go forward to victory without them, and they will have no part in its triumph" (RH Extra, Dec. 23, 1890).

While reading, Prescott felt so moved that several times he stopped because of tearful emotion. His life would never be the same. He had been an Adventist, but that day he had met Christ as his Savior. Thereafter he linked arms with Ellen White, Jones, and Waggoner in preaching Christ and His love. Prescott had taken seriously the counsel to repent and be zealous.

THE BAPTISM OF ADVENTIST EDUCATION—1

Behold, I stand at the door and knock; if any one hears my voice and opens the door, I will come in to him and eat with him, and he with me. Rev. 3:20, RSV.

In December 1890, as we saw yesterday, Christ came to William Warren Prescott and knocked on the door of his heart. The young educator opened it. And he would never be the same. And neither would Uriah Smith. One result of Prescott's conversion was a ministry to Smith that led to his public confession and a healing between him and Ellen White.

And so it is that the message of Christ changes lives and reshapes them. But in the case of Prescott the reshaping not only affected individual lives but also had a mighty impact on Adventist education.

You see, Prescott was not merely the president of Battle Creek College—he was also the head of the Seventh-day Adventist Educational Association and would soon be the president of both Union College and Walla Walla College. Being leader of the association and president of three colleges at the same time, the articulate Prescott was in a position to make serious changes in Adventist education.

He would initiate the transformation of Adventist education at an educational convention he sponsored at a little place called Harbor Springs in northern Michigan during July and August 1891.

Up to that point Adventist education had struggled with its mission and identity. Although Adventists had founded it to be distinctively Christian and to prepare ministers and missionaries, from its beginning at Battle Creek College in 1874 it had been held captive to the pagan classics and the study of Latin and classical Greek. Some reforms had been attempted, but most yet remained to be accomplished.

That would begin to change with the conversion of Prescott. The truth of Prescott's story is that God uses people to change His church. But He can only work through those willing to let Him use them.

That is where you and I come in. God wants to take our lives and shape us in such a way that He can use us to reach out and affect others and the larger church.

Now, I know that some of you are saying that you have no influence. Not so! Each of us touches other people in some small way every day. It is through bits and pieces of such influence that the snowball of change eventually comes about.

THE BAPTISM OF ADVENTIST EDUCATION—2

He who has an ear, let him hear what the Spirit says to the churches. Rev. 3:22, RSV.

The Holy Spirit had a great deal to say to the church and its educational program during the 1890s. Not only were Ellen White, A. T. Jones, and E. J. Waggoner taking the message of Christ and His righteousness to the churches and camp meetings, but the General Conference had also established an annual ministers' institute, in which Adventist clergy could meet for several weeks each year to study the Bible and the plan of salvation.

The newly energized Prescott decided to do the same for the denomination's educators during the summer of 1891 at Harbor Springs. W. C. White described the sessions in terms of spiritual revival, stressing the emphasis on spontaneous personal testimonies. He noted that each day began with Jones's expositions of the book of Romans. Ellen White also spoke on such topics as the necessity of a personal relationship with Christ, the need for spiritual revival among the educators attending the convention, and the centrality of the Christian message to education.

Prescott asserted at the 1893 General Conference session that Harbor Springs had marked the turning point in Adventist education. "While the general purpose up to that time," he claimed, had been "to have a religious element in our schools, yet since that institute, as never before, our work has been *practically* [rather than theoretically] upon that basis, showing itself in courses of study and plans of work as it had not previously."

Before Harbor Springs the teaching of Bible had held a minor place in Adventist education. The convention, however, adopted a recommendation calling for four years of Bible study for students in Adventist colleges. Specifically, the delegates decided that "the Bible as a whole should be studied as the gospel of Christ from first to last." The convention also recommended the teaching of history from the perspective of the biblical worldview.

There is a side lesson of great importance as we think of the changes brought about in Adventist education at Harbor Springs. That is, when we really understand the centrality of Christ to our lives, it will affect everything we do as both individuals and as a denomination. Educationally, if our salvation depends on Christ, we had better get to know Him.

The "Adventizing" of Adventist Education: The Avondale Experiment—1

It is written in the Prophets: "They will all be taught by God." Everyone who listens to the Father and learns from him comes to me. John 6:45, NIV.

The first step in the transformation of Adventist schools took place at the Harbor Springs educational institute in the summer of 1891. The next one began when Ellen White and her son W. C. White sailed for Australia in November 1891. Remaining there until 1900, they would have opportunity to work with some of the most responsive of Adventism's reform leaders.

One of the most important endeavors of the Adventists in Australia in the 1890s was the founding of the Avondale School for Christian Workers (today known as Avondale College). Australia had the advantage of being beyond the reach of the conservative Adventist leadership in the United States. In addition, it was a new mission field for Seventh-day Adventists. Thus the fledgling denomination there had no established traditions to contend with. As a result, it piloted several innovations in Australia during the nineties that would have been much more difficult to experiment with in the United States.

The church forged a new type of Adventist school at Avondale. By the end of the century Ellen White was so impressed that she referred to Avondale as an "object lesson," a "sample school," a "model school," and a "pattern" (LS 374; CT 349). In 1900 she categorically stated that "the school in Avondale is to be a pattern for other schools which shall be established among our people" (MS 92, 1900).

Milton Hook, the historian of Avondale, concluded that two main goals undergirded the Avondale School. The first was the conversion and character development of its students. "Higher education," as defined at Avondale, was that which prepared individuals for eternal life.

The second goal was the training of denominational young people for Christian service both in the local community and in worldwide mission outreach. Both goals reflect a distinct move away from the strictly academic orientation of Battle Creek College and the schools that came under its influence.

Here's a question that we still need to ask: Why do we value Adventist Christian education? The only important answer is that it makes a difference in the lives of our children. Its primary purpose is to introduce them to Jesus Christ as Savior and Lord. When it does so, Adventist education has a value beyond money.

THE "ADVENTIZING" OF ADVENTIST EDUCATION: THE AVONDALE EXPERIMENT–2

All your sons shall be taught by the Lord, and great shall be the prosperity of your sons. Isa. 54:13, RSV.

As we noted yesterday, Ellen White spent a great deal of her time during the 1890s working closely with the development of the Avondale school in Australia as a pattern, whose principles the church could apply to other institutions.

In early 1894 she wrote that "our minds have been much exercised day and night in regard to our schools. How shall they be conducted? And what shall be the education and training of the youth? Where shall our Australian Bible School be located? I was awakened this morning at one o'clock with a heavy burden upon my soul. The subject of education has been presented before me in different times, in varied aspects, by many illustrations, and with direct specification, now upon one point, and again upon another. I feel, indeed, that we have much to learn. We are ignorant in regard to many things" related to education (FE 310).

Mrs. White was giving serious thought to the proposed Australian facility because she saw the possibility of developing a school outside the sphere of influence of Battle Creek College. In her keynote testimony regarding it she set the tone for thinking about a new type of Adventist school. It would be a Bible school that emphasized missionary activities and the spiritual side of life. In addition, it would be practical, teach young people how to work, and have a rural location.

After 20 years of trial and error, Ellen White was more convinced than ever regarding the type of education that the church needed. From her growing understanding of her own testimonies during the past two decades, she had already explicitly affirmed that the Bible must be at the center and that Adventist schools should not follow the false leads of classical education. It had, she wrote, "taken much time to understand what changes should be made" to establish education on a "different order" (6T 126), but the process of understanding and implementing that understanding would develop rapidly between 1894 and 1899.

As we have noted again and again during the past few months, God leads His people step by step. He does not give all understanding at one time. God directs us to the next step at the proper time. So it was in the field of education. By the 1890s Adventism was ready for an educational revolution.

THE "ADVENTIZING" OF ADVENTIST EDUCATION: THE AVONDALE EXPERIMENT—3

All shall know me, from the least of them to the greatest. Heb. 8:11, RSV.

Part of the new covenant experience reflected upon in Hebrews 8 is educational. Central to the new covenant is knowing God and His will. With that in mind, it is no accident that the post-Minneapolis revolution that had begun to transform Adventist thinking on the place of Christ and the Bible in Adventism would also mightily shape the denomination's educational philosophy.

It was in the light of the Avondale experiment that Ellen White wrote that "human productions have been used as most essential" in prior Adventist education "and the word of God has been studied simply to give flavor to other studies" (FE 395).

That model, she asserted, must come to an end. "The Bible should not be brought into our schools to be sandwiched in between infidelity. The Bible must be made the groundwork and subject matter of education. . . . It should be used as the word of the living God, and esteemed as first, and last, and best in everything. Then will be seen true spiritual growth. The students will develop healthy religious characters, because they eat the flesh and drink the blood of the Son of God. But unless watched and nurtured, the health of the soul decays. Keep in the channel of light. Study the Bible" (FE 474).

Again, "higher education is an experimental [i.e., experiential] knowledge of the plan of salvation, and this knowledge is secured by earnest and diligent study of the Scriptures. Such an education will renew the mind and transform the character, restoring the image of God in the soul. It will fortify the mind against . . . the adversary, and enable us to understand the voice of God. It will teach the learner to become a coworker with Jesus Christ. . . . It is the simplicity of true godliness— our passport from the preparatory school of earth to the higher school above.

"There is no education to be gained higher than that given to the early disciples, and which is revealed to us through the word of God. To gain the higher education means to follow this word implicitly; it means to walk in the footsteps of Christ, to proclaim His virtues. It means to give up selfishness and to devote the life to the service of God" (CT 11).

Now, there is the platform of revolutionary education for a Christian life.

THE "ADVENTIZING" OF ADVENTIST EDUCATION: THE AVONDALE EXPERIMENT–4

You are yourselves taught by God to love one another. 1 Thess. 4:9, REB.

Spiritual revival in the church and its teachings had led in the 1890s to a call for a similar reformation in Adventist education. The denomination's schools were to be both more specifically Christian and Adventist than they had been in the past.

Ellen White's numerous testimonies on education during her Australian years continued to give direction to the Avondale School. Furthermore, living adjacent to the campus during its formative stages, she was able to take part in developing the institution in a way that was unique in her experience. Beyond that, W. W. Prescott, who had collected and edited the manuscripts for *Christian Education* (1893) and *Special Testimonies on Education* (1897), spent several months on the campus in the mid 1890s. During that period, he and Ellen White had extended conversations on Christian education. They both benefited by being able to come to a fuller grasp of the implications of the testimonies and how one might implement their principles. She wrote to her son Edson that Prescott drew out her mind and thoughts as her husband had done earlier. Their conversations, she claimed, enabled her to clarify her thinking and to say more than otherwise. "We could see some matters in a clearer light" (MS 62, 1896).

Not only did the Avondale experiment help place the Bible, student spirituality, missions, and service to others at the focal point of Adventist education, it also urged it to be rural wherever possible. Thus in place of the few acres at the edge of town that had sufficed for Battle Creek College, the new institution would be established on the 1,500-acre Brettville estate in a rural location. The acreage and rural location not only allowed the students to be away from the problems of the city and close to nature, but it also provided the school ample room for the teaching of practical skills for the world of work. Adventist education would never be the same after the establishment of Avondale. Not only did the denomination now have a massive amount of material on educational ideals from the pen of Ellen White, but it had a real-world model that it could pattern after in other parts of the world.

Given the importance of education to the church, we who are older need to take a larger interest in our young people and our church schools. We not only must support them with our funds, but also help them become what they can and should be.

THE RISE OF ADVENTIST ELEMENTARY SCHOOLS—1

And these words which I command you this day shall be upon your heart; and you shall teach them diligently to your children. Deut. 6:6, 7, RSV.

One of the most exciting developments in Adventist education in the 1890s was the elementary school movement. Up through the middle 90s Adventists had largely neglected elementary education except at localities where they had a college or secondary school. That indifference would change by the end of the decade, and Adventists have ever since supported a strong system of local church (elementary) schools.

The General Conference had called in 1887 and 1888 to begin a system of elementary schools, but nothing had come from the resolutions.

In 1897, however, Ellen White challenged the church with a renewed demand for elementary schools. The Australian situation had alerted her on the topic. "In some countries," she asserted, "parents are compelled by law to send their children to school. In these countries, in localities where there is a church, schools should be established if there are no more than six children to attend. Work as if you were working for your life to save the children from being drowned in the polluting, corrupting influences of the world.

"We are far behind our duty in this important matter. In many places schools should have been in operation years ago" (6T 199).

Again she wrote: "Wherever there are a few Sabbathkeepers, the parents should unite in providing a place for a day school where their children and youth can be instructed. They should employ a Christian teacher who, as a consecrated missionary, shall educate the children in such a way as to lead them to become missionaries. Let teachers be employed who will give a thorough education in the common branches, the Bible being made the foundation and the life of all study" (*ibid.,* 198).

Those words proved to be some of the most important and most influential counsel in all of her long ministry. In the next few years Adventist churches around the world established schools, even if they had only five or six children to attend. Their salvation and future became a focal point of Seventh-day Adventism as the church took seriously its evangelistic responsibility to prepare its own children for God's kingdom.

From such a perspective, education was evangelism. That is an insight that we dare not lose.

THE RISE OF ADVENTIST ELEMENTARY SCHOOLS–2

I have singled [Abraham] out so that he will direct his sons and their families to keep the way of the Lord and do what is right and just. Gen. 18:19, NLT.

Education for the faith has a long history in the Judeo/Christian realm. In fact, God chose or singled out Abraham, the father of the faithful, because of his willingness to educate his family in the ways and teachings of the Lord.

But old though the command to educate one's children in the faith may have been in the Bible, it was a late comer in Seventh-day Adventism. The denomination would be more than 50 years past the Great Disappointment of 1844 before it began to develop an elementary education system.

The stimulus, as we saw yesterday, came from Ellen White's summons in far-off Australia to form local church schools even if a congregation had but six to attend.

Such individuals in America as Edward Alexander Sutherland and Percy T. Magan, the reform leaders who would move Battle Creek College into the country in 1901, took that admonition to heart. Years later Sutherland recalled with some exaggeration, "Magan, Miss DeGraw, and myself practically at the end of every week would pick up a teacher and go out and establish three schools before Monday morning."

Exaggeration or not, the statistics on Adventist elementary education shot practically straight up beginning in the second half of the 1890s. Watch the curve: In 1880 the denomination had one elementary school with one teacher and 15 students; in 1885 it had three schools with five teachers and 125 students; in 1890 7 schools with 15 teachers and 350 students; in 1895 18 schools with 35 teachers and 895 students; and in 1900 220 schools with 250 teachers and 5,000 students. And the growth didn't stop there. By 1910 the numbers had swollen to 594 schools with 758 teachers and 13,357 students. In 2006 the figures stood at 5,362 schools, 36,880 teachers, and 861,745 students.

The elementary school movement also stimulated expansion in the church's secondary and higher education. In part that growth came about because of the increased need for Adventist elementary teachers. But, more importantly, the elementary movement gave publicity to the belief that every Adventist young person should have a Christian education.

Thank You, Lord, for our school system. Help me to do my part to help every young person in my congregation to have an education that will fit each for eternity.

EDUCATIONAL EXPLOSION

*From childhood you have known the sacred writings which are able to give
you the wisdom that leads to salvation through faith which is in Christ Jesus.
2 Tim. 3:15, NASB.*

We might call the 1890s the decade of Adventist education. Beginning with
the revival at Minneapolis in 1888 and running up through the start of
the educational reformation at the Harbor Springs Convention in 1891 and flowing into the Avondale experiment and the elementary school movement, the
1890s would shape Adventism educationally for the rest of its stay on earth.

And we haven't even yet talked about the mission explosion of the 1890s that
took Adventism and its educational system quite literally to every corner of the
globe. Nor have we explored the impact of the Avondale model on Adventist
schools in other parts of the world.

One small aspect of that influence was the making of Adventist education at
the secondary and higher education levels into a largely rural system. E. A.
Sutherland and P. T. Magan, for example, transferred Battle Creek College from
its restricted campus to the "wilds" of Berrien Springs, Michigan, where it became
Emmanuel Missionary College in 1901. Likewise, the directors of Healdsburg
College moved the institution during the early twentieth century to the top of
Howell Mountain, where it became Pacific Union College. Not only were the in-
stitutions isolated from the problems of the city (as students at Pacific Union
College in the early 1960s we quipped that the school was located 10 miles from
the nearest known sin), but they were both built on hundreds of acres of land.

And so it was with Adventist education around the world. The reverberations
from Avondale have never ceased. And they have had some interesting side effects. As population increases have expanded the cities and pressured land prices,
Seventh-day Adventist schools often find themselves on priceless property hold-
ings that they could never hope to purchase in today's market.

God has led His people in unique and special ways. When we survey the various aspects of the Adventist program around the world we can only praise His name
for the guidance He has given in our past history. Now we need to pray that we
might have the conviction and the courage to follow His direction in present history.

Father, help us to be as responsive to Your leading as the reformers of past eras.

TURNING EDUCATION ON ITS HEAD

If any man desire to be first, the same shall be last of all, and servant of all. Mark 9:35.

Our ideas of education take too narrow and too low a range. There is need of a broader scope, a higher aim. True education means more than the pursual of a certain course of study. It means more than a preparation for the life that now is. It has to do with the whole being, and with the whole period of existence possible to man. It is the harmonious development of the physical, the mental, and the spiritual powers. It prepares the student for the joy of service in this world and for the higher joy of wider service in the world to come" (Ed 13).

Thus read the opening words of the book *Education,* one of Ellen White's most important contributions to Adventism. It is no accident that the book came off the press in 1903. After a decade of thinking and writing on the topic of education, she was ready in the early years of the new century to develop a book that would give direction to one of the denomination's most important sectors. *Education* provides the Adventist school system with its philosophical marching orders. And in the process it sets forth ideals of education quite at odds with traditional programs.

Whereas traditional education aimed at preparing people for a successful life here on earth, *Education,* while not denying that important function, claimed that such a preparation was not enough. More vital yet was preparing students to live with God for eternity.

Whereas traditional education tended to focus on developing the mental aspects of its students, *Education* called for the improvement of the whole person.

And whereas traditional education prepared people to position themselves advantageously for getting ahead in the world, *Education* argued for the goal of service to God and others. The service theme brackets the book. On its last page we read that "in our life here, earthly, sin-restricted though it is, the greatest joy and the highest education are in service. And in the future state, untrammeled by the limitations of sinful humanity, it is in service that our greatest joy and our highest education will be found" (*ibid.,* 309).

The book *Education* turned traditional education on its head. And in the process it put forth a philosophy of education and life that we need both to understand and to live. It is a philosophy that puts into practice the values of the One who said, "if any man desire to be first, the same shall be last of all, and servant of all."

EDUCATION EVANGELISM

So God created man in his own image, in the image of God he created him; male and female he created them. Gen. 1:27, RSV.

E llen White's book *Education* takes the topic of pedagogy out of the realm of the mundane and transfers it to a crucial issue in the great controversy.

On its second page it provides Adventist education with its ultimate purpose. "In order to understand what is comprehended in the work of education," we read, "we need to consider both [1] the nature of man and [2] the purpose of God in creating him. We need to consider also [3] the change in man's condition through the coming in of a knowledge of evil, and [4] God's plan for still fulfilling His glorious purpose in the education of the human race" (Ed 14, 15).

At that point the book begins to treat those four points, indicating that (1) God created human beings in His image to be like Him, and (2) that they had infinite potential.

Next it gets very specific and quite pertinent to the human situation. "But [3] by disobedience this was forfeited. Through sin the divine likeness was marred, and well-nigh obliterated. Man's physical powers were weakened, his mental capacity was lessened, his spiritual vision dimmed. He had become subject to death. [4] Yet the race was not left without hope. By infinite love and mercy the plan of salvation had been devised, and a life of probation was granted. To restore in man the image of his Maker, to bring him back to the perfection in which he was created, to promote the development of body, mind, and soul, that the divine purpose in his creation might be realized—this was to be the work of redemption. This is the object of education, the great object of life" (*ibid.*, 15, 16).

Later in the book Ellen White puts it even more bluntly when she notes that individuals "can find help in but one power. That power is Christ. Cooperation with that power is man's greatest need. In all educational effort should not this cooperation be the highest aim? . . . In the highest sense the work of education and the work of redemption are one." The "teacher's first effort and his constant aim" is to introduce students to Jesus and His principles (*ibid.*, 29, 30).

With those thoughts in mind, it is no wonder that Adventists have supported Christian education for both their own children and those of others through sacrificial giving. They have recognized the truth that education is in actuality evangelism.

PROTESTANT MISSION EXPLOSION

And the Good News about the Kingdom will be preached throughout the whole world, so that all nations will hear it; and then, finally, the end will come. Matt. 24:14, NLT.

World mission stood at the heart of nineteenth-century Protestant Christianity. The modern mission movement began in 1792 when William Carey published *An Enquiry Into the Obligation of Christians to Use Means for the Conversion of the Heathens.*

That might not seem so revolutionary to us, but it was in 1792. The next year saw the establishment of the first missionary society for sponsoring foreign missionaries and the sending of Carey to India, where he worked for seven years without an Indian convert.

But even though his efforts began slowly, they rooted themselves firmly. By the time of his death in 1834 Carey had not only established a strong Christian church in India, but he had fathered the modern mission movement that would take Protestantism around the world. The first great wave of Protestant mission to the world peaked in the 1830s, but it didn't stop there. Rather, it increased in magnitude during the latter part of the century. Kenneth Scott Latourette has labeled the nineteenth century as "the great century" of Protestant missions, while Sydney Ahlstrom, a leading student of American church history, has noted that "the closing two decades of the nineteenth century witnessed the climactic phase of the foreign missions movement in American Protestantism."

One of its main stimulants was the Student Volunteer Movement for Foreign Missions, which grew out of an appeal by evangelist Dwight L. Moody in 1886 for college students to devote their lives to mission service. One hundred took their stand that first year. That number increased to 2,200 in 1887, and within a few years many thousands of young people had pledged their lives to mission service. The movement's motto was "the evangelization of the world in this generation."

It stimulated, claims Ernest R. Sandeen, "the greatest demonstration of missionary interest ever known in the United States." As a result, American Protestants began to see such places as Africa, China, and Japan as their spiritual provinces.

Such a movement did not catch Adventists sleeping. God had opened the way through the Protestant initiative, and the Seventh-day Adventists would rapidly reach out "to every nation, and kindred, and tongue, and people" with the messages of the three angels.

ADVENTIST MISSION EXPLOSION—1

Then I saw another angel flying high in the air, with an eternal message of Good News to announce to the peoples of the earth, to every race, tribe, language, and nation. Rev. 14:6, TEV.

It must be confessed that the Seventh-day Adventist Church did not begin as a mission-oriented people. To the contrary, their earliest years found them as what we might call the antimission people.

Between 1844 and 1850, holding to the shut-door theology, they felt no burden to preach to any but those who had been in the Millerite movement of the 1840s.

Shortsighted! you might say. Yes, but an essential stage in the development of Adventism. This period of Adventist mission (1844-1850) freed up scarce resources from potential missions to build a doctrinal platform. In other words, first came a very distinct message, and only after that could they spread that message.

The second stage of Adventist mission (1850-1874) restricted itself to North America. That was also a necessary step in the progression of Adventist mission. Those years allowed for the development of a power base in North America that could eventually support a foreign missions project.

We might think of the third stage (1874-1889) as mission to the Christian nations. Thus Seventh-day Adventists sent their first official denominational missionary to Switzerland to call people out of Babylon. And even when they went to such places as Australia or South Africa, the Adventists always began their work among the Christians of those nations. Limited as it was, the third stage functioned to establish additional power bases among the various Christian populations scattered around the world. As a result, those nations were prepared to act as home bases for the sending of missionaries at the beginning of the fourth stage of Adventist missions, which began in 1890. We might regard that stage as mission to the world—not just to Christian populations around the earth, but to all peoples.

Step by step, without anyone being conscious of what was taking place in the overall development of Adventist missions, God positioned the Seventh-day Adventist Church where it could take advantage of the Protestant mission explosion that detonated in the last years of the nineteenth century.

God leads even when we aren't aware of it.

ADVENTIST MISSION EXPLOSION—2

Thou must prophesy again before many peoples, and nations, and tongues, and kings. Rev. 10:11.

From the perspective of Adventist history, the 1890s was an excellent time for a Protestant mission explosion that would nearly complete its penetration to the remote corners of the earth. As we saw yesterday, the development of Adventist mission mentality through three stages had positioned the denomination to take advantage of the new impulses surging through the larger Christian community.

Beyond that, Adventists had published their first book on foreign missions—*Historical Sketches of the Foreign Missions of the Seventh-day Adventists*—the same year (1886) that D. L. Moody stimulated the birth of the Student Volunteer Movement.

Then in early 1889 the denomination sent S. N. Haskell and Percy T. Magan on a two-year itinerary around the world to survey opportunities, problems, and possible mission sites in various parts of Africa, India, and the Orient. They fully reported their tour to the church through the pages of the *Youth's Instructor* (the forerunner of *Insight*). Thus mission and mission service began to capture the hearts and minds of Adventist youth in a manner similar to the way the non-Adventist student movement affected thousands of young people in the larger Protestant world.

In November 1889 the General Conference session took the momentous step of creating the Seventh-day Adventist Foreign Mission Board "for the management of the foreign mission work" of the denomination. The same year saw the *Home Missionary* developed as a periodical aimed at promoting the various aspects of missionary service.

The establishment of the Foreign Mission Board was more than symbolic. It proclaimed that Adventists were at last ready to take their mission mandate seriously. Never again would Seventh-day Adventists be backward about foreign missions. To the contrary, they would become known for their efforts to reach the entire world with their special message of the three angels, spreading not only it but their publishing, medical, and educational institutions wherever they went.

Lord, we appreciate the importance of the final message of warning that You have given Your church. Help us to support it with our prayers, our money, and even our lives if You call.

The Rise of the Missionary College

How are men to call upon him in whom they have not believed? Rom. 10:14, RSV.

That is a good question. And both the larger Christian community and Seventh-day Adventists in the 1890s began to take unprecedented steps to spread the teachings of God's Word as the seedbed of faith.

Part of the preparation for broader mission among Protestants was the development of missionary colleges and Bible institutes. Such schools aimed to prepare large numbers of workers as quickly as possible to staff mission outposts both at home and overseas. The new institutions focused on practical training and Bible knowledge. The first such school appeared in 1883 as the Missionary Training College for Home and Foreign Missionaries and Evangelists.

Events within Adventism paralleled those in the evangelical educational realm. Thus mission outreach had a direct effect on the expansion of the denomination's schooling. The church looked to its educational institutions to supply staff for its rapidly expanding worldwide program.

John Harvey Kellogg was apparently the first Adventist to develop a missionary school. He established the Sanitarium Training School for Medical Missionaries in 1889, followed by the American Medical Missionary College in 1895.

Meanwhile, the Avondale School for Christian Workers (1894), the training schools founded by E. A. Sutherland and Percy Magan, and the Adventist missionary colleges (such as Washington Missionary College, Emmanuel Missionary College, Southern Missionary College, and the College of Medical Evangelists at Loma Linda) soon were dotting the Adventist landscape—all of them similar in intent to the institutions spawned by the evangelical mission movement.

Mission expansion affected Adventist educational growth in at least two ways. First, it greatly increased the number of schools and students in North America, since most of the denomination's early workers came from the United States. Second, Adventists began to establish schools around the world so that the church could train people in their home fields. By 1900, therefore, not only had Adventist educational institutions exploded in number, but the system had been internationalized.

No one can doubt the mission orientation of Adventist schools in the 1890s. The challenge in our time is to keep that focus at the forefront of our schools at all levels. The nature of mission has changed in the past century, but not the need to tell a world about hope in Christ.

ADVENTISM ON THE MOVE–1: RUSSIA

And how are they to believe in him of whom they have never heard?
Rom. 10:14, RSV.

G od at times uses strange ways to help people hear His Word. Such was the case of the arrival of Adventism in Russia. As in so many areas of the world, converts to Adventism in America among immigrant populations first stimulated the beginning of Adventism in Russia. In wanting to share their faith they often sent doctrinal tracts back home to family and friends.

Thus it was in 1882 when a Crimean neighbor of Gerhardt Perk notified him that he had some interesting but dangerous literature that had come from America in 1879. After much pleading the neighbor loaned Perk J. N. Andrews' *The Third Angel's Message*. Reading it in secret, Perk wrote to the American publishers for more information. Soon he had read himself into conviction on Adventist doctrine, but he hesitated to start observing the Sabbath.

About that time he became an agent of the British and Foreign Bible Society. While traveling from place to place selling books, Perk escaped disaster several times through what he believed was divine protection. At that point he was convicted that if he expected God's care, he should live up to all the Bible truth that he had. As a result, he added Adventist literature to the Bibles he was selling.

But Perk was not the only person spreading Adventist doctrine in south Russia. Another was a German-Russian convert to Adventism from South Dakota. Even though he was more than 80 years old, had a speech impediment, and had no money, he returned to Russia to share his faith, selling his boots to pay for part of his fare.

To say the least, he was creative. Pleading poor eyesight, he would enter a village marketplace and request people to read to him. If the reader became interested in the topic, he gave the tract to him or her.

Passing out such material, however, was against the law in Russia. But when the local priest wanted to have the old man arrested, the people stoned the cleric for thinking that a nearly blind old man could be dangerous. The "harmless old man" evangelized for more than a year in this manner.

Such was the beginning of Adventism in Russia. It appears that God can use almost anyone in almost any condition by almost any method to spread biblical truth. He can probably even use us.

ADVENTISM ON THE MOVE–2: RUSSIA

And how are they to hear without a preacher? Rom. 10:14, RSV.

A nd preachers there were. One of the most significant was L. R. Conradi, a German-born immigrant to America where he found the Advent message. In 1886 he returned to Europe as a minister.

Almost immediately he faced a request from Gerhardt Perk to visit Russia. Since the authorities would not admit a minister to the country, Conradi, having worked for a while at the Review and Herald Publishing Association in Battle Creek, declared himself as a printer.

But no matter what he called himself, once Conradi got into the country he began to preach the Seventh-day Adventist message openly. He and Perk located about 50 Sabbathkeepers, and Baptist and Lutheran congregations often greeted them with open arms. At other times the two Adventists found themselves met with stones, especially when they introduced the Sabbath question.

But in all of his activities Conradi was violating Russian law, which forbade preaching and proselytizing. Still things went well until they arrived at Berde Bulat, where they organized a church and held a public baptism in the Black Sea. The rooftops were crowded with spectators who desired to watch the novel scene.

That was too much for the local authorities. They arrested Conradi and Perk and charged them with the teaching of Jewish heresy, of public baptism, and of proselytizing Russians. For 40 days the two men endured a cramped cell, poor food, and intimidating threats. But finally the American embassy in St. Petersburg secured their release.

And what did they do? More preaching as they spread the Advent message in a difficult place to do evangelism.

Conradi would eventually locate in Germany, where he would lead the Adventist denomnation in Europe for the next 35 years.

Meanwhile, back in Russia more returning Adventist immigrants arrived to preach the message they loved. Some of them would end up banished to Siberia, but it was through such sacrifices that the Seventh-day Adventist message took root and began to grow in Russia.

Lord, most of us today have it so easy. Help us to learn to remember the sacrifices of those who have gone before in the spreading of the messages of the three angels.

ADVENTISM ON THE MOVE—3:
THE PACIFIC ISLANDS

And how can men preach unless they are sent? Rom. 10:15, RSV.

B ut some went without being sent. One of that group was John Tay, a ship's carpenter who had long dreamed of visiting tiny Pitcairn Island, where the infamous mutineers of the *Bounty* had finally settled in 1790. Working his way on some six ships, Tay finally arrived on Pitcairn in 1886.

Ten years earlier James White and John Loughborough had heard of the island and had sent a box of Adventist literature in the hope that its inhabitants would read it. But they didn't. For 10 years the box sat in storage. Finally some of the younger people rediscovered it. To their surprise, they learned that Saturday was the true Sabbath. But even though they were impressed with the Bible evidence, they hesitated to make a change.

It was at that point that Tay arrived, requesting permission to remain on Pitcairn until the next ship arrived. Asked to speak at church on the first Sunday he was there, the self-sent "missionary" discussed the seventh-day Sabbath. Many were convicted, yet others remained doubtful. But Bible study by Tay convinced all. By the time he left the island five weeks later, all its adult inhabitants had accepted the spectrum of Seventh-day Adventist doctrines.

The exciting news of the conversion of the Pitcairn Islanders inspired the Adventists back in the United States. They took the event to be a sign from God that it was time to open up the Adventist work in the South Pacific.

But how? Part of the problem was that steamship connections in much of the region were at best irregular. Thus it was that the 1887 General Conference session authorized the spending of $20,000 to buy or build a ship as soon as possible.

But such was not to be. Not yet anyway.

Hoping to move with more speed, they sent Tay back to Pitcairn to strengthen his converts. But after attempting the task, he finally returned to San Francisco unable to locate a ship to take him to the isolated island. More disastrous was the experience of A. J. Chudney, who was also sent to Pitcairn. When he couldn't find a boat going his way, he bought one at a bargain price. But he, his crew, and the boat went down in the Pacific.

That sobering catastrophe brought the church leaders back to the idea of constructing their own missionary ship.

ADVENTISM ON THE MOVE—4:
THE PACIFIC ISLANDS

Let them give glory unto the Lord, and declare his praise in the islands. Isa. 42:12.

The Chudney disaster and the frustration of John Tay in not being able to find a ship to take him to Pitcairn Island reoriented the General Conference to the need to build a seaworthy vessel for service to the multitude of South Pacific islands.

That mission boat was a project that stirred the enthusiasm of the Sabbath schools across the United States as nothing had ever done before. Adults brought their quarters and dollars and children sold baked goods so that they might have a part in buying the needed nails, boards, and canvas.

Sabbath school members were even invited to suggest a name for the ship. Some opted for *Glad Tidings,* but others finally decided to name it for the island that had stimulated the project. Thus Adventists christened their first missionary vessel the *Pitcairn.*

In October 1890 the 100-foot, 120-ton, two-masted schooner set sail with a crew of seven and three missionary couples. The first stop, appropriately enough, was Pitcairn Island, where E. H. Gates and A. J. Read baptized 82 of the islanders and organized a church.

Several weeks later the mission ship moved on to the Tahiti, Rarotonga, Samoa, Fiji, and Norfolk island groups. At each location those aboard it held meetings, distributed literature, and awakened interest.

After two years the *Pitcairn* returned to San Francisco, its first voyage a success. But there had been a cost in human lives. John Tay, who had remained to pioneer the Adventist mission in Fiji, died after only five months into his work. And Captain J. O. Marsh had passed to his rest while his ship was being refitted in New Zealand.

But the work went on. Altogether the *Pitcairn* made six voyages between 1890 and 1900. At that point steamship schedules had improved to the extent that the denomination no longer needed its mission boat.

But in those 10 years not only did the church establish itself in the Pacific islands, but the adventures of the intrepid *Pitcairn* inspired Adventists toward missions and mission giving more than any other single thing in their history.

ADVENTISM ON THE MOVE—5: SOUTH AFRICA

Store up for yourselves treasures in heaven. Matt. 6:20, NIV.

Some treasure seekers find more than they are looking for. So it was with William Hunt who while prospecting for gold in California in the 1870s had accepted the Sabbath through J. N. Loughborough.

Years later Hunt, by then searching for diamonds in South Africa, met two Dutch farmers who had independently become convinced through Bible study that Saturday, the seventh day, was the Sabbath.

The meeting really seemed to be accidental but the eye of faith might call it providential. George van Druten, one of the farmers, came across Hunt while on a Saturday afternoon stroll. But he noticed something strange about this prospector. Instead of working his claim the man was reading his Bible. And thus it was that two Sabbathkeepers met in the diamond fields of South Africa.

Hunt put van Druten and another independent Sabbathkeeper by the name of Pieter Wessels in contact with the Seventh-day Adventists in America. The two South Africans fired off an appeal to Battle Creek for a Dutch-speaking missionary. With their request they sent the sizable sum of £50 (the better part of a year's salary for a laborer) to finance the voyage.

Someone read their "Macedonian call" before the 1888 General Conference session. It so moved the delegates that they spontaneously rose and sang the doxology. The next July a missionary party of seven under the leadership of D. A. Robinson went to Cape Town. Meanwhile, the South Africans raised up a body of some 40 believers on their own.

The South African mission took a turn for the better after the discovery of diamonds on the farm of Johannes Wessels, Pieter's father. Made a millionaire overnight, Father Wessels invested heavily in the Adventist program in his homeland. Before long the young church had a publishing house, a college, a sanitarium, and other institutions.

It seems more than accidental that two of the handful of Sabbathkeepers should meet in the midst of a South African diamond field. God was leading His people. And the good news is that He still does.

ADVENTISM ON THE MOVE–6:
RHODESIA

Their voice has gone out to all the earth, and their words to the ends of the world.
Rom. 10:18, RSV.

It was one thing to begin a mission among European immigrants in South Africa and quite another to herald the Advent message to the indigenous peoples of the great African continent. A first step toward that broader mission took place in Rhodesia (now Zimbabwe).

In 1894 the General Conference, at the urging of the Wessels family, decided to try to obtain a mission station in Matabeleland in the territory north of South Africa. This was just after the British had crushed the powerful Matabele tribe.

Named Rhodesia after Cecil Rhodes, empire builder and premier of the Cape Colony of South Africa, it was a land fresh to European influence. A. T. Robinson and Pieter Wessels received a sealed envelope after the close of what they feared had been a rather unsatisfactory meeting with Rhodes. The Adventists were more than a little surprised to discover that the letter granted them more than 12,000 acres near the town of Bulawayo.

Obtaining the grant had actually been the easy part in developing what would become the Solusi Mission. One challenge to the Solusi project came from North America, where A. T. Jones spearheaded an attack on those who would accept government favors and thus blur the boundary between church and state. According to Jones and the other editors of the *Sentinel of Religious Liberty,* the missionaries had "sold themselves for a mess of African potage." If the denomination was inconsistent, Jones asserted, that fact would soon get around to its enemies and would weaken the Adventist argument against those who would Christianize America through such things as Sunday laws. The influential Jones even got the 1895 General Conference session to vote to deny the gift on the basis of separation of church and state.

On the other side of the ledger was Ellen White, who wrote to the General Conference leaders from far-off Australia, recommending that Jones and others read the book of Nehemiah. "The Lord," she penned, "still moves upon the hearts of kings and rulers in behalf of His people, and it becomes those who are so deeply interested in the religious liberty question not to cut off any favors, or withdraw themselves from the help that God has moved men to give, for the advancement of His cause" (Lt 11, 1895).

ADVENTISM ON THE MOVE—7: RHODESIA

I have been found by those who did not seek me; I have shown myself to those who did not ask for me. Rom. 10:20, RSV.

With Ellen White's pointing out that Nehemiah had "prayed to God for help, and God heard his prayer" and "moved upon heathen kings to come to his help" (Lt 11, 1895) the General Conference reversed its ruling against accepting the Solusi gift. Thus the internal challenge to the mission had been overcome.

But the political situation remained. Not long after the arrival of the missionaries the recently conquered Matabele tribe revolted against the British, causing the missionaries to withdraw for five months. And if that wasn't problem enough, soon after their return they had to face a famine among the local people and an outbreak of rinderpest, which destroyed the few mission cattle that had survived the recent war.

And the mission encountered yet another serious problem—malaria. I still remember standing by the little graveyard at what is today Solusi University. Nearly all of the original missionaries had died because they had refused to take quinine, the only known preventative of malaria in the 1890s.

Why had they refused to use the life saving medicine? Because, not fully understanding the context of Ellen White's counsel against taking harmful drugs, they inflexibly rejected the one thing that could have helped them. They were "faithful health reformers" unto death.

Of the original seven who had arrived in 1894, only three survived in 1898, and two of those were at the Cape recovering from malaria.

The remaining missionary had been the "unfaithful" one. He had used quinine on the basis that taking some of a harmful drug was better than remaining vulnerable to the full force of a lethal disease. He was in effect using the "common sense" that Ellen White advocated in such difficult situations. As a result, he continued to serve and witness at Solusi Mission.

As of 2007 that toehold in Africa has grown to more than 5 million baptized believers in the three world divisions of the church that serve that continent.

The lessons for us surrounding the Solusi Mission are many. One of the most important is that God is still leading His church in spite of the flawed humans He has chosen to use in His work.

Lord, we live in a complex world. Please help us in our struggles to keep both eyes open, along with the eye of faith.

ADVENTISM ON THE MOVE—8:
INTER AMERICA

So faith comes from what is heard, and what is heard comes by the preaching of Christ. Rom. 10:17, RSV.

Here are lots of different ways of hearing the Advent message. That is the lesson we learn from the entrance of Seventh-day Adventism into the tropical world bordering the Caribbean.

Things got started in 1883 when an Adventist in New York City persuaded a ship captain to deliver a bundle of printed material to Georgetown, British Guiana. The captain's delivery style left much to be desired but it did the trick. Flinging the parcel out on the wharf, the good man deemed that he had fulfilled his obligation. Meanwhile, a bystander gathered a few of the papers as they began to scatter. He not only read them, but shared them with his neighbors.

Several of them began to observe the Sabbath, and one woman sent copies of the rescued *Signs of the Times* to her sister in Barbados. Here they reached a woman who years before had told her children that the true Sabbath would be restored.

Meanwhile, on the other side of the Caribbean, Mrs. E. Gauterau, who had been converted to Adventism in California, returned in 1885 to her native Bay Islands off the coast of Honduras. After she had shared her faith for six years, the denomination sent Frank Hutchins to care for the people she had influenced. The Sabbath schools, in the *Pitcairn* spirit, provided him funds to build a mission schooner (the *Herald*) to spread the Advent message along the Central American coast.

In Antigua it was Mrs. A. Roskrug, who had accepted Adventism in England, who began to plant the seeds of a church upon her return to her native island in 1888. Before long an Adventist book sold in Antigua found its way to Jamaica.

The Adventist message in Mexico got its start in 1891 with an Italian-American tailor who became a colporteur. Not finding anything to sell in Spanish, he peddled English copies of *The Great Controversy*.

It appears from these stories that God is able to employ just about anyone or any method to spread His message. He can even use us if we are willing.

ADVENTISM ON THE MOVE—9:
SOUTH AMERICA

As my Father hath sent me, even so send I you. John 20:21.

M any of Adventism's pioneering missionaries did not have the support of any "organization." Rather, the Spirit impelled them to go on a self-supporting basis. So it was for South America.

Interestingly enough, even though the principal languages of that continent are Spanish and Portuguese, the first converts to the church were from German- and French-speaking immigrants to Argentina, Chili, and Brazil. To a large extent that was due to the fact that the denomination lacked both material in and speakers of Spanish and Portuguese.

The first Seventh-day Adventists to reach South America were Claudio and Antonieta de Dessignet, who had accepted Adventism in France through D. T. Bourdeau and immigrated to Chili in 1885.

About that same time two families in different regions of Argentina discovered Adventism through periodicals received from Europe. In northern Argentina an Italian couple, the Peverinis, read an article making fun of *Les Signes des Temps'* (*The Signs of the Times*) claims that the end of the world was near. Mrs. Peverini obtained a copy of the Adventist magazine from her brother in Italy, and they began to read themselves into the Seventh-day Adventist faith. Farther to the south, Julio and Ida Dupertuis, residing in a Swiss-French Baptist colony, had a similar experience.

The Dupertuis family not only accepted the new beliefs, but they also convinced several other families in the colony of the truth of what they were discovering. Around 1889 they contacted the Seventh-day Adventists in Battle Creek. Their inquiries stimulated the leaders of the denomination to consider initiating a mission to South America. But where to get the money? That was the perennial problem. The perennial solution eventually came to be the Sabbath School Association. The Association gladly took on the task, devoting its collections during the last half of 1890 to the South American Mission.

God works in ways that we often don't expect. He takes humble people who have no training for ministry and uses them to spread His truth in low-keyed ways. That happened in the past and it continues on in our day as people open their hearts and lives to His Spirit.

ADVENTISM ON THE MOVE—10:
SOUTH AMERICA

And . . . God . . . opened a door of faith to the Gentiles. Acts 14:27, RSV.

Yesterday we noted that the Sabbath School Association devoted offerings from the last half of 1890 to initiate the denomination's South American Mission.

Here we need to stop for a moment. Most of us have participated in the Sabbath school mission offerings, but few of us recognize how they got started. The first Sabbath school gifts to missions took place in 1885, as the Adventist Church began in Australia. But mission offerings did not stir much enthusiasm until the *Pitcairn* project in 1889 and 1890. After that project the Sabbath school would never be the same. The firm supporter of Adventist missions around the world, its second large giving project would be for the South American Mission in 1890. From that point the Sabbath school has never stopped financially encouraging missions to every part of the world.

That brings us back to the beginnings of Adventism in South America. Early in 1890, before the church could send any denominationally supported missionaries, George Riffel led four German-Russian farm families from Kansas as self-supporting missionaries to Argentina. A new convert to Adventism, Riffel had written of his new faith to German-Russian colonists in that country. One wrote back that he would observe the Sabbath if he had someone to keep it with him. That was enough to lead Riffel into a life-changing move.

Late in 1891 the Seventh-day Adventist Church sent its first "official" missionaries to South America. None of them spoke Spanish or Portuguese, so those three colporteurs made their way selling German and English books to a population that read another language.

The calls from the Dupertuis family, the reports of the colporteurs, and requests from the Riffels stimulated the General Conference in 1894 to dispatch F. H. Westphal to oversee the Adventist mission in Argentina, Uruguay, Paraguay, and Brazil. Westphal would spend more than 20 years working in those countries and Chile.

Small ideas lead to big results. And humble laypeople sharing literature with others did much to spread Adventism around the world. These are things that we can all participate in.

ADVENTISM ON THE MOVE–11:
INDIA

Go out and train everyone you meet, far and near, in this way of life.
Matt. 28:19, Message.

As in so many other places in the world, colporteurs early spread the Seventh-day Adventist message in India. William Lenker and A. T. Stroup landed in Madras in 1893 to sell books among the English-speaking inhabitants of India's major cities.

But as was also the case in so many places, Lenker and Stroup were not the first Adventists in the country. While in London on the way to India Lenker learned to his joy that Adventist believers already lived there. As he put it, "my heart was made to rejoice to learn that the truth has gone before to India, and has begun with encouraging omens."

How the Adventist message got there is not known. But presumably it did so through tracts sent from America, Europe, or Australia. Those silent messengers did more than all other things combined to spread the Adventist teachings "to every nation, and kindred, and tongue, and people" (Rev. 14:6).

By 1894 at least five colporteurs worked in India, three of them from Australia. The books sold well, and before long people requested their translation in Tamil and other local languages.

The first regular Seventh-day Adventist employee was Georgia Burrus (later Georgia Burgess), a young Bible instructor from California who arrived in India in January 1895 as the sole official representative of the church in that complex land.

The General Conference had planned that D. A. Robinson would lead the mission, but he was delayed in England. That didn't hinder the intrepid Miss Burrus, who proceeded alone even though only her passage had been paid. While learning Bengali, she worked on the side to survive. But soon someone from Africa promised her financial aid. Georgia would spend 40 years in her adopted country spreading the Advent message.

Other missionaries reached India in late 1895, and in 1898 William A. Spicer (who would become General Conference president in 1922) arrived to begin the publication of the *Oriental Watchman*.

One thing strikes the student of the spread of Adventist missions. That is, they were international from the beginning. Even though the movement throughout the nineteenth century was largely North American, we find people, literature, and funds coming from everywhere and going to everywhere. That is still the dynamic in Adventist mission.

ADVENTISM ON THE MOVE–12:
EASTER ASIA

Many shall come from the east and west, and shall sit down with Abraham, and Isaac, and Jacob, in the kingdom of heaven. Matt. 8:11.

Abram La Rue (1822-1903) is one of the truly fascinating people in an Adventism casted with a fair number of picturesque individuals. Having amassed a fortune in the gold fields of California and Idaho, by the 1880s he had managed to lose it and was working alternately as a sheepherder and woodchopper when the Adventist message took hold of him.

Immediately after his conversion, La Rue, who was short on neither boldness nor enthusiasm, requested a mission appointment to China from the General Conference. But given the fact that he was both a new convert and had reached retirement age, the leaders declined his offer, suggesting he go as a self-supporting Adventist to one of the Pacific islands.

After sprinting through a term at Healdsburg College, La Rue worked his way to Honolulu in 1883 or 1884. His success there led the denomination to send W. M. Healey to Hawaii to organize the church in the islands.

By 1888 the exuberant pioneer was off to Hong Kong, where he set up a seamen's mission and for 14 years did colporteur work. He concentrated on the many ships in the multinational harbor, but during his Hong Kong years La Rue managed to fit in missionary tours to such places as Shanghai, Japan, Borneo, Java, Ceylon, Sarawak, Singapore, and once even to Palestine and Lebanon. Needless to say, he sold books and tracts wherever his ship stopped. In his spare time he also arranged to have the first Adventist tracts published in Chinese.

Meanwhile, back in California, W. C. Grainger, one of La Rue's early converts, had become president of Healdsburg College. But inspired by his mentor, he was soon off under official appointment to Japan. There in league with a former student of Japanese descent, T. H. Okohira, he established a foreign language school to teach English through Bible reading to university students. In that move Grainger began a mode of evangelism that has been productive in the Far East to the present day.

One of the lessons of the La Rue story is that God can use "old" people to spread His message. The good news is that life for God is not over at retirement.

MISSION TO BLACK AMERICA—1

In Christ Jesus you are all sons of God, through faith. Gal. 3:26, ESV.

A unique aspect of Adventist mission extension during the 1890s was an outreach to Black Americans. Although some Blacks participated in the Millerite movement (including Pastor William Foy, who filled a prophetic role from 1842 to 1844), early Sabbatarian Adventism was largely a White movement. In fact, it was roughly a half century after the Great Disappointment before Seventh-day Adventism got under way among North American Blacks with any real success.

Denominational historians have estimated that only about 50 Black Seventh-day Adventists existed in the United States in 1894, but by 1909 that number had climbed to 900. That growth in Black membership largely resulted from several mission projects aimed at evangelizing Blacks during the 1890s.

The 1870s and 1880s witnessed sporadic work among Southern Blacks in Texas, Tennessee, Georgia, and other states, with the first Black congregation officially organized at Edgefield Junction, Tennessee, in 1886. But White "Yankees" from the North were somewhat at a loss as to how to face the peculiar and difficult racial problems of the South. They not only faced suspicion among Southern Whites for being Northerners (remember these people had recently fought a bloody Civil War related to the race issue), but were in a quandary on how to handle such issues as segregation.

Their work often met with violence from local Whites who feared that the intruders might be preaching the "dangerous" doctrine of racial equality. Given the difficulties, the Adventist leadership finally concluded that it would be best to follow social convention by establishing separate congregations for the two races. Charles M. Kinny, whom we met earlier in the year as the first African-American ordained as a Seventh-day Adventist minister, concurred with the decision. While Kinny did not see separate congregations as the ideal, he did believe that solution to be preferable to segregating Blacks to the back pews of White churches.

Lord, we pray today and every day for a healing between the various races of the world. If it doesn't happen in the world at large, help it to take place in our hearts.

MISSION TO BLACK AMERICA—2

For as many of you as were baptized into Christ have put on Christ. Gal. 3:27, ESV.

By 1891 Ellen White had become concerned over the lack of Adventist activity among American Blacks. On March 21 she presented a "testimony" on the topic to the delegates of the General Conference session. She especially called for more work among Southern Blacks. Her appeal soon went into print as a 16-page tract entitled *Our Duty to the Colored People*.

"The Lord," she told the delegates, "has given us light concerning all such matters. There are principles laid down in His Word that should guide us in dealing with these perplexing questions. The Lord Jesus came to our world to save men and women of all nationalities. He died just as much for the colored people as for the white race. . . . The same price was paid for the salvation of the colored man as for that of the white man, and the slights put upon the colored people by many who claim to be redeemed by the blood of the Lamb . . . misrepresent Jesus, and reveal that selfishness, tradition, and prejudice pollute the soul. . . . Let none of those who name the name of Christ be cowards in His cause. For Christ's sake stand as if looking within the open portals of the city of God" (SW 9-18).

In spite of her plea to aggressively extend Adventism's mission to southern Blacks, nothing happened until 1893. That year James Edson White "discovered" the document. Her oldest living son, Edson, had recently experienced conversion in his mid-40s. In his zeal he became convicted that he should take the Adventist message to the ex-slaves of the Deep South.

Apparently inspired by the *Pitcairn,* the ever-creative Edson soon linked up with Will Palmer (another recent convert with a dubious background) to build a "mission boat" and to enter into one of the most exciting chapters of North American Adventist missions.

The two unlikely missionaries built the *Morning Star* in Allegan, Michigan, in 1894 at a cost of $3,700. Their vessel would eventually serve as a residence for its Adventist staff. In addition, it provided space for a chapel, library, printshop, kitchen, and photography lab. In short, it was a mission station on water.

The fact that God could use troubled Edson and Will astounds me. It is an aspect of His grace. Beyond that, it is a beacon of hope for those who have children who have not yet found the Way.

MISSION TO BLACK AMERICA–3

There is neither Jew nor Greek, there is neither slave nor free . . . , for you are all one in Christ Jesus. Gal. 3:28, ESV.

Edson White's mission boat had one major problem. It was hundreds of miles from his target audience and at least 20 miles from any large body of water.

No problem for the inventive Edson. He floated his craft down the Kalamazoo River to Lake Michigan, across Lake Michigan to the Chicago area, across Illinois on the river system linking Lake Michigan to the Mississippi, and down the Mississippi River to Vicksburg, Mississippi, in the American South, where he set up headquarters.

But White had one other problem—money! Not being trusted by the Adventist Church leaders, he and his colleagues were self supporting in their mission. But like his father, one of Edson's talents was raising money.

One project he used to finance the mission was the publication of the *Gospel Primer*, a book simple enough to use in teaching illiterates to read while conveying Bible truth in the process. The sale of that successful little volume helped finance the mission.

From Vicksburg the work spread to the surrounding countryside, often in the face of White resistance and violence. By the early years of the twentieth century the mission had nearly 50 schools in operation. In 1895 Edson's self-supporting mission organized as the Southern Missionary Society. Then in 1901 the society became a part of the newly established Southern Union Conference. Eventually the publishing arm of the enterprise also came under denominational ownership as the Southern Publishing Association, headquartered in Nashville, Tennessee.

The mid-1890s also saw the establishment of a training school for Black workers. The General Conference opened Oakwood Industrial School in 1896 on a 360-acre plantation near Huntsville, Alabama. Oakwood soon became the center for training Black leaders, becoming a senior college in 1943 and a university in 2007.

The tardy mission to Black America harbors a much-needed lesson. It is all too easy to get excited about going as, or sending, a missionary overseas, while at the same time neglecting our neighbors next door.

Lord, help us to get our people values straight and to let You use us right where we are today to shed Your love.

WOMEN OF THE SPIRIT—1

There is neither . . . male nor female, for you are all one in Christ Jesus.
Gal. 3:28, ESV.

S he has accomplished more the last two years than any minister in this state. . . . I am . . . in favor of giving [a] license to Sr. Lulu Wightman to preach, and if Bro. W. is a man of ability and works with his wife and promises to make a successful laborer, I am in favor of giving him a license also." Such were the words of Pastor S. M. Cobb writing to the New York Conference president in 1897.

Because the bulk of Adventism's ministry has consistently been male, too few have recognized the contribution to the church made by women who have served as ministers and in other official positions.

The role of Ellen White, of course, was central to the establishment and development of Adventism. Even though the denomination never formally ordained her, as early as 1872 it listed her as an ordained minister. Believing that her ordination came from God, she does not appear to have been concerned about the human laying on of hands. What is beyond doubt, however, is that she was the most influential minister ever to serve the Seventh-day Adventist Church.

Many other women participated during the late nineteenth and early twentieth centuries as licensed ministers. One of the first may have been Sarah Lindsay, licensed in 1872. The denominational yearbooks list more than 20 additional women as being licensed ministers between 1884 and 1904—the first two decades of the yearbook.

In spite of the fact that those women faced discrimination at times, they often made major contributions to the church.

Minnie Sype, for example, established at least 10 churches. And beyond her evangelistic work she performed such ministerial tasks as baptizing, marrying, and conducting funerals. On one occasion when attacked because she was presuming to preach as a female, Minnie replied that after His resurrection Jesus had commissioned Mary to notify the disciples that He was alive. Minnie claimed that she was following in Mary's footsteps, telling people that Jesus was not only risen but coming again.

God is able to use both men and women to spread the good news of salvation in Christ. That is what ministry is all about. The church would be better off if it had more women and men doing the ministry of the risen Savior.

WOMEN OF THE SPIRIT—2

"Mary!" . . . "Go to My brethren and say to them, 'I ascend to My Father and your Father, and My God and your God.'" John 20:16, 17, NASB.

Yesterday a resolution was adopted by the [Missouri] House of Representatives inviting Mrs. Wightman to address the representatives on 'The Rise of Religious Liberty in the United States.' I believe this action upon the part of the Missouri legislature is unprecedented in the history of our people."

Such was a part of the impact of the ministry of the impressive Lulu Wightman, one of Adventism's most successful female evangelists. Credited with starting at least 17 churches, she far outdistanced most of her male contemporaries.

Another woman of the Spirit was Jessie Weiss Curtis, who presented 80 converts for baptism at the conclusion of her first evangelistic campaign. The Drums, Pennsylvania, church originated in that effort. She extended her influence by training ministerial interns for the conference. One of those young men was N. R. Dower, who later became director of the General Conference Ministerial Department.

In addition to those women who held ministerial credentials, many others served the denomination in various ways. Most, of course, had such usual female roles as teachers and nurses, but others held less-traditional positions. Among them was L. Flora Plummer, who became executive secretary of the Iowa Conference in 1897 and served as acting president for part of 1900. In 1901 she became the corresponding secretary for the newly organized General Conference Sabbath School Department. In 1913 she became the department's director, a position she held for the next 23 years.

And then there was Anna Knight, who pioneered the Adventist educational program among Southern Blacks. She also had the distinction of being the first African-American female missionary sent to India from America.

Scores of other Adventist women in the late nineteenth and early twentieth centuries served in such elected offices as conference treasurers, conference secretaries, educational department leaders, and Sabbath school department leaders. And beyond those are the millions of unsung women who form the backbone of most effective congregations.

The commission of Jesus to Mary is still being carried out.

RETHINKING CHURCH ORGANIZATION—1

The word of God increased; and the number of the disciples multiplied in Jerusalem greatly. Acts 6:7.

Growth is generally a good thing. But in churches it has traditionally called for rethinking the structures that allow a religious body to perform its function. So it was in Acts 6, when change led to the appointment of deacons.

Seventh-day Adventism has experienced dynamic growth ever since its inception. The period from 1863 up through 1900 saw unprecedented expansion of the denomination, partly because of its organization. Adventism entered that time period with six conferences and 30 evangelistic staff, all located in the northeastern quarter of the United States. The denomination exited that time span with 45 local conferences and 42 missions with 1,500 evangelistic staff spread around the world.

Beyond growth in the conference area, the denomination's institutional sector also rapidly developed. Between 1888 and 1901 alone the number of major medical institutions jumped from 2 to 24, ending with some 2,000 employees. By 1903 the denomination could report 464 Adventist schools from elementary to collegiate, employing 687 teachers and having an enrollment of 11,145. In addition to health and educational institutions, an ever-increasing number of publishing houses had begun operating around the world.

That unprecedented expansion in all sectors of the church brought about an administrative situation that the 1863 organizational format was ill-prepared to handle. Most people seemed to be pleased with the two levels above the local congregation structure. But they soon discovered certain inherent problems.

One was the centralization of decision-making in the few individuals that formed the small executive committee of the General Conference (never more than 8 members before 1897 when it changed to 13) that seldom met. Thus most major decisions fell on the denomination's president. It didn't help matters that James White and George I. Butler had tendencies to dominate anyway. Thus a perpetual problem with the 1863 structure was that it lent itself to what Ellen White repeatedly referred to as "kingly power."

By 1900 nearly everybody recognized the need for a change.

Rethinking Church Organization—2:
The Call to Congregationalism

The head of every man is Christ. 1 Cor. 11:3, RSV.

The post-1888 years would see the development of two main approaches to reorganizing the church. The denomination's leading and most influential theologians during the 1890s—A. T. Jones, E. J. Waggoner, and W. W. Prescott—promoted the first avenue to reform. They conceived a theological ecclesiology that basically held that the church did not need a president since Christ was its head and would direct every born again individual.

As Waggoner put it, "Perfect unity means absolute independence. . . . This question of organization is a very simple thing. All there is to it is for each individual to give himself over to the Lord, and then the Lord will do with him just as he wants to. . . . 'Receive ye the Holy Ghost.' The Holy Ghost is the organizer." "If we get it right," Prescott claimed, "there will be no officials here." "All ye are brethren" is the biblical ideal.

To Prescott, Jones, Waggoner, and their colleagues such a scheme was not anarchy but true biblical organization. They would push their ideas with great vigor at the 1897, 1899, 1901, and 1903 General Conference sessions.

Their greatest success came in 1897. Fueled by an 1896 quotation from Ellen White (taken out of the context of her general statements on the topic) that "it is not wise to choose one man as president of the General Conference" (Lt 24a, 1896), the reform element urged either no president (their preference) or multiple presidents. During 1897 they pushed through a resolution for three General Conference presidents—one each in North America, Europe, and Australia.

In practice, things didn't work out to the desire of the reformers. But their ideas were firm, and they would advocate them strongly in 1901 and 1903.

A. G. Daniells, who would eventually become the denomination's president, quipped that the ideas of Jones and Waggoner on organization would work in heaven but certainly not on earth. And Ellen White must have wondered at the strange twist that the two men had given her original statement.

Help us, Lord, as we think about the purpose of organization as it relates to the mission of Your church here on earth.

RETHINKING CHURCH ORGANIZATION—3: THE SOUTH AFRICAN EXPERIMENT

This good news of the kingdom will be proclaimed to men all over the world as a witness to all the nations, and then the end will come. Matt. 24:14, Phillips.

The second avenue to organizational reform in the 1890s would emerge in the denomination's mission fields and would focus on pragmatic necessity rather than theology. It is not that theology was absent. Rather it was not central. The theological foundation of this approach was eschatology. Since Adventists needed to preach the three angels' messages to all the world before the Second Advent, this second approach focused on the mission of the denomination as it related to its eschatological goal.

The first element of the reform began in the newly established South African Conference in 1892 under the leadership of A. T. Robinson. His major problem involved a shortage of personnel. In no way could he staff all of the legally independent auxiliary organizations that had developed in Battle Creek. Where, for example, was he to find leadership for the Publishing Association, the General Tract and Missionary Society, the Educational Society, the General Sabbath School Association, the Health and Temperance Association, the General Conference Association, and the Foreign Mission Board?

Robinson's solution was born of necessity. He would not create independent organizations, but would develop departments under the conference system.

Both O. A. Olsen, General Conference president, and W. C. White felt concerns over the suggestion and the General Conference wrote to Robinson not to create the departments.

But it was too late. Because of the large amount of time it took to communicate by ship's mail in those days, by the time the instruction from the General Conference arrived Robinson had already instituted the program and found that it worked.

Later in the 1890s Robinson transferred to Australia where he was able to sell the departmental idea to A. G. Daniells and W. C. White. They in turn would take the idea to the 1901 General Conference session as part of a reorganization plan.

Innovation is often the origin of progress. While structure and rules are necessary for any stable organization, the ability to improvise is essential for continued vitality.

Help us, Father, to find the proper balance between regulations and innovations in both our daily life and in our church.

MEET ARTHUR G. DANIELLS

One thing I do, forgetting what lies behind and straining forward to what lies ahead, I press on toward the goal. Phil. 3:13, 14, RSV.

If I have accomplished anything worthwhile in the cause of God, it is because in my youth I set my eyes upon the goal, and . . . by the grace of God I have never allowed anything to divert my mind or take my eyes from that goal," Arthur G. Daniells wrote near the close of a long and fruitful life. He was a leader par excellance because he not only knew his goal but persisted in achieving it.

Born in 1858 to a father who died in the American Civil War, Daniells accepted Adventism at age 10. Like all young people, he faced the daunting question of what to do with his life. After attending Battle Creek College for one year, he was teaching public school when he received a call to ministry.

That wasn't what he was looking for. He felt unprepared, but like so many across the ages, Arthur could not escape conviction.

Daniells began his ministry in Texas in 1878, where he served as secretary to James and Ellen White for one year. In 1886, while doing evangelism, he received a request to go to New Zealand and Australia, where he served as a church administrator for 14 years. While "down under" he worked closely with W. C. White and his mother. He and Willie developed the structures that Daniells would put forth in 1901 for the reorganization of the church.

Elected General Conference president in 1901, Daniells remained in that position for 21 years, longer than any other individual. Partly because of the more efficient organization adopted in 1901/1903, Adventism grew rapidly during his administration.

Later he developed the General Conference Ministerial Association, through which he influenced a generation of young preachers to emphasize Christ and salvation through Him in their lives and ministry. His book *Christ Our Righteousness* revived the 1888 issues related to salvation and is an Adventist classic.

Daniells was a person with a goal. In that he followed both Paul and Jesus.

I need to be that kind of person.

Help me, Lord, today and every day to "press toward the mark for the prize of the high calling of God."

RETHINKING CHURCH ORGANIZATION—4: THE AUSTRALIAN EXPERIMENT

There is one body and one Spirit—just as you were called to one hope when you were called—one Lord, one faith, one baptism; one God and Father of all. Eph. 4:4-6, NIV.

How do we maintain both unity and efficiency in a world church? Not an easy task. But an important one.

Part of the difficulty the rapidly spreading denomination faced in the 1890s was one of communication. In the name of unity, operating policy decreed that church headquarters in Battle Creek had to approve all decisions above the conference level.

A. G. Daniells spoke to the problem of time lag in communication and decision-making from the perspective of 1913. The difficulty was that at its best the mail took four weeks each direction and often arrived to find the members of the General Conference Executive Committee away from their offices. "I remember," Daniells noted, "that we have waited three or four months before we could get any reply to our questions." And even then it might be a five- or six-line inquiry saying that the General Conference officers really didn't understand the issue and needed further information. And so it went until "after six or nine months, perhaps, we would get the matter settled." By that point in his argument, Daniells' audience had no trouble understanding his meaning when he claimed that "we found continually that our work was hindered."

Ellen White also had problems with the 1861/1863 structure and its centralized decision making. Having spent years in the church's mission fields, she recognized that "the men at Battle Creek are no more inspired to give unerring advice than are the men in other places, to whom the Lord has entrusted the work in their locality" (Lt 88, 1896).

But how to decentralize and at the same time maintain unity was the challenge. The answer was the union conference, "invented" in Australia during the mid-1890s. The Australasian Union Conference consisted of the various local conferences and missions in its territory and served as an intermediary unit between the General Conference and the local conferences. With executive power to act within its territory, it regionalized decision-making while at the same time maintaining unity.

By the time the Australian church leaders had devised the union conference, A. T. Robinson had arrived from South Africa with the departmental system. Australia also adopted the latter.

Most of us don't think much about the mechanics of running a world church. Perhaps we should. Even in that rather "mundane" area we see God's guiding hand.

Rethinking Church Organization—5: The 1901 General Conference Session

By a prophet the Lord brought Israel out of Egypt, and by a prophet was he preserved. Hosea 12:13.

Some things seem almost impossible to do. One of them was the restructuring of the Adventist Church in 1901. The leading ministers had sparred on the topic for more than 10 years but had accomplished nothing.

That would all change beginning with a meeting of denominational leaders chaired by A. G. Daniells in the Battle Creek College library on April 1, 1901. Daniells told those assembled that some of them had met the evening before, but that they wanted to open up the discussion to additional people and also to allow "Sister White . . . to be present and place before us any light that she might have for us."

Ellen White, however, did not want to take charge of the meeting. "I thought," she told Daniells, "I would let you lead out, and then if I had anything to say, I would say it." He replied that he and his colleagues didn't want to discuss the issue of reorganization further until they had heard from her.

Mrs. White countered by saying, "I would prefer not to speak today, . . . not because I have not anything to say, because I have." Then she presented for about one and one half hours one of the most influential talks of her ministry.

In no uncertain terms she called for "new blood" and an "entire new organization" that broadened the governing base of the denomination. Opposing the centralization of power in a few individuals, she left no doubt that "kingly, ruling power" and any administrator who had a "little throne" would have to go. She urged "a renovation without any delay. To have this conference pass on and close up as the conferences have done, with the same manipulating, with the same tone and the same order—God forbid! God forbid, brethren" (MS 43a, 1901).

The next day, the opening meeting of the General Conference session, saw her take the floor and request reorganization in no uncertain terms, even though "just how it is to be accomplished [she could] not say" (1901 GCB 25). From her perspective, it was her duty to urge reform, but the responsibility of the delegates to develop the structures.

Here we find some interesting insights on Ellen White's prophetic role. In this case she functioned as the spark plug to get things moving. Without her igniting function in 1901 the church probably would not have taken any firm action on reorganization. The prophetic gift is one way God guides His people.

RETHINKING CHURCH ORGANIZATION–6: THE 1901 GENERAL CONFERENCE SESSION

Here we have no lasting city, but we seek the city that is to come. Heb. 13:14, ESV.

This earth is not our home. That underlying motif and the necessity of mission drove the winning faction at the 1901 General Conference session.

G. A. Irwin, the president, opened the meetings by recognizing the strength of Ellen White's plea for reform, but he stopped at generalities.

At that point A. G. Daniells took charge and moved that "the usual rules and procedures for arranging and transacting the business of the conference be suspended" and that they appoint a general committee to develop recommendations related to reorganization of the denomination and other topics of concern. His motion carried.

The officers appointed Daniells chair of the reorganization committee. And he and W. C. White were the leading voices in the reorganization, even though the Jones and Waggoner coalition sought to shift the process in their direction.

When Daniells spoke of reorganizing the church, he meant restructuring its administration for more successful mission outreach. He made his point clear on the second morning of the 1901 session when he told the delegates that unless something definite was done "it will take a millennium to give this message to the world."

The 1901 General Conference session resulted in some of the greatest changes in the history of the denomination. The most important organizationally were five in number: (1) the creation of union conferences and union missions that had supervision of local conferences and missions and thereby dispersed the administrative authority of the General Conference officers; (2) the discontinuance of most of the auxiliary organizations and the adoption of the departmental system; (3) the General Conference Committee increased to 25 members; (4) ownership and management of most institutions shifted from the General Conference to the union conferences; (5) and the General Conference would have no president, only a chairperson whom the executive committee could remove at any time it desired.

The church had made major changes based on the mission experience of Daniells and W. C. White. And leadership had made a difference. God still works through people, both collectively and individually, to guide His church.

RETHINKING CHURCH ORGANIZATION—7:
THE 1903 GENERAL CONFERENCE SESSION

What causes fights and quarrels among you? James 4:1, NIV.

Excellent question!

The answer is universally perverted human nature. We want our own way. We want to protect our turf.

That's true of individuals everywhere, whether it be in their family or professional lives. In the church such strife can arise when the "mission" of individuals supersedes the gospel mission commanded by God.

Two structural problems continued after the 1901 meetings. The first was that the powerful medical branch under the control of Dr. John Harvey Kellogg still remained outside the departmental system. The second was the issue of presidency.

By 1902 a major power struggle had developed between A. G. Daniells, the "chair" of the General Conference executive committee, and Kellogg. It resulted from the fact that Daniells called for fiscal responsibility while the doctor had plans for unlimited spending as he increased his medical empire.

The solution to the difficulty seemed clear to Kellogg, who controlled one third of the votes in the executive committee and had influence over others. Dump Daniells and replace him with A. T. Jones, who was favorable to Kellogg's point of view.

The thunderous sounds of struggle shook the denomination in November 1902. The issue: who would control the church and for what reasons. We can be thankful that Daniells won a battle that would determine the purpose of Adventism in the twentieth century.

Meanwhile, finding that for legal purposes it was almost a necessity, Daniells had resumed using the title of "president."

Such were the struggles that set the stage for the 1903 General Conference session. Those meetings made the medical program a department of the church, restored the presidency, and set the stage for schism.

All too often in church history the mission becomes me and my program. Such is the death of peace and spirituality. The devil is always on hand to encourage us to push for our individual agendas. Each of us finds ourselves tempted to be central, to sit on our little throne.

Lord, help us to examine our motives as we work for You. Save us from our "selves."

PERSPECTIVE ON THE 1901/1903 RESTRUCTURING

I will increase the fruit of the trees and the crops of the field. Eze. 36:30, NIV.

The restructuring of the church set it up for productivity and efficiency as its worldwide mission program sped forward in a way that would have been impossible with the problems of the old structure.

We should note, however, that the 1901/1903 organization was not a new structure. It retained the general outline of the 1861/1863 plan, but modified it to meet the needs of an evolving church.

Modification, however, was not the ideal that some of the delegates brought with them in 1901/1903. The Jones/Waggoner faction had sought total revolution. In the end their bid for a drastic reshaping of the church lost out for several reasons. Not the least was that their model was theologically inadequate in the sense that it focused on the individual church member and left no room for a practical approach to unified action. Theoretically, it sounded fine to say that every person would work in harmony with every other person if they were converted, but the biblical picture reflects both less perfectionism and a more complex view of sin than did Adventism's would-be revolutionaries.

The revolutionary party also regularly took Ellen White's quotations out of their literary and historical contexts and thereby made her say things that she did not believe. She, for example, had no problem with the title of "president" and regularly used it.

The approach of Daniells was more down to earth and was quite in harmony with that of James White who had engineered the 1861/1863 organization. Both men looked for an efficient structure that would complete the task of carrying the Adventist message to the ends of the earth in as short a time as possible so that Christ might come.

Efficiency for mission is the keyword in Seventh-day Adventist organizational history. While most delegates at the 1903 session agreed with its final conclusions, M. C. Wilcox made an important point when he noted that the church should not be organizationally inflexible. It should leave itself open to adapt as the needs of mission demanded.

Thank You, Father, for a church structure that can reach out to the entire world in a unified manner. We want Jesus to come more than anything else.

Reinventing Babylon

Therefore is the name of it called Babel; because the Lord did there confound the language of all the earth. Gen. 11:9.

After 1903 A. T. Jones became unrelenting in his attack on A. G. Daniells, Ellen White, and church structure. For him religious liberty had become freedom from church organization.

By 1907 Daniells noted that Jones and others aimed "to sow disaffection among the separate churches; wherever they can find a church that is out of joint with the body, they will fan the disaffection to a flame, and if possible, induce them to separate from the general organization."

As to the General Conference, Jones predicted that "there was going to be such a complete smash and breakup of that thing, that there would be nothing left of it."

Ellen White perceived that in their drive to congregationalism, Jones and his associates were seeking to take Adventism back to the Babylon of confusion that she and her husband had worked so hard to get the movement out of in the 1850s. "Oh," she penned in January 1907, "how Satan would rejoice if he could succeed in his efforts to get among this people and disorganize the work at a time when thorough organization is essential and will be the greatest power . . . to refute claims not endorsed by the word of God! We want to hold the lines evenly, that there shall be no breaking down of the system of organization and order that has been built up by wise, careful labor. . . . Some have advanced the thought that as we near the close of time, every child of God will act independently of any religious organization. But I have been instructed by the Lord that in this work there is no such thing as every man's being independent" (TM 489).

In 1909, the year that the church had to disfellowship Jones, she spoke of "deceived souls" advocating "the spirit of disorganization." While leaving room for independent judgment, she went on to firmly state that "God has ordained that the representatives of His church from all parts of the earth, when assembled in a General Conference, shall have authority" (9T 257, 259-261). Thus she sided with Daniells in no uncertain terms, even though she continued to warn him of exercising too much personal control. Her ideal was unity in diversity.

Now you know why it is important to reject the periodic appeals to congregationalism within Adventism. Reformation is one thing, but revolution toward disjointed action is quite another.

Disaster and Disorientation

In my distress I called upon the Lord;
  to my God I called.
From his temple he heard my voice,
  And my cry came to his ears. 2 Sam. 22:7, RSV.

Adventism felt much distress during the first years of the twentieth century. And in the midst of distress there was much calling upon God.

The century began with the massive, world-famous Battle Creek Sanitarium burning to the ground on February 18, 1902. That was bad enough, but a second fire on December 30 destroyed the Review and Herald publishing building and the General Conference offices.

The question was whether to rebuild in Battle Creek or move the denomination's institutions elsewhere. Dr. Kellogg, for his part, determined to reconstruct the Sanitarium bigger and better than ever, despite the fact that the church leaders opposed such an extravagant move at a time when the denomination verged on bankruptcy because of overly rapid expansion in mission fields around the world. Money and the question of who was in control would soon divide Daniells and Kellogg in what became a struggle to the finish.

But money and power weren't the only issues to separate them. The doctor by this time also had theological aberrations related to pantheism, a view that made God a force within, rather than above, nature. Thus Kellogg could write in his *Living Temple* that "there is present in the tree a power which creates and maintains it, a tree-maker in the tree, a flower-maker in the flower."

Kellogg was not alone in his pantheistic perspective. E. J. Waggoner of 1888 prominence taught at the 1897 General Conference session that Christ "appeared as a tree, or as grass." And at the 1899 session Waggoner proclaimed that "a man may get righteousness in bathing, when he knows where the water comes from."

The struggle between Kellogg and his colleagues with the Daniells faction lasted for several years. Ellen White tried for some time to bring peace, but by 1903 she increasingly sided in public and in her writings with Daniells. Finally Kellogg left the Adventist Church, being disfellowshipped from the Battle Creek congregation in 1907 and taking with him A. T. Jones, E. J. Waggoner, and others.

Times of trouble have always come to God's people. The question for each of us is where to focus on during such times. Our only safety is Jesus and His principles.

OUT OF THE ASHES—1

Let the peoples renew their strength; let them approach, then let them speak.
Isa. 41:1, RSV.

R enewal and rebuilding were at the forefront of Adventist thinking in the early years of the twentieth century. Not only had disastrous fires destroyed the institutional presence of the denomination in Battle Creek; not only had the denomination lost J. H. Kellogg, A. T. Jones, E. J. Waggoner, and others; but in the process Kellogg had wrested ownership of the rebuilt Battle Creek Sanitarium and the church's medical school (the American Medical Missionary College) from the denomination.

It was time not only for rebuilding, but for doing so in a new location. By the beginning of the twentieth century the continual migration of Adventists to Battle Creek had become a definite problem. Instead of living in various places where they could witness to their faith, a large portion of the Adventist membership had congregated in the city, gossiping among themselves and hindering Adventist mission in other ways.

Beyond that, Battle Creek had become overly centralized as the power base for world Adventism. Not only were the church's largest and most influential institutions located there, but also the world headquarters. A handful of men sitting on interlocking boards "ruled" Adventism everywhere. In short, by 1900 Battle Creek had become to Adventism what Jerusalem was to the Jews and what Salt Lake City is to the Mormons. The new century, however, saw the breakup of Adventism's "holy city."

Ellen White had been urging it since the early 1890s. Not many, however, had responded. The first institutional leaders to initiate a departure from the city were E. A. Sutherland and P. T. Magan, who had transferred Battle Creek College to Berrien Springs, Michigan, in 1901.

The 1902 fire that destroyed the Review and Herald plant provided the necessary impetus to move both the publishing program and the General Conference headquarters out of the city.

Where to go became the major issue for many. At first it appeared that New York City might be the appropriate location, but by 1903 Washington, D.C., had become the favored site.

Congregating in Adventist "centers" has plagued the Adventism's witness practically from its beginning. Perhaps part of our commission is for more of us to move into areas where we can witness to our neighbors. Think about it.

OUT OF THE ASHES—2

Your wounds I will heal, says the Lord. Jer. 30:17, RSV.

Healing is a wonderful thing, whether it be to a human body or the body of the church. In fact, sometimes the healed body is stronger than before. So it would be for Adventism headquartered in its new location far from the influence of Kellogg and Jones and their dissident teachings and divisive ways.

The next few years saw the establishment of a new center of operations just inside the Washington, D.C., boundary. Not only did the denominational leaders establish the General Conference headquarters and Review and Herald Publishing Association in the District of Columbia, but a couple miles down the road in Takoma Park, Maryland, they built the Washington Sanitarium and the Washington Training College. The latter institution they rechristened in 1907 as the Washington Foreign Missionary Seminary. Thus the new headquarters soon sported a full array of typical Adventist institutions.

Washington, D.C., and Takoma Park remained the headquarters for world Adventism for nearly nine decades. The Review and Herald Publishing Association eventually moved to Hagerstown, Maryland, in 1982-1983, and the offices of the General Conference transferred to Silver Spring, Maryland, in 1989. The sanitarium and college have remained at their original locations. The former is now known as Washington Adventist Hospital and the latter as Columbia Union College.

The breakaway from Battle Creek brought with it a major shift in the Adventist medical program, and this time the forceful Kellogg was not in control.

The first aspect of the new Adventist medical work consisted of a new generation of Adventist sanitariums. The focal point in medical activities shifted from Michigan to southern California.

Ellen White had begun pointing to California in 1902, even before Kellogg's difficulty reached a crisis level. God, she penned, "is preparing the way for our people to obtain possession, at little cost, of properties on which there are buildings that can be utilized in our work" (Lt 153, 1902). Rather then one "mammoth institution" (7T 96), Ellen White counseled that the denomination establish many smaller sanitariums in different locations.

No matter how deep the wound, we serve a God who can heal. *Thank You, God, for that aspect of grace.*

GOD STILL LEADS—1

Like an eagle teaching its young to fly,
  catching them safely on its spreading wings,
the Lord kept Israel from falling.
  The Lord alone led his people. Deut. 32:11, 12, TEV.

God's guidance.

Sometimes we think that's ancient history. Not so. One of the interesting stories of divine leading in early twentieth-century Adventism relates to the reestablishment of the medical branch of the denomination after the loss of the Battle Creek Sanitarium and the American Medical Missionary College to Kellogg.

Even before that loss, as early as the summer of 1902, Ellen White was urging the need of a medical outreach in California. On September 5 she wrote to the General Conference president that "constantly the Lord is keeping southern California before me as a place where we must establish medical institutions. Every year this region is visited by many thousands of tourists. Sanitariums must be established in this sector of the state" (Lt 138, 1902).

Three weeks later she penned that "for months the Lord has given me instruction that He is preparing the way for our people to obtain possession, at little cost, of properties on which there are buildings that can be utilized in our work" (Lt 153, 1902).

Mrs. White had no doubt that Adventism needed "smaller sanitariums in many places" "to reach the invalids flocking to the health resorts of Southern California." After all, "our sanitariums are to be established for one object—the advancement of present truth" (7T 98, 97).

Those were good ideas. But where would the money for them come from? The denomination, partly because of rapid worldwide expansion in the previous decade, trembled on the verge of bankruptcy. It had ended 1900 with only $32.93 in the General Conference treasury. Beyond that, even the $32.93 represented borrowed money. For several years the General Conference had existed on a hand-to-mouth program of deficit spending. And that was before the fires that burned the Battle Creek institutions to the ground.

So just where was the money to come from in this era of near bankruptcy and rebuilding?

Now here is a first class question to which there wasn't even a fourth class answer. Without God's leading there would not be that new generation of sanitariums that enthused Ellen White.

But He can do the humanly impossible.

GOD STILL LEADS–2

In all thy ways acknowledge him, and he shall direct thy paths. Prov. 3:6.

Yesterday we left Ellen White with her "impossible" dreams of acquiring several properties in southern California.

And it was an excellent time to buy such properties. Late in the nineteenth century others had built many beautiful sanitariums in the area. But then came prolonged droughts. Without water the institutions began to shut down. Those closings presented an opening for the Adventists. But even a good bargain isn't of much help to those without money.

Well, they did manage to dig up some. The first property purchased for the church was San Fernando College, obtained for $10,000 in 1902—less than one fourth its original cost.

The second was an inactive sanitarium in Paradise Valley near San Diego, consisting of a three-story building on 20 acres of land. Its developers had spent much money on the property, but hard times had come and the building had remained unoccupied for more than 10 years. When Ellen White first visited Paradise Valley, she was convinced that the Adventists would purchase it.

The main building had cost $25,000, but now its owners offered the entire property for $12,000. But where could local Adventists get the money? They couldn't look to the General Conference. And the Southern California Conference with its 1,100 members was $40,000 in debt and had recently purchased the San Fernando property. Those amounts of money look small today, but for those times they were huge. No way could the conference raise $12,000.

Even when the price dropped to $8,000 and then to $6,000 it still seemed hopeless. But when it went to $4,000, Mrs. White personally borrowed $2,000 from the bank at 8 percent interest, got a close friend to put up $2,000, and telegraphed to buy the property.

The first step had been taken toward establishing the church's southern California medical program. That first step, of course, was the easy one.

And just how does God lead His church?

The short answer is by guiding individuals to see His vision of what can be done. He opens the doors. It is up to us to walk through them.

GOD STILL LEADS—3

He leadeth me. Ps. 23:2.

Soon after the purchase of the Paradise Valley Sanitarium God revealed to Ellen White that an Adventist sanitarium needed to be established near Los Angeles. Finding the property was the easy part. Pastor John A. Burden soon discovered the castlelike 75-room Glendale Hotel. Built at a cost of $60,000 in 1886, it now had a price of $26,000. Burden believed that acceptance of his offer of $15,000 would be a sign of God's approval. All doubts vanished when the owners told him that he could have it for $12,000.

But the Adventists faced the same old question: Where to get the money? The small conference was all but bankrupt. It had recently bought the San Fernando and Paradise Valley properties. And the $20 that Burden had taken out of his own pocket for an initial payment certainly didn't go very far. The conference couldn't even pay the $1,000 down payment, and the conference constituency had rejected the purchase.

Under those discouraging circumstances, Burden and the conference president personally advanced the down payment out of their own savings. At that point a letter arrived from Ellen White asking why the work was being delayed. The conference president read it to his constituency. That broke the wall of resistance. They pledged enough to purchase the Glendale property.

Obtaining the Paradise and Glendale properties had occurred through a combination of vision and sacrifice. But the real test was yet to come.

The church had acquired both properties in 1904. But Mrs. White asserted that God had still another one for the church. Back in October 1901 she had claimed that God had distinctly shown her in a vision a sanitarium property in southern California consisting of "an occupied building" with "fruit trees on the sanitarium grounds." So real was the vision that she seemed to be living there herself (MS 152, 1901).

Yet she didn't know the property's exact location.

God is a person of timing. He knows when the occasion is right for certain moves that will rapidly forward His cause on earth. But He wants us to be in tune with His timing so that He might use us in unexpected ways.

GOD STILL LEADS—4

[He] guided them in the wilderness like a flock. Ps. 78:52.

Yesterday we noted that Ellen White in 1901 had seen in vision a third sanitarium property in southern California that the denomination needed to acquire. Yet she didn't know the location of the property. And neither the Glendale nor the Paradise purchases met the qualifications.

Soon Adventists discovered a location called Loma Linda. The place had cost its owners $150,000, but because of financial failure it now went on the market for $110,000, and then dropped to $85,000. But it might as well have been $1 billion to a conference that couldn't even raise $1,000 and had recently become involved with major properties in San Fernando, Paradise Valley, and Glendale.

It is not difficult to imagine the increasing perplexity of the conference officers when Mrs. White began urging the purchase of a third sanitarium property within a few months after acquiring two others. Wouldn't she ever stop? But she was adamant. She was confident that the purchase of the Loma Linda property was God's will.

The good news was that the owners soon reduced the price to $40,000. But even that didn't help people with no money.

Unfortunately, time wasn't standing still. They had to come up with a down payment right away or lose the Loma Linda property. Ellen White, who still hadn't seen Loma Linda, telegraphed John Burden to make an immediate down payment.

He did so, recognizing that the conference had explicitly told him that they could not be obligated. The good elder, realizing that he could lose the $1,000 down payment, decided to follow Ellen White's advice rather than that of the conference officers. Catching her vision that the securing of the Loma Linda property was God's will, he stepped out in faith.

Thinking big is not an inherited trait for many of us. Yet all down through Adventist history it has been thinking big that has propelled the church forward.

Help us, Lord, to be able to think larger, to be able to envision what You have in mind, and to have a part in the energizing of Your work.

GOD STILL LEADS—5

I am the Lord your God, who teaches you what is good and leads you along the paths you should follow. Isa. 48:17, NLT.

Adventism in southern California in mid-1905 had reached the end of its financial rope. Yet after the purchase of three major properties, Ellen White now urged a fourth.

The terms of the Loma Linda property were $5,000 down (due June 15), with like amounts on July 26, August 26, and December 31. The remaining $20,000 would be due in three years. But, as you know by now, there was no money in sight. Truly faith in this case was built on things "not seen" (Heb. 11:1)—except in vision.

Meanwhile, Mrs. White made her first visit to the Loma Linda property on June 12. "Willie," she said as she stepped out of the wagon that brought her, "I have been here before."

"No, Mother," he replied, "you have never been here."

"Then this is the very place the Lord has shown me," she said, "for it is all familiar."

She had no doubt in her mind. Looking at the church leaders examining the property, she declared, "We must have this place." As the group surveyed the buildings and the grounds Ellen White repeatedly stated, "This is the very place the Lord has shown me." And as she and Burden entered the recreation building she prophetically noted, "This building will be of great value to us. A school will be established here. . . . Battle Creek is going down. God will reestablish His medical work at this place" (see A. L. White, *Ellen G. White*, vol. 6, p. 18).

But words and visions aren't cash. They had but three days to raise the balance of the first $5,000, or they would lose both their option on the property and the $1,000 Burden had deposited.

Now, here is a proposition for the fainthearted. How do we respond to life when the going gets tight? With three days to go and no money on the horizon the most sensible thing would be to give up and say that we had done enough. But then there is the path of faith. We are told somewhere that "prayer moves the arm of omnipotence." And it does. It did so at Loma Linda, as we will see in the next couple days, and it can do so in our personal affairs. Our Father encourages and rewards faith.

God Still Leads—6

He led you through the vast and dreadful desert, that thirsty and waterless land.
Deut. 8:15, NIV.

God still leads His people through some difficult terrain. And they have only two choices: stay with Him or return to the "easy" life in spiritual Egypt.

There Adventist leaders in California stood with three days to raise the $5,000 for the purchase of Loma Linda, and with nothing but financial sand in view.

But they did have one possible lead. A couple weeks earlier Burden and Pastor R. S. Owen had heard about a person who might have some means. After taking the train to near his home, they walked the final mile and a half. But no one was home.

They returned to the train stop and waited. But for some reason they failed to signal it, and the train passed them at full speed. With two hours on their hands before the next one, the men walked back to the cabin, which now had a light on in it.

"Praise the Lord!" the farmer shouted as Burden explained the situation. "I have been praying for months for the Lord to send me a buyer for my place, that I might get out of the city and devote my means to advance His cause. A few days ago a man came and purchased my place, and the money is now lying in the bank. The devil has been tempting me to invest it again in land, but I am sure the Lord wants it to secure this property." At that point he offered the astonished ministers $2,400.

Then just before the June 15 due date Burden solicited a loan from a woman named Baker, who had also caught the vision. "Are you willing to risk $1,000?" he asked.

"Yes," she replied.

"You may lose it," he reminded.

"Well," she said, "I will risk it."

Next, Burden conferred again with R. S. Owen. "I don't have the money," he declared, "but I'll mortgage my house for it." With Owen's loan they finally had the first $5,000 on the very day it was due.

So far so good. But the next $5,000 was due in five weeks, and now they were truly out of good prospects for more money.

Sometimes the deserts of life are more estensive than we expected. But just because the going gets tough doesn't mean that God isn't with us.

GOD STILL LEADS—7

Remember how the Lord your God led you all the way in the desert these forty years, to humble you and to test you in order to know what was in your heart, whether or not you would keep his commands. Deut. 8:2, NIV.

The date for the second installment on the down payment for the Loma Linda property on July 26 rapidly approached the struggling Adventist leaders. In fact, the day arrived and they still saw no hope in sight.

That morning the conference leaders met in deep perplexity. At that point, Pastor Burden recalled, "It was easy and natural to blame and censure those who had pressed the matter through against what appeared to be sound reason and good judgment."

But he and others couldn't forget the affirmation regarding the property that had come through Ellen White. "Let's wait for the morning mail," someone suggested.

The postman soon arrived. Opening a letter from Atlantic City, New Jersey, they found a draft for $5,000—just the amount needed to make the payment.

"Needless to say," Burden tells us, "the feelings of those who had been critical quickly changed. Eyes filled with tears, and one who had been especially critical was the first to break the silence. With trembling voice, he said, 'It seems that the Lord is in this matter.'"

And surely He was. They immediately paid the second $5,000—once again on the very day it was due.

Now they faced the challenge of the third $5,000, due in 31 days. Once again they sought to raise the money without success. But a few days before the August 26 date a man in Oregon learned of the project and wrote that he had just sold some property and could make $4,500 available. The third payment took place on time.

The ball was rolling now. They had three months to raise the final $5,000, but they were offered a $100 discount for immediate payment. That was enough to inspire camp meeting gifts for the December installment, which they paid a few days after the August payment.

Father, it is so easy for me to be critical of others when things don't work out the way I think they should. Give me the grace of patience when things do work out and the grace of forgiveness when You solve problems some other way.

GOD STILL LEADS—8

Do not be afraid or discouraged, for the Lord is the one who goes before you. He will be with you; he will neither fail you nor forsake you. Deut. 31:8, NLT.

With the down payment cared for, the final payment of $20,000 for Loma Linda was a merciful three years off. But with momentum up and the previous owners offering a $1,000 discount if the Adventists paid the remaining money at once, the conference leadership moved quickly.

The impetus for the final push came from a non-church member who came to stay at the sanitarium even before it was ready for patients. It was inconvenient, but the staff did their best to make her feel comfortable. "As she was out on the grounds the next day," Burden writes, "we noticed that she seemed to look lonesome, so we thought to cheer her up. As we remarked about the beauty of the place, she said, 'I was just thinking how happy I would be to live in a place like this. I am all alone. My husband is dead. I am so lonesome I almost wish I were dead.'

"We suggested that she might make her home there. She asked how much it would cost. On [our] stating the amount she said, 'Why, I have that much in cash,' We went to the office and wrote out a life annuity."

The amount, of course, was far less than the needed $19,000, but the unexpected blessing encouraged them. They soon found a church member able to loan them $15,000 for three years.

Modern miracles still happen. In less than six months the church had raised the entire $40,000, and the Loma Linda property belonged to it. "The counsel" of Ellen White "had been confirmed," Burden enthused. "As we moved forward in faith, the Lord opened the way before us, and the money came from unexpected sources. Nearly all were at last convinced that truly God was carrying forward the enterprise."

Loma Linda, as predicted, later developed into a full-fledged medical school whose graduates have blessed people around the world with both physical care and the love of Jesus.

God still leads His church, even though it is less than perfect and even though its members and leaders may disagree on how to move forward. In spite of it all, the Lord still guides.

THE PASSING OF ELLEN WHITE

For I know whom I have believed, and am persuaded that he is able to keep that which I have committed unto him against that day. 2 Tim. 1:12.

W e saw early in the year that Joseph Bates, James White, and Ellen White were the founders of the Seventh-day Adventist Church. Bates passed away in 1872 and James in 1881, but Ellen continued to guide the Adventist church until 1915. Although she never held an official administrative position in the denomination, she possessed immense charismatic authority. Her writings and counsels had special meaning for both individuals and corporate Adventism.

On July 16, 1915, "the little old woman with white hair, who always spoke so lovingly of Jesus" (in the words of her non-Adventist neighbors) died at age 87. The last words that her family and friends heard were "I know in whom I have believed" (LS 449). Her passing, her son Willie noted, "was like the burning out of a candle, so quiet."

She may have died quietly, but her long life had been one of constant activity and accomplishment. Remarkably active in her old age, she attended her last General Conference session at Washington, D.C., in 1909. After the meetings she visited her old hometown in Portland, Maine, where she had begun her prophetic ministry some 65 years earlier. It was her last trip to the eastern United States. Although advanced in age, she still spoke 72 times at 27 locations during the five-month journey.

Returning home to southern California, she devoted her remaining years to the development of such books as *The Acts of the Apostles* (1911), *Gospel Workers* (1915), *Life Sketches of Ellen G. White* (1915), the final version of *The Great Controversy* (1911), and *Prophets and Kings* (published in 1917 after her death).

On the morning of February 13, 1915, Ellen White tripped and fell in her Elmshaven home. An X-ray examination disclosed a fractured left hip. She spent her last five months in bed and a wheelchair. On July 24 she was buried beside her husband in the Oak Hill Cemetery in Battle Creek, Michigan. Side by side they await their resurrection at the Second Coming—a teaching for which both of them had given their lives.

My hope is to meet them on that day as we all greet Jesus in the air.

UNPARALLELED MISSION GROWTH: 1900-1950–1

It grew and became a large tree. Luke 13:19, NKJV.

The beginnings of Seventh-day Adventism were indeed like the proverbial mustard seed. But how it grew once the roots were finally established!

Having spread around the world in the 1890s, by the early years of the new century Adventism was ready for an explosive expansion guided and held together by its beefed up organizational structure.

Part of the reason for success was that for the first three decades of the twentieth century two of the denomination's most mission-oriented leaders held its top positions. Arthur G. Daniells served as General Conference president from 1901 to 1922, and then as General Conference secretary for the next four years. Meanwhile, William A. Spicer was secretary between 1903 and 1922 and president from 1922 to 1930.

The presidential office is obviously important in setting directions, but in Adventism the secretariat is equally vital in terms of foreign missions, since that office took over the function of the denomination's Foreign Mission Board in 1903.

Spicer and Daniells not only were able leaders, but were dedicated to missions and the preaching of the third angel's message "to every nation, and kindred, and tongue, and people" (Rev. 14:6).

It is difficult to grasp the magnitude of the changes in Adventist mission outreach. In 1880 the denomination had 8 overseas missions. The same number held for 1890, but in 1900 it was 42, by 1910 it had increased to 87 missions, with the number rising to 153 and 270 in 1920 and 1930, respectively. The expansionary dynamics were beginning to transform Seventh-day Adventism from a North American church into a worldwide movement. The 1890s were the crucial decade for mission development. Before that period the church had witnessed little growth in the number of missions, but beginning in the 1890s the number advanced rapidly. That continuous spread into all the world not only altered the geographical boundaries of the church but increasingly it changed the nature of Adventism itself.

How surprised the pioneers of Sabbatarian Adventism would have been if they could have viewed it from the perspective of 1930. But massive transformation had just begun. The leaders of 1930 would find the denomination today unrecognizable. And I imagine today's leaders would experience the same shock if they could be transported to 2030. Adventism is a church on the move.

Unparalleled Mission Growth: 1900-1950—2

It had been planted on good soil by abundant waters, that it might produce branches and bear fruit and become a noble vine. Eze. 17:8, ESV.

By 1900 rapid growth had become the Adventist way. Its roots had been set, its branches had been established, and it began to develop abundant fruit around the world.

In 1890 Adventism had 255 evangelistic workers and 27,031 members in North America and 5 workers and 2,680 members outside. But by 1910 the North American statistics show 2,326 evangelistic workers and 66,294 members, while the non-North American membership stood at 38,232, served by 2,020 workers. Two decades later the numbers were 2,509 workers and 120,560 members in North America and 8,479 workers and 193,693 members overseas. And by 1950 the number of evangelistic workers in North America stood at 5,588 and the membership at 250,939. The non-North American numbers were 12,371 and 505,773.

Those rather startling figures indicate not only rapid growth but a shift in the proportion of Adventists outside of North America. During the mid-1920s the denomination passed the point where it had more members outside the continent of its birth than it did within. Thus the church not only preached worldwide but was beginning to become internationalized, a process still under way.

Some of the implications of internationalization were already becoming evident by 1900. One was an expansion of home bases for the sending of foreign missionaries. While that practice had begun during the nineteenth century, Daniells consciously sought to develop Adventism further in such nations as Germany, England, and Australia, in order to make them stronger home bases for additional expansion.

The early decades of the twentieth century witnessed the German church, under the leadership of L. R. Conradi, pioneer Adventism in the Middle East and East Africa. Australian missionaries, meanwhile, rapidly spread the message throughout much of the South Pacific. And British Adventism, with its nation's global empire and strongly developed missionary tradition, rapidly moved to plant Adventism in many parts of the world. As the century progressed, more and more missions in both developed and undeveloped nations became self-sustaining conferences that could function as home bases for additional mission outreach.

Step by step God was still leading His people.

Unparalleled Mission Growth: 1900-1950—3

Tell the children of Israel to go forward. Ex. 14:15, NKJV.

The children of Israel would have never made it to Canaan without a faith in God's leadership that gave them courage to step into the Red Sea. In like manner, the command to preach the three angels' messages to all the world combined with a faith in prophetic mission and God's empowerment gave the early Adventists the courage and enthusiasm to do the impossible for God. And they did it!

Or at least God did it through them. But we should note that the Lord did not do it without them. Not only did they give their lives for mission service, but their tithes and mission offerings fueled the denomination's ever-aggressive mission outreach. It was a program in which every member could take a part.

Part of their support went to the new media ministries that help speed the Adventist message to the ends of the earth. In the mass media tradition of Joshua V. Himes, H.M.S. Richards envisioned the possibilities inherent in radio. In 1930 he began *The Tabernacle of the Air*. Renamed *The Voice of Prophecy*, it became one of the first religious programs to enter the national broadcasting field.

In a world in which TV was still a new and largely untried medium of communication, William Fagel's *Faith for Today* program first aired in May 1950, soon followed by George Vandeman's *It Is Written*.

Adventists speaking a multitude of languages have duplicated those pioneering media efforts around the world. In addition, beginning in 1971 Adventist World Radio began to develop powerful radio stations in various parts of the world with the idea of blanketing the planet with the three angels' messages. And the late 1990s saw the church move into such strategic areas of outreach as the Internet and the development of a worldwide satellite television communication network with downlink locations in thousands of locations.

Truly the first angel is flying through "the midst of heaven, having the everlasting gospel to preach unto them that dwell" in every part of the earth (Rev. 14:6).

The age of miracles is not over yet.

ARRIVING AT MATURITY—1

Let us press on to maturity. Heb. 6:1, NASB.

Not only do individuals grow and develop, so do churches. We have spent a year examining the birth of Adventism, its childhood as it searched out the Bible doctrines that came to define it as a people, and the adolescent flexing of its muscles as it began to spread around the world.

By the 1950s and 1960s it had reached a level of maturity that all the previous decades had been moving toward. One sign of it was a more genuine internationalization of the denomination than had been seen in the past. In part that has meant that "foreign missionaries" from the United States, Europe, Great Britain, Australia, New Zealand, and South Africa no longer control the work in the newer fields of Adventist labor. Rather, the church has developed indigenous leaders in nearly every area of its far-flung mission program.

Today the administration of geographical sectors of Adventism up through the General Conference divisions is indigenous to the regions they lead. That means that Asians direct the church in Asia, Africans in Africa, and Latin Americans in South and Central America. The leader of each world division is also a vice president of the General Conference.

Beyond that, individuals from parts of the world that only a few years ago were still dependent on North American leadership now hold some of the most important positions of the General Conference's central administration.

That type of internationalization is a far cry from the "missionary" mentality largely maintained into the 1950s and 1960s. In fact, the very concept of missionary has changed. Whereas a few years ago being a missionary meant going as a European or North American to some non-Christian or non-Protestant land that might be quite primitive, at the present time the term implies working in a place other than one's native land. And mission has become a two-way street with "missionaries" not only going from America to Africa but some coming from Africa to serve in the United States. "From everywhere to everywhere" reflects the current shape of Adventist mission more adequately than does "missionary." The church around the world is growing up.

And in its maturity our prayer must be that it does not forget where it is going.

ARRIVING AT MATURITY—2

As for what was sown on good soil, this is he who hears the word and understands it; he indeed bears fruit, and yields, in one case a hundredfold, in another sixty, and in another thirty. Matt. 13:23, RSV.

Seventh-day Adventism has found a great deal of fruitful soil in nearly all parts of the earth. Gone are the days when it was largely a North American church. In fact, in 2007 only about 8 percent of the world's Adventists lived in North America. The land that first sent the missionaries stands dwarfed by the size of its children. Presently more than 5 million of the church's approximately 16 million members live in Africa, more than 5 million in Central and South America, and more than 2.5 million in Eastern Asia and India. By way of contrast, the North American Division has only recently topped the 1 million membership mark.

And the shape of world Adventism continues to transform as various parts of the world enter growth spurts. One surge has recently taken place in India, where church membership in the Southern Asia Division sprinted from 290,209 in 1999 to more than 1 million by the end of 2005.

And membership numbers are only one index of Adventist worldwide dynamics. A glance at the General Conference statistical report indicates that as of January 2006 it had 661 union and local conferences/missions, 121,565 congregations, 5,362 primary schools, 1,462 secondary schools, 106 colleges and universities, 30 food industries, 167 hospitals and sanitariums, 159 retirement homes and orphanages, 449 clinics and dispensaries, 10 media centers, and 65 publishing houses. The various institutions employed some 203,508 personnel. The church's publications appear in 361 languages and it uses 885 in its oral work.

And things haven't slowed down. To the contrary, growth has been accelerating. At the present growth rate we might expect to find 20 million Adventists in 2013 and 40 million between 2025 and 2030, if time should last.

Let's hope it doesn't. After all, God never raised up Adventism to grow a big church with lots of toys (institutions). To the contrary. He doesn't want any Seventh-day Adventists on earth. He desires us to enter the heavenly kingdom. That is the goal—what all the activity and sacrifice is about. The good news is that God has led His people in the past beyond their wildest dreams. And He will do so in the future if we don't forget who we are and why we are here.

THE MEANING OF IT ALL

And when in time to come your son asks you, "What does this mean?" you shall say to him, "By strength of hand the Lord brought us out of Egypt." Ex. 13:14, RSV.

And what does it mean? That was the question of the Jewish Passover with its strange meal and the spreading of blood on the doorposts. God was concerned that His ancient people not lose contact with His leading in their past.

The same God rules today. And "we have nothing to fear for the future" except we "forget the way the Lord has led us, and His teaching in our past history" (LS 196).

We have spent nearly one year meditating upon that history. So far we have seen Adventism birthed by the movement of William Miller, struggling to find an identity in the post-1844 period, flexing its youthful muscles in the 1850s through the 1870s, transformed and reoriented by the 1888 message, and advancing on into maturity in the twentieth century.

To put it mildly, the denomination is all but unrecognizable from its early years. In fact, even the past 60 years have reshaped it in ways that the leaders of the 1940s could hardly have envisioned. And the coming decades will undoubtedly do the same—probably even more so.

From a handful of scattered believers with no structure of institutions, Seventh-day Adventism has become a worldwide church of some 16 million people with an accelerating growth curve.

Starting out as a frowned-upon minority, in some nations today it is a leading or even the dominant denomination, though in most countries it still has and probably always will have minority status.

But why are we here? The answer is obviously not to create a strong denomination that is socially aware and provides a comfortable place of fellowship for its members. Those are good things, but not sufficient. The reason Adventism exists is to prepare people for a better world and to preach God's final messages to the world before the Second Advent.

During the last few days of the year we will meditate upon the meaning of Adventist history, including the questions of "What happened to all those Millerites?" and "Why" did Seventh-day Adventism succeed where others failed?

God's people still need to ask the Exodus question of "Why."

AND WHAT HAPPENED
TO ALL THOSE MILLERITES?—1

Establish your hearts, for the coming of the Lord is at hand. James 5:8, NKJV.

We have spent nearly a year meditating on the Lord's leading of the Advent movement. During it we have seen Seventh-day Adventism expand from nothing to some 16 million members worldwide. The pathway between zero and maturity was not a straight one. Nor was it one without difficulties. But step by step truth was uncovered and preached "to every nation, and kindred, and tongue, and people" (Rev. 14:6).

But what does it all mean? What lessons can we glean from Adventist history? And what might those lessons mean for the future of the movement? It is to such questions that we turn in the final few days of our journey through Adventist history.

The first thing we will do in our quest for perspective is to look at the post-Millerite denominations. Between 1844 and 1848, we noted some months ago, three diverse strands of Adventism evolved. The first was the spiritualizers, who gave up the literal interpretation of Scripture and spiritualized the meaning of even concrete words. Thus they could claim that Christ came into their hearts spiritually on October 22, 1844.

The second group was the Albany Adventists, who organized in 1845 to create distance between themselves and the fanatical spiritualizers. The group's proponents eventually abandoned any firm belief in Miller's prophetic scheme.

A third group, the Sabbatarians, continued to hold to a literal Second Advent (unlike the spiritualizers) and to Miller's principles of prophetic understanding (unlike the Albany Adventists). Thus the Sabbatarians came to see themselves as the only true heir of pre-Disappointment Adventism.

Between 1844 and 1866 six denominations arose out of the three branches of Millerism. The Albany group gave birth to four: The American Evangelical Conference (1858), the Advent Christians (1860), the Church of God (Oregon, Illinois) (1850s), and the Life and Advent Union (1863). The Sabbatarian movement resulted in two: the Seventh-day Adventists (1861-1863) and the Church of God (Seventh Day) (1866).

The spiritualizers, with their diversity, extreme individuality, and lack of organization, formed no permanent bodies. Various spiritualizers eventually gravitated to other "isms" or more stable Adventist groups, or vanished back into the larger culture.

But what happened to the rest? And why? Those questions lead directly to important thoughts on the meaning of the Adventist journey through time.

WHAT HAPPENED
TO ALL THOSE MILLERITES?–2

Unto them that look for him shall he appear the second time without sin unto salvation. Heb. 9:28.

While precise membership statistics are not available, it seems safe to suggest that the Evangelical Adventists and the Advent Christians were by far the most numerous during the early 1860s, with the Advent Christians constantly gaining over the Evangelicals. One reason for the Advent Christians' relative greater success seems to be that they had unique doctrines that gave them something to stand for. Their doctrines of the unconscious state of people in death and the final destruction of the wicked provided a focal point for their identity, eventually surpassing their emphasis on the Advent.

The Evangelicals, on the other hand, had only the premillennial Advent to separate them from the general Christian populace. When a significant portion of conservative Protestantism also adopted forms of premillennialism in the decades after the American Civil War, Evangelical Adventism had little reason to continue a separate existence. By the early twentieth century what had probably been the largest post-Millerite body in the early 1860s had vanished as a separate religious body.

In 1860 the first Adventist census estimated some 54,000 believers, with about 3,000 of them observing the seventh day. But by 1890 the United States government census indicated a radical shift in the relative size of the Adventist denominations. The once-minute Seventh-day Adventists had by then achieved predominance, with 28,991 members in the United States. The Advent Christians were next, with 25,816. The other four denominations ranged between 647 and 2,872 adherents each.

A century later only four of the six Adventist denominations still existed. In the opening years of the twenty-first century the Seventh-day Adventists reported more than 1 million members in the United States and more than 15 million worldwide, while the Advent Christian claimed 25,277 in the United States and practically none outside of North America. The other two surviving Adventist denominations reported 3,860 and 9,700 members.

Thus by 2006 the Seventh-day Adventists dominated the post-Millerite world. As Clyde Hewitt, an Advent Christian historian, put it, "the tiniest of the Millerite offshoot groups was the one which would become the largest."

And once again we are left with the question of What was it that propelled the Seventh-day Adventists in their mission that the others lacked?

THE "WHY" OF SUCCESS—1

The ground produces a crop by itself, first the blade, then the ear, then full grain in the ear. Mark 4:28, REB.

W hy do some things grow and others fail to do so? Why did the minute Sabbatarian movement with its unpopular doctrines not only survive but prosper?

That question is impossible to answer with absolute certainty, but the historical data suggest several reasons. Before exploring them, however, we need to look at a closely related query: why Millerism succeeded. It appears that the two movements experienced success for largely the same reasons.

A series of non-Adventist scholars have also asked the question of the "why" of growth, especially in terms of Millerism. One of them suggests that the movement arose at the right time. Thus natural disasters (such as changing weather patterns) and economic/social crises (such as the panic or depression of 1837) provided a climate in which people were looking for solutions in times of stress and tension. In short, Miller's message supplied hope in a world in which human effort had failed to achieve the expected results. In other words, the worse things get, in human terms, the more feasible millennial options appear to be. We find that truth illustrated in Seventh-day Adventist history by the upsurge in evangelistic results during World War I and other troublesome periods of the twentieth century.

A second non-Adventist scholar saw the success of Millerism in its orthodoxy—its essential harmony with other religious forces of the day. Millerism's one essential "heresy" was its view of the premillennial Advent. But the movement's very orthodoxy in most matters left the populace open to its one unorthodox message.

A third answer to the success of Millerism is that it grew up in an era of revivalism that provided it a method to proselytize, an atmosphere of millennial hope that gave direction to the movement, and a pervasive temperament of faith that enabled people to respond to the revival and accept the vision of the new world to come.

Those external factors certainly provided the soil in which both Millerism and Seventh-day Adventism could prosper. But even more important were the internal forces (which we will examine the next few days) that drove Millerism and Seventh-day Adventism in the success of their respective missions.

Those same forces, I might add, inspire not only movements to action, but also individuals. They thus have meaning for our lives in the twenty-first century.

THE "WHY" OF SUCCESS—2

[The kingdom of God] is like a mustard seed which, when it is sown on the ground, is smaller than all the seeds on earth; but when it is sown, it grows up and . . . shoots out large branches, so that the birds of the air may nest under its shade. Mark 4:31, 32, NKJV.

One factor that makes a movement successful is that it makes sense to both those inside and outside of its borders.

Here is a point at which some millennial groups have a problem. After all, apocalyptic movements tend to attract two personality types. On the one hand we find the rationalism that unpacks the biblical prophecies and develops the apocalyptic scheme of events. On the other congregate the emotional types that gravitate toward the excitement of the apocalyptic expectancy and often dive into fanatical, irrational extremism.

A movement disintegrates whenever the rational forces are not strong enough to stem the forces of irrationalism and emotionalism. It was in that area that the spiritualizer wing of Adventism came to nothing. To put it bluntly, once the fanatics and "nuts" get in charge, the movement spins out of control and loses direction.

One of the strengths of Millerism was its rational development of its central doctrine. That element drew believers to its cause through its very logic. Millerism at its best, however, also made room for religious emotionalism, but that emotionalism ideally took place within the bounds of a rational approach to life. The combination gave both vitality and stability to the movement and heightened its appeal.

Seventh-day Adventism has partaken of the same balance, although at times it appears to wander too far toward the purely rational pole. Both Millerism and Seventh-day Adventism, of course, have had their excitable and fanatical elements, but the stability of their success can largely be attributed to their ability to appeal to the rational element in people. Thus they have aimed at converting people to the "truth."

And I have to admit that as an adult convert from a reasoned agnosticism to Seventh-day Adventism, one thing that appealed massively to me in the Adventist message was that it made sense in a mixed-up world. As a 19-year-old I found the logic and coherence of the denomination's major teachings to be compelling. They not only made sense, but they held together as a package—a package of hope in a God of love who will bring about the end of the mess of sin in a manner that is in harmony with His character.

THE "WHY" OF SUCCESS—3

Grow in the grace and knowledge of our Lord and Savior Jesus Christ.
2 Peter 3:18, NKJV.

Another factor that led to the evangelistic success of Millerism and Seventh-day Adventism is the content or doctrinal element in their view of truth. Thus Millerism had what it considered to be an important Bible understanding to offer to individuals searching for meaning—the premillennial return of Christ. As a result, Millerism was not just a part of the ecclesiastical woodwork—it stood for something distinctive from other religious groups. It had a message to preach. And many responded to it.

As noted previously, one of the reasons Evangelical Adventism died out was that it had lost its doctrinal distinctiveness once a significant portion of American Protestantism accepted premillennialism. After that, Evangelical Adventism had no reason to exist. On the other hand, the Advent Christians adopted conditional immortality as a focal point that lent a reason for a separate denominational existence.

By way of contrast, the Seventh-day Adventists developed a whole arsenal of unconventional beliefs that they saw as their special mission to share with the world. And just as a kite flies against the wind, so there is a dynamic in religious movements vitalized by differences and even opposition. Being different gives individuals and social groups a sense of identity and meaning.

Clyde Hewitt, in seeking to explain Seventh-day Adventism's growth in contrast to his Advent Christian community's lack of growth, notes that "the distinctive beliefs and practices of the [Seventh-day Adventist] denomination, while causing it to be viewed with suspicion by many traditional Christian believers, have seemingly given its faithful members a resoluteness of individual and group character that goes far to explain their success." On the other hand, Seventh-day Adventism (like Millerism) is close enough to orthodoxy in most central doctrines to get a hearing among other Christians.

It's OK to be different (but not "strange"). That is true as long as the major differences rest upon sound principles—biblical and otherwise. One of the great strengths of Adventism is the lifestyle and doctrinal commitments that set it apart as a unique movement. It stands for something biblical, something true, something worth living for. That is part of the attraction of the Adventist message for people who are looking for the answer to life's most perplexing problems.

THE "WHY" OF SUCCESS—4

Choose able men from all the people, such as fear God, men who are trustworthy and who hate a bribe; and place such men over the people as rulers of thousands, of hundreds, of fifties, of tens. Ex. 18:21, RSV.

The children of Israel didn't make it to Canaan without organization. In fact, no task of great magnitude can be accomplished without it.

A third element that led to the evangelistic success of Seventh-day Adventism was an organizational structure sufficient to carry on the mission and meet the challenges of its message.

It was the lack of sufficient organization that spelled the demise of the spiritualizers and caused the lack of growth of the two Church of God Adventist denominations. Without sufficient organization they could not concentrate their resources for mission or maintain unity. Costly schism was the result.

It is at the point of viable organization that the Advent Christians and the Seventh-day Adventists also parted ways. The Seventh-day Adventist Church was the only one of the Adventist denominations to place significant authority at any ecclesiastical level above that of the local congregation. Clyde Hewitt, in bemoaning the plight of the Advent Christians, indicates that the lack of a "strong centralized organization" is one reason that "contraction threatens to overcome expansion" in their denomination. As a result of their congregational structure, Hewitt points out, the Advent Christians were unable to mobilize for united action. Had they had proper organization, he suggested in 1990, the Advent Christians might be "a growing and not a dying denomination."

By way of contrast, studies of Seventh-day Adventist organizational structure indicate that the denomination's structure was consciously designed with mission outreach in mind in both 1861-1863 and 1901-1903.

The worldwide commission to the church at the end of time to take the message of the three angels of Revelation 14:6-12 "to every nation, and kindred, and tongue, and people" demands an organizational structure sufficient for the task.

The mission of Adventism is not merely to local congregations or communities, but to all the world. We can thank God that He has given us a structure equal to the task. Perhaps we don't always appreciate it as we should. But both Bible principles and Adventist history demonstrate that it didn't come about by accident.

THE "WHY" OF SUCCESS—5

And I saw another angel flying through the heavens, carrying the everlasting Good News to preach to the people who belong to this world—to every nation, tribe, language, and people. Rev. 14:6, NLT.

The final, and by far the most important, factor in the rapid spread of Millerism was its sense of prophetic mission and the resulting urgency generated by that understanding.

Millerism was a mission-motivated movement. A sense of personal responsibility to warn the world of its soon-coming end literally drove William Miller, Joshua V. Himes, and their Millerite colleagues to dedicate everything they had to announce the world's impending judgment. Himes put it nicely in an editorial in the very first issue of the *Midnight Cry*. "Our Work," he wrote, "is one of unutterable magnitude. It is a mission and an enterprise, unlike, in some respects, anything that has ever awakened the energies of men. . . . It is an *alarm,* and a cry, uttered by those who from among all Protestant sects, as Watchmen standing upon the walls of the moral world, believe the WORLD'S CRISIS IS COME—and who, under the influence of this faith, are united in proclaiming to the world, 'Behold the Bridegroom cometh, go ye out to meet him!' "

That overwhelming sense of urgency, we must emphasize, rested upon an interpretation of the prophecies of Daniel and the book of Revelation. The Millerites believed with all their hearts that they had a message that people *must hear.* That belief and the total dedication that accompanied it pushed the Millerites into tireless mission.

That same vision, based upon the same prophecies, also provided the mainspring of Seventh-day Adventist mission. From their beginning Sabbatarian Adventists never viewed themselves as merely another denomination. To the contrary, they understood their movement and message to be a fulfillment of prophecy. They saw themselves as a prophetic people with God's last-day message to take to the entire world before the harvest of the earth (Rev. 14:14-20).

It is the loss of that very understanding that is robbing so much of present-day Adventism of any real significance and meaning. The eroding of that vision slows church growth and will eventually transform Adventism from a dynamic movement into a monument of the movement and perhaps even a museum of the monument of the movement.

THE "WHY" OF SUCCESS—6

"Fear God," he shouted. "Give glory to him. For the time has come when he will sit as judge." Rev. 14:7, NLT.

Not just another denomination!
A movement of prophecy!

A profound belief that Miller's basic prophetic understanding had been correct fueled both understandings. From the Sabbatarian perspective the other Adventist groups had lost their way and eventually their mission because of their denial of Miller's principles of prophetic understanding.

That denial took two different directions. One involved a rejection of the obvious interpretation of scriptural passages that clearly seemed to be quite literal in intent. Thus the belief that Christ had already come sapped the missiological strength of the spiritualizers. After all, if Christ had already arrived, what was the reason for any kind of mission at all?

On the other hand, the Albany Adventists spurned the stimulus to mission that had convicted and empowered Millerism when they abandoned Miller's principles of prophetic interpretation in their rejection of the great time prophecies of Daniel and the Revelation. Without that certainty of the flow of prophetic history, they lost a sense of conviction and urgency. They finally had to find meaning for existence in other doctrines, such as conditional immortality. That may have been good enough for a sort of status quo denominational existence, but the Albany group had abandoned the mainspring that had aggressively propelled Millerite mission.

By way of contrast, the Sabbatarians founded their movement on that very mainspring. They not only maintained Miller's prophetic scheme of interpretation, but they extended it in such a way as to give meaning both to their disappointment and to the remaining time before Christ's advent. Central to that extended interpretation were Christ's work in the heavenly sanctuary and the progressive nature of the three angels' messages of Revelation 14.

Father in heaven, help us as we think of Adventist pasts and Adventist futures to recognize the importance of apocalyptic prophecy for the Adventist present. We realize that a renewed understanding of the relevance and importance of apocalypticism for the twenty-first century is the only hope for a vibrant Adventism.

THE "WHY" OF SUCCESS—7

Worship him who made heaven and earth, the sea, and all the springs of water.
Rev. 14:7, NLT.

While the Sabbatarian Adventists saw William Miller and Charles Fitch, respectively, as the initiators of the first and second angels' messages, they regarded their own movement with its emphasis on the commandments of God as beginning the third. Their view of the end-time struggle over the commandments of God pictured in Revelation 12:17 and the fuller exposition of that verse in Revelation 13 and 14 reinforced their conviction that not only were they heirs of Millerism, but that God had predicted that their movement would preach the three angels' messages to all the world immediately before Revelation 14's end-time harvest.

As a result, that prophetic understanding eventually drove them to mission. By the early twenty-first century the conviction that their movement was a fulfillment of prophecy had resulted in one of the most widespread outreach programs in the history of Christianity. They had established work in 204 of the 230 nations then recognized by the United Nations.

That kind of dedication did not come by accident—it was the direct result of a prophetic conviction of their responsibility. Central to it was the imperative of the first angel of Revelation 14:6 to preach "to every nation, and kindred, and tongue, and people" and the command of Revelation 10:11 that the disappointed ones "must prophecy again before many peoples, and nations, and tongues, and kings."

Clyde Hewitt, in seeking to explain the success of the Seventh-day Adventists as opposed to the attrition faced by his Advent Christians, touched upon an essential element when he noted that "Seventh-day Adventists are convinced that they have been divinely ordained to carry on the prophetic work started by William Miller. They are dedicated to the task."

In contrast, Hewitt's father wrote in 1944 that the Advent Christians had given up Miller's understanding of Daniel 8:14 and the 2300 days and had no unanimity on the meaning of the text. And in 1984 I interviewed another leading Advent Christian scholar who noted that his denomination no longer even had an agreed-upon interpretation of the millennium—the very heart of Miller's contribution.

Lord, help Your modern church to realize that Bible prophecy is not dead history, but the only understanding that will make it alive to its fullest as earth's trajectory moves toward its climax.

THE "WHY" OF SUCCESS—8

This means God's holy people must be patient. They must obey God's commands and keep their faith in Jesus. Rev. 14:12, NCV.

When the Albany Adventist denominations and the spiritualizers stepped off Miller's prophetic platform, their understanding of end-time events began to deteriorate, and with that erosion came a lack of vision and mission. By way of contrast, the Seventh-day Adventist branch of Millerism took prophecy seriously.

We should note that merely holding the conviction that they had the "correct doctrine" does not fully explain the spread of Sabbatarian Adventism. After all, the Seventh Day Baptists preached the seventh-day Sabbath with conviction, but their 4,800 members in the United States in 2003 is less than what they had in 1840. As one nineteenth-century Seventh Day Baptist preacher told Bates, the Baptists had been able to "convince people of the legality of the seventh-day Sabbath, but they could not get them to move as the Sabbath Adventists did."

Likewise, many of the nonsabbatarian groups preached a premillennial Advent, but without the same results as Seventh-day Adventists. Clyde Hewitt notes that his "Advent Christian people have not been an evangelistic church and have not made much of an impact on the world." The result, he points out, has been smallness—not just in numbers, but most importantly "in dreams, in visions. Smallness breeds smallness." He also indicates that Advent Christians cannot attribute their lack of growth to unpopular doctrines, since the Seventh-day Adventist list of unpopular doctrines "includes all those of the Advent Christian faith and adds several more." Rather, he roots Seventh-day Adventist success in their conviction that they have a prophetic mission in the tradition of William Miller.

In short, the mainspring of success is much more than merely the fact that the Sabbatarians believed they had the "truth" on the Sabbath and the Second Advent. *The driving force undergirding Seventh-day Adventism has been their conviction that they were a prophetic people with a unique message concerning Christ's soon coming to a troubled world. That prophetic understanding of their mission, integrated with their doctrines within the framework of the three angels' messages, provided Sabbatarians with the motive power to sacrifice in order to spread their message far and wide.*

It is that very understanding that Adventism is in jeopardy of forgetting in the early twenty-first century.

AND WHAT HAPPENED
TO ALL THOSE MILLERITES?—3

Where there is no vision, the people perish: but he that keepeth the law, happy is he.
Prov. 29:18.

And what did happen to all those Millerites? Plenty, but not much. Several of the post-Millerite denominations have died and been buried. Others are in the process of dying. That is certainly the inference of Richard C. Nickels' 1973 history of the Church of God (Seventh Day), which concludes with a section entitled "A Dying Church?" The treatment's ominous last words are from Christ's message to the Church at Sardis: "It was alive, yet dead!" Similarly, the final section of Clyde Hewitt's three-volume history of the Advent Christians (1990) is "Should a Denomination Be Told It's Dying?"

Those thoughts bring us back to young Ellen White's first vision in December 1844. Before going there, we should point out that she made very few predictions. But perhaps her most interesting one is found at the very beginning of her ministry.

Writing of the post-Disappointment experience of the Adventists, she noted that I "saw a straight and narrow path, cast up high above the world. On this path the Advent people were traveling to the city, which was at the farther end of the path. They had a bright light set up behind them at the beginning of the path, which an angel told me was the midnight cry. This light shone all along the path and gave light for their feet so that they might not stumble. If they kept their eyes fixed on Jesus, who was just before them, leading them to the city, they were safe. But some soon grew weary. . . .

"Others rashly denied the light behind them and said that it was not God that had led them out so far. The light behind them went out, leaving their feet in perfect darkness, and they stumbled and lost sight of the mark and of Jesus, and fell off the path down into the dark and wicked world below" (EW 14, 15).

The Midnight Cry, we noted earlier, was God's guidance in the prophetic understandings leading up to the October 1844 disappointment. The facts of history are that every post-Millerite denomination except the Seventh-day Adventists gave up the "light behind them" and came to nothingness or almost nothingness (i.e., they "fell off the path"). So it was with the once-powerful Evangelical Adventist Conference, the Advent Christians, and the others.

By way of contrast, the one group that maintained the prophetic foundation continues to prosper as a dynamic worldwide movement. The only thing it has to fear is forgetting the Lord's leading in its past history.

THE OLD STONES STILL SPEAK

And those twelve stones, which they took out of the Jordan, Joshua set up in Gilgal. And he said to the people of Israel, "When your children ask their fathers in time to come, 'What do these stones mean?' then you shall let your children know, 'Israel passed over this Jordan on dry ground.'" Joshua 4:20-22, RSV.

We began our year's journey through Adventist history with this text. It is no accident that we are closing with it. God's truth hasn't changed with the passage of time. The Bible is a historical book. It traces the great points in salvation history from the creation to the Second Advent.

Thus the Bible is a book of remembrance of God's miraculous leading of His people.

And that leading is not over. It continues on and will do so until the final victory has been won.

It is when churches lose the significance and reality of God's leading in their past history that they are in trouble. Just as it was so in Bible times, so it is today.

And it was no accident that the aging Ellen White alerted her readers to the topic: "In reviewing our past history," she penned, "having traveled over every step of advance to our present standing, I can say, Praise God! As I see what the Lord has wrought, I am filled with astonishment, and with confidence in Christ as leader. We have nothing to fear for the future, except as we shall forget the way the Lord has led us, and His teaching in our past history" (LS 196).

Lest we forget! As Seventh-day Adventists, we have nothing to fear for the future unless we forget God's guidance in our past.

The pathway from the past indicates the way into the future. When Christians forget God's past leading, they also lose their sense of identity in the present. And that loss of identity causes a loss of mission and purpose. After all, if you don't know who you are in relation to God's plan, what do you have to tell the world?

Christian history, we noted 364 days ago, is littered with religious bodies who have forgotten where they have come from, and, as a result, have no direction for the future.

Now, at the end of the year, we know that Adventist history is littered with dead and dying bodies, all of which have forgotten their prophetic past.

That forgetting is one of Seventh-day Adventism's greatest temptations. But we have nothing to fear for the future, *unless we forget!*

TITLES OF READINGS—MARCH

TITLES OF READINGS—APRIL

TITLES OF READINGS—JUNE

TITLES OF READINGS—JULY

Titles of Readings—August

TITLES OF READINGS—SEPTEMBER

TITLES OF READINGS—OCTOBER

TITLES OF READINGS—NOVEMBER

The Apocalyptic Vision and the Neutering of Adventism

Why does George Knight say **this is the most important book** he's ever written?

Does the Adventist Church have any reason for existence if it has lost that which makes it different from all the rest of Christianity?

Why were the early Seventh-day Adventists so passionate about evangelizing the world?

How can we rekindle in our own lives that passion for spreading the gospel?

Could a revitalization of the apocalyptic vision provide the answer as the world and the church move toward the Second Coming?

Accept Knight's challenge to go back to your roots for the answers. (But beware—you may have to uproot yourself from the pew to be truly Adventist!) Paperback, 400 pages.

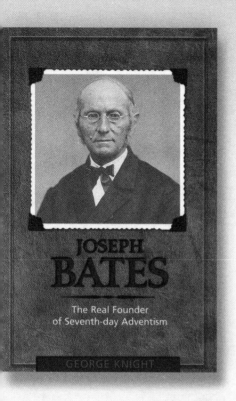

Lest We Forget ...

"We have nothing to fear for the future, except as we shall forget the way the Lord has led us, and His teaching in our past history." —ELLEN G. WHITE.

JOSEPH BATES
The Real Founder of Seventh-day Adventism

George Knight sheds new light on the first theologian and real founder of the Adventist Church—a man who gave his estate to the Advent movement and spent the rest of his life in unpaid service to his King. 0-8280-1815-4.

3 WAYS TO SHOP

- Visit your local ABC
- Call 1-800-765-6955
- www.AdventistBookCenter.com

REVIEW AND HERALD ®
PUBLISHING ASSOCIATION
Since 1861 | www.reviewandherald.com

Lest We Forget …

"We have nothing to fear for the future, except as we shall forget the way the Lord has led us, and His teaching in our past history."—ELLEN G. WHITE.

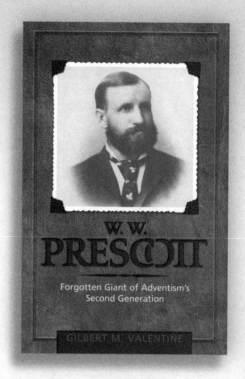

W. W. PRESCOTT

Forgotten Giant of Adventism's Second Generation

Gilbert Valentine examines Prescott's impact on the church's educational system and how he helped reshape the church's theology and policies during a critical era. 0-8280-1892-8.

3 WAYS TO SHOP

- Visit your local ABC
- Call 1-800-765-6955
- www.AdventistBookCenter.com

Prices and availability subject to change. Prices higher in Canada.

Lest We Forget ...

"We have nothing to fear for the future, except as we shall forget the way the Lord has led us, and His teaching in our past history." —Ellen G. White.

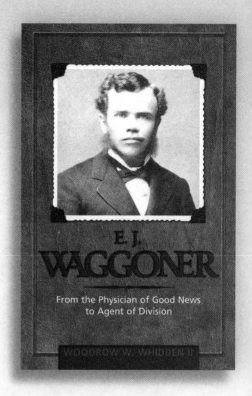

E. J. WAGGONER
From the Physician of Good News to Agent of Division

Woodrow Whidden traces the life and public ministry of one of Adventism's most controversial pioneers—a man who received both stern rebuke and emphatic support from Ellen White and whose theological contributions have shaped, and divided, the Adventist Church. 978-0-8280-1982-8. Hardcover, 368 pages.

3 WAYS TO SHOP

- Visit your local ABC
- Call 1-800-765-6955
- www.AdventistBookCenter.com

Prices and availability subject to change. Prices higher in Canada.

REVIEW AND HERALD®
PUBLISHING ASSOCIATION
Since 1861 | www.reviewandherald.com

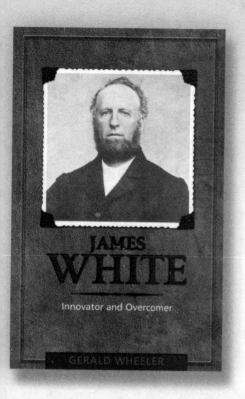